The INSEAD–Wharton Alliance on Globalizing

The INSEAD–Wharton Alliance combines the insights of two leading global business schools to examine the forces that are driving firms to globalize, the consequences – positive and negative – that accompany increasing globalization, and their managerial and political implications. Written by experts in diverse management disciplines – including leadership, finance, marketing, and operations management – the book is an important contribution to contemporary business strategy. In contrast to strident and often heavily rhetorical debates, this volume focuses on the managerial strategies involved in globalizing businesses, including leadership, market entry, and managing risks. The non-partisan treatment of the issues will be of interest to managers wrestling with the many challenges of globalizing, to policymakers interested in whether and how to either slow or accelerate the process, and to those in non-governmental organizations concerned with understanding global business challenges.

HUBERT GATIGNON is Research Director of the Alliance and Director of the Alliance Center for Global Research and Development. Dr. Gatignon is the Claude Janssen Chaired Professor of Business Administration and Professor of Marketing at INSEAD and is also INSEAD's Dean of the PhD Program.

JOHN R. KIMBERLY is Executive Director of the Alliance. Dr. Kimberly is the Henry Bower Professor of Entrepreneurial Studies and Professor of Management, Health Care Systems, and Sociology at the Wharton School of the University of Pennsylvania.

The INSEAD–Wharton Alliance on Globalizing

Strategies for Building Successful Global Businesses

EDITED BY HUBERT GATIGNON AND

JOHN R. KIMBERLY

WITH ROBERT E. GUNTHER

CAMBRIDGE
UNIVERSITY PRESS

PUBLISHED BY THE PRESS SYNDICATE OF THE UNIVERSITY OF CAMBRIDGE
The Pitt Building, Trumpington Street, Cambridge, United Kingdom

CAMBRIDGE UNIVERSITY PRESS
The Edinburgh Building, Cambridge, CB2 2RU, UK
40 West 20th Street, New York, NY 10011–4211, USA
477 Williamstown Road, Port Melbourne, VIC 3207, Australia
Ruiz de Alarcón 13, 28014 Madrid, Spain
Dock House, The Waterfront, Cape Town 8001, South Africa

http://www.cambridge.org

First published 2004

Printed in the United Kingdom at the University Press, Cambridge

Typeface Sabon 10/13 pt.   *System* LATEX 2$_\varepsilon$ [TB]

A catalogue record for this book is available from the British Library

Library of Congress Cataloguing in Publication data
The INSEAD–Wharton Alliance on globalizing : strategies for building successful
global businesses / [edited by] Hubert Gatignon and John R. Kimberly with
Robert E. Gunther.
     p.   cm.
Includes bibliographical references and indexes.
ISBN 0 521 83571 2
1. Strategic alliances (Business).   2. International business enterprises – Management.
I. Title: Strategies for building successful global businesses.   II. Gatignon, Hubert.
III. Kimberly, John R. (John Robert), 1942–   IV. Gunther, Robert E., 1960–
V. INSEAD–Wharton Alliance.
HD69.S8A4345   2004
658′.049 – dc22   2004040755

ISBN 0 521 83571 2 hardback

Contents

List of figures   *page* viii

List of tables   x

Notes on contributors   xi

Foreword   xxi

Acknowledgments   xxii

1   Globalization and its challenges   1
     Hubert Gatignon and John R. Kimberly

Part I   Leading the global organization

2   The changing international corporate governance
     landscape   23
     Mauro F. Guillén and Mary A. O'Sullivan

3   Corporate governance and leadership in a globalizing
     equity market   49
     Michael Useem

4   Leadership in a global organization: a cross-cultural
     perspective   78
     Mansour Javidan, Günter K. Stahl, and Robert J. House

5   The globalization of business education   104
     Arnoud De Meyer, Patrick T. Harker, and Gabriel
     Hawawini

Part II   Global market participation

6   Globalization through acquisitions and alliances: an
     evolutionary perspective   129
     Harbir Singh and Maurizio Zollo

7   Developing new products and services for the global
    market   159
    Reinhard Angelmar

8   Managing brands in global markets   184
    George S. Day and David J. Reibstein

9   Global marketing of new products   207
    Hubert Gatignon and Christophe Van den Bulte

10 Global equity capital markets for emerging growth firms:
    patterns, drivers, and implications for the globalizing
    entrepreneur   229
    Raphael Amit and Christoph Zott

    Part III   Managing risk and uncertainty

11 Cross-border valuation: the international cost of
    equity capital   255
    *Gordon M. Bodnar, Bernard Dumas, and Richard
    Marston*

12 Managing risk in global supply chains   288
    Paul R. Kleindorfer and Luk N. Van Wassenhove

13 Global recombination: cross-border technology and
    innovation management   306
    Philip Anderson and Lori Rosenkopf

14 From corporate social responsibility to global citizenship   331
    Eric W. Orts

15 Colliding forces: domestic politics and the global economy   353
    Ethan B. Kapstein and Stephen J. Kobrin

16 Global implications of information and communication
    technologies (ICT)   378
    Arnoud De Meyer

    Part IV   Implications and conclusions

17 Globalization and its many faces: the case of the health
    sector   395
    *Lawton R. Burns, Thomas D'Aunno, and John R.
    Kimberly*

18 Conclusion: The continuing process of globalizing 422
    Hubert Gatignon and John R. Kimberly

Author index 431
Subject index 438

Figures

1.1 Globalizing decisions   *page* 2
3.1 Value of foreign equity held by US residents, and of
    US equity held by foreign investors, 1990–2002   53
3.2 Percentage of value of Japanese shares held and traded by
    foreign investors, 1990–2002   54
3.3 Foreign direct investment in the United States,
    1990–2002   54
3.4 Share of institutional ownership of 1,000 largest US
    companies, 1987, 1995, and 2000   56
3.5 Compensation of top seven or eight managers at
    forty-five US manufacturing firms, 1982–2003   60
3.6 Median change in CEO wealth per $1,000 change in
    company value, 1980–94   61
4.1 Cultural dimensions   91
5.1 Four models for globalization   108
6.1 Cisco's corporate development choice   135
6.2 Managing the post-agreement phase: overlapping
    challenges   143
7.1 Profit impact of global new product strategy options   172
8.1 Distribution of price premium for a strong brand   190
8.2 Brand strategy spectrum   193
9.1 Global marketing of new products   208
10.1 Domestic vs. non-domestic IPOs   231
10.2 Evolution of Nasdaq   232
10.3 Neuer Markt   233
10.4 The increasing share of non-domestic IPOs on Nasdaq
     and the Neuer Markt   234
10.5 Number of foreign countries represented on Nasdaq and
     the Neuer Markt (cumulative IPOs)   235

10.6 Number of non-domestic IPOs on Nasdaq by country of
origin (cumulative number of listings
for the period 1988–2001) 237
10.7 Number of non-domestic IPOs on the Neuer Markt by
country of origin (cumulative number of listings for the
period 1997–2001) 239
10.8 Issue price vs. first price (average), Neuer Markt,
1997–2001 239
10.9 Percentage difference between the issue price and the first
price, Neuer Markt, 1997–2001 240
10.10 Issue price vs. first price (average), Nasdaq,
1990–2001 241
10.11 Percentage difference between the issue price and the first
price, Nasdaq, 1990–2001 242
11.1 Equity returns around the world, 1900–2000 259
11.2 Testing the CAPM across countries 262
11.3 Testing the CAPM across countries and currencies 263
11.4 The world investor population 269
12.1 The supply chain 290
12.2 The supply chain's impact on ROA 291
12.3 The supply chain's balancing act 292
13.1 Four capabilities for successful global recombinative
innovation 312
17.1 The healthcare value chain 398

Tables

2.1 Stock market capitalization for selected advanced
    economies   *page* 32
2.2 Stock market capitalization for selected economies
    classified as "developing" at beginning of period   33
3.1 Members of the boards of directors of Enron, Tyco,
    and WorldCom before and after their scandals,
    2001, 2003   67
4.1 Jack Brown's action items/talking points for different
    parts of the world   92
5.1 Globalization of top business schools   105
7.1 Types of global segments   165
8.1 Value of global brands   192
9.1 Three international segmentation approaches   213
9.2 Waterfall vs. sprinkler strategies   216
11.1 Segmented and integrated views of Thalès   261
11.2 Required US dollar premium on Thalès according
     to the "hybrid model" incorporating world and
     country factors   264
11.3 Joint βs and hybrid pricing model for selected
     US firms   265
11.4 Joint βs and hybrid pricing model for selected
     French firms   266
11.5 Required US dollar premium on Thalès according to
     the IAPM incorporating world and currency factors   270
11.6 Required euro premium on Thalès according to the
     IAPM incorporating world and currency factors   271
11.7 A multi-beta model that prices political risk   273
15.1 Irreconcilable differences on privacy?   360
15.2 Information technology in the US economy   370

Contributors

RAPHAEL AMIT (WHARTON SCHOOL) Dr. Amit is the Robert B. Goergen Professor of Entrepreneurship, Professor of Management, Academic Director of the Goergen Entrepreneurial Management Programs, Director of the Wharton Electronic Business Initiative (*WeBI*). His research areas are in entrepreneurship, strategic management, venture capital financing, and e-business. Currently he is investigating business model design and performance, family ownership, control and management, and firm performance, growth of emerging businesses, digital transformation, and strategic alliance activity and firm performance. Among many publications, he is co-editor of *Creating Value: Winners in the New Business Environment* (2002).

PHILIP ANDERSON (INSEAD) Dr. Anderson is the INSEAD Alumni Fund Chaired Professor of Entrepreneurship, Director of the 3i Venturelab, and Director of the International Center for Entrepreneurship. His research interests include the formation of entrepreneurial firms, managing growth, processes of technological evolution, managing change and innovation, and strategies for private equity investors. He is co-author of *Managing Strategic Innovation and Change: A Collection of Readings* (1996; and 2nd edn. 2004), and *Inside the Kaisha: Demystifying Japanese Business Behavior* (1997).

REINHARD ANGELMAR (INSEAD) Dr. Angelmar is Professor of Marketing. His current research interests focus on the pharmaceutical industry. He is the co-author of three books, and has also written many case studies, which are used in business schools around the world, including "Advanced Drug Delivery Systems: The Partnership between Ciba-Geigy Pharmaceuticals and Alza Corporation" (with Y. Doz), and "Zantac" (with C. Pinson), which was the winning case in the 1998 European Case Clearing House Awards.

GORDON M. BODNAR (THE JOHNS HOPKINS UNIVERSITY)
Dr. Bodnar is the Morris W. Offit Professor of International Finance
at the Paul H. Nitze School of Advanced International Studies (SAIS),
The Johns Hopkins University. His research focuses on international
and corporate finance. Specific topics include corporate exchange
rate exposure, foreign exchange risk management, the valuation of
multinational operations, and financial disclosures. He is also an
occasional consultant to the financial industry, multinational firms,
and international research organizations.

LAWTON R. BURNS (WHARTON SCHOOL) Dr. Burns is the
James Joo-Jin Kim Professor, Professor of Health Care Systems and
Management, and Director of the Wharton Center for Health Management, and Economics. He is conducting research on integrated
healthcare, supply chain management, healthcare management,
formal organizations, physician networks, and physician practice
management firms. His current projects include examining the
healthcare supply chain, the structure, process, and outcomes of
integrated delivery systems in healthcare, and hospital ownership
conversions. He is the author of *The Health Care Value Chain*
(2002).

THOMAS D'AUNNO (INSEAD) Dr. D'Aunno is the Novartis
Chaired Professor of Healthcare Management, Director of
INSEAD's Healthcare Management Initiative, and Professor of
Organizational Behavior. His research focus is on organizational
behavior and the performance of healthcare organizations. Dr.
D'Aunno has conducted national studies in the United States that
were funded by the National Institute on Drug Abuse (NIDA),
the Agency for Health Care Quality and Research, and the Pew
Memorial Trust.

GEORGE S. DAY (WHARTON SCHOOL) Dr. Day is the Geoffrey
T. Boisi Professor, Professor of Marketing, Co-Director of the Mack
Center for Technological Innovation, and Director of the Emerging Technologies Management Research Program. His research
areas include market-driven competitive strategies in global markets, new product development and management, market structure
and competitive analysis, strategic planning processes and methods, and marketing management. His current projects are centered

around competitive strategies in markets for emerging technologies, including how firms survive shake-outs; how innovative organizations choose their growth directions; building market-driven organizations; and capabilities for forging customer relationships. He is the author of *Market-Driven Strategy* (1990) and *The Market-Driven Organization* (1999), and he co-edited *Wharton on Managing Emerging Technologies* (2000).

ARNOUD DE MEYER (INSEAD) Professor De Meyer is the Akzo Nobel Fellow of Strategic Management, Professor of Technology Management and Asian Business and Comparative Management. He is also INSEAD Deputy Dean and Dean of Administration. His main research interests are in innovation management, technology strategy, the implementation of new manufacturing technologies, and the management of R&D. He has authored or co-authored several books, including *Creating Customer Advantage* (1992) and *The Bright Stuff: How Innovative People and Technology Can Make the Old Economy New* (2002).

BERNARD DUMAS (INSEAD) Dr. Dumas is the Rothschild Chaired Professor of Banking and Professor of Finance. He specializes in research in the fields of international finance (investments and portfolio management), international corporate finance, international economics (trade and balance of payments), continuous-time dynamic finance, and capital markets. He is the co-author of *Financial Securities: Market Equilibrium and Pricing Methods* (1996) and *Les titres financiers: équilibre du marché et méthodes d'évaluation* (1995).

HUBERT GATIGNON (INSEAD) Dr. Gatignon is the Claude Janssen Chaired Professor of Business Administration, Professor of Marketing, Dean of the PhD Program, Research Director of the INSEAD–Wharton Alliance, and Director of the Alliance Center for Global Research and Development. His research areas include modeling the factors influencing the adoption and diffusion of innovations and measuring how the effects of marketing mix variables change over conditions and over time. His current research deals with innovation strategies, as well as international marketing strategy. Dr. Gatignon recently published *Statistical Analysis of Management Data* (2003) and he is also a co-author of *MARKSTRAT3: The*

Strategic Marketing Simulation (1997) and *ADSTRAT: An Advertising Decision Support System* (1991).

MAURO F. GUILLÉN (WHARTON SCHOOL) Dr. Guillén is the Felix Zandman Professor of International Management and Professor of Management and Sociology. His research areas are multinational and comparative management, organizational behavior, and sociology of organizations. His current projects include patterns of corporate governance around the world and development of the Internet across countries. Among his recent publications is *The Limits of Convergence: Globalization and Organizational Change in Argentina, South Korea, and Spain* (2000).

PATRICK T. HARKER (WHARTON SCHOOL) Dean Harker is the Reliance Professor of Management and Private Enterprise, Professor of Operations and Information Management and Systems Engineering, and Dean of the Wharton School. His research areas include service operations management and economics, the performance and design of financial institutions, and information technology. His current projects are in the field of productivity and quality in services, customer relationship management (CRM), service quality, and computational equilibrium modeling. He is co-author of *Performance of Financial Institutions* (2000).

GABRIEL HAWAWINI (INSEAD) Dean Hawawini is the Henry Grunfeld Chaired Professor of Investment Banking, Professor of Finance, and Dean of INSEAD. His research interests include corporate finance; value-based management; valuation and risk estimation, and corporate strategy and financial markets. He is the author of twelve books, including *Mergers and Acquisitions in the US Banking Industry* (1991) and *Finance for Executives: Managing for Value Creation* (2nd edn., 2002).

ROBERT J. HOUSE (WHARTON SCHOOL) Dr. House is the Joseph Frank Bernstein Professor of Organizational Studies and Professor of Management. His research involves the topics of leadership, motivation, personality and performance, and cross-cultural organizational behavior. He is principal investigator for the Global Leadership and Organizational Behaviour Effectiveness (GLOBE) research project. Among many publications, he is co-author of "Culture, Leadership, and Organizational Practices," in

Advances in Global Leadership (1999), and "Cross Cultural Leadership," in *Cross Cultural Organizational Behavior and Psychology* (1997).

MANSOUR JAVIDAN (UNIVERSITY OF CALGARY) Dr. Javidan is Professor of Strategic Management and Chairman of the Strategy and Global Management Area. His research interests are in the areas of strategic management, top management performance, cross-cultural leadership, mergers and acquisitions, and e-business strategy. He is a member of the coordinating team for the Global Leadership and Organizational Behavior Effectiveness (GLOBE) research project and a co-principal investigator of the GLOBE Phase 3 research program.

ETHAN B. KAPSTEIN (INSEAD) Dr. Kapstein is the Paul Dubrule Chaired Professor of Sustainable Development and Professor of Economics and Political Science. He is a specialist in international economic relations. He is the author or editor of eight books, the most recent of which is *Sharing the Wealth: Workers and the World Economy* (1999).

JOHN R. KIMBERLY (WHARTON SCHOOL) Dr. Kimberly is the Henry Bower Professor of Entrepreneurial Studies and Professor of Management, Health Care Systems, and Sociology. His research areas are organizational design, organizational change, institutional creation, health policy, and managerial innovation. His current projects include processes and consequences of firms' internationalizing activities, competition and collaboration among healthcare organizations in local markets, structure and mobility of managerial elites, and competition and change in business education. His recent publications include *The Quality Imperative: Measurement and Management of Quality in Health* (2000) and "Emerging Technologies and the Customized Workplace" in *Wharton on Managing Emerging Technologies* (2000).

PAUL R. KLEINDORFER (WHARTON SCHOOL) Dr. Kleindorfer is the Anheuser-Busch Professor of Management Science, Professor of Decision Sciences, Economics, and Business and Public Policy, Chairperson of the Operations and Information Management Department and Co-Director of the Risk Management and Decision Processes Center. He is conducting research on pricing and capacity policies for capital-intensive industries, governmental regulation, and energy and environmental policy and strategy. Currently he is examining the topics of risk management for the energy sector, the economics of postal and delivery services, environmental strategy, and natural hazards insurance and mitigation. He co-authored *Decision Sciences: An Integrative Perspective* (1993) and *Future Directions in Postal Reform* (2001).

STEPHEN J. KOBRIN (WHARTON SCHOOL) Dr. Kobrin is the William H. Wurster Professor of Multinational Management. His research areas include international political economy, globalization, the politics of cyberspace, and privacy. He is currently examining the political and social impacts of the information revolution, the governance of cyberspace, global governance, the US–EU data privacy dispute, and cyberspace and territoriality. He is author of "Sovereignty @ Bay: Globalization, Multinational Enterprise and the International Political System," in *The Oxford Handbook of International Business* (2001), and "Economic Governance in an Electronically Networked Global Economy," in *The Emergence of Private Authority: Forms of Private Authority and Their Implications for Global Governance* (2002).

RICHARD MARSTON (WHARTON SCHOOL) Dr. Marston is the James R. F. Guy Professor of Finance, Professor of Economics, and Director of the Weiss Center for International Financial Research. His research interests include international investments, international asset pricing, and foreign exchange risk management. Currently, he is investigating the topics of international asset pricing and exchange rate exposure of firms. He is the author of *International Financial Integration* (1995).

MARY A. O'SULLIVAN (INSEAD) Dr. O'Sullivan is Associate Professor of Strategy. Her broad research interests include political economy, the history of economic thought, and economic history. She is currently co-directing a three-year research project funded by the European Commission on "Corporate Governance, Innovation, and Economic Performance" (http://www.insead.fr/projects/cgep/). She is the author of *Contests for Corporate Control* (2000).

ERIC W. ORTS (WHARTON SCHOOL) Dr. Orts is the Guardsmark Professor, Professor of Legal Studies and Management, and Director of the Environmental Management Program. He conducts research on corporate and securities law, corporate governance, and environmental law and policy. His current projects include research on a social theory of the business enterprise, and informational regulation of the environment in the digital age. He is co-author of *Environmental Contracts: Comparative Approaches to Regulatory Innovation in the United States and Europe* (2001).

DAVID J. REIBSTEIN (WHARTON SCHOOL) Dr. Reibstein is the William Stewart Woodside Professor and Professor of Marketing. His research areas include competitive marketing strategies, electronic commerce resource allocation, promotion evaluation, market segmentation, product variety, and brand equity. He is currently engaged in examining competitive marketing strategies. Among many publications, he is author of *Marketing: Concepts, Strategies, and Decisions* (1985), and co-editor of *Wharton on Dynamic Competitive Strategy* (1997).

LORI ROSENKOPF (WHARTON SCHOOL) Dr. Rosenkopf's research interests include technological and organizational evolution, innovation diffusion, and learning in interorganizational networks. Her current projects include understanding how networks of technical professionals and firms shape technological evolution; tracking connections between technical committee activity, director/officer interlocks, and alliances in the cellular industry, and exploring how and when social capital of individuals accrues to firms. Dr. Rosenkopf wrote "Managing Dynamic Knowledge Networks," in *Wharton on Managing Emerging Technologies* (2000).

HARBIR SINGH (WHARTON SCHOOL) Dr. Singh is the Edward H. Bowman Professor of Management and Co-Director, at the Mack Center for Technological Innovation. His research interests include the areas of strategies for corporate acquisitions, corporate governance, joint ventures, management buyouts, and corporate restructuring. He is co-author of *Knowledge@Wharton on Building Corporate Value* (2002) and *Innovations in International and Cross-Cultural Management* (2000).

GÜNTER K. STAHL (INSEAD) Dr. Stahl is Assistant Professor of Asian Business and Comparative Management. His research extends into the areas of leadership and leadership development, cross-cultural management, and international human resource management. His current research interests also include international careers, trust within and between organizations, and the management of mergers and acquisitions. He has co-authored several books, including *Developing Global Business Leaders: Policies, Processes, and Innovations* (2001). Currently, he is co-editing a new book, *Mergers and Acquisitions: Managing Culture and Human Resources*.

MICHAEL USEEM (WHARTON SCHOOL) Dr. Useem is the William and Jacalyn Egan Professor, Professor of Management, and Director of the Center for Leadership and Change Management. His research areas include leadership and governance, corporate change and restructuring, and institutional investors. He is currently examining decision-making in leadership, leadership development, company leadership in a globalizing equity market, leading organizational change and restructuring, leadership during periods of challenge, stress, and uncertainty, and lateral and upward leadership. He is the author of *Upward Bound: Nine Original Accounts of How Business Leaders Reached Their Summits* (2003), *Leading Up: How to Lead Your Boss so You Both Win* (2001), and *Investor Capitalism: How Money Managers Are Changing the Face of Corporate America* (1996).

CHRISTOPHE VAN DEN BULTE (WHARTON SCHOOL) Dr. Van den Bulte is Assistant Professor of Marketing. His research interests encompass the fields of new product diffusion, social networks, and industrial marketing. His current projects include studying the impact of social contagion and population heterogeneity in the diffusion of innovations, investigating variations in the speed of transfer of best practices within organizations, and examining patterns of product-market entry and subsequent performance in the US mutual fund industry.

LUK N. VAN WASSENHOVE (INSEAD) Dr. Van Wassenhove is the Henry Ford Chaired Professor of Manufacturing and Professor of Operations Management. His research is concerned with integrated operations management, time compression, quality, and continual improvement and learning. Among his recent publications are *Industrial Excellence: Management Quality in Manufacturing*

(2003) and *Quantitative Approaches to Distribution Logistics and Supply Chain Management* (2002).

MAURIZIO ZOLLO (INSEAD) Dr. Zollo is Associate Professor of Strategy and Management. His work is concerned with researching and teaching on the management of corporate development processes, from strategy implementation (acquisitions and strategic alliances) to organizational learning and social responsibility issues. The managerial insights from his research have been featured in several book chapters.

CHRISTOPH ZOTT (INSEAD) Dr. Zott is the Rudolf and Valeria Maag Fellow of Entrepreneurship and Associate Professor of Entrepreneurship. His research interests are centered on the process of business creation, on the design of business models, and on venture capital finance. Articles he has written on these subjects have appeared in several books. Dr. Zott has been an academic advisor to companies that have been created by recent INSEAD graduates, including PangoSystems, iFox, and NetVestibule.

Foreword

THE Wharton School of the University of Pennsylvania and INSEAD are delighted to contribute to advancing scholarship and business practice through our ambitious Alliance. From its start, the Alliance was focused not only on education but also on developing the knowledge to meet the challenges of a changing global business environment. This book is the fruit of our collaboration.

We are proud of the contributions this volume makes to addressing the complex challenges of globalizing business. We are especially pleased that the theme of the book corresponds precisely to our objectives as leading business schools: to create a model for delivering life-long business education through a global knowledge network. This book is a reflection of the depth and breadth of insights from the combined faculties of two leading business schools. We would like to thank our colleagues on both sides of the Atlantic – each an expert in a specific discipline – for joining together with us to create this much broader view of global management.

DEAN PATRICK HARKER
The Wharton School
University of Pennsylvania
Philadelphia, USA

DEAN GABRIEL HAWAWINI
INSEAD
Fontainebleau, France

Acknowledgments

THIS book was the product of a true collaboration between the faculties of the Wharton School and INSEAD, and we are grateful for the enthusiasm for this project of faculty from both schools and across many different departments. In particular, we would like to acknowledge the wisdom and guidance of our colleagues on the Steering Committee for this book project: George Day, Yves Doz, Bernard Dumas, Pat Harker, Gabriel Hawawini, Richard Herring, Bruce Kogut, and Subi Rangan. We are especially grateful to Deans Patrick Harker and Gabriel Hawawini for their vision and dedicated support of the Alliance and this project. It has been our personal pleasure to work with the authors on this project.

We have benefited from the enthusiasm and insights of Chris Harrison and Katy Plowright of Cambridge University Press. We would also like to acknowledge the hard work of Susan Almstead-Treffel at INSEAD in supporting this project in many ways.

Globalization is reshaping our world in ways that create many new challenges for managers and business researchers, as discussed on the following pages, but these changes also create wonderful opportunities for broader and richer collaboration. This book has represented one such opportunity, and we are very grateful to have had the chance to join such an outstanding group of colleagues in making it a reality.

HUBERT GATIGNON
Fontainebleau, France

JOHN R. KIMBERLY
Philadelphia, USA

1 | Globalization and its challenges

HUBERT GATIGNON
INSEAD

JOHN R. KIMBERLY
Wharton School

W HILE debates about globalization rage in the media, at international conferences, and in the streets, managers still have work to do. They need to create profitable businesses and generate returns for investors by entering global markets, compete against international rivals, make investments, and find opportunities in the shifting tableau of a world in continuous transformation. And they need to do this in a way that is environmentally and socially responsible. The global arena is where the extraordinary opportunities lie, but it is also where complexity and risk abound.

Although some government leaders may feel they have a choice about whether to participate in this process of globalization, it is not a matter of choice for businesses. All but the most insular business leaders recognize that in a world in which markets are global, they need to be actors on the world stage. In fact, apart from a few wealthy individual investors, firms are the economic entities that *must* create value across national boundaries. Firms are responsible for producing and delivering the goods and services that benefit the people of the world. And firms are the actors that can create new opportunities for sustainable economic development.

Even as the political debate continues between proponents of *globalization* and its "discontents,"[1] companies are wrestling day-to-day with the process of *globalizing*. The debate over globalization is itself part of the context for world business, but managers of global corporations face other complex problems. They need to lead and govern far-flung international enterprises, enter diverse international markets, and manage risks and uncertainties that range from global supply chains to financial risks to geopolitical risks.

Our objective in this book is to illuminate and understand more fully the challenges that confront managers today in firms that are globalizing. To this end, faculty from Wharton and INSEAD probe deeply

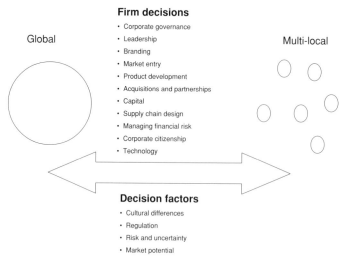

Figure 1.1. Globalizing decisions.

into issues of leadership, finance, marketing, operations, mergers and acquisitions, and entrepreneurship that are encountered as firms globalize.

Decisions without borders

To consider just one dimension of globalizing, managers need to decide whether to pursue a global or multilocal strategy in a variety of business areas, as summarized in Figure 1.1. Should the company develop global brands or tailor branding to the quirks of individual markets? To what extent can the company create more uniform global products? What are the opportunities and risks of establishing global supply chains? How can the company successfully complete a merger that joins together diverse organizational and national cultures? How can the company be a good "corporate citizen" when it is expected to be a citizen of so many different nations? How should its leadership be tailored to the demands of individual cultures while addressing the concerns of global investors? Among the factors that might influence such decisions are the extent of cultural differences across regions in which the company operates, the regulatory regimes that apply, perceptions of risk and uncertainty, and estimates of market potential. These and many other factors in the environment and within the organization will shape the choice of strategy for globalizing.

As complex as the decisions presented in Figure 1.1 may be, the figure itself is a heuristic that necessarily oversimplifies the reality that managers face. In practice, they are faced with a wide array of options, from creating a wholly owned subsidiary to becoming a small shareholder with one partner.[2] They may create a portfolio of brands and products, some of which are global and others of which are local, depending on factors such as the specific products, cultures, and targeted segments. Furthermore, decisions about globalizing occur within the context of broader business considerations such as ensuring returns on investment, recognizing organizational constraints, or addressing competitive threats.

Global challenges represent complex and interwoven puzzles. Although each of the following chapters of this book focuses on a different set of decisions, in practice these decisions are closely linked. Leadership and governance, for example, cannot be separated from regulation. Product development must go hand-in-hand with supply chain design and management. Listing the firm on different international exchanges affects the role of investors in shaping governance. Advances in telecommunications and other technologies have facilitated the rise of global outsourcing, with an estimated 3.3 million white-collar jobs and $136 billion in wages being expected to move from the United States to other countries by 2015.[3] As security has become a greater national priority for the United States and other nations, the "Washington Consensus" of the 1990s, which promoted increasing globalization and the establishment of a "new world order," has begun to unravel (accelerated by the tragic events of September 11, 2001). The emerging "new world disorder" has increased political, economic, and financial risks,[4] raising the importance of companies' tactical, globalizing decisions in areas such as market entry, branding, or operations.

To add further to the complexity, the global environment is not static. For example, once a company has made a decision to enter a specific market, managers might then need to rethink their decisions about other issues such as product development, supply chain and financial risks, or corporate citizenship. There are dynamic changes in the environment, including economic crises, new regulations, or political rebellions that can have a significant impact on these decisions over time. Regulatory changes such as the passage of Sarbanes–Oxley in the United States, for example, have had significant, and often unexpected, impacts on firms in Europe and other parts of the world.

Understanding the process of globalizing

The process of "globalization," which has grabbed the headlines, refers to the big-picture process that draws products, services, and markets around the world closer together. It is a process that involves a complex array of actors and institutions, including firms, governments, NGOs, and consumers. This process is typically analyzed at the macroeconomic level, where the country is the unit of analysis. The primary focus of the often strident and heavily rhetorical debates about globalization has been on macroeconomic policies, as exemplified by the discussions on the Tobin tax, on the role of international institutions in influencing these policies, and on what some see as the exploitation of underdeveloped countries and their labor forces (or, from another perspective, the threats of outsourcing from these countries to domestic economies).

Globalizing, in contrast, refers to the process by which a given firm becomes increasingly global in its objectives and operations. Few, if any, firms are truly "global"; many, however, are globalizing. In our view, globalizing is a process that unfolds not at the level of the country but at the level of the firm, and consists of the actions firms have to take as they become more engaged in that process. This book focuses on the business side of the global challenge: managing the process of globalizing in today's increasingly interconnected, fast-moving international environment.

Globalization creates the context for globalizing

To understand the process of globalizing, we certainly cannot ignore the broader process of globalization. Our global political and economic systems create the context for our business enterprises. As Thomas Friedman writes in *The Lexus and the Olive Tree*, "the slow, fixed, divided Cold War system that had dominated international affairs since 1945 has been firmly replaced by a new, very greased, interconnected system called globalization."[5] This global system is quite different from the period of globalization that preceded World War II. In contrast to the pre-war global economy based on shipping, the current era of globalization is facilitated by technology and has made the flow of information and capital nearly frictionless. As Friedman points out, the post-Cold War global economy is also different politically, because it is based on an open international trading system. Technological advances combined with political openness have forged a dramatically different environment for business. While the process of globalization that Friedman chronicles has changed the world in significant and, sometimes, irreversible ways, recent political shifts may have begun to slow or even reverse what once appeared to be a rapid and relentless march to greater economic integration.

With the maturing of a global economy, there remains a basic mismatch between global financial markets and our political institutions, a gap that places deeper demands on business leaders to fill in the missing pieces. As George Soros notes in his book *On Globalization*, "the development of our international institutions has not kept pace with the development of international financial markets."[6] He points out, for example, that while capital can move freely around the globe, people cannot. As a result of this mismatch between regional regulation and global economic activity, current institutions such as the World Trade Organization have come under attack from both the left, where activists protest the destructive impact of globalization on local economies and cultures, and the right, where there are worries about the impact of these global institutions on restricting open markets.

This lack of global infrastructure also means that companies sometimes have to step into the gaps to create their own infrastructure or policy, or work as partners with global organizations and governments to create conditions in which they can conduct business. The relationships between government, NGOs, international agencies, and companies can be quite complex, particularly in the developing world. For example, the Chad–Cameroon oil pipeline project in Africa was developed through the cooperation of the World Bank, national governments, NGOs concerned about impact on the environment and indigenous cultures, and a consortium of major oil companies, who compete fiercely against one another in this region and other parts of the world.

Companies can and do influence the process of globalization in a variety of ways, although the extent of their impact is debatable. The highly visible success of global firms such as McDonald's and Disney has been a lightning rod for protesters concerned about cultural dominance and economic imperialism by US multinationals. Because firms can profit from globalization, they may contribute to the pressures on governments and international organizations to liberalize exchanges, a criticism that has been made of the influence of American lobbies especially on the negotiations of the World Trade Organization.[7] However, as we will see, other forces are probably more significant.

While the concept of giant multinationals practicing global corporate imperialism may be appealing to the popular imagination, these firms still depend upon a democratic process of attracting consumers who are free to vote with their dollars, rupees, euros, roubles, or yuan. Unless these global companies bring benefits to local markets and populations, their long-term prospects will be limited. Even as protesters around the world were targeting the storefronts of Western megabrands, consumers in these countries were continuing to purchase US products. For example, while students were protesting the US-led war in Iraq in 2003, they still headed to the theater in the evening, driving overseas box office receipts for American movies to near-record highs.[8] And although there will inevitably be highly visible instances where a firm's managerial practices clash with local cultures, part of the success of global firms is derived from the application of management practices developed elsewhere (and ideally adapted to local circumstances). Questions about the protection of a culture may fall largely into the political domain, but firms must take these cultural differences into account in the development of their strategies and in managing their operations. Adapting and responding to local markets is not only good global citizenship; it is good business.

This global context is dynamic and uncertain. The breakdown of WTO negotiations in Cancun and the vote in Sweden against adopting the euro have a significant impact on integration of global and European markets. The agreements that are forged at these meetings, or fail to be forged, not only affect the progress of individual nations but can also rapidly improve or limit the prospects for specific and even local global firms.

Global economic interdependencies and opportunities continue to increase with the rapid rise of offshoring of service operations. Through business process outsourcing (BPO), companies are shipping out call centers, transaction processing, claims processing, data entry, MIS reporting, cash-flow forecasting and insurance yield and risk analysis.

Gartner Research estimates that offshore business process outsourcing services will grow from $1.3 billion to $24.3 billion from 2002 to 2007, an 80 percent compound average growth rate.[9]

These shifts have tremendous impacts both at home and abroad. As Marcus Courtney, an organizer with the Washington Alliance of Technology Workers, an affiliate of the Communications Workers of America, told *Knowledge@Wharton*, "America's leading high-tech companies such as Microsoft and IBM are exporting our country's best-paying high skilled jobs in order to slash labor costs. This trend will only increase job insecurity, lower wages and mean fewer benefits for America's white-collar professionals."[10]

Even if businesses are not actively engaged in the debates over globalization themselves, they cannot ignore them. In this book, we explore how firms can best respond to the opportunities offered by the globalization of world markets for the good of the people of the world as well as for their own sustainable economic development. We also discuss how firms must take into account the implications of less positive trends such as the highly visible and sometimes violent reactions of protest groups, even if these reactions are frequently more directed at governments and international organizations like the IMF than at individual firms. To understand the context for globalizing decisions, we begin with an analysis of some of the forces that are driving globalization in general.

Forces driving globalization

To understand the dynamic unfolding of globalization, we need to consider the complex forces that are driving this process. While recent writings on globalization have focused more narrowly on the proactive role of international organizations such as the IMF or the WTO in the liberalization of markets,[11] many other factors are impelling or impeding this process of globalization, including:[12]

• *Liberalization of capital markets:* With the digitization of capital, investments have flowed ever more freely across international borders. Much of the attention has focused on problems resulting from this liberalization, such as financial crises in Asia in 1997, the Russian crisis, and the Argentinian crisis of 2002, which sparked criticism of IMF policies. Opponents of liberalization criticized the free movement of capital across countries and, most particularly, the hot money characterized by short-term speculative cross-currency movements. Proposals such as the Tobin tax or the Chilean tax on short-term capital have been made to limit these speculations. Without in any way denying the problems of speculation and the macroeconomic remedies that may be applicable, there have also been benefits from this liberalization. For example, one of the benefits of liberalization is greater access to funds for individual entrepreneurs or small and medium-sized firms. Outside of the United States, banks are very often under the control of governments that favor lending to institutions they control more or less directly or formally.[13] This has been the case in South Korea,[14] and also in France, as the scandals of the Crédit Lyonnais during the 1980s illustrated. While more government controls may be placed in the future, as recommended by highly respected economists, it will be difficult, considering economic history over the long term and the increased flow of goods and services across nations, to prevent further liberalization of the capital markets. This liberalization of capital markets has clearly created many opportunities for investment, but also increased risks from currency fluctuations and interlinked financial markets.

• *Advances in technology and accelerating information flows:* Rapid technological progress has had direct and indirect impacts on globalization. Among its direct impacts has been the shift to manufactured products from agriculture, especially for the developing countries that have difficulty in competing in food products with heavily subsidized rivals from the United States and Europe (receiving 20 percent to 35 percent subsidies, respectively).[15] Communication and information technologies have facilitated exchanging information and conducting transactions quickly and cheaply, diminishing the barriers of distance and international borders. These changes have spawned new industries and created new opportunities, as well as sparked debate about legislation to control them. The flow of information, in turn, accelerates the diffusion of innovation between countries. Diffusion occurs at different rates in different countries, and business leaders need be concerned about the rate of transfer of technologies between countries to manage cross-border innovation, develop new products and services for a global market, and protect intellectual property. They also need to look at the potential opportunities and threats created by the Internet and other technologies, particularly their second-order and third-order effects in transforming business models and markets. The costs and risks of moving too slowly or too quickly can be enormous, as telecom companies found in sky-high bidding for G3 wireless licenses in Europe at a time when the industry was retrenching.

• *Mobility of people:* While people, at present, remain for the most part bound to their homeland, we can expect a sharp increase in labor movement over the coming decades. The movement for a free labor market started with the unification of Germany and the dismantling of the Communist bloc.[16] Several factors support a continuation of this trend. The populations of industrialized countries are getting older, creating a demand for labor, while poorer countries with young, active populations have a labor supply growing beyond what they can absorb. Moreover, these cheaper workers in some emerging countries have received the best education, which makes them competitive in the world labor market. The populations of the most industrially advanced countries are more diverse than ever. Migration is increasing, driven by factors such as wars and political dissent as well as economic opportunities. Some have argued that an increase in the freedom of labor movement will be indispensable in the future.[17] A smaller, but nevertheless critical phenomenon is a significant increase in passenger traffic for business and tourism. Increasing movements of people around the globe have obvious implications for human resources decisions of companies, and also affect the diffusion of products, ideas, and culture.[18]

• *Mobility of products:* Barriers to trade are falling, in large part because of the role of the GATT and the World Trade Organization. There are still limitations, mostly due to the effects of lobbies, either for business or for cultural protectionism or both. Nevertheless, in general, the possibility of selling any product anywhere in the world is becoming a reality. This creates opportunities for businesses to enter diverse markets more easily. But competitors have the same opportunities so it has led to new threats from aggressive global competitors who can move much more easily into an established firm's markets at home and abroad. Competition can come from unexpected quarters.

• *Decline in transportation costs:* Part of the reason for the mobility of people and goods is the decline in transportation costs. Increased capacities and new technologies have reduced costs to the point that materials that were too bulky to transport long distances are now manufactured in a single location and shipped to the rest of the world. The new Beetle, produced in Puebla, Mexico for export around the world is a good example. Reduced transportation costs have major implications for the localization of manufacturing facilities and global sourcing. As long as energy costs are low, this trend is likely to continue.

• *Global regulatory harmonization:* Two major factors motivate a greater harmonization of regulations. First, as firms transact more across country boundaries and compete on a global basis, the need for homogeneous regulation increases, as seen in the standardization of international accounting rules. Second, greater diffusion of concerns about environmental issues such as the emission of toxic gases in industrialized countries and deforestation in developing countries is leading to greater harmonization of global regulations in this area. Businesses often feel the greatest impacts of these regulations, both positively and negatively. On the one hand, clear and uniform regulations can help reduce uncertainty and level the playing field across international markets. On the other hand, new regulations can restrict a business or destroy it, or impose significant additional costs, from environmental compliance or from taxation, on companies.

• *Cultural convergence (cultural context and identity):* Similarities among cultures can be expected to increase in the future on account of sharing of products, experiences, travel, and communications, and the use of the English language as an international mode of communication. This does not mean, however, that all cultures will move towards a single culture. While globalization is sometimes accused of leading to cultural hegemony, or at least homogenization, it is not clear what is the cause and what is the effect.[19] There are clearly a number of factors which explain cultural convergence – such as economic development, urbanization, and mass media coverage – that have nothing to do with globalization. History and languages are also intimately linked to cultures and are very resilient. There may also be greater differences among groups of people within countries than across. For example, rural populations in a given country may be more similar to rural dwellers in other nations than urban populations in the same country. Increasing uniformity can facilitate the development of mass markets, while awareness of cultural differences can help companies identify niche opportunities. Cultural convergence is also a key concern of critics of globalization, and companies need to be aware of and respond to these concerns about respect for local cultures as they build global businesses.

• *Emerging markets and economic development:* During the last two decades, a number of countries have reached levels of development that place them well within the set of industrialized countries. Mauro Guillén cites South Korea as an example of a country that went from a "backward developing country" to an "export and foreign investment power" with fourteen Korean firms within the Fortune Global 500 list published in the mid nineties.[20] The end of the Communist regimes in Russia and in Eastern Europe as well as the opening of China to a market economy have created a new set of opportunities for development within these countries and in collaboration with the rest of the world. The impact of opening markets is not uniform. China's revenue per inhabitant has continuously increased while Russia's economic situation is critical, with a GDP currently inferior to what it was under the Communist regime. These emerging markets are heterogeneous, and to be successful, businesses must understand the peculiarities of each, as demonstrated by the experience in China. Economic development in these countries can open significant new markets and also create new players in global markets, as has been seen in electronics, automobiles, and other industries.

• *Increased interdependency:* The utility derived from a particular product may depend on network effects across countries. For example, the utility of the telephone increases with the number of users in all countries. As mobility and communication increases, these global externalities become greater at the international level. This has clear implications for the production and marketing of products such as telecommunications that depend upon these network effects, and these effects also serve to increase the interdependency of different parts of the world.

• *Global consolidation:* Through mergers and acquisitions, we have seen the rapid consolidation of businesses across borders. As firms compete more in multiple geographical markets and face the same competitors, size has become a critical factor. Coordination also is important, so relevant information about markets must be transmitted to managers in different countries. To achieve this coordination, companies that once had arm's-length relationships with local companies are now seeking ownership (as well as strategic alliances and joint ventures). Business leaders face many challenges in managing these organizations that span diverse organizational and ethnic cultures and face multiple and sometime conflicting business and regulatory environments.

• *Corporate social responsibility:* Concern about corporate social responsibility, which has been on the business agenda for at least a decade or two, has been raised to a new level in global markets. This is due, in large part, to the failure of the international organizations (especially the IMF and the World Trade Organization) to provide balanced economic development to poorer countries. For balanced globalization to become a reality, government leaders would need to agree to some international principles, such as the proposal by Tina Rosenberg for "nine new rules" for the global economy.[21] These agreements will necessarily focus on a number of controversial issues such as mobility of people and environmental protection. Business leaders need to recognize and respond to these new demands for global corporate responsibility. In addition to working with governments and other firms to tackle broader issues, companies also need to address individual responsibilities such as designing policies for local compensation and benefits to avoid exploitation.

While these driving forces are propelling the world toward greater globalization, we also see some countervailing trends moving the world toward greater separation. Concerns about security, cultural and religious differences, and protests against the process of globalization itself are among the forces that are driving in the opposite direction. While the overall trend may be toward greater globalization, there are times when these countervailing forces will slow the trend or reverse it, particularly in certain regions or time periods.

How can managers chart a course through these driving forces of globalization? What challenges do these forces create for managers engaged in globalizing their firms? At times, corporate leaders, like sailors, can use the crosswinds of globalization to propel their businesses forward. At other times, they need to avoid being blown off course.

Charting a course through the crosswinds of globalization

What do we know about the process of globalizing? Business researchers have been working with leaders of global firms to explore global challenges and best practice for decades. Much of this research, however, has focused on a single aspect of the overall process – such as entering new markets or considering financial risks. This book takes a broader view, drawing upon the experience and research of experts from diverse disciplines and perspectives to address many key management challenges faced by firms as they become more global. It offers a multifaceted perspective on the processes and strategies for success.

The following chapters examine a number of strategic issues facing firms as they globalize. The authors offer both broad perspectives and practical insights to any manager involved in global business as well as to students, policymakers, leaders of NGOs, and others seeking to understand better the complex challenges facing business leaders. Our objective in publishing the book is to stimulate informed dialogue among those who are key actors in the unfolding story of globalization and managers facing the immediate struggles of globalizing their businesses. In particular, the following chapters explore management responses in three broad areas that cut across typical management functions:

(1) Leading the global organization
(2) Global market participation
(3) Managing risk and uncertainty.

Leading the global organization

- *The changing international corporate governance landscape*
- *Corporate governance and leadership in a globalizing equity market*
- *Leadership in a global organization: a cross-cultural perspective*
- *The globalization of business education*

Part I of the book examines corporate governance and leadership in the global context. In the first chapter, Mauro Guillén and Mary O'Sullivan look at the challenges of corporate governance. In a world of poorly developed global governmental structures, business leaders are directly exposed to the challenge of global governance in all its dimensions. The leadership of such companies is critical and complex. In the wake of recent scandals, there has been intense discussion in nations around the world about the role of corporate governance and best practices for boards. But how do these practices need to differ internationally and are they converging to a uniform model? How do companies that compete in multiple markets need to design their corporate governance to meet the challenges of globalization and diverse standards? Is there one best answer to the question of governance? The best approach may depend on a variety of factors related to its strategy and the structure and pace of change in its industry, as well as its global context. There is not a one-size-fits-all approach to governance.

In the second chapter of this part, Mike Useem explores the impact of globalization of equity markets and the new demands of leadership, particularly from institutional investors. In the last two decades, equity markets have been transformed from markets dominated by orphans and widows to markets dominated by professional money managers. In the process, stockholders have taken the upper hand in the relationship with publicly held companies, giving investors more power over the destiny of companies. There has also been an increasing movement of equity investments across national borders. This chapter examines some of the implications of these changes, through stories of companies such as Vivendi Universal, Daimler Chrysler, and Toyota. Useem points out that the combination of these changes in ownership influence and global capital flows has made leadership and governance more important at all levels of the organization, increased the attention of investors to these issues, demanded that leaders focus more attention on equity markets, and moved governing boards in many parts of the world to greater transparency and greater independence.

What kind of leadership is needed for global firms? Former General Electric CEO Jack Welch commented that "The Jack Welch of the future cannot be me . . . The next head of General Electric will be somebody who spent time in Bombay, Hong Kong, in Buenos Aires. We have to send our best and brightest overseas . . ." In the third chapter in this part, Mansour Javidan, Günter Stahl, and Robert House examine the role of leadership in a global context, based on insights from one of the most extensive studies of global leadership. The Global Leadership and Organizational Behavior Effectiveness (GLOBE) project started in 1993 with funding from the National Science Foundation to examine the way effective leadership in different countries and cultures is similar or different. The project has involved 160 researchers from 62 countries, and 18,000 middle managers in food processing, banking, and telecomms. Based on this research, the authors consider examples of the different attributes of leadership needed in Singapore, Denmark, Argentina, and the United Kingdom.

Finally, the last chapter in this part offers insights from the deans of Wharton and INSEAD on the globalization of business education. The authors examine different models business schools have used to globalize, providing perspectives for managers on organizing or expanding global knowledge networks.

Global market participation

- *Globalization through acquisitions and alliances: an evolutionary perspective*
- *Developing new products and services for the global market*
- *Managing brands in global markets*
- *Global marketing of new products*
- *Global equity capital markets for emerging growth firms: patterns, drivers, and implications for the globalizing entrepreneur*

In his famous discussion of global marketing in the 1980s, Theodore Levitt foresaw a world of global brands and global products. The world was moving toward convergence, he contended, and companies that tailored their products and services to local markets were following misguided marketing research. He urged companies to organize according to a global model. The world that has since emerged is much more complicated than this initial vision. In Part II of the book, authors explore the complex terrain of global market entry, branding, and capital markets.

Companies need to make alliances or acquisitions to move into global markets, but the success rate, globally and domestically, continues to hover around 40 percent. Yet some companies do much better. The first chapter in this part, by Harbir Singh and Maurizio Zollo, explores the choice of acquisition or alliance and the capabilities needed for success, particularly in a global context. They consider the different approaches used by companies such as Hewlett Packard, Corning, Cisco, and Nationsbank to manage and structure alliance and acquisition capabilities. The authors point out the importance of post-acquisition integration and find that companies with better relational capabilities not only have higher success rates but also have more positive market reactions to their transactions – as much as $40 million in added return for companies with strong relational capabilities.

When Levitt urged managers to create global products, he pointed to Japanese companies such as Honda as an example of the opportunities. But, as Reinhard Angelmar points out in Chapter 7, the irony is that Honda ultimately moved away from its standardized global products after it ran into trouble using this approach. When Honda tried to please everyone with its 1994 Accord, it ended up pleasing no one. The model turned out to be too small for Americans and not stylish enough for the Japanese. In 1996, Honda remodeled the car for the US market, where it was a great success; but it was less successful in its home market. The company then did exactly what Levitt had advised against, developing three very different models – one for the United States, another for Japan, and a third for Europe. Angelmar examines how the development of new products needs to be tailored to diverse national markets, based on customer distinctiveness (how customers perceive things differently) and commonality inside the product (how much of the product is based on common parts and processes). Different companies have very different migration paths. Some move to sets of products that are very different technologically, but not highly differentiated by customers. Others have products that appear to be quite different to customers but actually share many common parts and processes. The chapter explores the reasons for different migration paths and the tradeoffs between distinctive product features and the cost and complexity of design and manufacturing.

In the next chapter in this part, George Day and David Reibstein paint a similarly multifaceted picture of another aspect of Levitt's philosophy: the creation of global brands. The authors note that contrary to Levitt's expectations that brands would become more global – with consistent names, identities, positionings, and target markets in every country – two decades of experience show that this is often not the case. The authors conclude that there are very few truly global brands, and that the forces promoting globalization and standardization are being blunted by countervailing forces that encourage adaptation and local identity. They explore how global companies are managing their brands, and how organizational innovations are facilitating the coordination process.

Once you have a new product, you could sell anywhere in the world. How do you roll it out? In the next chapter in this part, Hubert Gatignon and Christophe Van den Bulte explore the complex decisions about market entry, such as order of entry, and marketing mix strategies in different countries. Decisions about the selection and order of countries to enter with new products may be based on different views of segmentation and a consideration of diffusion patterns. The authors consider conditions that favor using a "waterfall" strategy (rapid and aggressive market entry across multiple markets) rather than a "sprinkler" strategy (a slower rollout across global markets).

As capital markets have become global, managers face a richer set of options in financing entrepreneurial ventures, as discussed by Raphael Amit and Christoph Zott in the final chapter of Part II. About 9 percent of new issues on the US Nasdaq exchange in the period 1998–2001 were for non-US firms and about 17 percent of the issues on the German Neuer Markt in the period 1997–2001 were for non-German companies. The expansion of global capital markets raises some very complex questions for managers financing new ventures. What are the advantages of non-US companies in listing on the US Nasdaq? What are the benefits for a US firm in listing on the German Neuer Markt? Drawing on an extensive database of offerings on exchanges in the United States and Germany, the authors explore the implications of globalizing capital markets and the implications of global capital markets for entrepreneurial firms.

Managing risk and uncertainty

- *Cross-border valuation: the international cost of equity capital*
- *Managing risk in global supply chains*
- *Global recombination: cross-border technology and innovation management*
- *From corporate social responsibility to global citizenship*
- *Colliding forces: domestic politics and the global economy*
- *Global implications of information and communication technologies (ICT)*

With the complexity of global markets come greater risk and uncertainty, which is the focus of Part III of the book. One of these risks comes from cross-border valuation of the international cost of equity capital, as examined by Gordon Bodnar, Bernard Dumas, and Richard Marston in Chapter 11. Managers have traditionally used the Capital Asset Pricing Model (CAPM) for valuation, which allows for a systematic comparison of the costs of equity in various traded securities. But international markets present many more dimensions of risk than can be captured by the CAPM. In this chapter, the authors examine these other sources of risk and explore new models that incorporate them into an assessment of the global cost of equity capital. The authors consider the implications of home vs. world stock market risk, currency risk, and political risk. The authors propose a "hybrid" CAPM containing several risk premia for home and world risks.

Sourcing in the global context provides many options for the international firm, especially with low cost transportation, but it also increases risks as supply chains are stretched around the globe. In Chapter 12, Paul Kleindorfer and Luk Van Wassenhove investigate the opportunities and challenges raised by global sourcing. One set of risks global supply chains face comes from mismatches between supply and demand, which are especially important in capital-intensive industries where short-term scalability is impossible and where utilization is a central driver of profitability. Another set of risks relates to disruption of the supply chain through major accidents or economic disruptions such as strikes or terrorist acts. The authors examine two ways to manage these risks and capitalize on the emerging upside opportunities of global supply chain revolutions: the design of the supply chain and contractual innovations. The authors also explore risk analysis for global supply chains, a process including identifying underlying sources of risk, determining the pathways by which such risks can materialize, estimating the potential consequences of those risks under various scenarios, and providing the means for mitigating and coping with these consequences.

Just as the supply chain is stretched across borders, so is R&D, intellectual property, and the flow of new ideas. How can companies manage cross-border technology and innovation knowledge, when it flows across national borders as well as across companies? In Chapter 13, Philip Anderson and Lori Rosenkopf examine how business leaders can understand and better design and manage knowledge networks to facilitate the diffusion of innovations across the organization and around the world.

Global businesses answer to a complex set of stakeholders, including government regulators and citizens of the home countries in which they operate, non-governmental organizations (NGOs), investors, partners, and customers. Companies are expected to demonstrate "corporate citizenship," but these stakeholders may have very different views of what this means. Further, because national citizenship still matters very much, companies very often find themselves wrestling with "multiple citizenship" as they try to meet different regulations and expectations in different countries. In Chapter 14, Eric Orts examines the meaning of global citizenship and its implications for managers and their firms. What does it mean to be a global corporate *citizen* in contrast to earlier discussions of corporate social *responsibility*? How much should companies identify with their local markets and how much should they consider themselves global?

Government actions sometimes create the greatest risks and uncertainties for business. Changes in regulations or regimes, and international agreements on issues from trade to the environment can reshape the competitive playing field for companies. In Chapter 15, Ethan Kapstein and Steve Kobrin explore the impact of government in shaping the business environment by looking at two cases. The first case considers issues related to global pharmaceuticals and the tension between the desire of governments in emerging economies to provide vital medicines to their populations and the need for companies to protect intellectual property to support future innovations. The second case examines the challenges of divergent privacy legislation around the world, particularly the gulf between the United States and European nations on regulations related to data privacy and personal information. Multinational companies that operate in Europe and the United States are subject to both sets of rules. If European privacy regulations were strictly enforced, for example, a US visitor might not be able to use an American bank card in a European ATM.

Finally, one of the key sources of uncertainty and global change is the spread of information and communications technology, particularly the rise of the Internet. In Chapter 16, Arnoud De Meyer explores the importance of web-related technologies in the global economy and the potential of these technologies for creating new business models and service innovations. Among the opportunities are the facilitation of "overnight globalization," creating geographically independent knowledge-based services, making the customer the locus of innovation, and enabling peer-to-peer communities.

Implications and conclusions

- *Globalization and its many faces: the case of the health sector*
- *The continuing process of globalizing*

How do all these complex forces and management responses fit together? What can we expect in the future? The concluding part of the book, draws together insights in an integrative case and discusses some of the future prospects for globalization and the challenges for managers in continuing to globalize their firms.

In Chapter 17, Lawton Burns, Thomas D'Aunno, and John Kimberly look at the interrelated challenges of globalizing business through the lens of the healthcare industry. This is an industry that is especially global from the universal nature of the needs it satisfies, but also because of the scale of the operations from R&D to marketing, and because of the fundamental human rights that it addresses in determining the life and death of entire populations. They point out that diverse players at various points in the value chain experience different rates of globalization. The authors consider some of the common forces shaping healthcare, some leading to increasing globalization – such as rising costs and payer concerns with cost containment – and others leading to greater local divergence. How can managers make decisions about their global organizations in the context of this complex and rapidly changing industry?

Finally, in the closing chapter of the book, we consider some of the challenges of the ongoing process of globalizing. This chapter provides reflections on key insights from throughout the book and identifies some of the future challenges for managers and researchers in addressing the unfolding challenge of globalizing.

The importance of globalization

Our subject matter is hardly academic. The fates and fortunes of companies hang upon decisions about globalizing, particularly as large portions of the developing world come rapidly online. For example, decisions by the People's Republic of China about wireless communications standards could shake the largest global telecommunications firms to their foundations given the size of the Chinese market. Markets such as China become the tail that wags the dog of global business, and participation is not merely a question of growth but of survival for some firms. Yet while the risks of *not* participating may be great, there are also very significant risks of participating in these markets. The choices for acting in these markets can be quite complex. Companies neither want to be left behind nor find themselves on the "bleeding edge" of developing these new markets.

The following chapters propose a multifunctional perspective of managerial responses to globalizing. Even though some of the chapters may appear to reflect traditional management functions, they are treated from interdisciplinary perspectives and address the complex drivers of globalization described above. While typical international management books concentrate on single management functions (e.g. global marketing, international finance, the global organization), the Alliance between INSEAD and Wharton offers the possibility of presenting the expertise of specialists in diverse disciplines from different parts of the world within the same book. We hope that this volume will help you better meet the challenges of designing, improving, and managing globalizing enterprises.

Notes

1 J. E. Stiglitz, *Globalization and its Discontents* (New York: W.W. Norton & Company, Inc., 2002).
2 E. Anderson and H. Gatignon, "Modes of Foreign Entry: A Transaction Cost Analysis and Propositions," *Journal of International Business Studies*, 17, 3 (Autumn 1986), pp. 1–26.
3 Forrester Research Inc. estimate by John C. McCarthy, reported in P. Engardio, A. Bernstein, and M. Kripalani, "Is Your Job Next?," *Business Week*, February 3, 2003, p. 52.
4 N. Checa, J. Maguire, and J. Barney, "The New World Disorder," *Harvard Business Review*, August 2003, pp. 71–79.
5 T. L. Friedman, *The Lexus and the Olive Tree* (New York: Anchor Books, 2000).
6 G. Soros, *On Globalization* (New York: Public Affairs, 2002).
7 T. Rosenberg "The Free-Trade Fix," *New York Times*, August 18, 2002.
8 G. Khermouch and D. Brady, "Brands in an Age of Anti-Americanism," *Business Week*, August 4, 2003, pp. 69–71.
9 "Business Opportunity vs. Backlash: Perspectives on BPO," *Knowledge @Wharton: Special Section on Business Process Outsourcing*, at http://knowledge.wharton.upenn.edu/100803_ss1.html.
10 "Hard Time for Labor," *Knowledge@Wharton: Special Section on Business Process Outsourcing*, at http://knowledge.wharton.upenn.edu/100803_ss3.html.
11 Stiglitz, *Globalization and its Discontents*; Soros, *On Globalization*.
12 Guillén takes the position, however, that globalization is not a uniform and inexorable trend, but a discontinuous process leading to changes in opposite direction, although creating stronger mutual awareness rather than conformity. M. F. Guillén, *The Limits of Convergence*, (Princeton, NJ: Princeton University Press, 2001).

13 Ibid.

14 Ibid.

15 Rosenberg, "The Free-Trade Fix."

16 J. Story, *Frontiers of Fortune: Predicting Capital Prospects and Casualties in the Markets of the Future* (London: Financial Times / Prentice Hall, 1999).

17 For example, among her nine new rules, Tina Rosenberg believes that the rule about "letting the People go" is "probably the single most important change for the developing world." Rosenberg, "The Free-Trade Fix."

18 M. S. Granovetter, "The Strength of Weak Ties," *American Journal of Sociology*, 78 (1973), pp. 1360–1380; H. Gatignon, J. Eliashberg, and T. S. Robertson, "Modeling Multinational Diffusion Patterns: An Efficient Methodology," *Marketing Science*, 8 (1989), p. 231.

19 Guillén, *Limits of Convergence*.

20 Ibid., p. 31.

21 Rosenberg, "The Free-Trade Fix."

2 | *The changing international corporate governance landscape*

MAURO F. GUILLÉN
Wharton School

MARY A. O'SULLIVAN
INSEAD

Even as interest in corporate governance has increased around the globe, there are still great debates about differences in governance models. Are practices converging or diverging? What is best practice? While some commentators asserted in the late 1990s that US productivity and employment demonstrated the superiority of shareholder-oriented systems of governance, corporate scandals a few years later have raised many new questions about what constitutes an "ideal" system. In this chapter, the authors examine the arguments and evidence about global differences and similarities in governance models. They find that, despite popular perceptions, there is little evidence of convergence, although rigorous studies are largely lacking and research in this area is inherently hard to design. To explore differences in governance in different parts of the world, the authors examine the changing role of the stock market in four countries: France and Germany in the developed world, and the emerging economies of South Korea and Argentina.

C ORPORATE governance has been widely discussed and debated over the last two decades in the United States and Britain. While governance initially attracted much less attention in Europe, Asia, and other parts of the world, by the late 1990s, it had become a major, and highly contentious, issue in all of the advanced economies and in emerging economies and developing countries. However, while discussions have raged about governance within individual countries and regions, there has also been a broader question: are governance practices converging toward or diverging away from a common norm?

In what way is corporate governance different in developed and developing nations and what are the implications of these differences?

During most of the 1990s, the Anglo-American model of widely held share ownership, liquid stock markets, and (what appeared at the time to be) shareholder-friendly regulation became the reference point in discussions about corporate governance. In many countries, changes in corporate governance were stimulated by the rising importance of the stock market as a source of funds, for facilitating mergers and acquisitions, as a basis for corporate compensation, and as a mechanism to gauge corporate performance. In this chapter we review the nature and implications of these changes, and the debates about the best way to govern the business corporation. We focus our attention on two advanced countries (France and Germany) and two emerging economies (South Korea and Argentina), noting how local institutions have shaped the impact of the rise and fall of stock markets during the 1990s and early 2000s.

Debates on comparative corporate governance

The intense global interest in corporate governance is not surprising, given the role that corporate enterprises play in shaping economic outcomes through decisions about investment, employment, and trade. The way corporations allocate resources has an important influence on an economy's performance and the allocation of the returns from corporate activities has an important effect on the distribution of incomes and wealth.

Discussions of corporate governance are concerned with the institutions that influence how business corporations allocate resources and returns. Specifically, a system of corporate governance shapes who makes investment decisions in corporations, what types of investments they make, and how returns from investments are distributed.[1]

The case for convergence

Contemporary research on comparative corporate governance initially was preoccupied with the question of differences in national systems of corporate governance. In the 1980s and early 1990s, there was a debate about the strengths and weaknesses of different national systems for generating favorable outcomes for corporations themselves as well as the national economies in which they were based. In the 1980s, for example, there was considerable interest in the apparent strengths of the German and Japanese systems of corporate governance, as compared with their US counterpart, in supporting economic performance and social cohesion.

With the decline of Japan and the emergence of a "new economy" in the United States, however, proponents of the alleged virtues of the US model of corporate governance, and specifically of the merits of "shareholder value" as the primary objective of corporate enterprises, largely drowned out other voices. Now empirical analysis is focused less on exploring differences and more on the question of whether the process of globalization is reducing the diversity in corporate governance systems around the world by creating growing competitive pressures on national systems of corporate governance to converge.

Undoubtedly, the most influential argument for convergence contends that heightened global competition will lead enterprises, and ultimately countries, to converge on a set of "best practices" in corporate governance.[2] From this perspective, increased pressures for convergence have been generated by the process of globalization, commonly understood as the development of markets to permit the free flow of economic resources from one use to another across national economic borders.

These discussions of convergence have paid particular attention to the effects of the global integration of financial markets on systems of corporate governance across countries. Financial markets are perhaps the most thoroughly globalized markets in the world. Capital movements are, compared to those of goods or people, much less constrained. Moreover, capital can move almost instantaneously and costlessly, while goods and people take time and effort to move around. For some commentators on corporate governance, financial globalization implies that countries and firms without an investor- and shareholder-friendly system of corporate governance would suffer from a scarcity of funds; thus, financial starvation would sort out "efficient" from "inefficient" corporate governance practices. Even if countries were unwilling to adapt their corporate governance systems to make it easier for companies to get access to capital, the companies themselves, by seeking foreign listings, would contribute to a process of functional convergence.[3] The growing assertiveness of institutional investors both in the United States and around the world during the 1990s, discussed in more detail by Michael Useem in Chapter 3, was seen as a sign that countries and firms would need to change their ways if they wanted to remain competitive.

A second type of argument emphasizes political rather than economic globalization that creates pressures for convergence of corporate governance practices. In this view, the world's hegemonic economic, political, and military power is supposed to be able to impose on other countries the kind of economic model and practices that advance its own interests. At the turn of the century, the argument goes, few would doubt the supremacy of the United States in global affairs, and its attempts, either directly or indirectly through multilateral organizations such as the World Bank or the IMF, to entice or openly coerce countries into adopting rules about capital mobility and corporate governance consistent with the return-maximizing goals of its leading companies and financial institutions. With respect to the economic repercussions of the global integration of financial markets, scholars who emphasize the political dimension of globalization typically reject efficiency arguments. Rather, they contend that financial globalization often fosters heightened speculation that at certain times and places can have extremely damaging effects on real economies.[4]

Finally, a sociological argument contends that convergence is driven by the emergence of a global business elite since the 1980s, with shared dispositional, educational, cultural, and perhaps even political backgrounds. This global elite has become more cohesive with the increasing importance of the MBA degree as a key credential to get ahead in the business world, the rise of the international financial press, and the internationalization of many business corporations, which now hire managers globally as opposed to in their home countries. An important element of this argument is that most of the top business schools in the world happen to be located in the United States or the United Kingdom, as are virtually all of the most influential financial newspapers, magazines, and newswire services.

The case for divergence

The three arguments outlined above suggest that the pressures toward convergence in corporate governance are very real and likely overpowering. Some scholars argue, however, that systems of corporate governance around the world will continue to *diverge*. Two distinct types of argument are relevant in this regard.

While those who argue for convergence contend that economic efficiency leads to increasing similarity, some scholars turn this argument on its head. They contend that a deeper understanding of the foundations of economic performance suggests the persistence of diversity in systems of corporate governance. Loosely grouped into what might be called a "varieties-of-capitalism" perspective, they emphasize the importance of institutional diversity for shaping enterprise behavior and economic performance. These scholars reject the assumption that there is a single best way to organize economies and, in particular, they oppose the idea that the free flow of economic resources through "perfect" capital, labor, and product markets will lead to optimal economic outcomes.

The dominant view expressed by these scholars, although there are disagreements among them, is that to the extent that heightened global competition affects national governance systems it does so only through the prism of existing institutional configurations. Since different systems of capitalism will produce different responses to similar pressures, convergence is unlikely to occur. Rather the behavior and performance of enterprises will continue to differ depending on the institutional context in which they are embedded. A corollary of the basic argument is that to the extent that enterprises or nations attempt to import governance principles from other institutional settings, they may undermine the basis of their own success.[5]

Research on varieties of capitalism predates the debates on comparative corporate governance and its scope, being concerned with the broad range of institutions that support capitalism in different times and places, and typically going beyond systems of corporate governance alone. Nevertheless, the notion that there are different institutional foundations for economic success has obvious implications for comparative corporate governance. Recently, some scholars have explicitly made the connections between the varieties-of-capitalism literature and debates on comparative corporate governance.[6]

These economic arguments for continued divergence are closely related to recent research by political scientists, sociologists, and legal scholars on the comparative politics of corporate governance.[7] Claims that differences in corporate governance are rooted in variations in political organization do not imply that systems of corporate governance do not change. They do suggest, however, that significant changes are likely to occur only in response to major political transformations. The convergence of systems of corporate governance, therefore, seems at best to be a distant possibility and more likely a very remote one if substantial political differences persist.

Recent changes in systems of corporate governance

With compelling arguments on both sides of the convergence/ divergence debate, it would be useful if empirical evidence could offer insights into how corporate governance actually is evolving around the globe. Unfortunately, while contemporary research has generated a variety of different theoretical perspectives on the dynamics of systems of corporate governance, the link between these perspectives and empirical evidence is quite weak. In some cases, theoretical positions are advanced with nothing more than what one critic called "bald assertion" as evidence.[8] In other cases, only the most sweeping empirical claims are made to support theoretical positions.

National pride and hubris play no small part in the distortions that enter into such discussions. Perhaps the leading example in this regard was the assertion of the superiority of shareholder-oriented systems of corporate governance based on statements about US macroeconomic indicators such as productivity and employment in the second half of the 1990s. Recent scandals involving some of the poster boys of shareholder value during the 1990s have naturally generated skepticism about the merits of convergence towards that "ideal."

Whatever one's position on this point, the question of how much convergence has already occurred remains a crucial one. Addressing this question from an empirical perspective is complicated by the dearth of widely accepted and readily available empirical indicators for measuring change in corporate governance. The studies that do exist vary in the range of indicators used, the nature of the indicators, and the number of countries included. With only a couple of exceptions, the extant literature on cross-national corporate governance practices is generally based on evidence drawn from a small number of countries. Moreover, most studies tend to rely on qualitative indicators to a much greater extent than quantitative ones. Finally, few studies provide longitudinal indicators of the various dimensions of corporate governance that would allow us to systematically analyze the extent to which change has occurred.

The empirical studies that do exist show only limited evidence of convergence in corporate governance over the last fifteen years. For instance, while share ownership, institutional investors, long-term incentives for CEOs, the market for corporate control (hostile takeovers), and equity financing (as opposed to debt) have increased in importance in countries that already had strong equity markets and shareholder-friendly corporate governance systems as of 1985, few other countries have joined the trend. A recent survey of the evidence found that only France and, to a lesser extent, Belgium, the Netherlands, and the Scandinavian countries, seem to have embarked on a convergence trajectory with countries such as the United States and the United Kingdom.[9] And even in those cases, the question of whether the movement toward convergence will be thwarted by the recent collapse of stock market indices worldwide and the string of corporate scandals is clearly a pertinent one.

There is certainly something to be said for an injection of sobriety into a debate that has more than its fair share of extreme, unsubstantiated empirical claims. Yet we must be careful, in assessing the extent to which change has occurred in systems of corporate governance, not to ignore the forest for the trees. In a review of three studies of globalization, Susan Strange put her finger on the problem: "To sum up, all that these three books say about the overselling of globalization by firms and by observers may be true. But the litmus test that none of them really apply is whether there is, or is not, change." She went on to say "Sure, it takes more than one swallow to make a summer. But the moral for researchers may be to pay more attention to the newspapers and less attention to out-of-date and inappropriate statistics."[10]

Certainly data on corporate governance systems pose a particular problem in terms of their timeliness. Breakdowns of share ownership, for example, are typically only available with a few years' delay. The main problem with critical empirical work on globalization, however, is not so much its reliance on data that are often outdated as its focus on outcomes. The processes that lead to a shift in governance regimes take decades to unfold. In assessing whether fundamental change in corporate governance systems is under way, and whether it will lead to a convergence in these systems over the long haul, it is crucial that we focus not only on the outcomes of the change that has already occurred but on the extent to which the structural underpinnings of extant systems of corporate governance continue to be viable. It is only in that way that change in corporate governance can be identified and understood as it is happening rather than after the fact.

Forces challenging the structural foundations

To step back and look at the forest rather than the trees, it does seem as if there are a number of important forces at work that challenge at least some of the structural foundations of extant systems of corporate governance. These forces are both internal and external to the firm. They include the rise to top executive positions of managers with a finance background, the growing importance of the stock market as a source of financing, declining unionization of labor, enhanced global competition, faster technological innovation, and privatization of state-owned enterprises.

Three main internal changes have affected the preferences and relative power of the actors that seek to participate in the governance of the firm. Starting in the United States and the United Kingdom during the 1980s, managers with a finance background have risen to prominence in corporations, bringing with them a desire for autonomy to undertake diversification, acquisitions, and divestures, actions that have redressed the balance of power within the firm. A second change has had to do with the growing importance of the stock market as a source of financing for both established firms and entrepreneurial startups, a concomitant decline of banks as large shareholders, and the rise of new institutional investors. Finally, labor unionization is on the decline in most countries around the world, reducing this stakeholder's power. While these three changes are mutually reinforcing, they have separate roots and follow different dynamics.

Three important external changes have also put pressure on corporate governance. Perhaps the most salient is the intensification of global competition, which has tended to expose inefficiencies and enable firms to engage in cross-border arbitrage as they look for the best location to secure inputs, produce, and sell. A second trend is the acceleration in the rate of technological innovation, which imposes on firms the need to be flexible and adaptable, and to commit to the long term. Finally, the withdrawal of the state from the ownership and management of companies in many industries has not merely expanded stock market capitalization, but, in many cases, contributed to the unwinding of inter-corporate relations.

Corporate governance has been directly affected by each of these changes. Toward the end of the 1990s – just before the collapse of the "new economy," the beginning of the downturn in the stock market, and the wave of corporate scandals – the combination of finance-oriented managers, rising stock prices, and declining worker power seemed to be inexorably moving corporate governance in the direction of an emphasis on "shareholder" value. Stock options for both managers and employees appeared to many observers to be the optimal way to attract the best talent. While many of these changes have now slowed or reversed, certain corporate governance practices have been transformed around the world.

While we can make general statements about pressures for change in corporate governance, it is hard to understand their precise character and implications without studying them in some detail. In the next section, we look at the specific ways one important source of pressure – the changing role of the stock market – is changing corporate governance in four national economies. In this way, we illustrate how pressures for change are manifested in the dynamics of corporate governance in different countries.

The changing role of the stock market in different national economies

The stock market is central to systems of corporate governance based on shareholder value, and it is toward this type of system that many commentators believed convergence was occurring. Toward the end of the twentieth century, and especially during the 1990s, there were certainly signs of an expansion of the role of the stock market in a considerable number of countries in which it had historically played a modest role. If we look at data on the capitalization of the stock market as a percentage of gross domestic product (GDP), we see systematic evidence of change in the economic importance of the stock market.

The stock market assumed a position of much greater importance in many advanced industrial economies in the 1990s, as illustrated in Table 2.1. This was true in the United States and United Kingdom, where the stock market has always been a central focus, as well as in countries such as France, Italy, Germany, and Sweden, where the stock market had historically been less important. There is, however, considerable heterogeneity across countries in terms of the extent of that change. Finally, as mentioned, we have seen some retreat from a focus on the stock market after the decline in global stock markets from early 2001.

Table 2.1. *Stock market capitalization for selected advanced economies: total capitalization of domestic companies as percentage of GDP*

	1975	1980	1985	1990	1995	2000
Britain	37	38	77	87	122	184
France	10	8	15	26	33	112
Germany*	12	9	29	22	24	68
Italy	5	6	14	14	19	72
Japan	28	36	71	99	69	67
Netherlands	21	17	47	42	72	174
Sweden	3	10	37	40	75	145
USA**	48	50	57	56	98	153

Source: OECD; FIBV; * Association of Stock Exchanges; ** NYSE, Amex, and Nasdaq.

If we look at similar data for countries that were at earlier stages of economic development at the beginning of the period of observation, we also find evidence of considerable growth in the role of the stock market. In particular, for the sample of Latin American and Asian countries shown in Table 2.2, the last fifteen years of the twentieth century were a period of marked expansion in the stock market's role. In all cases, the stock market's share of GDP was much higher in 2000 than in 1985. However, for these developing nations, we observe much greater volatility in the stock market's economic importance, as compared with the advanced economies, with several periods of considerable advance in the role of stock market being followed by important reversals. As with the advanced economies there appears to be considerable heterogeneity among countries in levels and trends in the overall importance of the market. Finally, there has also been a marked downturn in stock market capitalization as a share of GDP in 2001 and 2002.

Other common measures of the stock market's economic importance, such as levels of trading in domestic shares as a percentage of GDP, display similar trends in equity markets around the world. However, market capitalization and trading activity, though commonly used proxies for stock market activity, really tell us only about the vibrancy of the secondary share markets, that is, the markets on which existing claims on corporate equity are traded. While liquid secondary markets may have indirect implications for economic activity, they do not

Table 2.2. *Stock market capitalization for selected economies classified as "developing" at beginning of period: total capitalization of domestic companies as percentage of GDP*

	*1975**	*1980*	*1985*	*1990*	*1995*	*2000*
Argentina	2	3	2	4	13	16
Brazil	n.a.	5	16	7	24	38
Chile	27	29	12	40	111	86
Mexico	6	7	2	11	39	22
Hong Kong	69	107	83	108	207	383
Indonesia	0.02	0.1	0.1	4	28	18
Malaysia	22	41	56	103	246	127
Philippines	9	9	4	18	73	34
South Korea	9	7	7	50	42	32
Taiwan	13	14	17	105	85	n.a.
Thailand	2	4	5	29	82	24

Source: Data for 1975–1995 from T. Beck, A. Demirgüç-Kunt, and R. Levine, "A New Database on Financial Development and Structure," *World Bank Economic Review* (Washington, DC, 2000); data for 2000 from IMF, *International Financial Statistics* (Washington, DC, 2001).
Note: * 1976 data for South Korea and Thailand; 1977 data for Philippines and Taiwan; 1978 data for Argentina, Mexico, Indonesia, and Malaysia; 1979 data for Chile.

themselves have direct economic implications for the real economy. A more detailed analysis of the evolving relationship between trends in the equity markets and corporate activity is therefore warranted if we are to understand how corporations' reliance on the stock market in different countries has changed in recent decades and the reasons for those changes.

To look more closely at these changes in the role of the stock market and their implications for governance, we take a closer look at four economies. Two – France and Germany – are advanced economies, with systems of corporate governance that are generally considered to be representative of a continental European model in which the stock market has played a rather modest role in the postwar period. We discuss the extent and nature of the transformation in the role of the stock market in these two countries in the last decade. We then consider the changing role of the stock market in South Korea and

Argentina, two emerging economies that have followed different paths to economic growth.

France

As indicated by Table 2.1, France experienced considerable growth in the role of the Bourse in the corporate economy since the mid 1980s, with total capitalization increasing from 15 percent of GDP in 1985 to 112 percent in 2000. When we look directly at the importance of the stock market for raising capital, we find that the French share markets reached an important turning point in the mid 1980s with all subsequent years registering higher levels of public share issues than had been seen until then. However, the volatility in the annual figures since the mid 1980s makes it difficult to conclude that public share issues have become steadily more important as a source of corporate finance since then. Only in the last five years of the 1990s did we see a steady rise in capital-raising by listed companies but it was from a rather low point in issuing activity in the mid 1990s.[11]

From the launch of the first French privatization program in 1986, the sale of state-owned companies has played a crucial role in driving the value of total share issues on the French Bourse. Privatizations accounted for thirteen of the largest twenty introductions (and 65 percent of the value of these transactions) to the Paris Bourse between 1981 and 2000. During the decade from 1990 to 1999, privatizations accounted for 31 percent of the proceeds of the public share issues undertaken on the Paris stock exchange.[12]

The second important category of public share offerings for cash – initial public offerings – is perhaps the one that people most readily associate with the stock market. In the late 1990s, there was a marked increase in the number and value of companies going public in France; during the period from 1995 to 1999, the average number of companies that went public in France each year was almost five times what it had been during the period from 1990 to 1994. By the late 1990s, the number of domestic companies introduced to the stock market each year in France hovered around the level attained in Britain.[13] The value of the proceeds raised in initial public offerings (IPOs) on the French stock market also expanded rapidly, with 1998, 1999, and 2000 breaking all previous records for funds raised on the stock market in these transactions. Particularly notable was the success of France's Nouveau Marché in attracting new listings, although the Premier Marché, France's main market, continued to play a crucial role in driving the value of proceeds raised in IPO activity.[14]

Moreover, in the 1990s, especially in the second half of the decade, a number of French corporations sought foreign listings on the London Stock Exchange, the Nasdaq, and especially on the US exchanges. By the end of 2000, a total of eighteen French corporations had listed American Depository Receipts (ADRs) on the New York Stock Exchange (NYSE) and a further fourteen had ADRs on the Nasdaq. Access to capital was the main motivation for most of the French companies that sought listings on Nasdaq. In most of the other cases, however, US listings were related to merger activity; either the listing came about as the result of a merger with a company that was already listed on a US exchange and/or it was undertaken to gain access to a currency for exchange in mergers and acquisitions (M&A) activity.[15] (For more discussion of some of the motivations for listing on foreign exchanges, see the exploration in Chapter 10 by Raphael Amit and Christoph Zott.)

In this sense, foreign listings by French companies are integrally related to the recent wave of M&A activity involving the French corporate sector in the late 1990s. Indeed, if there was a revolution in the role of the stock market in the French corporate economy, it was in facilitating M&A. French corporations are no strangers to acquisitions. A wave of M&A activity took place in the late 1980s and early 1990s as major French corporations attempted to reinforce their strategic positions in the context of European integration.[16] However, earlier activity pales in significance compared with the value of M&A activity that occurred from the middle of the 1990s.

A number of features of recent M&A activity involving French companies merits particular mention. The first is the growing scale of these transactions in the 1990s, particularly toward the end of the decade. A second tendency is the trend toward the use of shares rather than cash to conclude these transactions. Finally, there was a clear increase in the importance of cross-border M&A transactions involving French companies, with French companies displaying a distinct tendency to be the acquirer rather than the target.[17]

Another recent trend in the interaction between the stock market and the corporate economy in France was the growing use of shares as a basis for employee remuneration. The importance of stock options in France increased from the middle of the 1980s and, in particular, toward the end of the 1990s. In fact, data collected for 1999 and 2000 by the French business magazine *L'Expansion* on companies that are members of the CAC40 index show that France's largest enterprises are now the European leaders and, on a global scale, surpassed only by US companies, in the scale of their stock option awards to senior managers. Within Europe, large German enterprises come closest to the French but the difference between the two countries is enormous, with potential capital gains of senior French corporate managers forty times more valuable than those of their German counterparts.[18]

The other important mechanism linking the stock market to remuneration was employee shareholding. According to the French statistical office, INSEE, the number of employees holding shares in their own companies stood at about 700,000 by the end of the 1990s but most experts believe that this figure underestimated the true extent of employee share ownership in France. According to a survey by *L'Expansion* of the CAC40 companies alone, more than 1 million employees held shares worth FF157 billion at the end of 1999. Among the CAC40 companies, the level of employee ownership was highest in Société Générale, a fact that has received considerable attention given the important role that employee-shareholders played in thwarting an attempted hostile takeover of their employer by BNP.[19]

However, a recent study of employee ownership in France suggests that Société Générale is something of an exception. Of the 791 French companies listed on the Paris Bourse, in only 251 of them (that is, less than a third) did employees own shares. Moreover, the level of employee shareholding in these companies was relatively low; on average, employees held 3.7 percent of the capital of these companies, which is considerably lower than in the United States and Britain.[20]

Foreign listings by French companies and a rise in foreign ownership of listed French corporations in the wake of privatization have allowed foreigners to become an increasingly important presence in the shareholding structures of French corporations. That tendency has also been greatly facilitated by the trend toward the unwinding of their cross-shareholdings by leading French corporate enterprises that began in the mid 1990s. As a result, foreign institutional investors were able to move into the French share market to acquire the significant stakes in French corporate enterprises that were being sold off by corporations which previously formed critical nodes in the French cross-shareholding network. By 1997, foreign ownership accounted for 35 percent of stock exchange capitalization compared with 10 percent in 1985, and it has remained at that level since then. In leading French enterprises, foreign participation in their shareholding structures was even higher.[21] Notwithstanding these developments, certain aspects of the French structure of corporate share ownership remain relatively unchanged, notably the role of families as important shareholders in many leading French enterprises.

Germany

While the German IPO market experienced considerable volatility during the 1980s and early 1990s, the pace of IPOs accelerated with the creation of the Neuer Markt in 1997. The number of companies performing IPOs on the German stock market increased dramatically – 1998, 1999, and 2000 were all record-breaking years by this measure – and in 1999 and 2000 the proceeds raised in IPOs on the Deutsche Börse also broke all previous records. With the emergence of the Neuer Markt, the dominance of Germany's main market, the Amtlicher Handel, diminished. By 2000, indeed, almost twice as much money was raised in IPO proceeds and sixteen times more companies went public on Germany's new market than on its main market.[22]

In addition to heightened activity on the German stock exchange, some German companies sought listings on foreign exchanges, especially from the middle of the 1990s. By the end of 2000, thirteen German companies were listed on the NYSE and eight others had Nasdaq listings. As was the case for their French counterparts, German companies with listings on Nasdaq were often motivated by capital-raising opportunities in the US capital markets; in contrast, many of the NYSE listings were undertaken to gain access to an attractive currency to undertake acquisitions.[23]

Recent trends in merger and acquisition activity involving German companies were similar to those described for France. There was a spectacular increase in the value of these deals toward the end of the 1990s driven largely by a major increase in the average value of these deals rather than in the number of deals. Again, cross-border activity played a decisive role in driving these overall trends. There have been some prominent examples of foreign companies acquiring German companies in recent years, with the hostile takeover of Mannesmann by Vodafone in 1999 being undoubtedly the best-known case. However, an analysis of the summary statistics for M&A activity involving German companies shows that the German business sector, like its French counterpart, has in fact been a major net acquirer in cross-border activity; the value of acquisitions by domestic companies outweighed the value of foreign purchases of German companies. As in France, there seems to have been a trend in the late 1990s toward a greater reliance on shares as consideration in German M&A transactions.

Analysis of trends in the use of shares as the basis for employee compensation is hampered by the fact that, in Germany, as in France, corporations are not required to disclose detailed and systematic information on awards of share-based compensation (primarily stock options and long-term incentive plans) to individuals. From the data that are available, though, it does appear that the use of stock options increased in Germany. However, these developments were largely confined to large, listed corporations, as well as Neuer Markt companies. Overall, the penetration of stock options both across and within companies remains more limited in Germany than in France and certainly than in the United States.[24]

As far as share-based compensation other than stock options is concerned, German companies have made growing use of employee shares. According to figures available from the Deutsche Aktieninstitut, 1.6 million Germans held employee shares in the middle of 2001 compared with 1.7 million in 1998, 1.5 million in 1994, and 1 million in 1988. The rate of growth in employee shareholding was therefore steady but not spectacular and, as with stock options, the penetration of employee shares in Germany was lower than in the United States, Britain, and France.[25]

The traditional German share ownership structure has proven more resistant to change than the French one in recent years. There are, as yet, few clear signs of any unwinding of inter-company shareholding relationships by non-financial enterprises in Germany, notwithstanding changes in the tax law that seemed to encourage such a development. Nor have families ceded the central role that they occupy in the German shareholding system. Overall, the existing evidence suggests few grounds on which one could argue that insider control of the German corporate economy has broken down. The one area where there has been change, however, is in the relationship between financial enterprises in Germany and the rest of the corporate sector; in particular, there is evidence that some of the largest banks have been retreating from their role as important shareholders in the German corporate sector.[26]

South Korea

The corporate landscape in South Korea, quite different from that of France or Germany, is organized around some thirty large, highly leveraged, family-owned and controlled, diversified conglomerates – known as *chaebol* – that presently account for well over half of economic activity, and the bulk of stock market capitalization. As of the end of 2001, the affiliates of the four largest (Hyundai, Samsung, LG, and Sunkyong) accounted for 23 percent of all shares outstanding. Traditionally, the *chaebol* operated in rather secretive ways, and their equity was almost exclusively in the hands of family members.

Prior to the 1980s, the stock market played a very small role as a source of company finance. The Korea Stock Exchange has always been characterized by volatility and secretive deals, often in cash. However, during the 1980s, when financial deregulation enabled the *chaebol* to acquire stakes in banks and brokerage houses, member companies took an interest in floating shares on the stock market as a way of raising additional capital without having to give up control or to disclose information (securities regulations are lax and not enforced).

The increased importance of the stock market, however, has not resulted in a loss of control by the founders of the companies.[27] Each *chaebol* tends to float in the market only a small proportion of the shares of a few subsidiaries, and elaborate pyramidal ownership schemes are used to ensure that insiders from the founding family retain control. This is one of the reasons why M&As – whether friendly or hostile – have not increased: cross-shareholdings make them difficult. Hostile bids are so rare that entire years pass by without a single announcement. Even after the 1997 crisis, the largest *chaebol* continue to engage in cross-subsidization, at the expense of small shareholders who might be more interested in dividends and capital appreciation than in growth. Small shareholders do not have much say in corporate governance, which is essentially an affair of the owning family and state officials. The state is a powerful actor because, in spite of liberalization and privatization, much of the financial system remains orchestrated by the government, and former officials are appointed to the boards of companies.

Until the 1997 crisis, few domestic or foreign institutional investors were in operation, but since then some sources (e.g. the Economist Intelligence Unit) argue that foreign portfolio and hedge funds have become increasingly influential. It has been estimated that foreign ownership of shares at the Korea Stock Exchange presently stands at about 37 percent, a historical record. In 1996, the securities industry created the Kosdaq, modeled after the Nasdaq. Most investors outside Korea have stayed away from it because of the lack of regulation and oversight, so foreigners account for only about 10 percent of total capitalization. The Kosdaq index had more than trebled by late 1999, and then collapsed to just half of its original level. By the end of 1999, some 470 companies were listed on the Kosdaq. It has continued to expand, even after the Internet crash, with 166 new listings in 2001 and 122 in 2002.

Scholars agree that Korean corporate governance did not change substantially until the sobering 1997 financial crisis.[28] The meltdown, however, has induced important changes. Eleven of the top thirty *chaebol* were severely affected by the crisis, with five of them going bankrupt (including such powerhouses as Daewoo and KIA). As a result, some high profile M&As took place, including Hyundai's takeover of KIA, GM's of Daewoo Motor, and Ford's of Halla Machinery. The government of left-leaning President Kim Dae-Jung announced important new measures to introduce more transparency, including changes in accounting standards, independent auditing, and a minimum of 25 percent of outside directors; simplification of commercial laws to facilitate M&As; removal of foreign ownership ceilings; and a slight improvement in the protection of small shareholders.[29] Still, foreign and domestic fund managers remain skeptical as to whether these measures have actually increased transparency. The Korea Stock Exchange complains that "outside" directors continue to rubberstamp management and family decisions. Thus, while there have been both regulatory and actual changes in South Korea, corporate governance remains an affair of the large family owners and the state, to the exclusion of small shareholders and other stakeholders in the firm (fund managers, workers).

South Korea's changes offer an illustration of how the apparent global convergence of corporate governance – such as the public push for increased transparency – can be less extensive than it appears. The country's underlying systems, traditions, and cultures – which have been successful for many years – tend to subvert these changes, even when they are undertaken seriously by government leaders. To the casual observer, it may appear that Korea is moving toward a more shareholder-focused, Western system of governance, but underneath the reality is that the changes are perhaps not so profound. At the beginning of the new millennium, with the wounds of the Asian financial crisis fading and the Western corporate governance scandals still fresh, it seems even more likely that these reforms could slow further and perhaps reverse.

Argentina

The situation in Argentina is quite different from either South Korea or the two European countries we examined. Like the other three nations, the stock market has gained increasing prominence. From the mid 1980s, and especially in the 1990s, the capitalization of Argentina's stock market grew significantly as a share of GDP, but from a very low base – rising from less than 2 percent in 1985 to more than 16 percent in 2000. Privatization was the driving force of the increase. Argentina undertook one of the most ambitious privatization programs in the world, with most new entrants to the stock market in the 1990s being privatized firms. The largest three listed firms (Telefónica, SCH, and Repsol-YPF) account for 400 billion pesos of market capitalization (or 35 percent of the total in 2000). Both Telefónica and Repsol-YPF are privatized firms. The arrival of foreign portfolio investment often had the effect of increasing capitalization but foreign direct investment tended to have the opposite effect, as the foreign acquirer would de-list the target.

Even fuelled by all of this activity, Argentina's stock market capitalization remained one of the lowest among emerging economies, less than half the level of Brazil and less than a fifth of the level of Chile (see Table 2.2). Capital-raising activity by companies on the Buenos Aires stock exchange was also very modest in comparative perspective. While share issuance received an important boost in the 1990s from privatization, there is little evidence of any sustained increase in the role of stock issues as a source of capital for private enterprises in Argentina. The number of listed companies in Argentina actually declined in the last decade of the twentieth century from 179 in 1990 to 127 in 2000. That trend has been under way for a long time, with the stock market in decline since the 1960s when more than 600 firms were listed. Very few Argentinian firms had sought listings on the NYSE – a total of eleven by the end of 2001 of which five were privatized companies.

The apparent success of the government's currency peg with the US dollar during the 1990s attracted much foreign direct and portfolio investment to Argentina. Share prices were artificially high because of the huge inflows of money. After Brazil, Argentina's main trading partner, devalued its currency in early 1999, the economy went into a recession that undermined investor confidence to the point that the currency peg and the entire financial system collapsed at the end of 2001. Two years later, Argentina has not managed to enter into a comprehensive agreement with the IMF that would enable the country to reenter global financial markets on a regular basis. The limited role of the stock market and the rising importance of foreign-owned, unlisted companies in the Argentinian economy is yet another reason why corporate governance practices in the country have changed little over the last two decades. Argentina continues to be, in many ways, isolated from developments in the rest of the world.

Conclusions: the implications of the changing role of the stock market for corporate governance

For the two advanced economies that we have considered, it is clear that the role of the stock market has substantially increased in the last two decades, especially in the second half of the 1990s. However, even by 2000, the stock market remained much less important in France and Germany than in the United States and Britain.[30]

Furthermore, with the recent dramatic downturn in stock market activity in these two countries, there is a serious question about whether the trend toward the increased importance of the stock market in these national economies will continue in the future at anything like the pace witnessed in the 1990s. It is possible that the increased use of the stock market by French and German companies was a temporary phenomenon induced by speculative conditions in the late 1990s. Certainly, as boom has turned to bust, share issues by European companies have dried up. The decline of the new markets in both of these countries, and indeed the collapse and closure of the Neuer Markt in June 2003, is particularly notable given their importance in driving increased levels of capital-raising in the late 1990s. The sustainability of the trends toward higher levels of M&A activity in evidence in the late 1990s is also open to question with the recent collapse in the number and value of global M&A transactions. There are several examples of German and, especially, French companies, such as Alcatel, Vivendi, and Cap Gemini, whose enthusiasm for acquisitions in the bull market of the 1990s seems to have left many of their stakeholders with a rather bad hangover in the cold light of the new millennium.

While companies were actively using, and therefore reliant on, the stock market as a source of capital, for facilitating mergers and acquisitions and as the basis for corporate compensation, it is clear that they had to appear to be responsive, at least, to the demands of portfolio shareholders. Even then, certain examples of companies that were heavily dependent on the market in this way, like Vivendi, suggest that corporate managers still retained considerable room for strategic manoeuvring. To the extent that companies' reliance on the stock market diminishes in the new millennium, it would seem that portfolio shareholders would find companies less receptive to their demands.

As we saw from our discussions above, while France and Germany apparently faced similar forces and patterns in the transformation of their financial markets and governance, the outcome, particularly in relation to inter-company shareholdings, was quite different. German companies were less likely to dismantle these interrelationships than their French peers. We need to know much more about the source of these differences but even on the basis of existing evidence the different outcomes recorded for these two countries suggest the importance of domestic factors in determining changes in corporate governance. Based on their analysis of French companies' sales of their holdings in other enterprises from the mid 1990s, Morin and Rigamonti[31] suggest that companies were motivated to liquidate these stakes by several factors. While some of these motivations were international in nature, others such as the financial difficulties of some prominent French banks in the wake of the French real estate crisis, reflected features of the domestic economy that were not present in the German case.

The different experiences of South Korea and Argentina also cast some doubts on the argument that global financial markets exert similar pressures around the world. It is clear that domestic political structures and prevailing corporate governance practices shape the way in which global pressures play a role. As a result, little convergence has taken place in these two countries. The case of Argentina is clear in this respect. For about ten years, the country introduced some of the most liberal economic policies, including privatization, deregulation, and trade opening. The local stock market, however, has not developed into an important source of company finance nor have Argentinian companies displayed any dramatic tendency to raise equity capital overseas by securing foreign listings.

As in Argentina, it is not clear that globalization has made the Korean business sector become more similar to the US system. Korean firms saw in the globalization of financial markets during the 1980s and 1990s an opportunity to obtain funds at relatively low cost. While Korea's development in the 1960s and 1970s had been fuelled by foreign debt inflows orchestrated by the government, during the last twenty years it was Korean firms that obtained funds directly from abroad, predominantly in the form of debt as opposed to equity. Given the lack of accounting transparency, increased borrowing from abroad did not generate many efficiencies because foreign creditors were in no position to provide an effective selection mechanism for allocating capital to the most promising or the best managed ends. South Korea has also been under pressure from the United States to liberalize its financial markets and practices, especially as the country tried to "polish" its résumé in order to become a member of the OECD. Scholars agree that South Korea's financial liberalization actually gave firms more autonomy and reduced accountability, largely because the government's supervisory role was greatly reduced and no alternative mechanism (such as accounting standards or auditing) was put in place.

It is clear that an array of financial and economic global forces have influenced corporate governance dynamics around the globe. Our four-country journey, however, has exposed some of the ways in which local institutions and politics have altered the effects of such forces. Even in emerging economies, in which foreign capital tends to play a very important role, one observes a resilience of indigenous patterns of corporate governance. While financial markets are certainly important and influential, they are not the only institution that shapes corporate governance.

Implications for managers

It is clear that there are no sweeping generalizations that can be made about global corporate governance in reference to convergence. As business leaders enter or invest in global markets, they need to think through the issues related to governance on a country-by-country basis.

The following are some of the implications of the above discussions for leaders of global organizations:

• *Be aware of differences in governance across nations:* As indicated by our discussion, there are compelling arguments for and against global convergence of corporate governance, and even these arguments have been thrown into question by recent corporate scandals. If you assume that the historical differences in governance systems in different countries have been largely erased, you are in for a rude awakening or a harsh encounter with highly specific national institutions and practices. An awareness of history and the evolution of factors such as the rising importance of the stock market can offer a more nuanced perspective on the level of convergence of a specific country or the harmony of the governance of a specific foreign company with the governance of your own firm.

These micro-level considerations are vital to conducting business in global markets. As Harbir Singh and Maurizio Zollo point out in Chapter 6, mismatches in corporate cultures and systems are often the kiss of death for alliances and acquisitions. National culture and practices inform the culture and practices of specific companies, so an awareness of the governance environment in a particular country can provide valuable perspectives on potential challenges and opportunities in cross-border alliances, acquisitions, or other activities.

• *Don't believe everything you hear about revolutions in corporate governance:* Sometimes the changes that appear extensive on the surface are less dramatic upon closer inspection. Also, there are pendulum swings and fads in governance that can later be reversed. As our discussions of South Korea, Argentina, France, and Germany indicate, it is important to look a bit more deeply at the evolution and dynamics of each specific country. By understanding the drivers of changes in governance, such as the rising importance of the stock market, you can make a more thorough assessment of changes in governance in other countries and how they might affect your investments and interactions with companies there.

• *Understand the key players and drivers of governance changes:* While we make generalizations about governance at our peril, we can round up a set of "usual suspects" who drive the evolution of practice and governance in a specific country. These include major corporations, the families and other owners behind them, government regulators, institutional investors, investor activists, foreign stakeholders, banks and other types of lenders, employees, and broader investors in public capital markets. By examining these diverse players more carefully, you can gain insights into the drivers that are shaping governance in a particular country.

Corporate governance is a dynamic process, and the one certainty is that it will continue to evolve. The portraits we have presented of our four countries are for illustration purposes only. Stock markets and governance in France, Germany, South Korea, and Argentina will continue to change with shifts in the environment. Globalization is a powerful factor in driving these changes. The rising importance of institutional investors, as discussed by Mike Useem in Chapter 3, is one of the forces driving governance reforms, and there are others we have analyzed in this chapter.

Notes

1 M. O'Sullivan, *Contests for Corporate Control: Corporate Governance and Economic Performance in the United States and Germany* (Oxford: Oxford University Press, 2000).

2 H. Hansmann and R. Kraakman, "The End of History for Corporate Law," *Georgetown Law Journal*, 89 (2001), p. 439.

3 J. Coffee, "The Future as History: The Prospects for Global Convergence in Corporate Governance and its Implications," *Northwestern University Law Review*, 93 (1999), p. 641.

4 P. G. Cerny (ed.), *Finance and World Politics: Markets, Regimes and States in the Post-Hegemonic Era* (Aldershot, UK: Edward Elgar, 1993); F. Chesnais (ed.), *La mondialisation financière: genèse, coûts et enjeux* (Paris: Editions Syros, 1996); P. Gowan, *The Global Gamble: Washington's Faustian Bid for World Dominance* (London: Verso, 1999); Susan Strange, *Casino Capitalism* (Oxford and New York: Blackwell, 1986); Susan Strange, *Mad Money: When Markets Outgrow Governments* (Ann Arbor: University of Michigan Press, 1998).

5 See, for example, S. Berger and R. Dore (eds.), *National Diversity and Global Capitalism* (Ithaca, NY: Cornell University Press, 1996); R. Boyer and D. Drache (eds.), *States against Markets* (New York: Routledge, 1996); P. Hall and D. Soskice (eds.), *Varieties of Capitalism: Institutional Foundations of Comparative Advantage* (Cambridge: Cambridge University Press, 2001); R. Hollingsworth, "New Perspectives on the Spatial Dimensions of Economic Coordination: Tensions Between Globalization and Social Systems of Production," *Review of International Political Economy*, 5 (1998), pp. 482–507.

6 Hall and Soskice (eds.), *Varieties of Capitalism*; M. Aoki, *Towards a Comparative Institutional Analysis* (Cambridge, MA: MIT Press, 2001); R. Dore, *Stock Market Capitalization: Welfare Capitalism: Japan and Germany versus the Anglo-Saxons* (Oxford: Oxford University Press, 2000); O'Sullivan, *Contests for Corporate Control*; W. Lazonick and M. O'Sullivan, "Le rôle du marché boursier dans les systemès nationaux de governance d'enterprise: les changements actuels en France envisagés dans une perspective historique comparative," Rapport final au Commissariat Général du Plan (responsible scientifique: Michel Aglietta), 2001; S. Vitols, S. Casper, D. Soskice, and S. Woolcock, "Corporate Governance in Large British and German Companies: Comparative Institutional Advantage or Competing for Best Practice," report prepared for the Anglo-German Foundation for the Study of Industrial Society, Anglo-German Foundation, London, 1997.

7 See, in particular, J. Cioffi and S. Cohen, "The Advantages of Forwardness: The Interdependence of the State, Law, and Corporate Governance in an Age of Globalization," in G. Boyd and S. Cohen (eds.), *Corporate Governance and Globalization* (Cheltenham, UK: Edward Elgar, 2000); M. Rhodes and B. van Appeldoorn, "Capitalism in Western Europe," in M. Rhodes, P. Heywood and V. Wright (eds.), *Developments in West European Politics* (New York: St. Martin's Press, 1997), pp. 171–189; N. Fligstein, *The Architecture of Markets: An Economic Sociology of Twenty-First Century Capitalist Societies* (Princeton, NJ: Princeton University Press, 2001); M. F. Guillén, "Corporate Governance and Globalization: Is There Convergence across Countries?" *Advances in Comparative Management*, 13 (2000), pp. 175–204.

8 D. Branson, "The Very Uncertain Prospect of 'Global' Convergence in Corporate Governance," *Cornell International Law Journal*, 34 (2001), p. 321 (commenting on Hansmann and Kraakman, "The End of History for Corporate Law").

9 Guillén, "Corporate Governance and Globalization."

10 Strange, *Mad Money*.

11 M. O'Sullivan, "Equity Markets and the Corporate Economy in France: Recent Developments and their Implications," INSEAD working paper, 2001.

12 Ibid.

13 M. O'Sullivan, "A Revolution in European Corporate Governance? The Extent and Implications of Recent Developments in the Role of the Stock Market in Five European Economies," INSEAD working paper, 2001.

14 O'Sullivan, "Equity Markets and the Corporate Economy in France."

15 Ibid.

16 V. Schmidt, *From State to Market? The Transformation of French Business and Government* (Cambridge: Cambridge University Press, 1996), pp. 358–368.

17 O'Sullivan, "Equity Markets and the Corporate Economy in France."

18 *L'Expansion*, September 14, 2000; September 13, 2001.

19 *L'Expansion*, January 20, 2000.

20 J.-P. Balligand and J.-B. de Foucauld, "L'epargne salarialé au coeur du contrat social," Rapport au Premier Ministre, Paris, 2000, p. 89.

21 F. Morin and E. Rigamonti, "Evolution et structure de l'actionnariat en France," *Revue francais de gestion*, 28, 141 (2002), pp. 155–181.

22 O'Sullivan, "A Revolution in European Corporate Governance?"

23 "Allianz Keeps Eye Out for US Buys," *Financial Times*, July 21, 2001, p. 21; "BASF Hopes US Listing Will Lift Stock," *New York Times*, June 7, 2000, p. 22.

24 U. Jürgens and J. Rupp, "The German System of Corporate Governance – Characteristics and Changes," CGEP working paper (January 2001), pp. 35–40.

25 Ibid., p. 37.

26 D. Wójcik, "Change in the German Model of Corporate Governance: Evidence from Blockholdings 1997–2001," University of Oxford Working Paper, 2001 (http://www.ssrn.com/).

27 S. J. Chang, *Financial Crisis and Transformation of Korean Business Groups: The Rise and Fall of Chaebols* (Cambridge: Cambridge University Press, 2003); M. F. Guillén, *The Limits of Convergence: Globalization and Organizational Change in Argentina, South Korea, and Spain* (Princeton, NJ: Princeton University Press, 2001); K. J. Fields, *Enterprise and the State in Korea and Taiwan* (Ithaca, NY: Cornell University Press, 1995).

28 Chang, *Financial Crisis and Transformation.*

29 Ibid., pp. 208–212.

30 International Federation of Stock Exchanges (http://www.world-exchanges.org/).

31 Morin and Rigamonti, "Evolution et structure."

3 | Corporate governance and leadership in a globalizing equity market

MICHAEL USEEM
Wharton School

The increasing globalization of capital markets and rising importance of institutional investors are leading to increased attention to governance and leadership. As a small number of institutional investors with a rising percentage of ownership seek to protect their large global investments they are defining new standards for governance and these standards are being exported around the world. The author discusses these trends and their implications for governance. He shows how research and practice are indicating that leadership at all levels is more significant to corporate performance, particularly in environments of rising uncertainty and in organizations with more diffused authority. In the wake of significant failures of leadership such as Enron's bankruptcy, investors are looking for ways to ensure that company leaders make good and timely decisions. These reforms have focused on changes in board composition and policies, establishing norms that are spreading globally. He concludes that the forces of institutionalization and internationalization are driving the world toward convergent standards of governance and leadership.

THE bankruptcy of Enron on December 2, 2001 starkly reconfirmed the importance of effective corporate governance and leadership. While its failure demonstrated the role that active shareholders and government regulators must play in calling company leaders to take responsibility for their actions – and the consequences of their failure to do so – it also shows how difficult it is for investors and regulators to monitor company executives and their directors.

The governing board of Enron had appeared to meet most contemporary investor standards of good governance. The board's thirteen directors made it neither too large nor too small, just two insiders served, and the outsiders included former chief executives of an insurance company and an international bank, a former accounting professor, a hedge fund manager, an Asian financier, and the former head of a US government commission.[1]

The governing board's decisions were badly flawed, however, as well documented by a board investigation after the firm's bankruptcy and by a US Senate investigation. Far more than the outward features of governance, it was boardroom and executive decisions that carried Enron into bankruptcy. Four months before the crash, Enron vice-president Sherron Watkins had met with chairman and CEO Kenneth Lay in his Houston headquarters to warn him that the company could "implode in a wave of accounting scandals." At that moment – August 22, 2001 – Lay could have taken specific actions that might have prevented bankruptcy and saved the jobs of thousands of Enron employees. That would have required a top management team that recognized the gravity of the moment, yet Lay barely had a top team at all. Chief executive officer Jeffrey Skilling had quit the company a week before. Chief financial officer Andrew S. Fastow had devised the improper accounting schemes. And other senior officers had been resigning in droves.[2]

Even without a well-functioning executive team, the board should have required immediate notification of its audit committee of the charges that Sherron Watkins had leveled against the chief financial officer. It then might have made up for the management shortcomings. Yet CEO Lay sought outside legal advice instead from a Houston law firm that Watkins herself had warned against, since it had already reviewed and approved many of CFO Fastow's financial practices. The outside counsel reported back to management on October 15 that Enron's accounting was "aggressive" but not "inappropriate," and only then did the chair of the board's audit committee finally learn of the Watkins accusations and the outside review. And even then, neither her memos nor her identity were revealed to the audit chair and other outside directors. Enron executives would only refer to the messenger as an anonymous employee. It was not until November 2 that the board finally learned from Enron's outside auditor of "possible illegal acts within the company."[3]

Enron directors had raised too few questions and challenged too few assumptions during its many meetings with management. It was a board that routinely relied on Enron executives and the outside auditor for information but made scant effort to verify it. The board quickly approved management's risky steps and illicit partnerships, and then exercised too little oversight of the execution that followed.

The Enron board had an opportunity to step in and aggressively clean house once the improper partnerships and accounting schemes became evident, but no such actions were taken. By contrast, a decade earlier when Salomon CEO John Gutfreund failed to report the illegal actions of a subordinate for more than three months, its board made a far more aggressive response. When the scandal broke, Gutfreund resigned and outside director Warren Buffett stepped in to resurrect the company and its shattered credibility. Buffett took decisive action, replacing the old management team and instilling a culture of impeccable ethics. Though Salomon paid dearly – customers fled, shares dropped, fines topped $290 million – the firm survived, prospered, and was later sold for $9 billion. Had outside director Buffett with the board's backing not cleaned house, 9,000 Salomon employees almost certainly would have lost their jobs and thousands of investors their equity. By contrast, no Enron executive or director stepped forward to avert what was to become the nation's largest bankruptcy.[4]

The Enron bankruptcy is a stark reminder that in the globalizing economy, the leadership of both executives and directors is essential. The primary function of Enron's board of directors was to protect investors' equity – and to pick great managers who would responsibly husband and grow that equity. The directors, however, approved the appointment of a chief financial officer who hid critical information from them, they appointed a chief executive who failed to supervise the CFO, they approved flawed accounting policies that they did not fully understand, and when it all unraveled, none came forward to spearhead a recovery.

In the wake of the collapse of Enron and other corporate scandals in the US and elsewhere, investor scrutiny of top leaders and company boards has intensified. While the scandals added momentum, intensifying attention to the quality of corporate leadership and governance was already well under way, driven, in particular, by transforming developments in equity markets around the world. In this chapter, we examine those drivers and consider how they are redefining corporate governance and leadership.

The rise of institutional and international investing

Well before Enron became the exemplar child of poor governance, the issues of leadership and governance were moving center stage in markets across the globe. The intensifying concern was driven in large part by the continuing rise of institutional investors and the increasing globalization of equity markets. Both of these developments placed a greater premium on governance and leadership among publicly traded companies worldwide.

First, many national markets have moved from domination by individuals and families to rule by institutions and analysts. In the process, professional investors have taken the upper hand in the market's relationship with publicly held firms, giving shareholders more power over the destiny of companies. Institutional holders expect more of company governance and leadership, and they are more capable of insisting that their expectations be met. Second, many national markets evolved from complete dominance by domestic owners to a growing presence of international holders. As a result, powerful institutional investors have acquired an increasing voice in the affairs of companies regardless of country setting, giving emergent world standards more currency everywhere. The size and reach of these institutional investors have made them a more potent monitor of company performance and a catalyst for transfer of best governance practices around the globe.

Internationalization of equity holdings

By virtually any measure, the world's equity markets pushed rapidly across country boundaries during the 1990s. National residents increasingly held foreign shares, and national shares were increasingly owned by non-residents. From 1990 to 1999, for instance, the value of foreign equity held by US residents rose from less than $198 billion to $2.03 trillion. During the same period, the value of US equity held by non-US investors grew from $244 billion to $1.61 trillion (Figure 3.1). During the early years of the 2000s, the value of those holdings contracted with the worldwide market decline, but the degree of internationalization remained large. In 1990, just 5 percent of US investor holdings were in non-US equities; by 2002 that had more than doubled to 11 percent, and another doubling may come in the decade ahead.[5]

A host of forces have driven the change, including enhanced availability of information on foreign companies, fewer regulatory barriers to cross-national investing, and more stock listings on foreign exchanges (a phenomenon Raphael Amit and Christoph Zott examine in more detail in Chapter 10). The number of non-US stocks listed on the New York Stock Exchange, for instance, rose from 96 in 1990 (5 percent of all listed companies) to 469 in 2003 (17 percent); the

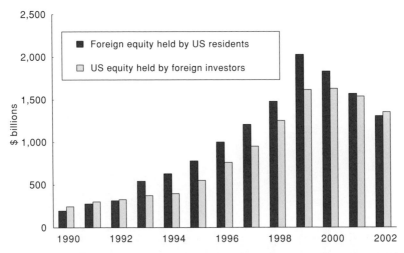

Figure 3.1. Value of foreign equity held by US residents, and of US equity held by foreign investors, 1990–2002. (*Data source*: US Federal Reserve, 2003.)

market valuation of the foreign companies on the exchange in 2003 reached $4.6 trillion, nearly a third of the value of the exchange's total capitalization.[6] None of the drivers behind these trends is likely to reverse in the near term, and cross-border equity investing is sure to continue its spread.

Even in Japan, legendary cross-holdings – stock held long-term by other companies within a firm's *keiretsu* such as Sumitomo or Mitsubishi – are gradually unwinding. In 1987, more than half of shares were so held in Japan, but the fraction had dropped to less than a third by 1999. At the same time, the fraction of Japanese shares held by foreign investors rose from just 9 percent in 1990 to 33 percent in 2002 (after extracting cross-held shares that are never exchanged), as shown in Figure 3.2.[7]

Paralleling the globalizing of equity investment is globalizing direct investment. Foreign direct investment (FDI) in the United States – the ownership of manufacturing and service operations in America by such companies as Japan's Toyota and Germany's Deutsche Bank – rose from $500 billion in 1990 to $1.5 trillion in 2002 (Figure 3.3). Net new foreign direct investment in China displayed a similar trend: in 1990, foreign companies invested $4 billion in facilities or acquisitions in China, in 1995 FDI reached $36 billion, and in 2002, $53 billion.

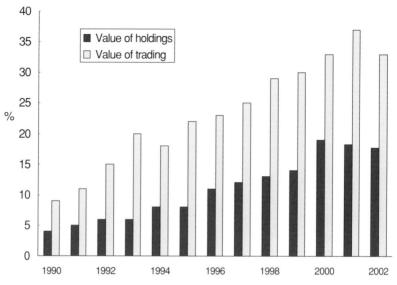

Figure 3.2. Percentage of value of Japanese shares held and traded by foreign investors, 1990–2002. (*Data source*: Mizuho Securities, 2003.)

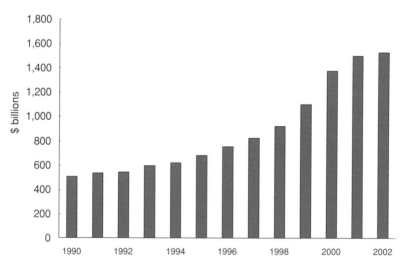

Figure 3.3. Foreign direct investment in the United States, 1990–2002. (*Data source*: US Federal Reserve, 2003.)

Companies in virtually all national markets were increasingly faced with international competitors.

Institutionalization of equity holdings

At the same time that investments are internationalizing, cross-border equity ownership has been moving toward more professional investment management. What is being left behind varies greatly from country to country: in the United States, it is the individual investor; in Japan, the *keiretsu* partner; in Germany, the lead bank. In each case, however, what are coming to the fore are the institutional holders. They are led in the United States by investment companies such as Fidelity and Vanguard, pension funds such as TIAA-CREF and the California Public Employees' Retirement System (CalPERS), and bank trusts and insurance companies.[8]

The emerging organization of professional investment varies from country to country, but the trend lines are much the same. The ownership transformation of the US equity market is illustrative of what is happening worldwide. The fraction of all shares overseen by institutions rose rapidly from 19 percent in 1970 to 56 percent in 2001. The proportion of shares of the nation's 1,000 largest companies held by institutions rose from 47 percent in 1987 to 61 percent in 2000 (Figure 3.4).

Since professional investment managers are more insistent on company performance than were individual investors, *keiretsu* members, or lead bankers, they are more demanding of company leadership and more concerned with company governance. And since these institutional holders are more frequently moving across national boundaries, the leadership and governance practices of publicly traded companies everywhere are more subject to rewards for high performance and to sanctions for under-performance. Moreover, since institutional investors with a global reach are relatively small in number – just several hundred – and they have collectively acquired the rudiments of a self-conscious professional community, the yardsticks for judging leadership and governance are becoming more standardized around the globe.

By virtue of their large assets, institutional investors have acquired the potential to influence company decisions, and many institutions

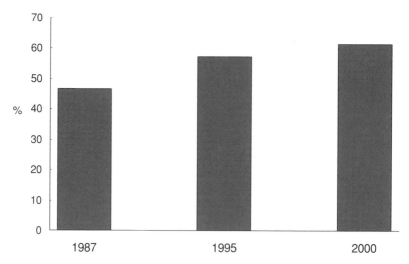

Figure 3.4. Share of institutional ownership of 1,000 largest US companies, 1987, 1995, and 2000. (*Data source*: Conference Board, 2003.)

have learned to leverage that potential through proxy challenges, public criticisms, sell orders, and direct negotiations. Among many studies showing the impact of investor activism, David Parthiban, Michael A. Hitt, and Javier Gimeno evaluated the effect of investor pressure on a firm's investment in research and development. They forecast that companies facing activist holders would increase their R&D budget since owners tend to favor long-term investments while managers prefer short-term payoffs. As they expected, their study of 73 large US industrial companies from 1987 to 1993 found that companies targeted by investors did increase their R&D spending as a percentage of sales. The investigators also found that the impact of that investor activism was greatest on firms that faced growth prospects and in high-technology industries that had been under-investing in R&D.[9]

Most institutional investors recognize that they should not be in the business of micro-managing R&D – or any other company decision for that matter. Professional money managers generally appreciate that they are expert at investment decisions but not management decisions. They would thus prefer to see good governance in place as a proxy for ensuring that good management decisions are made. Their prescription is textbook: investors elect directors to represent them in guiding everyday strategy and execution.

A premium on good governance

Many institutional investors worldwide place a premium on good governance since it fits their theory, saves them time, and lowers their risk. Such a premium for effective governance has been documented in several McKinsey studies. When McKinsey asked forty-two asset managers in Europe and the United States, eighty-four in Asia, and ninety in Latin America to weigh the value of governance and financial issues in evaluating companies for potential investment, the managers ranked governance nearly as important as financial performance – and even more so in the Latin region.

McKinsey also asked the asset managers to compare two hypothetical companies, both with good track records but recently languishing. The governance of one of the companies, however, was described as far superior to that of the other. A majority of its directors were outsiders without ties to management; its directors owned significant amounts of stock; a large portion of their compensation was in stock or options; they evaluated one another's performance; and the company responsively disclosed information to investors. The asset managers reported that they would place substantial premiums on the stock of the well-governed company relative to its poorly governed counterpart. In fact, they would pay as much as 20 percent or more for good governance, especially in countries such as Venezuela, Indonesia, and Italy.[10]

In another survey of sixty-nine company executives and fifty institutional investors, McKinsey found that the investors placed a stock-price premium of 11 percent on good governance. Explained one investor who specialized in picking undervalued companies, "A good board may help lift an underperforming stock and capture hidden value." Many of the investors said that in their experience, well-governed companies perform better over the long term and rebound from setbacks more quickly. Most company executives shared the investors' view: they set their own price premium for good governance at 16 percent. One chief executive explained why: if "two companies are in a daytime race – nothing goes wrong – then they're evenly matched. If the race goes past dusk, however, the company with good governance has the headlights to deal with the problem."[11]

A premium on good leadership

In a bygone era of regulated growth and domestic protection, companies needed great executives and directors, but their actions were less consequential since their world was more predictable. Globalizing product and equity markets have been putting executives and directors more on the line, making their leadership decisions both more difficult and more consequential. Institutional investors have consequently recognized that the quality of leadership throughout the firm has become more predictive of company performance than in the past. Their concerns are in line with recent scholarship on leadership.

Research confirms that leadership makes greater difference when markets are more uncertain. In a study of forty-eight large publicly traded US manufacturers, for instance, David A. Waldman, Gabriel G. Ramírez, Robert J. House, and Phanish Puranam asked two direct subordinates of the firm's chief executives to assess the extent to which their chief (1) was a visionary, (2) showed strong confidence in the subordinate and others, (3) communicated high performance expectations and standards, (4) personally exemplified the firm's vision, values, and standards, and (5) demonstrated personal sacrifice, determination, persistence, and courage. They then assessed the extent to which the firms faced markets that were unpredictable. Taking into account a company's size, sector, and other factors, they found that the strength of these five leadership capacities made a significant difference in the firm's net profit margins over the following years if the company confronted a highly uncertain environment – but far less so if the company faced a more certain world.[12]

Studies also reveal a flattening of organizational hierarchies with greater decentralization and devolution of authority, thereby placing greater leadership responsibilities on those in the ranks. A study by Raghuram G. Rajan and Julie Wulf of 300 large US firms, for example, found that the number of positions reporting directly to the CEO had risen from four in 1986 to seven in 1999, the levels between the lowest-level manager with profit-center responsibility and the chief executive had declined, and more division heads reported directly to the CEO. These changes came not from company growth, mergers, or diversification, nor from greater resources in divisional hands. Rather, the authors found, layers of management were simply being stripped from the chart. Managers that remained were rewarded with more long-term incentive compensation, consistent with the notion that their potential contributions were greater and more contingent upon their leadership capacities.[13]

Still other research has shown the importance of effective leadership even further down the ranks. In a study of nine restaurant chains, James H. Davis, F. David Schoorman, Roger C. Mayer, and Hwee Hoon Tan found that when employees had confidence in their superiors, their restaurants achieved higher levels of sales and profitability during the following quarter. They also found that the most trusted superiors were those that brought ability, integrity, and respect to the office. By implication, good leadership by the mid-level managers was a source of sustainable competitive advantage.[14]

Taken together, these studies imply that company leadership – not only at the top but also in the middle – has become more important for company performance as globalizing markets have created less predictability in the markets.

Leaders are more accountable for corporate performance

The rise of institutional investors has raised the bar on leadership, and the globalization of their holdings has meant that the bar is being lifted just about everywhere in the world. With this increased focus on leadership and its link to corporate performance, top executives are increasingly scrutinized and rewarded or punished for company performance. A study by Shehzad Mian of more than 2,000 company replacements of their chief financial officers from 1984 to 1997 found that CFOs were more likely to be dismissed at a company with poor performance and promoted at a company with good overall performance. The CFOs apparently were held personally responsible for their company's performance – implying that their leadership of it weighed heavily on the minds of their boss, board, and owners.[15]

Management compensation is also increasingly contingent upon company performance and decreasingly dependent on face-time and seniority. This can be seen in data collected annually by the compensation consulting firm Hewitt Associates on the senior seven to eight executives of forty-five large US manufacturing firms. In 1982, 63 percent

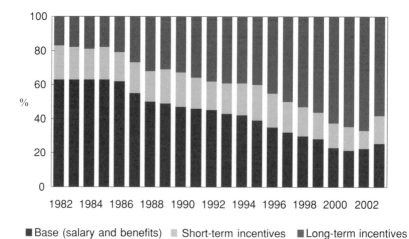

■ Base (salary and benefits)   ▨ Short-term incentives   ■ Long-term incentives

Figure 3.5. Compensation of top seven or eight managers at forty-five US manufacturing firms, 1982–2003. (*Source*: Hewitt Associates.)

of their pay was fixed and just 17 percent was based on long-term incentives. By 2003, that ratio was nearly inverted: just 26 percent was still fixed, and 58 percent had become on based long-term incentives (Figure 3.5).[16] This trend can be seen as well in data on the compensation of chief executives from 1980 to 1994. If a chief executive added $1,000 to the market value in 1980, the executive would see an additional $2.15 in the paycheck; by 1994, that had more than doubled to $5.29 (Figure 3.6).[17]

Training managers for leadership

The growing emphasis on the quality of corporate leadership at all levels has also been reflected in the spread of leadership development programs in recent years. General Electric has run one of the best-known programs for two decades, but other major companies have now joined ranks. Abbott Laboratories, a US healthcare firm with $17 billion in revenue and 71,000 employees, brings groups of thirty-five high-performing, high-potential directors and vice-presidents together for three weeks of leadership development over nine months. Degussa AG, a German specialty chemical company with €12.9 billion in revenue and more than 54,000 employees, provides high-potential

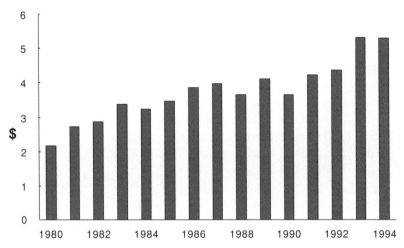

Figure 3.6. Median change in CEO wealth per $1,000 change in company value, 1980–94. (*Source*: Hall and Liebman, "Are CEOS Really Paid Like Bureaucrats.")

managers with leadership training in five capacities: passion for performance, making sense of the business world, making sense of the people, courage and determination, and delivering change and a climate for success. Toyota, the Japanese auto manufacturer with sales of $107 billion and 247,000 employees, periodically gathers its high-potential managers in Japan and the United States for several weeks of intensive development.[18]

For similar reasons, the Wharton School now requires that all incoming undergraduate students enroll in a course on leadership and communication, and that all new MBA students enroll in a class on leadership and teamwork. A decade ago, such courses were not in the curriculum. Today, all 2,000 Wharton undergraduates and 2,000 MBA students must pass such courses, and other business schools have recently incorporated similar requirements into their programs.

Companies are facing more fast-changing and unpredictable markets – and more vigilant and demanding investors who insist on mastery of those markets – and, as a result, they place greater emphasis on leadership at all levels. This in turn has led to the rise of performance-based compensation and the expansion of leadership development programs.

Sound governance for good decisions

Few institutional investors doubt the importance of good leadership for driving company performance. The best way to ensure effective leadership, however, remains a challenge. While investors and analysts can witness executive and director performance during their annual meetings, they are only observing the public veneer of their leadership. As seen in the case of Enron's Kenneth Lay, it is what the executives and directors decide in their private offices or boardrooms that fundamentally defines their leadership.

John F. Kennedy inspired a nation with his inaugural rhetoric, "Ask not what your country can do for you – ask what you can do for your country." But it was what he decided inside the Oval Office during the thirteen-day Cuban missile crisis that far better defined his presidency. Jack Welch became well known for his dictum that each of the General Electric operating companies must stand as number one or two in its market, but it was what he resolved in his executive suite around such issues as whether to sell Kidder Peabody or acquire Honeywell that better defined his reign.[19]

This extends to the board as well. Outward appearances are important: the board should be of limited size, the directors independent, the rewards commensurate. But it is what transpires behind the boardroom's closed doors that ultimately counts: do the directors set good strategy, appoint quality executives, prevent untoward behavior?

Institutional holders cannot control the decisions that are made in the privacy of the boardroom, nor should they want to do so. After all, they have designated the directors to take those actions as the shareholders' elected representatives. Investors can, however, create the context for these private leadership decisions through governance reforms, and that has become a primary focus of initiatives by institutional investors and government regulators. Their objective has been to design good outward foundations that promise sound inside judgment.

Investors have long focused on improving those outward foundations. It began in the United States during the late 1980s and early 1990s when a wave of hostile takeovers, leveraged buyouts, and executive shakeups pointed to the performance shortcomings of existing boardroom practices. That concern has spread to most other major economies as well during the last decade. When held up against the light of emergent global ideals of governance, however, most national systems still come up very short. A World Bank report in 2002 on governance in China, for example, warned that although "corporate governance has moved to the center stage of enterprise reform in China," relative to "practices in other countries, boards are less independent" and "Chinese capital markets lack mature users of financial information, such as institutional investors and analysts."[20]

The governance failures at Enron, Tyco, WorldCom, and other US companies in 2001 and 2002 further intensified the demands by institutional investors for governance reform. The New York Stock Exchange proposed a new set of governance rules for its more than 2,700 listed companies in 2002, and the Sarbanes–Oxley Act of 2002 did the same for the audit function. Their provisions and continuing debate about whether to separate chair and CEO, stagger director elections, and compensate directors with stock – revolve around the outward foundations that would best facilitate unbiased, thoughtful, hard-hitting, and timely decisions when the board convenes behind closed doors.

If we view outward governance principles as those practices that optimize inner company decisions for ultimate shareholder benefit, and if we keep in mind that investors are increasingly demanding great decisions from within, then companies will increasingly focus on two distinct outward foundations of good governance in the years ahead: board composition and board policies. Both are vital; neither is sufficient.

Board composition

The composition of the governing board revolves around two key elements: how many seats are in the boardroom and who fills the chairs. Once those seats are numbered and then occupied, much of the decision-making to follow has already been predetermined. This is analogous to asset allocation in investing: once a money manager has divided the assets between equities and fixed-income and then more finely among their sub-species, the fund's rates and risks of return are relatively preset. Active trading within the asset allocations modestly raises or lowers the rates and risks, but most of the outcome was pre-ordained by the initial allocations.

The research record points to smaller boards as better boards. A study by David Yermack of 450 large US industrial firms from 1984 to 1991 reveals that – adjusting for company size, manufacturing sector, and inside ownership – companies with smaller boards displayed (1) stronger incentives for their chief executive, (2) greater likelihood of dismissing an under-performing chief executive, and (3) larger market share and superior financial performance. The same is found by Martin Conyon and Simon Peck to prevail among large companies in Denmark, France, Italy, the Netherlands, and the United Kingdom.[21]

Though we have little direct evidence from inside the boardroom, research on teams consistently reveals that modestly sized teams are superior decision-makers. When a group of decision-makers is large, the engagement of each diminishes, their resolution of conflict is slower, and decisions are therefore less optimal and less timely. Policy groups have reached much the same conclusion from their own members' understanding. The Business Roundtable, America's premier association of top executives, avowed in a new set of governance guidelines in 2002 that "the experience of many Roundtable members suggests that smaller boards are often more cohesive and work more effectively than large boards."[22]

Though not necessarily informed by either the research findings or policy recommendations, many companies have modestly shrunk their boards on the premise that their decisions would be better and more timely. A few have cut radically: Sony Corporation, for instance, announced in 1999 that it was downsizing its board of directors from thirty-five to nine members as part of a broader restructuring to "create greater shareholder value." The reorganization, it said, was designed to achieve "quicker decision-making and execution in a rapidly changing environment" and "facilitate quick decision-making while maintaining steady corporate governance." During the same year, Japan Airlines took much the same step in response to its languishing performance, shrinking its board from twenty-eight directors to fifteen.

Counter-examples, however, remind us that board size is only a weak proxy for decision-making quality. Toyota Motor Corporation, one of the world's best performing manufacturers, has sustained its growth despite a governing body of sixty directors. General Electric, one the world's most successful conglomerates, has built its empire in spite of a board with nineteen directors. Still, the governing bodies of S&P 500 companies averaged fourteen directors in 1993; by 2003 the average size had dropped to eleven.[23]

Once the board size is determined – and companies are moving toward no more than a dozen directors – filling the seats with the

right occupants becomes the critical choice. Reformers have generally focused on the capabilities, experience, and independence of those
appointed to the board. New guidelines of the Business Roundtable, for
instance, have reemphasized the importance of picking the right directors. They stressed the importance of having "directors with relevant
business and industry experience" and a majority who are independent
of management "in both fact and appearance." The Conference Board,
an independent business research group that mobilized a commission
of prominent business executives (e.g. John Snow, subsequently US
Treasury Secretary; Andrew Grove, chair of Intel; John Bogle, founder
of Vanguard Group), similarly concluded in 2003 that "the board
should have knowledge and expertise in areas such as business, finance,
accounting, marketing, public policy, manufacturing and operations,
government, [and] technology," and "diversity in gender, race, and
background."[24]

Numerous investigations confirm that the composition of the governing body affects company performance. A study by George Kassinis
and Nikos Vafeas compared 209 US companies prosecuted for violation of environmental statutes from 1994 to 1998 with a set of matched
companies that were not prosecuted. Taking into account other factors
such as the firm's past financial performance, the researchers found
more environmental violations among companies whose boards were
larger, and fewer violations among companies whose directors held
additional directorships (thus broadening the directors' understanding
of good governance).[25]

The impact of the board's composition can take a subtle form as outside directors consciously or unconsciously shape the company in their
own image. This was revealed in a study by James Westphal and James
Fredrickson of 406 mid-sized and large publicly traded companies from
1984 to 1996, which showed that when directors replaced chief executives (usually when the company was troubled and needed redirection),
they often recruited the new CEO from companies whose diversification and globalization strategies resembled the strategies of the outside
directors' own firms. After the fresh CEO arrived, the company's diversification and globalization strategies soon came to resemble those of
the company from which the CEO was recruited. While considerable
credit is often attributed to a new outside CEO who brings new strategic thinking to overcome poor performance, this study suggests that it
is actually the outside directors that engineer the specific redirection.

Having outside directors who can draw upon their diverse experiences is the prerequisite for setting this process in motion.[26]

Recognition of the importance of board size and composition has been well illustrated by the reforms of Enron, Tyco, and WorldCom in the wake of their scandals. The new top management teams brought in to resurrect the companies following their debacles – and bankruptcies in the case of Enron and WorldCom – adopted the view that the failure of their boards to protect the company against executive malfeasance was partly a product of those who occupied the board seats and the presence of too many seats to begin with. Thus, all three companies completely replaced their incumbent slates and shrunk the slates as well (Table 3.1). They also rewrote their governance policies, but their complete compositional restructuring underscored just how seriously they viewed the identities and numbers of directors as a source of their disaster.

Comparable intervention restored Scandinavian Airlines (SAS) to health in 2001 when scandal had shattered its reputation. Its chief operating officer had conspired with his counterpart at rival airline Maersk Air to fix rates and routes. The COO initially denied doing so, but when an incriminating document surfaced after a night-time police raid on SAS headquarters, the board forced top management out. But even that cleansing had not gone far enough. Though SAS directors were eminent figures in Scandinavia and had served on the board for years, they concluded that only a wholesale makeover of the board itself would restore the credibility of its future decisions. They resigned *en masse*.

Research evidence, company experience, and corporate disgrace all point in the same direction. For good and timely governance decisions, increasingly demanded by institutional investors whatever the national setting, smaller boards and appropriate directors are the proven path to strong performance.

Governance policies

In addition to board composition, governance policies also shape the quality and timeliness of board and executive decisions. Contemporary standards set forward by the US Securities and Exchange Commission and the New York Stock Exchange – and comparable organizations in a host of other countries – stress policies such as full disclosure;

Table 3.1. *Members of the boards of directors of Enron, Tyco, and WorldCom before and after their scandals, 2001, 2003*

2001	2003
Enron Corporation	
Belfer, Robert A.	Ballantine, John W.
Blake, Norman P., Jr.	Haddock, Ron W.
Chan, Ronnie C.	McNeill, Jr., Corbin A.
Duncan, John H.	Troubh, Raymond S., Interim Chair
Foy, Joe H.	
Gramm, Wendy L.	
Jaedicke, Robert K.	
Lay, Kenneth L., Chair	
Lemaistre, Charles A.	
Skilling, Jeffrey K., CEO	
Urquhart, John A.	
Walker, Charles E.	
Tyco International	
Lord Ashcroft	Blair, Dennis C.
Berman, Joshua	Breen, Edward D., Chair & CEO
Bodman, Richard	Buckley, George W.
Fort, John F.	Gordon, Bruce S.
Kozlowski, L. Dennis, Chair & CEO	Krol, John A., Lead Director
Lane, Wendy	McCall, H. Carl
Pasman Jr., James S.	McDonald, Mackey J.
Slusser, W. Peter	O'Neill, Brendan R.
Swartz, Mark, Executive VP & CFO	Wijnberg, Sandra S.
Walsh Jr., Frank E	York, Jerome B.
Welch, Joseph F.	
Winokur, Herbert S., Jr.	
WorldCom, Inc. (renamed MCI)	
Allen, James C.	Beresford, Dennis
Areen, Judith	Katzenbach, Nicholas de B.
Aycock, Carl J.	Rogers, Jr., C. B.
Bobbitt, Max E.	
Ebbers, Bernard J., President, CEO	
Galesi, Francesco	
Kellett Jr., Stiles A.	
Macklin, Gordon S.	
Roberts, Jr., Bert C., Chair	
Sidgmore, John W.	
Sullivan, Scott D., CFO	

independent audit, compensation, and nomination committees; and either separation of the chair from the chief executive or appointment of a lead director. Such policy prescriptions are intended to focus directors on critical challenges and provide them with full and unbiased information for reaching decisions, regardless of how many and who they are.

Such policies are of value to institutional investors. When an abrupt decline of the Thai currency, beginning on July 2, 1997, triggered crises in Indonesia, Korea, Malaysia, the Philippines, and Thailand, many companies in the region experienced plunging stock values as investors fled the East Asian equity markets. In a study of 398 companies in these five East Asian countries, researcher Todd Mitton found that companies with rigorous disclosure and accounting standards were better able to weather the storm. He found that companies that listed their shares as an American depository receipt (ADR), which required the companies to meet strict disclosure standards, outperformed peers by 11 percent during the twelve months following the crisis. Similarly, companies that had retained one of the top six international accounting firms outperformed the others by 8 percent. Superior disclosure and accounting thus equipped companies in the East Asian markets better to ride out the 1997–98 bout of Asian flu.[27]

Governance policies that entrench management, by contrast, can have an adverse impact on company performance. This is the conclusion, for instance, of a study by Paul Gompers, Joy Ishii, and Andrew Metrick when they examined more than 1,300 publicly-traded US companies during the 1990s. They defined good governance policies to be the absence of twenty-four practices that ensconced managers and disenfranchised investors, ranging from staggered boards and secret ballots to poison pills and golden parachutes. The investigators found that an investor in 1990 who placed $1 into companies with fourteen or more of these negative practices (which researchers dubbed the "dictatorship portfolio") would have seen the holding grow to only $3.39 by December 31, 1999. By contrast, a $1 invested in the set of companies with five or fewer of these practices (which the researchers termed the "democracy portfolio"), would have done more than twice as well, achieving $7.07 in the same period. These gains were the equivalent of annualized returns of 14 percent and 23 percent respectively, a nine-point difference in annual yield over a full decade. Good governance policies help companies run better.[28]

It should be noted that governance composition and policies are not only additive in impact but sometimes multiplicative. That is, an element of both taken together can accomplish what neither achieves when taken singly. For instance, Sayan Chatterjee, Jeffrey Harrison, and Donald Bergh studied seventy-six companies that successfully resisted a takeover effort. They theorized that companies targeted for unwanted takeover were viewed by the pursuer as requiring strategic redirection. But they also reasoned that companies with vigilant boards were less likely to refocus in the wake of a defeated takeover since their boards presumably had actively challenged top management prior to the takeover threat, and top management in turn had already refocused its strategy or fine-tuned its operations. Less vigilant boards, by contrast, had arguably allowed top management the latitude to drift in less optimal directions, and the hostile takeover attempt thus served for them as a "wake-up call." The investigators measured restructuring as the extent to which the company refocused its operations through spin-offs or sales of divisions and plants. They found that companies with relatively low levels of stock ownership by the independent directors more often refocused their operations after the hostile bid than other companies, indicating that lower ownership levels were associated with less vigilant boards.[29]

While it is sometimes claimed that the composition and policies of governing boards have no impact on company performance, the research record confirms the contrary. And companies such as Tyco, Sony, and JAL have changed their composition and policies on their experience-based conclusions that they do make a difference. As institutional holders increasingly pursue their relentless search for high returns from equity investing around the world, they will be more intensively focusing on the extent to which publicly traded companies of any national incorporation have adopted board compositions and governance policies likely to optimize their directors' decisions and thus the company's performance.

The new arbiters of corporate governance

With an eye on protecting investor assets, watchdog groups, government commissions, blue-ribbon panels, and new legislation in many countries have recently sought to improve board composition and policies. Companies in the United Kingdom, for example, have benefited from several such initiatives, from a 1992 commission headed by Adrian Cadbury to two commissions formed in response to the Enron and like catastrophes. One, headed by Derek Higgs, urged greater director independence from management, and the other, led by Sir Robert Smith recommended stronger audit committees. Similar sets of recommendations were issued in 2002–03 by commissions in Brazil, Canada, France, Germany, Spain, and elsewhere.[30]

Many companies in many countries have restructured their governance in the wake of these initiatives, but it has remained for investors to reach their own conclusions regarding the quality of governance of the firms that are targeted for their portfolios. Some institutional investors have developed their own internal capacity for the systematic appraisal of governance – most notably TIAA-CREF whose proprietary assessments date back a decade. Many professional asset managers, however, until recently have of necessity chosen to ignore company governance or only glanced at it because of the high cost of obtaining the right information.

As a sign of the times, however, three intermediaries have stepped to the fore to provide systematic appraisals of the governance of publicly traded companies: Institutional Shareholder Services, Standard and Poor's Governance Services, and Governance Metrics International (see box). Their detailed appraisals of a single company's governance are labor-intensive, entailing extensive interviews with top executives and independent directors, and the cost can run to $100,000 or more per company. But these services have concluded that there is now a profitable market for third-party appraisals. In some cases the company pays for the service, in others the investor, but either way their rise is indicative of the conclusion on both sides that a company's governance makes a difference and it is worth disseminating or acquiring detailed information on the board's composition and policies.

Arbiters of good governance

Institutional Shareholder Services: Institutional Shareholder Services (ISS) has long provided institutional investors with independent advisory and appraisal services on company proxy proposals. It recommended for the merger of Hewlett-Packard and Compaq in a hotly contested proxy test in 2002, for instance, and its advice was seen as a critical catalyst for the merger since it convinced wavering investors to back the marriage. ISS has now added the Corporate Governance Quotient (CGQ) to its proxy advisories. The CGQ rates a company's governance relative to all large companies (such as the S&P 500) and also to industry peers within twenty-three sectors. Four of seven criteria concern board composition: who the directors are, how they are paid, what stock they hold, and what continuing education they are receiving. Two criteria concern the board's policies: its bylaw provisions, and the laws of its incorporating state. By early 2003, ISS had established ratings for more than 5,000 companies, accounting for 98 percent of domestic US equity.[31]

Standard and Poor's Corporate Governance Scoring Service: Standard and Poor's (S&P) has traditionally provided credit and debt ratings of larger companies, and now it draws on the OECD's *Principles of Corporate Governance* to rate their governance as well. It issues a Corporate Governance Score (CGS) that evaluates boards on their composition and policies using criteria similar to those of ISS. The CGS also takes into account a company's legal, regulatory, and market environments, that may vary from country to country.[32]

Governance Metrics International: Newly formed in 2002, GMI builds its governance rating from more than 600 points of data, including director accountability, disclosure policies, and shareholder rights. Its governance criteria also draw upon OECD and several international corporate advisory groups, and it too places a premium on appropriate board compositions and policies.[33]

Though originating in the United States, all three services are evaluating companies headquartered in a range of national settings, from Britain and Germany to India and Japan. Standard and Poor's, for instance, appraised the governance of BP, the British-based petroleum company, in 2001 and gave it a CGS score of 9.6 out of a possible 10. Contributing to its high score were the facts that at least half of BP's directors were non-executives; the CEO and chair were separate; BP maintained relatively independent audit, compensation, and nomination committees; the board had explicitly put forward a set of criteria for making its decisions; and BP regularly evaluated the performance of the board and its directors.[34] Orix Corporation, one of Japan's largest financial services firms, received a CGS score of 7.8. S&P explained that even though Orix was listed on the New York Stock Exchange, it did not disclose its director compensation, virtually all directors were executives, and the board lacked independent committees.[35]

Because of the worldwide visibility of such ratings and since they are based on global criteria, albeit with some appreciation for local context (the S&P report on Orix says, "it is important to note that Orix's score is constrained by a number of factors affecting the Japanese market as a whole"), their emergence and use by professional money managers in making investment decisions will bring mounting pressure for global standards for board composition and policies. A major law firm reviewed these developments for its clients in late 2002 and forecast that "there will eventually be a leveling of corporate governance practices among public companies." And, it warned, companies "must now seek to avoid a 'junk' governance rating."[36]

Toward convergence

Despite the rising investor focus on governance worldwide, significant national differences remain in governance, as Mauro Guillén and Mary O'Sullivan show in Chapter 2. The countervailing forces of deeply entrenched national cultures, regulatory regimes, and business customs are resisting investor demands and slowing cross-national convergence in both governance forms and leadership styles. Yet the forces for convergence in good governance and leadership are ineluctable. It will require years, but market forces ultimately dictate organizational form, and the institutional and international equity market is sure eventually to impose its own worldwide rules on the local forms of governance and leadership whatever the national setting.[37]

Institutional investors and the internationalization of markets are driving the convergence, and the associated arbiters of governance are now defining more clearly the standards toward which companies around the world are moving. Large investors have strong agendas and expectations for governance, and as they make global investments, they are increasingly exporting these ideals around the world. In the pursuit of high returns from public companies on the world stage, money managers have little patience for local variations that are not demonstrably productive. Their buy and sell decisions and political activism are likely to force companies everywhere to converge or at least accept a minimum set of governance principles. For James Shinn and Peter

Gouervitch, writing an assessment in 2002 of how governance should become a foreign policy issue, the "goal is to induce firms to produce better information – through accounting, audit, and disclosure – that will give investors incentive to discipline a firm when this information signals a governance problem," regardless of its national setting.[38]

When institutional money managers first entered markets abroad, they were reluctant to urge improved performance and better governance for fear that they did not sufficiently appreciate local mores or markets. That reluctance is fading. As they have become more comfortable with investing in foreign markets and more uncomfortable with foreign shortcomings, they have pressed for change. As awareness and interest in governance issues and acceptance of a shareholder model of the firm have spread, foreign investors can push for change without appearing to be insensitive to local differences or imperialistic. Given the accumulating assets and powers of the institutional holders and their movement onto the world stage, their performance expectations for company leadership and governance are sure to intensify.

Four practical implications of the globalizing equity market are evident for corporate governance and leadership whatever the national setting:

(1) Governance and leadership have greater impact on a company's performance than they did a decade ago, and investors are therefore paying closer attention to how a company is governed and led. The days of weak leadership and flawed governance will eventually be numbered as professional international investors press for better results and stronger boards.

(2) Leadership is being pushed down from the executive suite and developed deeper in the firm.

(3) Top executives are spending more of their time meeting with institutional investors and managing relationships with the international investment community.

(4) Governing boards are moving toward greater transparency, independence, and influence.

The thrust of these developments is to ensure that both directors and executives have the wherewithal to lead by making good and timely decisions in the privacy of their offices and boardrooms. Investors and regulators around the world are seeking to prevent recurrence of the governance and leadership failures of Enron CEO Kenneth Lay or

Salomon CEO John Gutfreund – and to encourage the type of decisive
and effective action demonstrated by Warren Buffett and the Salomon
board. Effective leadership and governance ultimately require coura-
geous and effective executives and vigilant and informed investors who
can put in place the right governance to ensure that the right leadership
decisions are reached behind closed doors.

Notes

1 J. A. Sonnenfeld, "What Makes Great Boards Great," *Harvard Business Review*, September, 2002, pp. 106–113.

2 W. C. Powers, Jr., R. S. Troubh, and H. S. Winokur, Jr., "Report of Investigation" by the Special Investigative Committee of the Board of Directors
of Enron Corp., February 1, 2002; US Senate, Permanent Subcommittee
on Investigations of the Committee on Governmental Affairs, *The Role of
the Board of Directors in Enron's Collapse* (Washington, DC: US Senate,
2002), http://news.findlaw.com/hdocs/docs/enron/senpsi70802rpt.pdf.

3 M. Useem, "Corporate Governance Is Directors Making Decisions:
Reforming the Outward Foundations for Inside Decision Making," *Journal of Management and Governance*, 7 (2003), pp. 241–253; M. Swartz
with S. Watkins, *Power Failure: The Inside Story of the Collapse of Enron*
(New York: Doubleday/Random House, 2003).

4 M. Useem, *The Leadership Moment: Nine True Stories of Triumph and
Disaster and Their Lessons for Us All* (New York: Random House, 1998).

5 US Federal Reserve Statistical Release Z.1, "Flow of Funds Accounts
of the United States: Annual Flows and Outstanding, 1985–1994,"
December 5, 2002, Table L.107, p. 59, http://www.federalreserve.gov/
releases/Z1/current/data.htm; US Federal Reserve Statistical Release Z.1,
"Flow of Funds Accounts of the United States: Annual Flows and
Outstanding, First Quarter, 2003," June 5, 2003, Table L.107, p. 67,
http://www.federalreserve.gov/releases/Z1/current/data.htm.

6 New York Stock Exchange, *Home Page* and *Fact Book Online*,
http://nyse.com/home.html and http://www.nyse.com/factbook/.

7 P. Dvorak, R. A. Guth, J. Singer, and T. Zann, "Frayed by Recession,
Japan's Corporate Ties Are Coming Unraveled," *Wall Street Journal*,
March 2, 2001, p. A1; Mizuho Securities, *Japanese Stock Market: Review
of Investor Activities* (Tokyo: Mizuho Securities, 2003), http://www.
mizuho-sc.com/english/ebond/equity/trends.html.

8 M. Useem, "Corporate Leadership in a Globalizing Equity Market,"
Academy of Management Executive, 12, 4 (1998), pp. 43–59; Michael
Useem, *Investor Capitalism: How Money Managers Are Changing the*

Face of Corporate America (New York: Basic Books/HarperCollins, 1996); Michael Useem, *Executive Defense: Shareholder Power and Corporate Reorganization* (Cambridge, MA: Harvard University Press, 1993).

9 D. Parthiban, M. A. Hitt, and J. Gimeno, "The Influence of Activism by Institutional Investors on R&D," *Academy of Management Journal*, February 2001, pp. 144–157.

10 McKinsey & Co., *Investor Opinion Survey 2000* (London: McKinsey & Co., 2000).

11 R. F. Felton, J. van Heeckeren, and A. Hudnut, "Putting a Value on Board Governance," *McKinsey Quarterly*, 4 (1996), pp. 1–8.

12 D. A. Waldman, G. G. Ramírez, R. J. House, and P. Puranam, "Does Leadership Matter? CEO Leadership Attributes and Profitability Under Conditions of Perceived Environmental Uncertainty," *Academy of Management Journal*, February 2001, pp. 134–143.

13 R. G. Rajan and J. Wulf, "The Flattening Firm: Evidence from Panel Data on the Changing Nature of Corporate Hierarchies," March 2003, http://www-management.wharton.upenn.edu/wulfresearch/Papers/Flattening_Firm_3_03.pdf.

14 J. H. Davis, F. D. Schoorman, R. C. Mayer, and H. Hoon, "The Trusted General Manager and Business Unit Performance: Empirical Evidence of a Competitive Advantage," *Strategic Management Journal*, 21 (2000), pp. 563–576.

15 S. Mian, "On the Choice and Replacement of Chief Financial Officers," *Journal of Financial Economics*, 60 (2001), pp. 143–175.

16 Hewitt Associates, personal communication.

17 B. J. Hall and J. B. Liebman, "Are CEOs Really Paid Like Bureaucrats?" *Quarterly Journal of Economics*, 113 (1998): 653–691.

18 See http://leadership.wharton.upenn.edu/l_change/other_organizations/index.shtml.

19 J. F. Welch with J. A. Byrne, *Jack: Straight from the Gut* (New York: Warner Books, 2001).

20 S. Tenev, C. Zhang, and L. Brefort, *Corporate Governance and Enterprise Reform in China: Building the Institutions of Modern Markets* (Washington, DC: World Bank, 2002); James Shinn and Peter Gourevitch, *How Shareholder Reforms Can Pay Foreign Policy Dividends* (New York: Council on Foreign Relations, 2002).

21 D. Yermack, "Higher Market Valuation of Companies with a Small Board of Directors," *Journal of Financial Economics*, 40 (1996), pp. 185–211; M. J. Conyon and S. I. Peck, "Board Size and Corporate Performance: Evidence from European Companies," *European Journal of Finance*, 4 (1998), pp. 291–304.

22 Business Roundtable, *Principles of Corporate Governance* (New York: Business Roundtable, 2002).

23 Spencer Stuart, *Board Index 2003* (New York: Spencer Stuart, 2003), http://www.spencerstuart.com/common/pdflib.SSBI-2003.pdf.

24 Conference Board, Commission on Public Trust and Private Enterprise, *Findings and Recommendations. Part 2: Corporate Governance* (New York: Conference Board, 2003), p. 17.

25 G. Kassinis and N. Vafeas, "Corporate Boards and Outside Stakeholders as Determinants of Environmental Litigation," *Strategic Management Journal*, 23 (2002), pp. 399–415.

26 J. D. Westphal and J. W. Fredrickson, "Who Directs Strategic Change? Director Experience, the Selection of New CEOs, and Change in Corporate Strategy," *Strategic Management Journal*, 22 (2001), pp. 1113–1137.

27 T. Mitton, "A Cross-Firm Analysis of the Impact of Corporate Governance on the East Asian Financial Crisis," *Journal of Financial Economics*, 64 (2002), pp. 215–241.

28 P. Gompers, J. Ishii, and A. Metrick, "Corporate Governance and Equity Prices," *Quarterly Journal of Economics* 118 (February 2003), pp. 107–155.

29 S. Chatterjee, J. S. Harrison, and D. D. Bergh, "Failed Takeover Attempts, Corporate Governance, and Refocusing," *Strategic Management Journal*, 24 (2003), pp. 87–96.

30 A. Cadbury, *Corporate Governance and Chairmanship: A Personal View* (Oxford: Oxford University Press, 2002); S. Ascarelli, "Corporate Reform through Tweaks," *Wall Street Journal*, January 21, 2003, p. A2.

31 Institutional Shareholder Services, Corporate Governance Quotient, http://www.isscgq.com/RatingCriteria.htm.

32 Organisation for Economic Cooperation and Development, *Principles of Corporate Governance* (Paris: Organisation for Economic Cooperation and Development, 1999); Standard and Poor's Corporate Governance Service, 2003.

33 Governance Metrics International, http://www.governancemetrics.com/.

34 Standard and Poor's Corporate Governance Service, *Corporate Governance Score: BP PLC*, United Kingdom, December 18, 2001.

35 Standard and Poor's Corporate Governance Service, *Corporate Governance Score: Orix Corporation*, Japan, August 1, 2002.

36 M. S. Brown, *The Corporate Governance Advisor* (Chicago: Katten Muchin Zavis Rosenman, 2003).

37 M. F. Guillén, *The Limits of Convergence: Globalization and Organizational Change in Argentina, South Korea, and Spain* (Princeton, NJ: Princeton University Press, 2001); M. F. Guillén, "Corporate Governance and Globalization: Is There Convergence Across Countries?" *Advances in Comparative International Management*, 13 (2000), pp. 175–204.
38 Shinn and Gourevitch, *How Shareholder Reforms Can Pay Foreign Policy Dividends*.

4 | *Leadership in a global organization: a cross-cultural perspective*

MANSOUR JAVIDAN
Haskayne School of Business, University of Calgary

GÜNTER K. STAHL
INSEAD

ROBERT J. HOUSE
Wharton School

How do the qualities of leaders vary across national cultures? In this chapter, the authors draw upon the GLOBE research program, a large-scale study of culture and leadership in sixty-two cultures, to offer insights on differences in leadership across three nations: Singapore, Denmark, and Argentina (with the United Kingdom as a reference point). Using a framework of value-based leadership, they show that, on average, employees in these cultures have different characteristics along the following dimensions: in-group collectivism, uncertainty avoidance, power distance, humane orientation, gender egalitarianism, institutional collectivism, assertiveness, future orientation, and performance orientation. The authors then explore the implications of these differences for leadership approaches in each country. For example, a leader might emphasize quick wins in Argentina because of its culture of short-term orientation, but might emphasize a longer-term view in Denmark. Finally, they examine a set of core capabilities needed by global leaders, and strategies for cultivating these capabilities.

J ACK Brown (disguised name), the newly appointed chief executive of a large business unit in a global corporation beamed with excitement as he looked out of the window of his office, overlooking Singapore's bustling shopping belt, Orchard Road. Later that afternoon, he would be giving his managers and staff in Singapore the good news that the board had decided to relocate the business unit's headquarters from the United Kingdom to Singapore, reflecting the critical importance of Asia Pacific to the company's global strategic objectives.

The company is a multi-billion dollar global corporation with extensive operations in Europe, North and South America, and Asia Pacific, operating as three global lines of business. Headquartered in the UK, it employs over 30,000 people and serves more than one million customers worldwide. Since early 2002, the company has been restructuring its businesses, moving from country-focused operations to global lines of business. In early 2003, the second phase of the transition was completed with the CEO's announcement that the positions of regional chief executives were to be abandoned. Jack, formerly the chief executive of Asia, was promoted to head the newly created global line of business.

While Jack was excited about his expanded responsibilities in the new position, he was also aware of the challenges ahead. As the chief executive of the new global business unit, he knew that what he did in the next few weeks could be crucial in the success of the unit's transition to a global line of business. Reflecting upon the challenges awaiting him, he thought that it would be an uphill battle to convince the country managers of the benefits of a global business line. Although there is no doubt that the new operating model would give the company a huge competitive advantage, the change would not necessarily benefit the country managers directly. In fact, they might even see it as an erosion of their power. So the big question to him was how he could gain their support and inspire them to work toward the business unit's global vision.

Jack felt that his key role during this difficult transition period was to communicate the new vision for the company and the global business line, and to guide the implementation process. It was clear to him that, rather than telling his country managers exactly how to do it, he had to encourage them to transform their operations in a way that was in line with the company's global strategic objectives.

In less than two hours, Jack would face his managers in Singapore – the first of a series of meetings with his country managers over the next few weeks. He felt that it should not be too hard to win the Singaporean managers over since he had been working closely with them for the past few years and knew quite a few of them very well. He also felt that he was sufficiently familiar with the local culture and their working style.

As Jack's thoughts moved on to his expanded responsibilities of managing the operations worldwide, especially those with which he had previously had little or no contact, he became a little apprehensive. In the next few days, he would be leaving for a ten-day business trip to visit the business unit's operations in Scandinavia, followed by a short visit to Argentina where the unit was in the process of acquiring a large family-owned company. "Getting the Danish and Argentinian managers' support and enthusiasm about the new global structure might be difficult," Jack thought. He had had some experience working with Scandinavians, but being a European himself, Jack was aware of the danger of falling into the trap of thinking that it would be easy to deal with the Danish managers. As for the Argentinian managers, they had gone through a series of mergers and acquisitions over the past two years, and were probably tired of the constant process of change and realignment that the company and its employees had to endure. "One thing's for sure, I have to tread the waters carefully and to display a considerable amount of cultural sensitivity in getting my country managers to align their operations with our global objectives. This will be a test of my cross-cultural leadership skills, no doubt about it."

Leading across cultures

The difficult and complex global tasks facing Jack Brown, which we'll return to later in this chapter, illustrate some of the challenges confronting leaders in today's highly competitive and rapidly changing global business world. As economic and political barriers come down and different countries come into closer contact, cultural barriers can act as a major obstacle.[1] The success of global corporations will depend not just on their competitive strategies but also on how effectively they manage to execute their strategies across multicultural organizations and workforces. Successful implementation in turn depends on the leadership abilities of top executives who need to navigate the global landscape and mobilize their cross-cultural workforces to move toward common objectives. They need a clear understanding of what it takes to be an effective leader and to what extent the criteria for effective leadership are universal or culture-specific.

In this chapter, we draw upon the findings of the GLOBE research program – one of the most far-reaching empirical studies of global leadership – to provide a better understanding of the impact of national culture on organizational leadership. We will explain the concept of value-based leadership and will demonstrate the effect of culture by examining how such leadership can be best implemented in different countries. The chapter will be of special value to executives managing multicultural units and researchers who are interested in cross-cultural challenges in management.

Value-based leadership

Like Jack Brown, executives of global corporations are faced with the challenge of communicating the company's strategy and vision to a multinational and culturally diverse workforce and implementing it in a highly uncertain, dynamic, and unpredictable environment. Even in a domestic context, building commitment to an overall corporate vision and aligning employees with a new strategy can be a daunting task.[2]

To better understand differences in leadership across cultures, we first must describe the framework through which we are considering these differences. In our global studies of leadership, we focus on a particular leadership style or way of influencing people, using values and vision to motivate others. While this genre of leadership theories has been referred to as "transformational," "inspirational," "visionary," and "charismatic," we use the term "value-based" because the leader reinforces the values inherent in the organization's vision. This view is in contrast to transactional leadership theories, which focus primarily on leader–follower exchange relationships, authority relations, and leader control and reinforcement behavior. In value-based leadership, vision is a central focus.

The distinction between transformational and transactional leadership is critical to understanding the motivational effects of value-based leadership.[3] While transactional leaders motivate followers by setting goals, monitoring performance, and promising rewards for desired performance, transformational leaders appeal to followers' intrinsic motives, idealistic goals, and emotions. With transformational leadership, the followers feel trust, loyalty, and respect toward the leader, and they are motivated to do more than they originally expected to do. In contrast, transactional leadership involves an exchange process that may result in compliance with leader requests but is not likely to generate follower commitment and enthusiasm. Transactional leaders are not perceived as inspiring, nor are they able to develop strong emotional bonds with followers; instead, they motivate followers by appealing to their self-interest.[4]

While early leadership studies emphasized the need for leaders to show a dual concern for task and relationships in their day-to-day pattern of behavior,[5] the role of vision and shared purpose was underexplored. Vision energizes and mobilizes people by providing them with a sense of belonging to something greater than themselves – "being a force of nature . . .; being used for a purpose recognized by yourself as a mighty one," as the Irish dramatist George Bernard Shaw put it.

Value-based leadership includes several important attributes, traits, and behaviors (see box for summary).[6] Note that these characteristics are not necessarily those of the "charismatic" leader portrayed in the popular media or leadership literature, where leaders are shown as dramatic orators or heroic figures with larger-than-life personalities. Jim Collins, in a study of the success factors of "great" companies, found that some of the most successful business leaders seem to be the exact opposite of charismatics, although they conveyed a strong sense of values.[7] The leaders of highly successful companies, like Darwin Smith, the former CEO of Kimberly-Clark, often have low-key personalities and possess a paradoxical mixture of personal humility and professional will. Another recent study on leadership, found that the most inspirational leaders possess atypical leader qualities – for example, they selectively show their weaknesses and expose some vulnerability, and they manage employees with a great deal of tough empathy.[8]

Characteristics of value-based leadership

Articulation of a clear and appealing vision: Inspirational leaders build commitment to a new vision or – in cases where a vision has already been articulated – they strengthen the existing vision. A vision consists of two major parts: core ideology and envisioned future.[9] The core ideology defines what an organization stands for and why it exists. It includes articulation of the organization's core purpose – the deeper reasons for its existence beyond just making money – as well as core values – the essential tenets of the organization. For example, Merck's core purpose to "preserve and improve human life" is reflected in its core values: social responsibility; science-based innovation; honesty and integrity; and profit, but profit from work that benefits humanity. The second part of vision, envisioned future, is what an organization aspires to become, to achieve, to create – something that will require significant change and progress to attain. It consists of a long-term, bold, even audacious, goal and a vivid description of the future – a better future for the organization and its members – a vibrant, engaging, and specific description of what it will be like to achieve the goal. For example, George Merck used vivid words to describe the envisioned future of his company and to illustrate his long-term goal to transform Merck from a chemical manufacturer into one of the preeminent drug-making companies in the world: "science will be advanced, knowledge increased, and human life win ever a greater freedom from suffering and disease."[10]

Use of strong, expressive forms of communication when articulating the vision: The success of a vision depends on how clear, well-communicated, and emotionally appealing it is.[11] For example, Jay Conger compares the rousing speech of charismatic Apple Computer founder Steve Jobs – who framed the strategic goal of his new computer company, NEXT, as revolutionizing the educational system of a nation – to the more pedestrian speech of a division head of a large corporation, who described his organization's mission for the next year in terms of operating goals, budgets, and policies.[12] Inherent in the visions of inspirational leaders such as Jobs are end values such as fairness, equality, or social responsibility, which appeal to people's emotions and have powerful motivational effects. The leader also needs to convince followers that the vision is more than just wishful thinking. It is important to make a clear link between the vision and a credible strategy for attaining it.[13]

Display of strong self-confidence and confidence in the attainment of the vision: A leader's confidence, optimism and enthusiasm can be contagious. When Carlos Ghosn, the President of Nissan Motor Company, announced in 1999 that he would turn around Nissan within eighteen months of taking over, or quit, few people believed he would succeed. At that time Nissan was close to collapse, and industry analysts were sure that his attempts to save the company would fail. But Ghosn succeeded, in part, because he firmly believed in himself and the vision he had created for Nissan, and his confidence convinced Nissan employees that they could pull it off.[14] In contrast, if a leader loses confidence and becomes hesitant, how can the leader expect followers to have faith in the vision?

Communication of high expectations for followers and confidence in their abilities: The motivating effect of a vision also depends on the extent to which followers are confident about their ability to achieve it. Leaders can create a self-fulfilling prophecy by having high expectations for their followers and showing confidence in their abilities. The term "self-fulfilling prophecy" refers to the well-known phenomenon that what we expect, very often, is exactly what we get; it explains how a belief or expectation, whether correct or not, affects the outcome of a situation or the way a person will behave. In the context of leadership, Eden found that increasing supervisors' confidence in their subordinates' abilities led them to perform better.[15] The principle underlying this effect is simple: managers form certain expectations of subordinates, they communicate those expectations with various cues (e.g. by what they say, how they say it, how they delegate authority and how they generally treat their subordinates), subordinates tend to respond to these cues by adjusting their behavior to match them, and the result is that the original expectation becomes true. The implications for managers are clear: by setting high expectations and showing confidence in their subordinates' abilities, they can create a self-fulfilling prophecy.

Role modeling behaviors that emphasize and reinforce the values inherent in the vision: A precondition for effective leadership can be summarized in the adage, "Lead by example." According to an old saying, actions speak louder than words. Some of the most admired military leaders have been ones who led their troops into battle and shared the dangers and hardships rather than staying behind in safety. Managers who ask subordinates to make personal sacrifices in the interest of the company's vision should set an example by doing the same. Gary Yukl tells a story about a top management team that asked employees to defer their long-expected pay increases, but awarded themselves fat bonuses. A more effective approach would have been to set an example by cutting bonuses for top management before asking for sacrifices from employees.[16]

Empower people to achieve the vision: When leaders commit themselves and their organizations to a huge, daunting challenge, they cannot do everything by themselves. Executives who are unable or unwilling to delegate are doomed to failure because they under-utilize the capacity of their subordinates. The essential role of upper-level executives is to articulate a vision, to credibly communicate that vision, and to guide the process by which the vision will be implemented. An important lesson learned from many failed change initiatives is that senior executives should encourage middle or lower-level managers to transform their units in a way that is consistent with the company's strategy and vision, rather than telling them exactly how to do it.

Research has shown that leaders described as transformational, visionary, or charismatic can motivate employees to perform above and beyond the call of duty. Further, value-based leadership can have a powerful effect on organizational performance, to the extent that the values inherent in the leader's vision are consistent with the firm's strategy and goals.[17] The effectiveness of value-based leadership has been demonstrated at different levels of analysis including informal groups, formal work units, and major sub-units of larger organizations, and for a wide variety of leaders including military officers, political leaders, educational administrators, middle managers, and senior executives.[18]

In the leadership literature, there is relatively little explanation of the process by which leaders "inspire" followers to do things that are not always in their self-interest. House suggested that values play a central role in this process. The values inherent in the visions of charismatic leaders are usually end values, which are intrinsically satisfying on their own.[19] Yet values differ from culture to culture and this makes value-based leadership across different nations – the type of challenge Jack Brown faces – quite complex and challenging. How can the values of the organization and the values of the national culture be brought together to drive the organization's progress?

Understanding national cultures – the GLOBE Project

Value-based leadership is particularly important for executives in large, diversified corporations operating in many countries around the world. A company's vision and core values provide the glue that holds the organization together as it grows, diversifies, and expands globally. A visionary company exports its core values and purpose to all of its operations in every country, but tailors its strategies, goals, and practices to local cultural norms and market conditions. For example, Wal-Mart exports its core value that the customer is number one to all of its operations overseas, but it does not necessarily export organizational practices such as the Wal-Mart cheer, which is merely a cultural practice to reinforce the core value. Cultural diversity can be a strength, but it must be rooted in a common understanding of what the company stands for and why it exists.[20]

While globalization creates many opportunities for corporations, it also produces significant managerial challenges. Success in dealing with people from other cultures requires that managers know about cultural differences and similarities among countries. They need the understanding and the skill-set to act and decide appropriately and in a culturally sensitive way. There is no shortage of advice on how this can be accomplished. Some experts call for open-mindedness and respect for other cultures.[21] Others suggest that relationship management and personal effectiveness are the secrets to success.[22] They suggest attributes like community building, conflict management, cross-cultural communication, influencing, and curiosity.

Still others have emphasized the importance of global perspective, local responsiveness, and cross-cultural interaction and awareness.[23] They suggest that global leaders need to understand the global business environment and must be able to adapt to living in different countries. Several other writers point to the importance of cognitive complexity and psychological maturity.[24] They suggest "walking in the shoes of people from different cultures," active listening, and a curiosity to learn about and from others.[25]

While such advice is useful, it is typically derived from small case studies or anecdotal information rather than empirical and scientific evidence. It is also too general and conceptual to be of direct value to executives. Managers are still left wondering how to be "open-minded" or how to "put oneself in somebody else's shoes" in a different culture. Small case studies or a small experience base are a problem in this context because there are few generalizations that can be made about "global" leadership. Different cultures are quite idiosyncratic, which means there are many shoes to walk in. For leadership, it is critical to understand how these cultures are similar or different and then design strategies tailored to the specific culture.

The GLOBE Project

The GLOBE (Global Leadership and Organizational Behavior Effectiveness) research program was designed to provide a richer view of global leadership challenges. It is a rigorous research effort intended to provide the kind of cultural understanding and sensitivity that help global managers succeed in their endeavors.[26] GLOBE is a multiphase, multimethod project in which investigators spanning the world are examining the interrelationships between societal culture, organizational culture, and organizational leadership. Close to 150 social scientists and management scholars from 62 cultures representing all major regions of the world are engaged in this long-term programmatic series of cross-cultural leadership studies. They have collected data on cultural values and practices and leadership attributes from 18,000 managers in telecommunications, food, and banking industries. (Further information about the project and its findings can be accessed through its website, at http://www.haskayne.ucalgary.ca/ GLOBE/Public/.)

Cultural dimensions

GLOBE identified and quantified nine cultural dimensions – including shared values, beliefs, and practices – that differentiate societies in meaningful ways and are transmitted across generations. These are aspects of a country's culture that distinguish one society from another and have important managerial implications. (Owing to space limitations, in this chapter we will focus on cultural practices rather than values.) The nine dimensions that will inform our subsequent discussions of global leadership are set out in the following paragraphs.

Assertiveness: Assertiveness is the extent to which a society encourages people to be tough, confrontational, assertive, and competitive rather than modest and tender. Highly assertive societies such as Argentina, the United States, and Austria tend to prefer strong and direct language. They admire winners and sympathize with the strong. Less assertive societies such as Denmark, Sweden, and New Zealand tend to prefer soft and collaborative relations. They have sympathy for the weak and prefer a less direct style of communication.

Future orientation: This dimension refers to the extent to which a society encourages and rewards future-oriented behaviors such as planning, investing in the future, and delaying gratification. Countries with strong future orientation, such as Singapore, Switzerland, and the Netherlands, are associated with higher propensity to save for the future and longer thinking and decision-making time-frames. Countries with shorter time horizons, such as Argentina, Russia, and Italy are less concerned with the future and more focused on immediate actions and decisions.

Gender egalitarianism: Gender egalitarianism is the extent to which a society minimizes gender role differences. Countries such as Denmark, Hungary, and Poland are reported to have the most gender-egalitarian practices. They have a higher percentage of women participating in the labor force and more women in positions of authority. In contrast, such countries as India, Egypt, and China are reported to have high degrees of gender differentiation. Men in those societies generally enjoy a higher status.

Uncertainty avoidance: This dimension refers to the extent to which a society's members seek orderliness, formalization, and regulation to cover situations in their daily lives. It reflects the society's reliance on social norms and procedures to alleviate the unpredictability of future events. Countries like Denmark, Singapore, and Germany have a stronger tendency toward structured lifestyles and rules. In contrast, in countries such as Argentina, Russia, and Greece, there is a strong tolerance of ambiguity and uncertainty. People are used to less structure in their lives and are not as concerned about following rules and procedures.

Power distance: Power distance is defined as the degree to which members of a society distribute, deploy, and react to application of power, authority, and status. It reflects the relationship between those who have the power and those who do not. Countries like Denmark and the Netherlands which practice low power distance, tend to be egalitarian and to favor stronger participation in decision-making. In contrast, countries like Argentina and Russia that are high on power distance, tend to expect obedience toward superiors and clearly distinguish between those with status and power and those without it.

Institutional emphasis on collectivism vs. individualism: This dimension reflects the degree to which individuals are encouraged to integrate into groups. Societies that strongly value individualism such as Argentina, Greece, and Italy, tend to value autonomy, individual freedom, and individual interest. In contrast, in collectivist countries such as Singapore and Denmark, group harmony and cooperation is paramount. Rewards are designed to recognize the group more than the individual. People in these societies tend to prefer similarity to others rather than distinctiveness. Group goals and interests are more important than individual goals and interests. Important decisions are made by groups rather than individuals, and organizations take responsibility for employee welfare.

In-group collectivism: This dimension is different from the institutional individualism/collectivism dimension described above. While the former reflects the extent to which a society's institutions favor individualism vs. collectivism, this dimension refers to the strength of ties within small groups like the family and a circle of close friends, and the organizations in which they are employed. In countries like Singapore and Argentina, being a member of a family and of a close group of friends, is very important to people. Family members and close friends typically have strong expectations of each other. In contrast, in countries like Denmark, Sweden, and New Zealand, the cultural practices are quite different. Family members and close friends do not have strong expectations of, nor obligations towards, each other.

Performance orientation: This dimension refers to the degree to which a society encourages and rewards group members for performance improvement and excellence. In high-performance countries like Singapore, Hong Kong, and the United States, people tend to feel a sense of urgency and prefer a direct and explicit style of communication. They value personal improvement and development. In contrast, countries like Argentina, Russia, and Italy are low on this dimension. They tend to view feedback as discomforting and pay attention to one's family and background rather than performance. They emphasize seniority and experience and prefer a lower sense of urgency.

Humane orientation: This dimension is defined as the degree to which a society encourages and rewards individuals for being fair, altruistic, generous, caring, and kind to others. In countries like Denmark and Malaysia, soft and supportive human relations and strong sympathy are highly valued. People tend to be friendly, sensitive, and tolerant. In contrast, in countries like Argentina and Austria people tend to be less caring and more confrontational. They are less sensitive and their tone of communication is harder and more direct.

The GLOBE study examined how different countries differ along these dimensions, and the results offer insights for leaders who need to motivate employees in these areas.

Value-based leadership in a global corporation: a cross-cultural perspective

How do the perspectives of value-based leadership from the GLOBE project address the challenges faced by Jack Brown described at the start of this chapter? Value-based leadership can help him mobilize the motivation and commitment of the business unit's multicultural workforce to implement the company's new global strategy. Yet his challenges are further complicated by the fact that the company's workforce consists of employees from different countries and he must tailor his leadership style to the specific characteristics of each culture. Country cultures influence the ways that leaders work with their followers, so to identify effective leadership in a country, one has to start with an understanding of the culture and its impact on leadership styles. How is value-based leadership put into action and executed in different cultures?

To address the challenges facing Jack Brown, and illustrate the use of GLOBE research, we focus on three countries – Singapore, Denmark, and Argentina – together with the United Kingdom as the reference country (Brown's native culture and the headquarters of his firm). These countries were chosen to represent a range of cultures and continents that are relevant to global executives. To provide specific action-oriented advice on the implications of culture for leadership, we need to look both at country cultures and at cultural differences between the global executive's country and the host country. The road to understanding of other cultures starts with a clear knowledge of one's own. Being an effective value-based leader in Singapore is probably easier for a manager from a country with a closer cultural profile than one from a more distant culture.

Figure 4.1 shows the country scores on the nine GLOBE cultural dimensions. The potential range for each dimension is from 1 (lowest) to 7 (highest). The higher the country score on each dimension, the stronger the country's practices are reported to be on that dimension. For example, Singapore has a score of 5.64 on in-group collectivism, meaning that cultural practices of the country are strong on in-group collectivism. In contrast, Denmark has a score of 3.53 on the same dimension, meaning that family ties are not as strong in that country.

As can be seen from Figure 4.1, Denmark has relatively high scores on institutional collectivism, humane orientation, and uncertainty avoidance. It has relatively low scores on power distance, assertiveness, and in-group collectivism. Argentina is high on individualism, power distance, assertiveness, and in-group collectivism but low on performance orientation, future orientation, uncertainty avoidance, and humane orientation. Singapore is high on performance

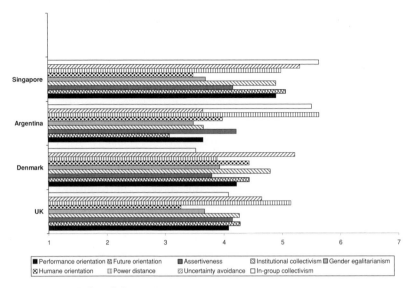

Figure 4.1. Cultural dimensions.

orientation, future orientation, in-group collectivism, uncertainty avoidance, and institutional collectivism. It is relatively low on humane orientation.

The cultural scores in Figure 4.1 are useful in helping us better understand how to pursue value-based leadership in different cultures. They also have implications for Jack Brown's approach to workers in different parts of the world. As he prepares to speak to employees, these insights will lead to a different set of action items or talking points for each country. While he may have a similar agenda in engaging employees in each region to the new global organization, he will need to tailor his actions and talking points to the specific country, as summarized in Table 4.1 and explored in more detail below.

Value-based leadership in Denmark

Denmark's high score on uncertainty avoidance means that people generally do not like to see major change. Moreover, in any change effort, they require a clear picture of the end point and need to see an explicit, detailed, and elaborate process spelling out what needs to be done, how, and by whom. The process of decision-making also

Table 4.1. *Jack Brown's action items/talking points for different parts of the world*

Denmark	Argentina	Singapore
• Avoid strong competitive language such as "killing the competition." • Stress egalitarianism, integrity, and democracy. • Involve employees in the process. • Stress that the company cares about employees and values their inputs. • Allow Danish employees to see how they fit into the new global strategy.	• Use strong competitive language. • Present the big picture, but stress short-term goals. • Create opportunities for cross-fertilization with other parts of company to counter strong in-group collectivism and individualism and elevate self confidence.	• Use strong competitive language • Communicate vivid, long-term goals. • Explain the role of Asia and Singapore in the company's global strategy. • Show strong confidence in employees and their capabilities. • Use quick wins as yardsticks and performance measures.

needs to provide ample opportunity for everyone to participate on account of the country's high score on collectivism and its low score on power distance. A heroic vision and strategy decreed from the top will be strongly resisted. Employees will want a say in any decision and will ask for a clear justification for any change. Furthermore, owing to their low assertiveness score, they would not resonate with strong competitive language such as global dominance or killing the competition or the enemy. They prefer mild language and a pace that is not seen to be too fast. They resonate with such values as egalitarianism, integrity, and democracy, and would be quite sensitive to any changes in the company's attitudes toward employees; they would look for empathy, sympathy, sensitivity, and being listened to. They value any efforts toward employee development to ensure job security. Because of their high score on humane orientation, employees would be concerned about job security not just for themselves, but also for everyone else.

The role of an effective value-based leader in Denmark is one of developing and managing a process where strategic decisions are made and implemented. Formulation and implementation of such decisions are directly and closely linked. The leader needs to provide sufficient information on the global company's change of strategy and its rationale, and to convey a message that the company cares about its employees and values their input. The leader also needs to be careful not to be perceived as elitist because that would create resistance among employees. One particular cultural dimension can be a major facilitator. The country's low score on in-group collectivism means that it may be easier to get employees to think globally. The new strategy and its benefits can be appealing if employees are given a chance to figure out how their Danish unit can contribute to it. On account of their low in-group score, Danish employees may show less resistance towards the idea of working closely with other units from other parts of the global corporation.

Value-based leadership in Argentina

The country's high score on power distance reflects the employees' willingness to accept authority. They expect their leaders to make decisions and communicate them. They are not used to taking part in the decision-making process. This makes it easier to explain the new strategy and its rationale. On the other hand, the country's low score on future orientation and performance orientation makes any strategy oriented to the long term hard to grasp and commit to. It is important to emphasize and communicate shorter-term milestones on the way to the ultimate objective. The leader also needs to plan for quick wins because they will reinforce the message to employees.

The high score on assertiveness points to the potential attractiveness of strong competitive language. The country's low score on uncertainty avoidance indicates that employees are not resistant to change. They can tolerate relatively high levels of ambiguity and will not be adversely affected by the notion of a new strategy. They also do not necessarily expect a clear and explicit process of decision-making regarding the new strategy and its implementation.

Two cultural dimensions need careful attention. The country's high in-group collectivism reflects the employees' potential resistance to working with employees from other parts of the global corporation. They may take a parochial view of their unit. At the same time, the high score on individualism means that employees will be more self-centered and will be concerned about their own jobs and development and advancement opportunities.

To address both cultural dimensions, leaders need to create opportunities for cross-fertilization between the Argentinian group and other parts of the company. One possibility is to provide for cross-system moves where employees, especially managers, from other parts of the company are transferred to Argentina and where Argentinian employees go to work in other parts of the corporation. This approach has important advantages. Working with foreign employees in Argentina, while not easy at the beginning, will help expand the notion of in-group collectivism beyond one's Argentinian colleagues. The in-group will eventually expand to include people from other cultures. To help sustain this, the value-based leader needs to provide regular and frequent information updates about events and outcomes in other parts of the world. The leader also needs to create a mechanism for regular meetings between the managers from the Argentinian unit and those from other countries. Employees' interest in this approach will be enhanced if there is an opportunity for them to move to other parts of the world. Being individualistic, they would see this as a valuable career development and promotion move. The company can further benefit by using the Argentinian managers as ambassadors for change. Given their low uncertainty avoidance score, they are more open to change and could be asked to help employees from other countries with high uncertainty avoidance scores, like Denmark, better cope with change. Of course, another benefit of this mechanism would be to help improve the performance standards in the Argentinian unit. Given the country's low performance orientation score, one can improve it by introducing global standards of performance and rewards and by familiarizing the group with the performance of the other groups within the company.

In sum, the value-based leader in Argentina presents the big picture and the broad strategy but focuses more on short-term actions and results. The leader is a change agent who is attempting to elevate the group's self-confidence and its contribution to the global corporation by exposing its members to the world around them and by showing that s/he is genuinely interested in helping them do better for themselves and the company.

Value-based leadership in Singapore

Singapore's high scores on future and performance orientation facilitate value-based leadership in the sense that the leader can emphasize and communicate a vivid and attractive long-term vision with bold goals. It is relatively easier to explain the company's new global strategy and its rationale. The leader can use strong competitive language and position the firm against its global competitors to better explain the new strategy. The leader can provide facts and figures about the company's and its main rivals' performances. While communicating a long-term vision and strategy is desirable, quick wins are also important because they act as performance metrics and create cohesion and commitment.

The country's high scores on collectivism and in-group collectivism indicate that a strong focus can be created on the company's major competitors as the enemies to beat. Furthermore, the leader needs to explain the important role of Asia and Singapore in the company's global strategies. The leader needs to create opportunities for Singaporean managers to come into face-to-face contact with their counterparts from other parts of the world to enhance the feeling of belonging to the whole corporation. A possible approach would be to identify topics that are of common interest across the organization. For example, safety, customer focus, innovation, and global multinational customers. The reward system should also reflect team-based and collective action. The purpose is to turn the global business unit into the in-group of the executives and employees in Singapore.

Singapore's high score on uncertainty avoidance means that they expect a clear plan with a time-line and schedule. They need to develop detailed action plans and require explicit policies or guidelines. While the low score on humane orientation reflects a lower degree of sensitivity and a weaker sense of caring, the culture's strong in-group collectivism requires the leader to be careful in the language that s/he uses. The issue is not as much about the welfare of the employee as it is about saving face and preventing embarrassment. Being a member of a group is highly prized and anything that jeopardizes that, such as direct language that could be embarrassing to a member, should be avoided.

To sum up, the role of the value-based leader in Singapore is one of communicating a vision, respecting in-group values and practices, showing strong confidence in employees and their capabilities, and mobilizing their collective energies to become a dominant global competitor.

Observations on cross-national differences from GLOBE

This discussion offers a number of important observations on the nature of cross-national differences. First, cultures may be different on some dimensions and similar on others. To assume that countries are totally different on all dimensions would be a misleading oversimplification. Denmark and Singapore are different in terms of in-group collectivism, but similar in terms of uncertainty avoidance. Argentina and Singapore share a strong degree of in-group collectivism. Thus the leader can sometimes take similar actions in different countries.

Second, our discussion of the three countries shows that the global leader requires a high degree of flexibility to adapt to different conditions. The same leader who takes an explicitly visionary role in Singapore, needs to play a much less explicit and more egalitarian and process-oriented role in Denmark. While this may sound easy, it is in fact very difficult, because managers learn from their experiences and develop their own ways of doing things. Modifying their ways of doing things in different countries requires a high level of capability, self-confidence, cultural empathy, and flexibility.

Third, an important message to global leaders is that they can sometimes turn cross-cultural differences into an advantage by encouraging employees in different cultures to learn from one another. Leaders need to inform employees from different countries about their own cultures and those of the other employees. They need to create opportunities for employees to learn from each other's cultures. To a typical Argentinian, uncertainty and ambiguity is not the end of the world. To a Danish employee, it may be. By bringing the two together, the leader can use the Argentinian employee to help the Danish employee better tolerate uncertainty.

Fourth, despite cultural differences, leaders may take exactly the same steps and actions in different cultures, but for different reasons. We suggested that Jack Brown use quick wins both in Argentina and Singapore. While the actions are the same, their rationale is quite different. Quick wins are important in Argentina because it is a culture oriented to the short term and does not resonate with long-term plans. They are also important in Singapore because they act as performance measures and yardsticks and as milestones in reaching long-term plans.

Fifth, it is not enough for a global leader to understand another culture. Leaders also need to know the extent to which the other culture is different from their own. As can be seen from Figure 4.1, a typical UK executive like Jack Brown will feel more comfortable in Denmark when developing and communicating long-term plans and performance targets, but will feel more at ease with authority and power issues in Singapore. At the same time, the leader will find it a challenge dealing with Singapore's strong in-group collectivism.

Finally, while the GLOBE project has shown that there are cultural attributes that distinguish among countries, it is important to recognize that there is still a range of cultural practices within a single country. Some Americans may be more individualistic than others and some Singaporeans may be less collectivist than others, but the American group on average will be more individualistic than the Singaporean group.

Global leadership competencies

Our analysis of the challenges facing Jack Brown, as he tries to mobilize his organization's cross-cultural workforce to move toward common objectives, illustrates that executives of global corporations must possess all the qualities of good domestic managers. But that is not enough. They must also understand the worldwide business environment from a global perspective; balance the often conflicting pressures for global integration and local responsiveness; communicate their company's strategy and vision to a multinational and culturally diverse workforce; and implement the strategy and vision in a highly uncertain, rapidly changing, and unpredictable environment. In other words, these leaders need specific global leadership competencies that go beyond their core management skills.

Leadership and cross-cultural management researchers have spilled much ink trying to delineate the competencies required for successful global leadership.[27] We do not intend to reiterate here the vast lists of global leadership competencies reported in the literature; rather, we will use the case of Jack Brown to illustrate the most important qualities needed by executives in a global arena. There are five such qualities, as described in the following paragraphs.[28]

Global business expertise: A global manager's technical and industry knowledge is the most fundamental quality that allows him or her to manage the day-to-day business successfully. This business savvy must include knowledge of the socio-political, economic, and cultural dimensions of the global environment. Executives such as Jack Brown must learn about the perspectives, trends, technologies, and approaches to conducting business in the countries in which their companies operate, and they need to understand what managing effectively in drastically different locations entails. Global business expertise also includes proficiency in line management outside the home country – a proven track record in successfully operating strategic business units and/or a series of major overseas projects.

Global organizing expertise: In addition to business savvy, global leaders need to have an intimate knowledge of the firm's capabilities and the ability to mobilize worldwide resources to capture market opportunities. They need to be familiar with the company's subsidiaries and competitive positions, and have established a network of contacts with key people in the worldwide organization. These global networking skills help them mobilize a culturally diverse workforce to accomplish the major mission and objective of the organization. An important aspect of global organizing expertise is the ability to act as a change agent – global leaders have a proven track record in successfully initiating and implementing strategic organizational changes. They also have the ability to recognize local market opportunities and to champion innovations that may offer transnational opportunities and applications.

Cross-cultural relationship skills: Executives of global corporations, such as Jack Brown, are faced with the difficult task of communicating the company's overall strategy and vision to a multinational and culturally diverse workforce, and of implementing the strategy and vision locally. They need skills to lead and motivate people from diverse cultural backgrounds, and to look for creative ways to leverage diversity toward greater organizational effectiveness. Managing relationships in an intercultural context requires cultural awareness and high levels of sophistication in adapting to different styles with different people. Further, it requires a clear understanding of what makes people tick in different cultures, and of the extent to which the criteria for effective leadership are universal or culture-specific.

Traits and values: The challenges facing executives of global corporations, as they mobilize a culturally diverse workforce to accomplish the major strategic goals of the organization, require a number of personality traits, values, and attitudes that managers operating in a domestic environment need to possess to a much lesser degree, such as inquisitiveness, open-mindedness, cosmopolitanism, behavioral flexibility, and learning orientation.

Global mindset: Successful global managers have a distinctive cognitive style, or way of perceiving the environment and processing information, which can be summarized as "global mindset." Global mindset includes the ability to scan the world from a broad perspective, an esthetic openness toward divergent ideas and experiences, and a predisposition to be more tolerant of other people and cultures. Other characteristics of a global mindset include the capacity to rethink boundaries, to consider diversity an asset, and to view uncertainty as an invigorating and natural part of business, rather than being threatened by it. Global leaders are able to balance tensions as they confront the dual pressures for global integration and local responsiveness, and they have a capacity to manage under conditions that are constantly changing and inherently complex.

Developing global leaders

It is clear that the challenges facing executives of global corporations are greater in magnitude (in the areas of connectedness, boundary-spanning, complexity, ethical challenges, dealing with tensions and paradoxes, etc.) and are qualitatively different from those faced in a domestic context (because some of the challenges are unique to a multicultural and global environment). Being constantly exposed to those challenges requires the development of new mental models – a global mindset.

How can this special breed of global leader be developed? It is not just sending people to business schools. HR scholars and practitioners agree that leadership qualities such as the ability to manage under conditions of uncertainty, cultural sensitivity, and a global mindset cannot be developed through classroom training alone – experience is the best teacher when it comes to global leadership development.[29] Assignments to cross-functional or cross-divisional teams, foreign travel, work in multinational teams, international MBA and executive education programs, global mindset training, and short-term assignments abroad can all be utilized for developing global leadership competencies.[30] In addition, HR practices in the areas of recruitment and selection of high-potential employees, performance management and compensation, organizational design, and global communication can support effective development of global managers.[31]

While the above practices and tools are essential elements of any effective global leadership development system, the "single most powerful experience in shaping the perspective and capabilities of effective global leaders" is a long-term international assignment.[32] This is why more and more companies, such as General Electric, Citigroup, Shell, Siemens, Nokia, and others, are beginning to use international assignments as a means of leadership development. They send their high-potential managers abroad, not only to fill local skill gaps, but also to give them the opportunity to improve their general management skills and to acquire a global perspective.

The insights from the GLOBE project, however, suggest that it is not enough for leaders with global responsibility to have experience in *one* country. They also need experience in a variety of different cultures, and the ability to reflect upon that experience. By having this breadth of experience, and depth in one or two cultures, the leader will have a better feel for the differences and the leadership requirements needed and the process of adapting rapidly to the different conditions. A US-born manager who has spent most of her career in Singapore, for instance, might still have trouble leading in Denmark or Argentina. This broader experience will ensure the leader has the breadth of skills and flexibility to meet different cultural demands and raise the leader's awareness about the factors that affect the quality of leadership in each country.

Notes

1 M. Javidan and R. J. House, "Cultural Acumen for the Global Manager: Lessons from GLOBE," *Organizational Dynamics*, 29 (2001), pp. 289–305; M. Javidan and R. J. House, "Leadership and Cultures around the World: Findings from GLOBE; an Introduction to a Special Issue," *Journal of World Business*, 37 (2002), pp. 3–10.

2 J. C. Collins and J. I. Porras, "Building Your Company's Vision," *Harvard Business Review*, 74 (1996), pp. 65–74; J. M. Kouzes and B. Z. Posner, *The Leadership Challenge* (San Francisco: Jossey-Bass, 1997).

3 B. M Bass, *Leadership and Performance Beyond Expectations* (New York: Free Press, 1985); B. M. Bass and B. J. Avolio, "Developing Transformational Leadership: 1992 and Beyond," *Journal of European Industrial Training*, 14 (1990), pp. 21–27.

4 G. A. Yukl, *Leadership in Organizations*, 5th edn. (Englewood Cliffs, NJ: Prentice Hall, 2002).

5 Ibid.

6 J. A. Conger amd R. Kanungo, "Toward a Behavioral Theory of Charismatic Leadership in Organizational Settings," *Academy of Management Review*, 12 (1987), pp. 637–647; Yukl, *Leadership in Organizations*.

7 J. Collins, "Level 5 Leadership: The Triumph of Humility and Fierce Resolve," *Harvard Business Review*, 79 (2001), pp. 67–76.

8 R. Goffee and G. Jones, "Why Should Anyone Be Led by You?" *Harvard Business Review*, 78 (2000), pp. 62–70.

9 Collins and Porras, "Building Your Company's Vision"; J. C. Collins and J. I. Porras, *Built to Last: Successful Habits of Visionary Companies* (New York: Harper Business, 1997).

10 Collins and Porras, *Built to Last*, pp. 203–207.

11 Yukl, *Leadership in Organizations*.

12 J. Conger, "Inspiring Others: The Language of Leadership," *The Executive*, 5 (1991), pp. 31–46.

13 Yukl, *Leadership in Organizations*.

14 *Fortune*, February 25, 2002.

15 D. Eden, "Self-Fulfilling Prophecy as a Management Tool: Harnessing Pygmalion," *Academy of Management Review*, 9 (1984), pp. 64–73; D. Eden, *Pygmalion in Management: Productivity as a Self-Fulfilling Prophecy* (Lexington, MA: Lexington Books, 1990).

16 Yukl, *Leadership in Organizations*.

17 Bass, *Leadership and Performance*; R. J. House, N. S. Wright, and R. N. Aditya, "Cross-Cultural Research on Organizational Leadership: A Critical Analysis and a Proposed Theory," in P. C. Earley and M. Erez (eds.), *New Perspectives on International/Organizational Psychology* (San Francisco: New Lexington Press, 1997), pp. 535–625.

18 R. J. House and B. Shamir, "Toward an Integration of Transformational, Charismatic and Visionary Theories of Leadership," in Martin Chemmers and R. Ayman (eds.), *Leadership Theory and Research Perspectives and Directions* (New York: Academic Press, 1993), pp. 81–107; D. A. Waldman, G. G. Ramirez, R. J. House, and P. Puranam,

"Does Leadership Matter? CEO Leadership and Profitability under Conditions of Perceived Environmental Uncertainty," *Academy of Management Journal*, 44 (2001), pp. 134–144; M. Javidan and D. Waldman, "Exploring Charismatic Leadership in the Public Sector: Measurement and Consequences," *Public Administration Review*, 63, 2 (March/April 2003), pp. 229–243.

19 House, Wright and Aditya, "Cross-Cultural Research."

20 Collins and Porras, *Built to Last*.

21 R. W. Kiedel, *Seeing Organizational Patterns: A New Theory and Language of Organizational Design* (San Francisco: Berrett-Koehler, 1995).

22 T. Brake, *The Global Leader: Critical Factors for Creating the World Class Organization* (Chicago: Irwin, 1997).

23 V. Pucik and T. Saba, "Selecting and Developing the Global versus the Expatriate Manager: A Review of the State of the Art," *Human Resource Planning*, 21 (1998), pp. 40–54.

24 S. Wills and K. Barham, "Being an International Manager," *European Management Journal*, 12, 1 (March 1994), pp. 49–58.

25 S. Wills, "Developing Global Leaders," in P. Kirkbride and K. Ward (eds.), *Globalization: The Internal Dynamic* (Chichester: John Wiley & Sons, 2001), pp. 259–284.

26 R. J. House, P. J. Hanges, S. A. Ruiz-Quintanilla, P. W. Dorfman, M. Javidan, M. Dickson, and V. Gupta , "Cultural Influences on Leadership and Organizations: Project GLOBE," in *Advances in Global Leadership* (Stamford, CT: JAI Press, 1999), vol. I, pp. 171–233; Javidan and House, "Cultural Acumen for the Global Manager"; Javidan and House, "Leadership and Cultures around the World"; R. House, M. Javidan, P. Hanges, and P. Dorfman, "Understanding Cultures and Implicit Leadership Theories Across the Globe: An Introduction to Project GLOBE," *Journal of World Business*, 37, 1 (Spring 2002), pp. 3–10.

27 Brake, *The Global Leader*; H. B. Gregersen, A. J. Morrison, and J. S. Black, "Developing Leaders for the Global Frontier," *Sloan Management Review*, 40 (1998), pp. 21–32; B. L. Kedia and A. Mukherji, "Global Managers": Developing a Mindset for Global Competitiveness, *Journal of World Business*, 34 (1999), pp. 230–251; M. E. Mendenhall, T. M. Kühlmann, and G. K. Stahl (eds.), *Developing Global Business Leaders: Policies, Processes, and Innovations* (Westport, CT: Quorum, 2001); Pucik and Saba, "Selecting and Developing the Global versus the Expatriate Manager."

28 M. Mendenhall and J. Osland, "Mapping the Terrain of the Global Leadership Construct," paper presented at the Academy of International Business Conference, San Juan, Puerto Rico, June 29, 2002.

29 N. J. Adler and S. Bartholomew, "Managing Globally Competent People," *Academy of Management Executive*, 6 (1992), pp. 52–65; A. K. Yeung and D. A. Ready, "Developing Leadership Capabilities of Global Corporations: A Comparative Study in Eight Nations," *Human Resource Management*, 34 (1995), pp. 529–547.

30 Gregersen, Morrison, and Black, "Developing Leaders for the Global Frontier"; M. E. Mendenhall and G. K. Stahl, "Expatriate Training and Development: Where Do We Go from Here?" *Human Resource Management*, 39 (2000), pp. 251–265; A. K. Yeung and D. A. Ready, "Developing Leadership Capabilities of Global Corporations."

31 P. Evans, V. Pucik, and J.-L. Barsoux, *The Global Challenge: Frameworks for International Human Resource Management* (New York: McGraw-Hill, 2002); Pucik and Saba, "Selecting and Developing the Global versus the Expatriate Manager."

32 J. S. Black, H. B. Gregersen, M. E. Mendenhall, and L. K. Stroh, *Globalizing People through International Assignments* (New York: Addison-Wesley Longman, 1999).

5 | The globalization of business education

ARNOUD DE MEYER
INSEAD

PATRICK T. HARKER
Wharton School

GABRIEL HAWAWINI
INSEAD

What does it mean to be a global business school? As business has become increasingly international, the demands of preparing business leaders for success in a global environment have forced leading business schools to reexamine their programs and structure. Schools have used a variety of strategies to raise the bar on internationalization. They have established programs and campuses around the world, brought in international students and faculty, and reshaped their organizations through alliances and joint ventures. The authors review four different models business schools have used to "internationalize" their programs: the import model, the export model, the partnership model, and the network model. They examine some of the key challenges of the process and strategies for success for each model. Finally, they explore some of the key leadership challenges for global business schools. While the focus is on education and research, the solutions of business schools to their global challenges offer insights for corporate managers on the development of global learning communities and managing international networks of knowledge workers.

BUSINESS schools are becoming more global. Our students and faculty are drawn increasingly from around the world. The content of what we offer to participants in our courses, be they full-time graduate students or executives, is gradually adapted to the needs of operating in an international environment. As shown in Table 5.1, of the top twenty schools listed in a recent *Financial Times* ranking, all drew at least a quarter of their students from outside their domestic markets, and with one exception, at least a tenth of their faculty members from abroad.

The percentage of international students in Wharton's MBA program more than doubled between 1980 and 2000, increasing from 18 percent to 39 percent. Over the same period, the proportion of

Table 5.1. *Globalization of top business schools*

	School	Country	International faculty (%)	International students (%)	International board (%)
1	University of Pennsylvania: Wharton	USA	29	42	49
2	Harvard Business School	USA	34	36	7
3	Columbia Business School	USA	50	30	35
4	Stanford University GSB	USA	35	36	14
5	University of Chicago GSB	USA	38	27	10
6	INSEAD	France and Singapore	85	92	71
7	London Business School	UK	71	83	57
8	New York University: Stern	USA	42	32	2
9	Northwestern University: Kellogg	USA	23	33	7
10	MIT: Sloan	USA	29	43	27
11	Dartmouth College: Tuck	USA	27	29	15
12	Yale School of Management	USA	29	34	6
13	IMD	Switzerland	98	96	70
14	University of Virginia: Darden	USA	13	26	18
15	Duke University: Fuqua	USA	40	32	12
16	Univ. of California at Berkeley: Haas	USA	31	35	9
17	Georgetown University: McDonough	USA	24	35	5
18	IESE Business School	Spain	25	61	80
19	Cornell University: Johnson	USA	12	23	35
20	UCLA: Anderson	USA	19	23	10

Source: Financial Times, 2003.

European students in INSEAD's MBA program dropped from 87 percent to less than 50 percent, while Asian students rose from a few participants to more than 20 percent of the total student population. International executive education also has grown over this period, driven both by the development of more courses on international topics as well as the growing numbers of international participants across all programs.

Forces driving the globalization of business education

As discussed in the introductory chapter of this volume, diverse forces are driving the globalization of business. With more global enterprises, there is an increasing need for managers who have global perspectives and experience right out of business school. The desire of students to emigrate to higher-paying jobs and regions also has led to increases in international applications and placement. At INSEAD, for example, up to 50 percent of graduates obtain a job in a country that differs from that of their nationality, while at Wharton more than 20 percent of the MBA class of 2003 took international positions.[1] National business and government leaders around the world also see the value of business education in driving economic progress for their nations, which has led to the development of a number of major new business school initiatives in China, India, Latin America, and other locations.

Recruiters are looking for culturally versatile graduates. As *Business Week* noted "Older, more experienced international graduates, who often speak several languages, give recruiters the flexibility to send them anywhere in the world, a particularly useful trait in recent times."[2] We need managers that are not only aware of global opportunities but are also capable of exploiting a diverse range of international opportunities simultaneously. Our colleagues Yves Doz, José Santos, and Peter Williamson point out that the traditional models of internationalization are not sufficient to explain how some of the most successful companies have been taking advantage of sensing and capturing new ideas all over the world, and combining these ideas into new value propositions that can be rolled out quickly throughout the world.[3] For example, how could a company such as Nokia be successful, starting in the "wrong" country, with a small home market that initially lacked the technological capabilities needed to support the business? In addition to language and cultural awareness, graduates need to develop a deeper sense of the answers to such questions and an appreciation of the strategic possibilities of global markets.

How can global managers be prepared for these challenges? Christopher Bartlett and Sumantra Ghoshal have pointed out that international experience is not sufficient in itself.[4] They note that initial corporate attempts to create "global managers" varied widely. Corning hired an American ex-ambassador to head its global division, but had to weigh the strong international contacts of this former diplomat against a lack of understanding of the corporation and its business. ITT took a different approach, setting up an educational program to encourage global perspectives in its international managers rather than insights into a particular country. The company found, however, that these generalists did not always have the specific knowledge to address the business concerns facing the company. Bartlett and Ghoshal recommend a team approach, using business, country, and functional managers, who play different roles in driving business strategies and creating businesses in specific countries.

Managers in every part of the organization need more knowledge and understanding of international business. But how do business schools need to change their structures and programs to accelerate this process of building global insights among students and faculty? How can these schools meet the resulting challenges of increasing the geographic and intellectual scope of their organizations? These questions have led business schools to develop a variety of different models to support international education.

Four models for internationalizing business education

Traditionally, business schools have been geographically anchored enterprises. The Wharton School has been on the campus of the University of Pennsylvania in Philadelphia since it was founded as the first collegiate school of business in 1881. Unlike a company that could consider outsourcing key parts of its business offshore or moving its entire manufacturing operations to Mexico or Asia, the school's ivory towers are firmly fixed in a certain location. Harvard means Boston, and the University of Chicago leaves little doubt about its location.

It is a difficult process to uproot the ivy and move the gothic towers, and yet business schools have found ways to overcome their geographic

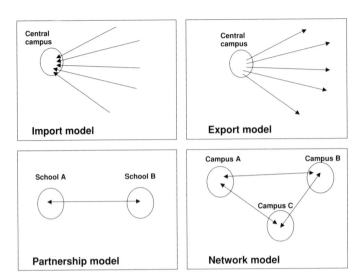

Figure 5.1. Four models for globalization.

limitations and forge international programs. We have identified four primary models business schools have used for internationalization, as illustrated in Figure 5.1:

(1) The import model
(2) The export model
(3) The partnership model
(4) The network model.

The importers

The first group of schools attempts to bring the world to the campus. They consider that there is a high value in co-location and getting students and faculty from different countries together in one location (the home campus). The degree to which they can be successful with this strategy depends very much on their brand image and their ability to disconnect themselves from the local environment. Indeed, their success in creating an international culture on campus is based on the quality of the participants, as well as the reduction of the pressure that the local environment exerts on the foreign students. With high-quality students who have the intellectual courage to defend their views of the world and respect their differences, one can indeed create an international culture.

This becomes even more feasible when the school is not identified with a particular country or political system.

Two visible and successful examples of this strategy are Harvard in the United States and IMD in Switzerland. Harvard attracts participants from all over the world and its faculty members have international experience. It has set up executive education "feeder programs" in different parts of the world (e.g. China, South Africa, and Latin America) to give foreign participants a flavor of the Harvard program and to encourage them to go to Boston for the full experience. Harvard has also created a few research outposts for the production of international case studies. The model is clearly successful, but may suffer from a bias toward a US view of the world. Many Harvard participants will admit that they have been groomed to be informal ambassadors for the US model of business and governance within their organizations.

IMD in Lausanne (Switzerland) sees itself as the forum where participants from all over the world can meet (thus creating a so-called "global meeting place"). Unlike Harvard, IMD is disconnected from the local socio-economic and political environment, and can claim to be at the crossroad of international ideas. Yet it still has a single strong campus to which it imports students, faculty, and ideas from around the world, excluding from its reach many companies and executives located in other parts of the world. The school has been very successful in this strategy, though more in the exchange of ideas than in the development of original research.

The exporters

A second group of schools will argue that it may be impossible always to bring all the targeted students together in one place, but these schools want to preserve the co-location of their key staff. These institutions also see their campus as the sole producer of their proprietary ideas, and have moved into exporting these ideas overseas by having traveling teaching staff. A very interesting example of this export strategy is the establishment of campuses in Barcelona and Singapore by the University of Chicago Graduate School of Business (Chicago GSB). The school is prepared to reach out to the students and teach in the local environment but strongly argues that the content is produced in and exported from its central location. The school's promotion argues that students in Barcelona and Singapore will get the best of Chicago, taught by Chicago faculty.

Many other schools from the UK and Australia have organized similar overseas programs in newly developing markets such as China or Eastern Europe. The strategy clearly has advantages: one can reach some of the best and the brightest students who do not have the means or willingness to relocate for their studies, while the school keeps its investment costs relatively low. The success of the strategy, however, is based on at least three critical conditions. First, the central location of the school must be recognized as a generator of knowledge; second, that knowledge has to be recognized to be relevant beyond the location of the school; and third, the faculty must be willing to travel. In the case of Chicago GSB with its outstanding faculty (including several Nobel Prize winners) the first condition is clearly fulfilled. Concerning the second and third conditions, the jury is out. Are the materials developed in Chicago indeed always relevant for doing business within the European Union or East Asia, and will the faculty be prepared in the long run to keep on traveling?

These questions may become even more difficult to answer for other schools that do not have the research reputation or strong brand image of Chicago GSB. Many of the second- and third-tier Australian and British schools that had relative success in Hong Kong, China, or Central and Eastern Europe, may have difficulties in defending their positions as these markets become more sophisticated and transparent, and as they have to rely more on local teachers.

Some of the top schools have developed a different angle on this export model. To cope with the difficulty of having to motivate faculty to travel abroad repeatedly, or to avoid the opportunity costs related to these constant absences from the campus, these schools have gone into some form of technology transfer. This is the case, for example, of the Wharton School and the newly created Indian School of Business (ISB), in which faculty of ISB benefit from the technological and pedagogical support offered by Wharton. This is different from a partnership, as discussed in the next subsection, in which there is more of a two-way exchange of both students and ideas. In the same vein, MIT has developed a technological approach to this export model. Rather than having the faculty travel, they teach through videoconferencing. While it does mean that generations of students are exposed to ideas flowing out of MIT, and may become loyal alumni, the benefits for faculty research are quite limited.

The partnering schools

A path to internationalization that has been chosen by many national champions and local players is the development of a portfolio of partnerships. Often the partnerships start as student exchange programs, offering students in undergraduate or graduate programs the possibility to spend some time (usually a semester) in the foreign institution. Since participation in these exchanges is usually limited to a few students, many schools are obliged to create a series of exchanges. In a few cases, schools have come together in a multilateral partnership to organize the exchanges among the different partners. The European Union has actually institutionalized undergraduate exchanges among universities within the Union.

Rarely do such partnerships go beyond student exchange to support faculty exchange or common research projects. Although this type of internationalization definitely benefits the students, the long-term learning for the institutions is not clear. Many of the exchanges are based on personal relationships, and the vigor of the partnership often disappears when the personalities change. Often the management of the partnerships becomes a complex challenge. Schools are not always of the same quality and this can lead to difficulties in comparing standards for graduation. There also is a risk that the foreign experience becomes a gimmick, an attractive personal experience, but not a source of deep learning.

More interesting are the partnerships in which universities design common programs. Alliances of this nature exist between London Business School and Columbia University, and among HEC (France), New York University, and the London School of Economics for executive MBA programs. The effort to design common programs and create interactions between the students during the whole length of the program offers the promise of longer-term partnerships in research and course development.

The Alliance between INSEAD and the Wharton School has created a deeper, multi-faceted relationship than either school had established in the past. While previous agreements with other institutions had often focused on limited educational exchanges, this alliance was designed to promote collaboration on educational programs across the board as well as on research. While past partnerships were often short-lived and based on personal relationships, the Alliance was conceived as a broader institutional partnership that involved many individual faculty members, students, administrators, and alumni. Further, while relationships in the past were focused on specific educational programs (such as an MBA exchange), the Alliance cut across many different programs, including MBA programs, doctoral programs, and executive education. This relationship – including education, research, and alumni activities – is one of the broadest and deepest of any business school. This deeper integration creates new opportunities for collaboration on projects such as this book.

The network builders

Finally some schools have gone one step beyond import, export, or partnership models. They follow what international companies or professional firms have done in the creation of overseas subsidiaries or offices. Given the fundamental characteristics of a business school, one can argue that these schools are in the process of building a network when they decide to station faculty abroad on a permanent basis. An interesting example of this is the French school ESCP-EAP. This school is the merger of two business schools, one of which (EAP) had from its beginning campuses in different countries. Currently, it has campuses in Paris, Madrid, Berlin, and Oxford. A second example is INSEAD, which made the decision in 1998 to establish a second full-fledged campus in Singapore in addition to its Europe campus[5] in Fontainebleau, France.

The difficulties of creating such a network cannot be underestimated. The investments can become relatively high, and the integration of a decentralized faculty is a major challenge. Few schools have done this before, so few role models are available, and most of the schools that experiment with a network of decentralized groups of faculty move very carefully into this uncharted terrain.

The payoffs can be equally high. Research can be localized and research results can be globally used in the educational programs of the school. It is easier to attract a diverse group of faculty, and the school can offer internal rotation and exchange programs. The new campus can also offer opportunities for students to understand better the region in which it is located and provide a stronger path for students from the region to come to other campuses. Such a strong presence in the country also provides greater access to opportunities for internships and work in the region in which the campus is located.

Strengths and weaknesses of internationalization strategies

Each of these models has distinctive advantages and disadvantages for education and research. They all require some degree of "entrepreneurialism" to get the process started and carried out. A "faculty champion" is often the key to successfully launching and sustaining the project. While many schools have focused on the impact of their global structures on education, they also need to give consideration to the implications for research. Some of the strengths and weaknesses of each model are discussed in the following paragraphs.

Import: The biggest challenge in managing a school using an import model is to keep faculty and students engaged in the world. It is difficult to escape the local culture. If students are not physically working and studying in other countries, how can the school provide that experience on campus? On the other hand, by placing all the international faculty and students in one location, there is more opportunity for direct interaction and one can preserve the critical mass that is so important for effective research.

Export: The challenge for the export model is managing the scarce resources of faculty time and attention as the school sends a core faculty around the world. This creates high opportunity costs, and the long-term sustainability depends on the school's image and renewal of content. There are also limited research opportunities abroad because faculty members are not based in the countries in which they are teaching. On the other hand, this model allows for strong integration of the faculty across the entire organization and permits the school to be more responsive to the needs of local students. It also creates strong bonds between students in the satellite programs and the main campus.

Partnership: The partnership model presents the challenges that exist in any alliance. There is increased management complexity and there

are potential conflicts because of differences in quality or philoso-
phies of the two institutions, and these issues can undermine the long-
term sustainability of these relationships. On the other hand, the partnership can offer the fastest and most inexpensive way to advance
internationalization across different regions. It offers real value to
students and facilitates research partnerships that can lead to rapid
results.

Network: The challenge of the network model is the high upfront
investment and commitment to building campuses in different parts of
the world. This model also presents challenges in managing a decentralized group of faculty and students. On the other hand, the network
facilitates the diffusion of proprietary knowledge and creates a stronger
presence and credibility with local partners and students. The commitment to a specific market can be an advantage for both education and
research, and the network is more likely to be open to accepting new
knowledge wherever it is developed, thus helping to avoid knowledge
imperialism.

Hybrid and evolving models

While these approaches are presented as four distinct models, in
practice many schools choose a combination of internationalization
strategies. For example, INSEAD has combined a network strategy of
campuses in France and Singapore with a partnership with the Wharton
School.

These models also evolve over time. INSEAD's presence in Asia
began with an "export model" in the early eighties with the establishment of its Euro-Asia Centre, which ran executive development programs throughout Asia. The programs were delivered either in rented
facilities or through a "virtual business school" within companies. This
center then became a springboard for the "network" model.

This evolution can also be driven by the costs and benefits of
different models. Duke University's Fuqua School of Business initially established a presence in Europe through a satellite campus in
Frankfurt, Germany. While the European campus gave the school a
strong foothold in Germany, it was an expensive strategy. As Dean
Douglas Breeden commented in *The Economist*, "we paid a lot of
blood for that."[6] When Fuqua sought to increase its presence in Asia,

it moved to a less resource-intensive alliance strategy, forging a partnership with Seoul National University in South Korea in 2003.

Despite its high cost and risks, the European campus helped Fuqua's Cross-Continent MBA program to create a distinctive approach to its executive MBA. Instead of simply exporting its faculty program abroad, the Cross-Continent MBA requires all students to complete parts of the program in both Frankfurt and the school's home campus in North Carolina, as well as using Internet-enabled distance learning.

Leading a global business school

These new models for promoting international education and research present a variety of challenges for business school leaders. Managing a global business school is not unlike managing a large multinational corporation. With multiple campuses, business school leaders need to be physically present in various locations. Schools that use a more centralized import or export model need to carefully manage the flow of knowledge, faculty, and students into and out of the main campus. Leaders need to define a common culture across the organization, yet respect and capitalize on international differences. Establishing a strong global brand is vital, although it is important also to have a strong local presence. Where a company CEO may spend time talking to investors, the business school dean will be meeting with diverse groups of alumni and donors who support the school around the world.

The leader of a global business school also needs to strike the delicate balance between autonomy and integration in the school's organization and culture. Is the school viewed as a mother campus with subsidiary campuses or is each part of the network equally central? Does the school replicate its centers of research excellence? How can school leaders best employ the talents of faculty for research and teaching? How can they use technology to connect different parts of the organization?

Among the key issues leaders of global schools need to address in promoting internationalization are: globalizing faculty and students; developing a global brand image; managing networks; creating globally oriented governance; facilitating international career management; and gaining support from alumni in cultures without a tradition of philanthropy. We consider each of these issues in the following discussions.

Attracting, developing, and retaining "global" faculty

Although there are many international students in doctoral programs, business schools face challenges in developing faculty with the right combination of global perspectives and regional expertise. It is easy to make mistakes in this context. For example, one cannot assume that a new faculty member who is a native of Korea and earned a PhD at a top US school will want to become the school's Korean expert. Faculty members often focus on a specific discipline and not on a region, and that needs to be respected.

There is little encouragement to develop research focused on global issues or specific regions. There are many distinguished academic journals that are discipline-based but few top ones that are devoted to international business (such as the *Journal of International Business Studies*). The process of academic research focuses on universal truths, so it runs counter to this tradition to find truths that apply only in Shanghai or the United States and not in other parts of the world.

Schools can counterbalance the disciplinary emphasis by creating new areas of focus. Research centers are one way to focus resources and attention on global issues. For example, INSEAD first established its Euro-Asia Centre and later on an Asian Business area (academic department) to draw faculty attention to this region, and thereby created the foundation for the school's campus in Singapore. At Wharton, the Weiss Center for International Financial Research has increased the attention of finance professors on global topics. While a strong disciplinary focus provides the depth and rigor to allow research to move forward, business schools have to find a way to build bridges between this disciplinary work and a regional and global focus.

Much of the faculty expertise developed in specific international markets is accidental. A professor might be working with colleagues in studying a specific business phenomenon in marketing or finance in Japan or France or Brazil, developing some familiarity with these countries in the process. In addition to this informal development of expertise, there can also be more formal processes for encouraging the global perspectives of faculty members. For example, early in Wharton's globalization process, the school established a weeklong international seminar for faculty that took professors with more limited global exposure for a week of presentations and interactions with business leaders in a specific region. INSEAD organized similar field trips to Tokyo and Seoul in the late eighties to prepare its faculty for the development of the school's activities in North Asia. As schools become more active in global teaching and research, this global exposure and interaction occurs much more naturally and informally. Yet schools still face a great challenge in understanding the global expertise of the faculty that is developed in this way – since it is not formal, it is often not tracked or codified.

Companies face a similar organizational challenge in deciding whether to organize along functional lines or by regions. Some have moved from a regional hierarchy to matrix structures where a functional organization is overlapped with a regional structure, so managers of certain parts of the business also have responsibilities as "lead country managers" in a specific nation and senior managers handle a line of business in a specific region.

In schools, however, it is not the organization of *business activity* that is the primary concern. Instead, it is the organization of *knowledge creation and dissemination* that is important. This knowledge has to be relevant to a specific discipline but also relate to global experience or be tailored to a particular region. It is no small challenge to encourage faculty members to marry global perspectives with their disciplinary expertise. The level of global focus may vary with the type of knowledge. To the extent that this knowledge deals with universal truths (business operations, human behavior, and financial analysis) a more centralized and disciplinary focus is appropriate. To the extent that this knowledge is affected by local markets, culture, regulations, and other idiosyncratic factors, specific regional or local insights are essential.

Organizations need to be aware of these lines of demarcation about types of knowledge and recognize when they are crossed. For example, researchers studying e-business from an abstract perspective might focus on issues such as technology adoption, online marketing, or new business models. From a global perspective, however, the impact of different views of privacy and regulation becomes vitally important. A global perspective is essential.

In developing the global perspectives of faculty and carrying out international research and education, business schools need to recognize the significant costs involved. Extensive faculty travel or relocation can lead to potential decreases in productivity. In addition to the resources needed for the travel and relocation itself, there may be a need to increase faculty to make up for the added time and attention required. Schools need to recognize these costs and give attention to creating organizational structures and support systems to make the transitions of this more nomadic life as smooth and efficient as possible.

Developing a critical mass of diverse students in each location

After developing a more global faculty, attracting the right mix of global students is the next critical challenge in building and sustaining global programs. Early on, when most programs were held on home campuses, defining what was meant by "international" students was relatively easy. The challenge at that point was usually to convince alumni with a domestic bias that there was value in inviting students from outside the home market into the school's classrooms, even if it meant giving up seats for domestic students. Ultimately, even the most adamant academic protectionists recognized the value of "minority" perspectives from different parts of the world, and today schools try to accept the best students regardless of their origins, while maintaining the right mix of diversity so there is no dominant group and all students benefit from this interaction.

When INSEAD opened its Singapore campus, there was concern that the Asia campus would be only for Asians. It turned out, however, that the Asian students wanted the exposure of the Europe campus while European and US students were very interested in having firsthand exposure to Asian thinking and markets. When Wharton and INSEAD began the Alliance, which allowed MBA students to move between schools, there was also a strong interest by students in experiencing the other campuses. The program quickly reached its capacity as students sought to move in both directions.

The success in creating diversity builds upon itself. Once there is a diverse mix at each location, it becomes very easy for individual students to choose the location where they can gain the most individual benefit. They no longer have to worry about feeling isolated in a foreign culture, because the business school has now become a region in which there are no "foreign" or "domestic" cultures.

For graduating students, global career opportunities are also a concern. If students can come to campus from anywhere in the world, they will also expect to be able to leave for work assignments in any part of the world. As pointed out earlier, up to 50 percent of INSEAD students take on a job outside their home country after graduation, and close to 70 percent embark on a career that will at one time in their life compel them to live abroad. Managers with global perspectives will expect to have career opportunities to match their talents, and this is a significant challenge for schools that tended to focus on domestic recruiting. Global alumni networks can be a help in this process, but global careers still run counter to the boundaries of the nation state.

Developing a global brand image

The brand is one of the most important assets of a business school. Managing and preserving the value and meaning of the brand is one of the great challenges of internationalizing a business school. As noted, most schools are so intimately associated with a particular location and campus that expanding their borders throws into question the entire meaning of the brand. Schools with brands that are not associated with a specific location seem to have an easier time of creating partnership and network models. INSEAD's decision to move away from its original Euro-centric acronym (based on the French translation of "European Institute for Business Administration") to the more open INSEAD brand made it easier to pursue its global strategy. Wharton also had a geographically independent name from the beginning. In contrast, the strong geographic link of the University of Chicago may have made it more difficult to move to a networked model and may have contributed to its decision to create an export model.

In essence, the branding challenges faced by globalizing business school are similar to those that face corporations. Companies ask these questions every time they create line extensions or use their brand in partnership with another. Some brands are strongly associated with a specific region. Consider the anti-American protests targeting US brands such as McDonald's or Disney. Although these companies have global businesses, their brands are clearly perceived as American. This association of the brand with a specific region can be a great strength, but also creates limits for these companies as for business schools. A key component of the positioning of the organization is globalization itself, and top business schools have actively built their global reputations even as they have enhanced their global activities and capabilities.

In addition to protecting the meaning of the brand, creating global visibility for the brand is also important. To be a global business school, one must have a global brand that is known in markets around the world. There is no other way to attract a diverse student body and top international faculty, and to create the opportunities for campuses and partnerships outside the home market. Among many strategies to raise their global visibility, Wharton and INSEAD have created online research newsletters (Knowledge@Wharton and INSEAD Knowledge) and magazines (*INSEAD Quarterly*) that help carry the schools' knowledge and brands out to a broad global audience.

The broader the global reach of the school – particularly as independent campuses are established – the greater the danger that the brand image may become diluted or confused. Does INSEAD in Fontainebleau mean the same thing as INSEAD in Singapore? How does the school ensure a common brand image while respecting the contributions and distinctive character of each local campus? In establishing its campus in Asia, one of INSEAD's most important challenges has been to ensure that the quality of work on the Singapore campus is at the same level as, if not better than, that of the Europe campus. Therefore it was decided to allocate some of the best faculty to the Asia campus and to have a "blind" MBA admissions process (admitting students to INSEAD independently of their choice of campus, and revealing only after the admissions had been confirmed the location the participant had chosen).

Managing networks effectively

The more schools move to networked models for research and education, the more skills in the management of the network itself become important. These challenges are well known to students of networks of international R&D laboratories in companies.[7] As usual, there is not one single best solution for this management challenge. What we know about industrial companies may, however, have some relevance for the networked business school campuses. We need to pay attention to four areas:

- Networks will work if the nodes in the network have credibility with each other, so attention should be given to activities that build credibility early on.

- Networks have value if the nodes in the network are sufficiently different from each other so that they can mutually enrich each other.
- Networks survive if management pays enormous attention to tools and methods for both formal and informal communication.
- Networks are complex and not limited to the internal relations between multiple campuses; outside partners that have contacts with the different campuses form an additional outside network that requires careful management.

While a central part of managing networks effectively is to exploit the innovations made in one node across the entire network, some innovations are specific to a particular location and are difficult to replicate. For example, INSEAD's Asia campus in Singapore is in an urban environment, and its proximity to the Singapore financial center and industrial parks has allowed it to attract managers to short breakfast conferences and workshops. The Europe campus is located in a rural area outside Paris, however, so these short meetings are not part of the heritage there because of the time needed to reach the campus.

At the same time, the school as a whole had to innovate because of the introduction of this new campus, with a significant increase in video conferencing for management meetings, research presentations, job interviewing, and teaching. Overnight, INSEAD had to become a specialist in virtual teamwork. The challenge is to diffuse innovations across campuses and among a wider group than the early users and trendsetters. In the end, innovation will be diffused, but the challenge is how to do this as fast as possible, to leverage these new innovations immediately.

Because these networks are designed to promote knowledge creation and dissemination, they must strike a delicate balance between a formal structure and an openness that permits individual initiative. The INSEAD–Wharton Alliance has a formal leadership structure to facilitate joint activities in education and research, including a designated champion in each department to encourage research collaboration. The Alliance also provides incentives for faculty research projects through grants for research by pairs or teams of faculty from the two institutions. This organizational structure and focus create a context for joint research and other collaboration. The approach is not to mandate such collaboration but rather to encourage it. The structures and incentives create a "market" environment in which the creation of new knowledge and value emerges. Further, the Alliance has become a central part of the culture of two institutions and has been supported through frequent meetings between the deans and other leaders of the two institutions, as well as other faculty, students, and alumni.

This type of broad collaboration with deep connections also takes time to develop. The Alliance from the outset was considered a broad experiment and the focus on both sides has been on learning from the experience. It was established with a three-year agreement, which proved to be too short a time in which fully to implement and test the relationship. Because it is a broad and complex relationship, the benefits can be much deeper, but this work is clearly taking at least five years to gain a firm footing.

Creating governance boards with global vision

Schools need board members who not only have global experience but also show global vision. If the board is US-centric or Euro-centric, leaders of the school will spend all their time explaining the requirements of globalization to the board. By appointing globally oriented members to the board, the schools can increase the flow of ideas and support for international initiatives.

One way to "seed" a traditionally domestically focused board is through the creation of separate regional boards. Wharton did this in creating three regional boards in East Asia, Europe, and Latin America. These boards brought high-level insights from these regions to the school and also formed a pool of potential members of the school's Board of Overseers. INSEAD has a single board that is very international (see Table 5.1) which is supplemented by National Councils in more than twenty countries around the world that keep the school close to local markets worldwide and help it develop its international position and strategy.

In developing their boards and building financial support, global schools also have to address the challenges of a more diverse group of stakeholders and "investors." As corporations have had to adapt to different financial markets and governance structures around the world (as discussed in Chapters 2 and 3), globalization presents similar funding challenges to private business schools. Schools have always relied heavily on alumni and other donors for support. As they become increasingly global, schools face the challenge of working with alumni in cultures that do not have a strong tradition of support for private education. To the extent that a school has been able to cultivate global perspectives in its graduates, these differences in cultural traditions may be bridged, but culture still represents a significant obstacle in developing the base of charitable support upon which many top schools depend. Schools either need to engage in an aggressive process of education of alumni to build a culture of philanthropy that creates the infrastructure for contributions, or reconsider their fundamental business models given the new realities.

Future challenges and requirements for success

The content and structure of global business education have changed dramatically in recent decades, and will continue to change. Among the forces shaping the future internationalization of business schools are competitive shifts, technological changes, and the emergence of new models for education.

Increasing competition

Graduate management education used to be offered by only a handful of top schools, primarily in the United States. Over the last two decades, there has been an explosion of MBA programs, full- and part-time, in the United States, Europe, Asia, and Latin America. Over the last five years, several dozen schools have launched MBA programs in China, for example. The costs of starting these programs were assumed to be minimal, since the buildings were there (fixed costs) and the faculty could be hired based on demand (variable costs). Students were willing to pay a relatively high tuition fee since there was a demand for good degrees. The governments of Australia, South Africa, Korea, Singapore, and Malaysia are actively working to attract new educational institutions and foreign students to their countries. Many of them see education as a growth sector. (For example, Australia's education sector accounts for 5 percent of its GDP.) They have recognized that it is a very attractive business to bring in foreign students, raising the image of their countries and contributing directly to their economies.

There is also new competition from outside the traditional industry, with the rise of private consultants and commercial schools, the growth of corporate educational programs, and participation of governments in business education.

The problem is that the competitive dynamics that made business education so attractive will also lead predictably to an oversupply, particularly in the lower and middle segment of the market. As oversupply leads to higher marketing and operational costs, we will see a shakeout in the industry in the long run, but the short run could be turbulent. Given that most of these schools belong to universities, which are measured by standards other than their financial contributions, they may be expected to be sustained longer than they would be otherwise. Given the national interest of governments in sustaining these schools to promote economic progress, the evolution of global business schools will be shaped by a complex mix of competitive, academic, and governmental interactions, making the outcome highly uncertain. Will we see an evolution of business schools that follows a similar trajectory to that of the airline industry with the creation of strong alliances? Or will the industry evolution look more like the consulting and auditing industry with its mega mergers and/or acquisitions?

New technologies

New technologies offer interesting possibilities for global education. Distance-learning technologies were initially seen as offering the potential to overcome the limits of geographical location – bringing the best teachers and experts in the world to students anywhere in the world. The technologies were viewed as a very efficient platform for international education without the significant financial and personal costs of moving students or faculty to different parts of the globe. Yet the progress of technology-based education has been less dramatic than its early proponents had expected. As businesses have also found, the technology is most useful in combination with opportunities for face-to-face interactions. This is even truer when the focal point of activity is education.

Education has always had elements of instructor-led learning and resource-based learning. Information and communication technologies dramatically increase the effectiveness of resource-based learning. This helps us to reach out more effectively to students that are geographically dispersed. Yet resource-based learning has never been a replacement for classroom learning. We all know that some topics, in particular the more complex and experiential ones, lend themselves better to instructor-led learning. Technology also is much better in conveying explicit knowledge than tacit knowledge. As any manager who has worked abroad knows, even a short experience of immersion in a country offers insights that cannot be gained from a book or long-distance encounters.

Learning technologies can be expected to gain wider acceptance and application as they continue to advance from their crude early models, as the automobile, computer, and other innovations have done. These advances will reshape the tools that schools have and allow the design of new approaches to global education and research. Technology can also make business research faster and more effective, with large databases and sophisticated tools that can significantly increase productivity and help to tailor empirical results to specific countries or regions. More effective technology will offer greater opportunities to supplement classroom education or in-person meetings and more tightly link the various campuses and activities of a school around the globe. Yet the need to combine resource-based and instructor-led education will likely mean that top business school programs will always blend technology and classroom interaction. That has been, at least, the recent experience of both INSEAD and Wharton.

Shifting educational needs and the emergence of global networks

The internationalization of business education is occurring in the context of other changes in business education. With a shorter half-life of knowledge, there is increasing demand for lifelong learning. Managers no longer feel they can be prepared for the challenges of today on the basis of a fixed degree that they earned two decades ago. Business school programs are changing rapidly, and managers recognize the need to change the way they learn.

The traditional model for business schools is a manufacturing model, in which high-quality inputs (talented students) are brought in one side and outputs (knowledgeable graduates) are delivered on the other. The network model, in contrast, is organized around a customer-centric service model, where members of the network participate in lifelong learning. It is less like a factory and more like a service station, where managers regularly top up their tanks with education anywhere in the world. The campus program becomes the first step to a set of ongoing interactions in diverse locations and online. Right now, these "top-ups" occur on an *ad hoc* basis through executive education programs for alumni around the world, alumni clubs in particular disciplines or regions, and publications. This ongoing development needs to become more formalized and sophisticated to meet the changing needs of managers.

The globalization of business also is contributing to this model of lifelong education. Today's corporate executives and entrepreneurs are more mobile than ever. As people move between companies as well as countries, their networks of family and friends can become very thinly stretched. Many people lack a sense of belonging, so a business school's worldwide network has a key role to play. Regional alumni clubs help support the social and career networking needs of the alumni. Broader alumni clubs focusing on topics such as private equity can address the specific concerns for ongoing professional development.

Conclusions

Business schools have no choice but to be international in a world in which business is global. While few would argue with this statement, there is considerable leeway in how different schools define and act upon this idea. There are diverse definitions of what it means to develop "global" programs, students, and faculty. There are also diverse models for designing and organizing a global business school and strategies for promoting the global insights and initiatives of faculty and students. While the demand for global knowledge is clear, this is a time of intense experimentation in discovering what this knowledge is and deciding how to create and disseminate it.

What are the implications for corporate managers? First, companies face similar challenges in developing the global perspectives of employees and sharing knowledge across the organization. Academic institutions, as knowledge-intensive organizations, have wrestled with the issue of managing a relatively independent group of knowledge workers with affiliations to their own institutions and their disciplines across institutions. The formal ties of these "knowledge entrepreneurs" are eroding. Universities may return to their medieval roots, in which "traveling mobile producers met with equally mobile knowledge customers."[8] In this view, the stars of this knowledge creation process will create their own brands and knowledge enterprises with "protégés" working under them. The challenge for business schools – and other organizations – is to manage knowledge workers with weak affiliations to the organization in a world in which no career – not even a tenured academic career – is guaranteed to be for life. To do this across global networks is the most serious challenge.

The emergence of these knowledge leaders, however, can also mean that any student or organization could have access to the best knowledge in the world (at the right price, of course) regardless of location or affiliation. While it may wreak havoc on individual institutions, particularly those unwilling to change, it also could represent a much more creative approach to the global creation and management of knowledge and knowledge workers – where knowledge flows in a marketplace with few artificial borders – to where it is needed most. The globalization of business education and research presents significant challenges to business schools for organization and leadership, but it also presents new opportunities for innovation and the broader creation, dissemination, and application of business knowledge.

Notes

1 "Wharton Careers: MBA Career Report 2003," The Wharton School, University of Pennsylvania.
2 *Business Week*, October 11, 2002.
3 Y. Doz, J. Santos, and P. Williamson, *From Global to Metanational* (Boston: Harvard Business School Press, 2001).
4 C. Bartlett and S. Ghoshal, "What is a Global Manager?" *Harvard Business Review*, September–October 1992, pp. 124–132.
5 The campuses are referred to as the "Europe campus" and the "Asia campus," rather than "European" and "Asian," to emphasize that they are not limited to a regional focus. Instead, while they are located in a specific region, they have a global focus.
6 "Old Friends, New Alliances," *Economist*, February 10, 2003.
7 A. De Meyer, "Tech Talk: How Managers are Stimulating Global R&D Communication," *Sloan Management Review*, Spring 1991, pp. 49–58.
8 H. Bouchikhi and J. R. Kimberly, "It's Difficult To Innovate: The Death of the Tenured Professor and the Birth of the Knowledge Entrepreneur," *Human Relations*, 54 (2001), p. 82.

6 *Globalization through acquisitions and alliances: an evolutionary perspective*

HARBIR SINGH
Wharton School

MAURIZIO ZOLLO
INSEAD

Although acquisitions and alliances are used increasingly to drive the growth in multinational activities, the success rates of both acquisitions and alliances continue to be considered low, both at home and abroad. How do companies make the choice between acquisitions and alliances as a mode of entry? How do they then approach the post-entry managerial challenges? And, most important, how do companies effectively learn to tackle these problems in a systematic way? The authors examine a variety of factors that might influence the entry choice, including feasibility, flexibility, information asymmetry, digestibility, time horizon, focus on core vs. periphery, and post-agreement hazards. They also explore distinctive post-entry competencies that affect the success of both alliances and acquisitions: an integration capability for the former dimension and relational capability for the latter. The authors stress the strategic value of deliberate investments in assessing and improving one's own capability levels in the management of these entry tools. For example, spending time on understanding one's own organization's less tangible qualities, such as its cognitive and cultural traits, needs to become part of the standard due diligence process. To achieve positive outcomes, the authors say, managers should invest in knowledge management mechanisms that can first identify, and then articulate and codify the processes idiosyncratic to their firms that produce positive results. These processes, along with skilled managers, constitute the competencies needed to achieve success more consistently in these external modes of globalization.

A
s geographic markets become more interconnected and operations become more far-flung, corporations have increasingly turned to global acquisitions and alliances to expand their businesses. Different companies have followed different paths of evolution that have affected their choices about acquisitions and alliances. Major corporations such as Unilever, Philips and Coca-Cola, which evolved to reach today's status as global organizations through patient development of increasingly important operations in locations across national boundaries, have used acquisitions and alliances more recently to change their product lines or geographic operations incrementally in response to new opportunities in local markets. Other firms, such as Cisco Systems, Electrolux and GE Capital, with a historically national or regional focus, have recently resorted to acquisitions and alliances as vehicles for more decisive and rapid globalization and growth.

In this chapter, we provide an evolutionary perspective on the international growth of the firm and how its path of evolution affects choices between different modes of growth. We also discuss opportunities and barriers to learning, and how firms can develop competencies to manage these modes of growth. We focus on three of the most pressing, yet still poorly understood, issues in the internationalization process. First, how do firms choose between the two external modes of growth: acquisitions and alliances? Second, how do they design and manage the post-entry adjustment period? And third, how do they learn how to manage the entry process through acquisitions and alliances?

An evolutionary perspective

This evolutionary perspective of global expansion builds on the work of Richard Nelson and Sidney Winter[1] as well as some recent refinements of the theory.[2] The globalization phenomenon, from the point of view of the firm, is an evolutionary process of activity and identity expansion,[3] taking on different sets of ambitions, forms, and velocities depending on the characteristics of the focal company and of the environment. Firms intensify their focus on international business activity from simple trading relationships with foreign partners, to the establishment of local sales and servicing units, to the location of operating activities of increasing strategic relevance, such as manufacturing and R&D.

Firms that began the process of geographic expansion several decades ago were able to internationalize at a moderate pace, starting well before the Second World War and evolving today to a state where the most subtle organizational aspects, such as values, shared beliefs, and cognitive mindsets are increasingly aligned across geographic locations.

On the other hand, some firms had a national or regional scope because of their prior historical decisions. For example, firms that started in smaller domestic markets, such as the Netherlands and Switzerland, sought scale economies by expanding geographically as soon as they could do so in their evolutionary path. In larger economies, instead, firms gained scale in servicing the large domestic market and looked for expansion abroad, having already reached the status of a large, multidivisional corporation. Over the last few decades, however, the opening of huge developing markets such as the former Soviet bloc, China, and India to foreign direct investments, coupled with rapid advances in telecommunication and information technologies, as well as with the growth in technological and managerial competence in many developing countries, changed the nature of the competitive game. Being a truly global organization became a strategic requirement to compete on multiple fronts: cost efficiencies, sales growth and, more recently, new product development. Most important, the initial logic of redeploying home-grown competitive advantages in foreign markets[4] has first been supplemented and is now gradually being replaced by logics based on different flows of knowledge: among foreign subsidiaries[5] and from the competence-rich periphery to the resource-rich center.[6]

In many industries, firms have rushed to build operating presence abroad pushed by a mixture of inward-looking learning[7] and outward-looking imitation processes.[8] The need for speed has forced them to prefer quicker means of market entry and expansion than the more incremental process of internal development. First, alliances with local competitors, especially if the host government would not look favorably on more aggressive moves, and more often outright acquisitions, have become standard tools for international expansions.

In a nutshell, evolutionary models study the way in which organizations change over time in their stable traits, such as operating routines, through variation, selection, and retention processes. In this perspective, the key drivers of behavior, decision-making, and performance become the presence and slow adaptation of routines, the semi-automatic application of heuristics to decision points, and the path-dependent development of competencies and incompetencies in operating processes, rather than the strategizing, planning, and radical change processes that have generated intuitive appeal for both practitioners as well as academics.

We intend to show that the application of an evolutionary perspective can help deepen our understanding of the choice of modes of growth by the multinational firm and of the most appropriate path to the implementation of a market entry strategy. Our goal in this chapter is to build on the recent theoretical and empirical contributions to show how the two alternative modes of growth (acquisition and alliance) compare in terms of competence requirements and of the relative efficacy of related learning processes.

Drivers of the acquisition vs. alliance choice

Why do firms choose alliances or acquisitions as modes of international growth? Current literature on the topic and our own clinical work offer a number of explanations. The adoption of an evolutionary perspective can provide additional insights on this question. We can think of the factors as being partly transactional, having to do with the deal being presented, and partly evolutionary, having to do with the path chosen by the firm and the set of choices presented as a result.

Research in this area is characterized by several fairly well-established explanations for choosing alliance or acquisition as the mode of entry:

(1) *Feasibility:* The first, and perhaps the simplest one of all, is related to the feasibility of an acquisition *vis-à-vis* an alliance as an entry mode. From a financial standpoint, this is fairly obvious: partnerships are the way to go if cash-flow constraints limit the scope for an acquisition. Perhaps slightly less obvious is the political version of the feasibility problem.[9] Foreign firms might encounter significant political barriers in their attempts to enter a certain country through the acquisition of a local competitor. Alliances are a natural way to reduce the risk of being held up by local government authorities[10] and were originally conceived during the 1960s and 1970s primarily for this purpose.

(2) *Flexibility:* A second, more recent, explanation for the choice is related to flexibility. Partnerships are characterized by significantly

lower resource commitments at the time of the agreement and these agreements often offer the possibility to scale up the commitment once the uncertainty is reduced.[11] This option-like feature suggests that alliances should be selected over acquisitions when uncertainty in the environment (e.g. technological evolution, demand shifts, regulatory changes, etc.) is particularly high and the advantages of flexibility are superior to those of full control of the venture.

Factors in dispute

In addition to these two, widely accepted considerations, two other drivers of the choice between acquisitions and alliances have been the focus of long-standing debate.

(3) *Information asymmetry:* Information asymmetries between the two firms could be a factor in the choice of entry mode.[12] In this view, acquisitions would be preferred when the resources and competencies of the counterpart are closely related to those of the focal firm. Otherwise, the high level of information asymmetry between the two firms and the presence of moral hazard suggest the use of alliances to mitigate the risk of dealing with opportunistic behavior from the counterpart, and with resources which are significantly less valuable than originally presented.

(4) *Focus (Digestibility):* Another potential driver of the entry choice is the extent of interaction and coordination between the two organizations needed to realize the strategic potential of the venture. Alliances, because they can be more selectively tailored, offer the advantage of focusing interactions between the two organizations on the specific sets of activities where the advantages from cooperation are maximized.[13] It follows that alliances are to be preferred when the strategic interdependence necessary to generate the expected rents is narrowly defined (and definable) around a small subset of the entire activities of the counterpart. On the other hand, acquisition might be a more likely choice if there is a large spectrum of cooperation, which would justify the costs and the risks inherent in the "digestion" of the entire organization through an acquisition.

These two views of the decision – information asymmetry and digestibility – have vigorously confronted each other in the literature,

which essentially succeeds in showing that both arguments are
supported to some degree by empirical evidence and that they are best
viewed as complementary, rather than substitute, explanations of the
choice between acquisitions and alliances.[14]

Additional criteria

While these four factors have been the primary focus of the theoretical
and empirical literature,[15] there are a few additional criteria for the
choice between acquisitions and alliances that show clear managerial
relevance.

(5) *Time horizon:* Alliances are inherently unstable governance solutions, as they are subject to the evolution of both partners' strategic
choices in response to changes in their own competitive environments.
If, therefore, the entry decision is purely exploratory or tentative in
nature, then alliances are the most sensible way to go. With a longer
time horizon, an acquisition may be attractive.

(6) *Core vs. periphery:* Another decision rule has been suggested to
us during a series of interviews we had with leading technology companies such as Hewlett Packard and Cisco. It argues for alliances as
superior governance choices if the counterpart's resources and capabilities are relatively close to the core competencies of the focal firm,
and for acquisitions if they are at the periphery. Thus, contrary to the
information asymmetry criterion, acquisitions are particularly good
tools for learning purposes (such as new product development in an
emerging market) in that they afford a complete internalization of the
knowledge resident in the counterpart organization. Alliances are better suited for explorations "closer" to known territory, where the risk
of being held up by the partner is relatively low. Cisco Systems pioneered this notion, leveraging, however, on a highly developed integration capability that allowed it to retain personnel and leverage the
sales and distribution network to "explode" the newly acquired and
developed products in its fast-growing markets (at the time). Figure
6.1 characterizes this relatively counterintuitive logic.[16]

One way to reconcile this apparent incongruence between the information asymmetry at the time of evaluation (suggesting an alliance

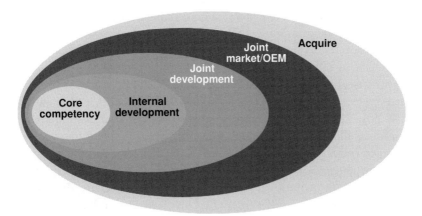

Figure 6.1. Cisco's corporate development choice. (Courtesy of Peter Ruh, VP Integration at Cisco.)

solution) and the post-transaction hazards of being exploited by the partnering firm (suggesting an acquisition solution) is to observe that the two alternative governance choices might be tied by complementary features in both their negotiation process and post-transaction dynamics. Advantages of one solution at the evaluation stage can turn into disadvantages after the negotiations are over and management issues take center stage.

The problem is particularly relevant with cross-border agreements, where the asymmetry in the knowledge endowment of the two counterparts is high by definition. Assessing both the actual worth of a counterpart's competencies as well as the likelihood of post-agreement tensions is particularly difficult in international market entry situations.

(7) *Post-agreement hazards:* This brings us to the last factor playing a potentially important role in the choice of the mode of market entry: the type and magnitude of post-agreement hazards. It is clear that the two modes of entry offer significant challenges to the realization of initial objectives, challenges that hide primarily in the interactions between the two organizations following the completion of the negotiation. One intuitive criterion for the choice of entry mode, therefore, is the evaluation of the risk of potential damage derived from failure in post-acquisition integration activities[17] *vis-à-vis* the potential difficulties related to spiraling cycles of worsening results, increasing

frustration and worsening trust among alliance partners.[18] All else being equal, the entry mode that would produce less expected frictions will be selected by the discriminant decision-maker.

In practice, however, this assessment of the risk of post-agreement hazards is very difficult. What factors influence the relative (or differential) risk posed by choosing a market entry strategy via acquisition rather than via alliance? While some argue that the relative differences in characteristics of the two firms (such as the degree of cultural distance or of product/market relatedness) are the most important drivers of these risks, an evolutionary perspective would emphasize the stand-alone characteristics of the companies involved: their competencies or lack thereof, their past decisions and the weight they carry on current decisions, their heuristics, shared beliefs, values, and so on. For example, consider how two factors – cognitive traits and cultural traits – might affect the choice of mode of growth:

Cognitive traits: In a way, this might represent the most (deceptively) simple decision criterion of all: choose the entry mode that corresponds to the most developed set of capabilities within the focal firm. An objective assessment of one's own capabilities in managing complex processes such as acquisitions and alliances, however, is extremely hard. It requires an uncommon willingness and capacity to self-assess the performance of prior experiences and to discriminate on the underlying causes. Was it our own good/bad decisions, or just unforeseeable events (good/bad luck)? Or were the decisions sensible but the way they were carried out suboptimal, or vice versa? Another related reason why this is more complicated than one typically expects is because, in the absence of solid performance metrics and monitoring systems, prior decisions end up being routinized "de facto". Lacking a clear signal against it, the simplest way to tackle a complex problem such as the selection between an acquisition or an alliance is to "do what we did last time." Unfortunately, only a minority of prior experiences can be clearly classified as "sure success" or "sure failure." In cases where there is no clear sense of the actual outcomes, of the performance implications of past decisions, or of the contingencies under which the various decisions have good or bad implications, the "weight of the past" will significantly influence the choice.

Cultural traits: An even more inward-looking evaluation criterion suggests that the cultural traits and managerial style of the focal company should be seriously considered in the choice of entry mode. More cooperative/consensus-based norms and leadership styles, for example, are inherently conducive to more effective alliances. On the other hand, more directive leadership styles might offer acquisition-based entries a better chance of success, relative to alliance alternatives. Other traits that can be more aligned with the post-formation requirements of alliances are a diffused tolerance for diversity and for risk-taking (including error-making). The more collectively humble the attitude of managers and employees in a company, the more one would expect alliances to fare relatively better than acquisitions. Again, though, making this call is all but easy for very similar reasons to those described above. If anything, assessing one's organization's cultural traits can be fraught with unavoidable biases to a greater extent than in the case of cognitive traits (skill self-assessments).

Building capabilities

The precision with which companies can assess their own cognitive and cultural traits is therefore a key antecedent to the quality of the selection of the mode of entry and, eventually, of its performance outcomes. However, precise self-assessments can be characterized as both a "blessing" and a "curse." Whereas the blessing part is clear, the "curse" might be worth elaborating. Essentially, being capable of selecting the most appropriate mode of corporate growth by taking the alternative that leverages on existing capabilities and cultural biases implies the existence of a "self-fulfilling prophecy." Like a tennis player with a strong forehand, a company that is strong in acquisitions continues to strengthen this capability with each new deal, but does not build strength in the "backhand" of other approaches such as alliances. In the long run, this self-reinforcing system can reduce the company's strategic flexibility and create biases.

There could, in fact, be an argument for continuing to experiment with unfamiliar entry modes to build future capabilities and slowly guide the evolution of cultural traits compatible with different practices.[19] Managers making this decision should recognize that the long-term consequences of these entry moves go beyond the immediate effects of redeploying existing resources or accessing new ones. These entries have a remarkable potential to establish and strengthen routinized behavior which, in the absence of clear performance feedback, can become an unconsciously accepted "way to do things."

An application to the automotive industry

To illustrate, the worldwide automobile industry is an interesting setting in which both acquisitions and alliances have been used both to globalize corporations and to consolidate capacity in a rapidly changing industry. Pressures to bring products ever faster to the market, coupled with the need for efficiency and increased quality, have resulted in large acquisitions and several inter-firm alliances to globalize players in the industry. The merger of Daimler Benz and Chrysler to form Daimler-Chrysler is an example of a major acquisition to create a global organization that would blend strength in Europe with strong positions in some key product lines in the United States. By contrast, Toyota steadfastly maintained that it would avoid large acquisitions, choosing *de novo* entry or alliances to pursue global opportunities, of which the alliance with GM in the NUMMI venture is perhaps the best-known success story.

Applying our evolutionary approach might reveal some of the explanations for such widely different performance outcomes from the two agreements. On the one hand, Daimler-Chrysler made several key errors in this purported merger of equals, starting with the public relations disaster consequent to the decision to announce the agreement as a merger of equals when it was actually an acquisition of Chrysler by Daimler. Its corporate culture, described at the time as self-absorbed and arrogant because of the enormous reputation and popularity of its key brands and a history of profitable growth, was clearly more in line with an outright acquisition, rather than a consensus-driven merger of equal partners. Second, Daimler Benz misjudged its own ability to manage an integration process on such a large scale. In particular, it failed to generate and leverage on early savings in overlapping functions or any other "quick win" that might have helped build a positive momentum. Even in the longer term, some of the most obvious sources of value, such as purchasing and IT systems, have not delivered on the potential, partly because of Daimler's cognitive biases against learning from external sources, partly because of its cultural traits, probably stiffened even more by the negative outcomes and the frustrating reactions by the markets and business counterparts (especially in the United States).

According to the concepts driving the choice of mode, we can see that there were significant concerns about flexibility, digestibility, cognitive traits, and cultural traits. It was likely that there would be severe integration and cultural problems, in addition to clashes in culture and possible delays in obtaining the needed synergies from such a transaction. The use of targeted alliances or of smaller-scale acquisitions (for example, of selected Chrysler assets) to achieve focused goals may well have been a better course of action, even based on information available prior to the transaction. The performance problems after merger have reinforced these concerns about the choice of acquisition as a definitive and radical step towards global presence in multiple product lines and price segments.

Toyota, on the other hand, chose a strategy that fitted well with the skills it had developed in its distinguished history. Toyota had pioneered the lean manufacturing process that demanded a high level of integration of operations with suppliers along the value chain, sharing technological knowledge, and seeking extensive efficiencies within firms not owned by Toyota, but having long-term trading relationships. This strategy nurtured capabilities that allowed Toyota to set up similar supply chains in countries it entered, adding capacity in ancillary industries and simultaneously upgrading those industries in its host countries. To counter resentment towards Japanese auto success in the United States in the 1980s, and to learn how to transfer their lean production process to the United States, Toyota entered into a joint venture to produce cars in the United States in California. The vehicle for the entry into US manufacturing was the New United Motor Manufacturing, Inc. (NUMMI) organization, jointly owned by GM and Toyota, in Fremont, California. Toyota was able to use the learning generated at NUMMI to set up its 100 percent owned production facilities in Kentucky a few years later, with similar success. On the other hand, GM was less successful in transferring the cutting-edge practices tested at NUMMI to its other existing plants, in spite of heavy investments to that end. The criteria examined above (feasibility, flexibility, digestibility, time horizon, cognitive and cultural traits in particular) all pointed to the use of targeted alliances to achieve globalization objectives.

Despite the seemingly incremental nature of the NUMMI transaction, it yielded more predictable and positive results than the more dramatic, newsworthy moves of Daimler-Chrysler into a full-line global auto company. Indeed, Toyota was able to leverage the experience relatively adroitly into new ventures. In this case, Toyota's capabilities and cultural biases were successfully matched with the entry mode, whereas the shock treatment experienced by Daimler-Chrysler seems to be at least partially explained by the poor assessment on the part of the acquirer of its own competencies and limitations, as well as its own cultural biases.

To summarize, taking an evolutionary perspective on the choice of entry mode forces the decision-maker to focus on the assessment of the specific post-agreement risks inherent in the two options, which in turn requires a highly developed consciousness of the company's cognitive traits (competencies and limitations) and cultural traits. We can then examine these two factors more in detail: the management of post-entry dynamics and the deliberate efforts to improve the firm's pre-dispositions towards these types of entry processes.

Managing post-entry dynamics

At first glance, the post-agreement phase in the case of a market entry through an acquisition looks very different from that in the case of an entry through an alliance. In the former, the emphasis is on the management of the transition phase through which the newly acquired subsidiary will merge, at least to a certain extent, into the structural, operational, and cultural identity of the acquiring organization. The problem is typically seen as a transitional one; that is, it will cease to exist once the integration objectives have been reached, and will then turn into a day-to-day management issue, as in all the other businesses in the acquiring entity.

On the other hand, alliances are typically approached from the opposite direction. Precisely because the nature of the agreement is typically limited to the short or medium term, the management challenge is seen as spanning the entire time horizon until the termination of the agreement. There is normally a set-up period to construct the necessary structures and operational routines, but no one would consider the problem "solved" once that period is over and the actual collaboration between the two organizations begins. On the contrary, that is when the challenge is greatest. As the cooperation unfolds, in fact, the initial conditions assume an increasingly marginal role and the adaptation of expectations, roles and governance arrangements to the perceived operating results and quality (or climate) of the relationship becomes the real name of the game.[20] From an evolutionary perspective, alliances are, almost by definition, arrangements through which two organizations co-evolve *vis-à-vis* each other and *vis-à-vis* the environment in which they compete.[21]

Although this fundamental difference in the approach to the post-entry challenge exists, the two modes share more similarities than might initially be apparent. In particular, both acquisitions and alliances face common challenges related to managing integration processes and to the establishment or preservation of a high-quality relationship between the two companies.

The level of integration: The first dimension is the extent to which the two organizations integrate their structures, align their activities, and attempt to converge in their cultural aspects. The decision on the level of integration is well identified in the literature on acquisitions,[22] but rarely considered in the academic work on alliances. This is not surprising, given the amount of attention dedicated to the fundamental issue of managing the ongoing relationship between the two partnering entities. The character of the collaboration is fundamentally determined by the degree to which the two organizations decide to structure their joint activities. In joint ventures, this is particularly evident: the two partners need to agree on how to organize the newly formed entity, and the degree to which each partner should contribute to each activity. Highly integrated JVs, for example, will see both partners contribute roughly equally to all the activities of the new entity. In less integrated ones, the division of labor between the two partners will be much higher, each being responsible for a specific set of activities, often strongly tied to the mother company's functions. While integration is obviously an issue in joint ventures, it is also quite important in other types of alliance. A collaborative agreement between two similar biotech firms that specialize in similar areas (a "horizontal" alliance) will be managed to a higher level of integration than a collaborative arrangement between a pharmaceutical company and a biotech firm (a "vertical" alliance, closer to subcontracting arrangements). To be sure, acquisitions can vary to a much larger extent along this dimension, as they can be managed at various points on the entire spectrum (from complete absorption to preservation of the acquired entity's structure, operations, and cultural identity). This does not mean, however, that one cannot compare and contrast the two entry modes along this dimension of the post-entry management problem.

The quality of the relationship: A second key dimension of the post-entry phase is the degree to which the two organizations (and particularly the acquirer, in the acquisition case) invest resources, time, and managerial attention to the monitoring and handling of the quality of the relationship between them. It can include several parameters, such as the degree to which the decision-making process is handled in an inclusive way, with open and frank discussion of expectations, responsibilities, and outcomes. This has long been recognized as a fundamental prerequisite of the success of alliances but has rarely been discussed as an important issue in the management of acquisitions as well.[23]

Part of the explanation for this goes back to the observation that the post-agreement problem in acquisitions is typically constrained to the transition period, after which the "acquired" personnel are supposed to be thinking and acting like all the other members of the acquiring organization. Some other explanations, though, might relate to cognitive biases in viewing absorption as "the way" to handle the typical post-acquisition challenge.[24] Whereas it might be true that in at least some of the cases where absorption approaches afford the possibility to downplay the importance of the quality of the relationship with the acquired counterpart, in many others that is certainly not the case. Think of acquisitions driven by cross-selling or innovation purposes, for example, or of mergers between equally sized organizations.

In the context of cross-border acquisitions, then, it is nearly never the case that the acquirer can achieve the strategic objectives of the entry move without paying attention to the quality of the relationship between the new subsidiary and the rest of the organization. Even alliances can vary in terms of requirements for investment in the quality of the relationship; think of subcontracting arrangements, and the solutions involving high division of labor to the role allocation problem. Even though one can expect on average larger investments in the

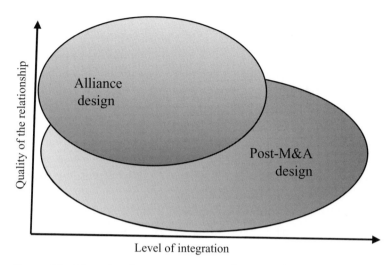

Figure 6.2. Managing the post-agreement phase: overlapping challenges.

quality of the relationship in the case of alliances, acquisitions can vary in the managerial approach along this dimension, from aggressive turnaround approaches to highly sensitive preservation ones. As with the level of integration, the quality of the relationship is not a distinguishing dimension between the different modes of entry.

As these discussions indicate, differences in the way acquisitions and alliances could be managed in the post-agreement period are a matter of degree along some common dimensions, rather than in the type of dimension relevant to the success of each type of venture, as illustrated in Figure 6.2. This shows the degree to which the two alternative modes of entry overlap in the two decision dimensions.

Initial empirical support for this overlap between acquisitions and alliances comes from a recent study of US bank mergers, in which data showed how alliance experience made a positive contribution to the performance of the focal acquisition when the post-acquisition phase was managed with a low level of integration and high relational quality, that is, in a way similar to a standard approach to managing an alliance. On the other hand, the higher the level of integration and the lower the relational quality (measured as the degree of replacement of the acquired bank's top management team), the more negative the impact of prior alliance experience on acquisition performance.[25] This result can be explained only if there are (a) common decision dimensions across the two tasks (such as the two identified above) and (b) overlapping decision alternatives along the common dimensions, as discussed and shown in Figure 6.2. Otherwise, the experience spillover between alliances and acquisitions could not assume this level of significance and, most importantly, could not be sensitive to the way the focal acquisition is managed.

The fact that the two market entry processes overlap substantially in the decision dimensions that managers need to take into consideration is an important departure from the established wisdom, which considers each mode of entry as characterized by a single core managerial problem: integration for acquisitions and relational quality for alliances. The next step is to consider the two dimensions together and to ask whether they can be viewed as independent decisions. The answer to this legitimate question has to be "no." In fact, the two decisions are likely to be strongly associated in a negative way. The higher the level of integration, in fact, the harder it will be to motivate the two organizations to work together, since autonomy is typically a major motivator in managers and employees. On the other hand, targeting a high-quality relationship between the two organizations can be significantly facilitated by a decision to accept lower integration levels. Trying to achieve both a high level of integration and high quality of relations between the two parties can therefore be particularly difficult, unless there are solid competencies already developed for this (see below).

Given the variety of options for level of integration and relationship quality in both acquisitions and alliances, and the negative interdependence between the two dimensions, how should managers approach the design of these relationships? The selection of the appropriate mix of integration level and relational quality can be thought of as a function of three sets of factors.

(1) *The value creation logic behind the agreement:* The more it relies on revenue enhancements as opposed to cost efficiencies, for example, the higher the requirements for relational quality and the lower those for the level of integration.

(2) *The relative characteristics of the two organizations:* Characteristics such as their degree of product and market relatedness or the

distance between the two corporate cultures will have an impact on these choices. In general, the lower the overlaps, the higher the expected relevance of relational quality and the lower that of level of integration.

(3) *Individual firm attributes:* The stand-alone, path-dependent attributes of the two organizations, such as their cognitive (skill-based) and cultural traits, also influence the design of acquisitions and alliances. The larger the expertise in alliances, for example, the more appropriate it will be to select and manage acquisitions in a cooperative and relatively low-integration fashion (all else being equal), since doing otherwise will raise the risk of erroneous generalization from the alliance experience to the acquisition context, with negative implications for performance. The same is true for cultural traits such as high tolerance for diversity or for risk: managing market entries against relevant corporate traits will lower the chances of appropriate design and execution.

This third family of factors is, of course, directly related to our theoretical understanding of how organizations evolve. Past decisions on how similar tasks have been managed will carry "weight" in the current decision context through the significance of path-dependence as an attribute of organizational evolution.[26] The presence of erroneous generalizations from one task to another with superficially similar, but deeply different, features also bears testimony to the power of routinized behavior, particularly when causalities between actions and outcomes are ambiguous.[27]

In conclusion, the comparison of the two entry strategies from a post-agreement management standpoint shows areas of uniqueness for each mode as well as overlapping decision dimensions and significant potential for both positive and negative influence of one company's cognitive and cultural characteristics. The degree of overlap in decision dimensions is particularly important from an evolutionary standpoint not only because it complicates considerably the identification of the most appropriate design to handle the post-entry phase, but also because it implies strong interdependencies among the learning processes through which companies develop competencies specific to the management of entry processes. We consider these learning processes in the next section.

Learning to manage market entries

Given the above discussion, it appears clear that (at least) two types of competency underlie the successful use of acquisitions and alliances to implement internationalization strategies. The first has to do with the management of the integration process, whereas the second is related to the establishment and protection of a high-quality relationship between the two companies involved. The questions of interest in tackling this learning problem are:

(1) What are the mechanisms at work in the development of these specific competencies?

(2) How do these mechanisms compare in regards to their relative effectiveness in developing these types of competency?

(3) How do these learning mechanisms compare with each other for each of the two competencies considered?

Finally, remembering that the evolutionary perspective indicates that a firm's capabilities evolve slowly, if ever, over time, what can companies do to speed up this learning process?

Several ways to learn

When it comes to tackling learning issues applied to alliances and acquisitions, the natural tendency of managers seems to be one of reliance on "learning-by-doing" mechanisms. The two entry processes are seen to be far too heterogeneous in their occurrences, too infrequent, and too context-specific to warrant a formal effort to disentangle the reasons for success or failure. However, that is a deceptive impression. Experience accumulation is only one of the learning mechanisms available for collective learning. Arrayed from the lowest to the highest level of intentionality in the learning process on the part of the organization, the full menu of learning mechanisms comprises experience accumulation, knowledge articulation, and knowledge codification.[28]

Consider, for example, two companies that have been seen as best-practice holders for the management of alliances: Corning and Hewlett Packard. Corning used a network of alliances over more than sixty years to allow its innovations in glass technology to reach new and different markets. As an innovator in glass technology, Corning created products which had applications in a variety of markets, including consumer products (plates and dishes), TV picture tubes, fiber optics cable, and test and measuring equipment (test tubes, etc.). Very early in its history, Corning used alliances (often with less than majority stakes) to partner with firms that had market knowledge, such as Owens Illinois (fluorescent tubes), Siemens (fiber optics), Samsung (picture tubes), Asahi (picture tubes), etc. Besides access to new product markets, Corning also obtained access to new geographic markets through alliances. Over the years, it built real expertise in handling such diverse alliances, with a high degree of mostly tacit knowledge on identifying partners, managing inter-firm boundaries, making its managers accountable for operations that the company did not wholly own, and in thriving in multiple cultural settings. This alliance capability afforded the company extensive flexibility, as it pursued markets that branched out from its pre-existing operations. In many ways, Corning was the epitome of successful alliance management and of the creation of a partnering capability. This capability, however, was developed through tacit apprenticeship processes and was strongly embedded in the culture of the firm, rather than explicitly codified in procedures or articulated through formal training programs.[29]

In contrast to Corning, Hewlett Packard developed alliance capabilities that are highly codified in manuals and procedures within the company. HP also has a strong track record as a highly successful alliance company. This came about as a conscious strategy in the mid to late 1990s in response to radical changes in the computer industry, where increasingly HP recognized the need for seamless inter-firm collaboration to respond to new customer needs. HP consciously invested in alliance management processes and training to become the most effective partnering company in its space. These processes stood the company in good stead as it expanded internationally in Europe and the Far East. On the product side, it had a highly successful alliance with Canon to make print engines for HP's dominant laser printers. Thus, deliberate investments in alliance capability allowed HP to grow across products and geographies using inter-firm relationships productively.

Enablers of learning

As these examples suggest, organizations use different approaches to learning – both experiential learning (Corning) and institutionalized learning (HP) – to develop relational capabilities and integration capabilities that are crucial to the success of both alliances and acquisitions.

Developing relational capabilities

How do organizations develop their relational capabilities? There are a variety of enablers that can facilitate this type of learning, and some of these are discussed in the following paragraphs.

Knowledge management: A key element of superior relational capability is knowledge management. Prashant Kale found that several key elements of knowledge management impacted capabilities and performance.[30] Specifically, relational capability and alliance performance had a positive relationship with the existence of an alliance management function that is responsible for developing both the tacit and codified knowledge associated with managing different stages of alliances. In addition, Kale identified four stages of the knowledge management process in the context of alliances: knowledge articulation, knowledge codification, knowledge sharing, and internalization. Firms that had well developed processes in each of these areas had significantly higher performance in their alliance ventures than those that did not.

Alliance management function: The creation of a corporate function specialized in alliance management, for example, has a significant positive effect on shareholder response to alliance announcements.[31] The differences are of the order of $50 million, or about 1 percent, in changes in market value (a statistically highly significant finding). Post-alliance performance results also indicate that firms which have an alliance function, and actively use it, tend to have higher performance than those without an alliance function. The implication is clear: external stakeholders tend to look for a well-developed function driving the alliance management process, and managers tend to observe higher levels of performance when there is an alliance management function in place within the firm.

Nature of experience: Another study of a large sample of biotech alliances shows that only partner-specific experience (that is the number of prior alliances made with the same partner) relates to superior alliance outcomes, whereas both generalized alliance experience and technology-specific alliance experience does not.[32] In addition, partner-specific experience interacts with governance choices (equity-based structures) to impact performance. The absence of equity protection enhances the positive implications of prior ties (i.e. partner-specific experience). These findings support the idea that it is the formation of interorganizational routines among partnering firms that explains the bulk of variation in alliance performance, as opposed to intra-firm learning processes based simply on experience accumulation.

Developing integration capabilities

While greater experience with alliances and acquisitions can lead to better integration capabilities, this is not always the case. It all depends on the ability of the organization to learn from this experience. This may be why the learning curve hypothesis (that experience accumulation should have a positive impact on the performance of the focal acquisition or alliance) has been tested several times with inconsistent results.[33] The development of a complete theoretical description of the learning mechanisms available to business organizations (and of their limitations) is in fact very recent.[34]

The most recent evidence found on the effectiveness of experience accumulation as a learning mechanism is that experience accumulation does not exhibit the hypothesized positive effect in many of the studies[35] and in some cases it shows evidence of non-linear effects.[36] More importantly, in the comparison between experiential learning and more deliberate forms of learning, the latter (knowledge codification processes) show strong and positive influence on performance, with increasing impacts as the level of integration rises.[37]

It appears that a simple view that more transactions imply better results (from automatic learning by doing) may not be true. Rather, there is a need for a disciplined process by which managers debrief and then articulate their understanding of the key drivers of success and failure in various phases of the decision process. These phases, such as due diligence and coordination of project work, can be common across acquisitions and alliances, while others, like pricing, are unique to acquisitions. The evidence points to the need for systematic learning in each of these phases, and the need for combining the lessons as needed in a particular transaction. There is a need both for articulation of knowledge from these transactions and for codification in a manner that can result in reliable implementation when needed.

Barriers to learning

Several factors affect the efficacy of learning processes in relation to managing acquisitions. Some are related to the characteristics of the task itself. Both acquisitions and alliances are typically highly infrequent events, presenting themselves each time with highly diverse characteristics and challenges (only some of which are actually apparent *ex ante*). They are inherently difficult to assess in their performance outcomes and the factors that explain their variation.[38]

Other characteristics of the process undermining the development of acquisition-related competencies are of a more manageable nature. These include:

(1) The fragmentation of the process among several actors simultaneously in charge of different, but interdependent, activities.[39]

(2) The lack of continuity in the presence of these actors through different stages of the acquisition process, from the selection of the counterpart to the deal-making and due diligence, to the integration planning phase, to the completion of the integration plan.[40]

(3) The lack of appropriate incentives for managers to link key preacquisition assumptions to post-acquisition decisions. Whether the actors are stable or not during the entire entry process, the projections generated during the internal justification and decision process are, once the entry is made, regularly discarded in favor of more "updated," and generally a lot less aggressive, ones.

(4) The distortions in the decision process leading up to overbidding for acquisitions.[41] These distortions occur because of incentive problems in the decision process, and are also due to escalating commitment to the acquisition, particularly when the decision-makers receive significant public attention in the process. More recently, Benjamin Powell, Phanish Puranam and Harbir Singh noted that the complexity of the decision process may result in poor information processing by decision-makers when faced with radical decisions on price in a short time-frame, as is typical in public acquisitions.[42] Thus, escalating commitment may be one of many explanations for why managers stay in the bidding game too long, and overbid, but it is not the only one. An equally compelling reason is the sheer complexity of the acquisition decision, and the compressed time-frame in which responses need to be made, resulting in erroneous decisions.

Investments in the creation and adaptation of guidelines and decision-support tools specific to the management of the integration process alleviate these learning impediments; but another benefit is that, as managers continue to invest in these activities, they attain an increasingly fine-grained understanding of the causal relationships between decisions, actions, and performance outcomes. Knowledge codification produces both potentially useful tools and, often tacitly, higher levels of understanding of the causal linkages between decisions and outcomes, as well as the contingencies to which they are subject.

It is also worth noting that, while most of the studies cited above work on samples of domestic alliances and acquisitions, the results are highly likely to be robust to the extension to cross-border activity, whether tied to entry or to expansion strategies. Preliminary results from the analysis of a sample of 161 mergers and acquisitions where the help of a leading consulting firm was used show remarkable stability both in the average performance outcomes of domestic and cross-border agreements, as well as in the impact of learning processes on the variance of the outcomes.[43] The sample covers all the most important sectors of activity, as well as country locations of both acquirers and targets fairly representative of the merger activity in the period 1998–2001. The presence of systematic and deliberate post-integration learning activities in the focal firm turns out to be the strongest predictor of performance in the sample studied, and that result is confirmed in the two sub-samples constituted by domestic and cross-border acquisitions.

Taken together, the implication of these studies is that raw experience in corporate development activities does not provide automatic access to superior performance. Deliberate learning processes, such as the articulation, codification, and sharing of knowledge derived from reflection upon prior activities are necessary in order to develop improved understandings of what makes them work or fail. A key element of a firm's capabilities for both alliances and acquisitions consists in the continuous investments in deliberate learning processes focused on the reasons for successes and failures in prior activity. Structural arrangements, such as the creation of an alliance management function, might improve alliance performance more for this learning-based rationale (i.e. they facilitate systematic learning and knowledge-sharing processes) than for pure coordination and project management advantages.

Conclusions

Managers confront both opportunities and challenges as they face discontinuous change in global markets. The pressures of rapid change have created the need for firms to extend their global reach through combinations of moves, including acquisitions and alliances. While the idiosyncratic historical path of the firm played a role in these choices, so did the characteristics of the transactions they considered in their decisions to acquire or partner with another firm. In this chapter, we discussed how managers can develop competence in managing these relatively more discontinuous processes of growth, in comparison to internal development. Three sets of factors play a role in this process of globalization through acquisitions and alliances: factors that influence the choice of mode, post-entry dynamics, and learning processes.

In the choice between the modes of growth, we suggested that several *types of factor* contribute to the decision. Transactional factors such as feasibility, flexibility, and time horizon play a significant role in the choice process. So also do information asymmetry, digestibility, and the extent to which the new resources being accessed are close to the core of the firm or to its periphery. An additional factor, not often thought about, is the presence and type of post-entry hazards, which tend to relate to cognitive traits and cultural traits of the firm. In sum, the choice between modes of growth – acquisition versus alliance – is influenced by transactional characteristics and firm-level traits, both of which play a significant role in the overall decision. In this sense, viewing the external mode of growth simply as a deal would be very limiting – in fact, the traits of the firm and its unique history play a significant role in the choice process. This points to a particular need for self-awareness, and a realistic appraisal of the firm's natural tendencies and preferences when managers consider the choice between acquisition and alliance as instruments of globalization.

An important insight from research and field observations is that the relative effectiveness of acquisitions and alliances as modes of growth is critically dependent upon the dynamics following the transaction. The *post-entry dynamics* following consummation of the deal significantly influence longer-term results. An insight from comparative work across different modes of entry is that there is, in fact, overlap in the post-acquisition and post-alliance management processes, even as there are significant differences. In particular, a key issue to examine is the *degree of integration* needed for the entry mode to achieve the desired results. Another important variable is the *relational quality* needed for the cooperative processes to take root. It is critically important for the decision-maker to have a sense of the degree to which integration would take place and the nature of cooperation (relational quality) needed to achieve the desired results. The better the decision-maker's understanding of the post-entry interventions needed, the greater the likelihood of achieving the desired results. Having clarity about the key drivers of value in the mode of entry and the key levers for achieving coordination is instrumental to success.

Perhaps the most important set of insights pertains to the role of *learning and capability building.* Here, we underscore the issue that simple learning from experience is insufficient to create acquisition and alliance capability. New research and field observation has shown that a disciplined process of decision-making, accountability of managers across various stages of the process, articulation and codification of knowledge, and effective sharing of knowledge link effectively with superior performance outcomes. Firms can have different paths to arrive at such results – some may stress the tacit knowledge of skilled managers, while others may rely more on codified processes. The higher the degree of integration of operations, however, the greater is the importance of codified processes of coordination to achieve the desired goals.

While the above learning processes are important elements of *capability building*, we also note that the creation of an alliance function relates strongly to positive performance, and expect the same to be true for acquisitions. These functions in combination can be seen as part of a corporate development function in the firm. Such a function exists in many corporations, but the main bet for conducting successful internationalization processes is made on the quality of the routines developed and constantly refined by the decision-makers in these positions. Our suggestion is that a disciplined process, based on a thorough understanding of the history of the firm involved and of the reasons for both successes and failures in its prior experience, as it relates to the transactional characteristics being considered, would strongly supplement the skills of people in such functions in the firm.

It is important to note some of the *barriers to learning*, which often result in continued replication of errors or poor outcomes. There is often a fragmentation of the process of decision-making, compromising the chance that a key manager will have a holistic view of the process of entry. A lack of continuity between the considerations of decision-makers in the earlier and latter stages of the process of entry can also compromise the outcomes. Often the decision-makers responsible for the strategic and financial considerations are no longer involved when the critical, post-entry issues are being faced. By the same token, those who will be responsible for running the post-entry activities are often excluded, or held in subordinate positions, during the selection and deal-making processes. A lack of incentive to revisit prior decisions and learn from prior mistakes is a third barrier to learning. This is often exacerbated by an organizational context that is quick to assign blame in the event of undesired outcomes.

Regardless of the mode of entry chosen, there is the need for managers to continue to invest in decision-support tools specific to the integration process. As they invest in these activities, they attain an increasingly fine-grained understanding of the causal relationships between decisions, actions, and performance outcomes. Codified knowledge produces a higher level of understanding of the contingencies under which particular interventions may be most effectively undertaken.

While we began our discussions by considering the choice of whether to grow globally through acquisitions or alliances, it is clear this choice cannot be considered in isolation from the characteristics, capabilities, and experience of the firms involved. Success appears to be as much a result of these underlying factors as of the choice of mode itself. This implies that, unfortunately, there are no simple recipes for successful internationalization strategies. Managers need to consider carefully the strategic situation and the cultural and cognitive traits of their own organizations as well as those of the potential partner. Once they make their entry choice, the key is to be constantly prepared to learn from the ongoing process and outcomes. As firms pursue the agenda of globalization and engage in external modes of growth, developing a full and rich understanding of the factors influencing the development of both integration and relational capabilities is likely to be a solid source of sustainable competitive advantage in an increasingly dynamic environment.

Notes

1 R. Nelson and S. Winter, *An Evolutionary Theory of Economic Change* (Cambridge, MA: Harvard University Press, 1982).

2 W. M. Cohen, R. Burkhart, G. Dosi, M. Egidi, L. Marengo, M. War-glien, and S. Winter, "Routines and Other Recurring Action Patterns of Organizations: Contemporary Research Issues. *Industrial and Corporate Change*, 5 (1997): 653–698; S. Winter, "The Satisficing Principle in Capability Learning," *Strategic Management Journal*, 21 (2000), pp. 981–997; M. Zollo and S. Winter, "Deliberate Learning and the Evolution of Dynamic Capabilities," *Organization Science*, 13 (2002), pp. 339–351.

3 Identity here is taken in the large sense as the union set of ambitions, strategies, structural arrangements, operating activities, beliefs, and values.

4 S. H. Hymer, "The International Operations of National Firms: A Study of Foreign Direct Investments," PhD. thesis, Massachusetts Institute of Technology, 1960; P. J. Buckley and M. C. Casson, *The Future of the Multinational Enterprise* (London: Holmes & Meier, 1976).

5 B. Kogut, "Foreign Direct Investment as a Sequential Process," in C. P. Kindleberger and D. Audretsch, *The Multinational Corporation in the 1980s* (Cambridge, MA: MIT Press, 1983).

6 Y. Doz and C. K. Prahalad, *The Multinational Mission: Balancing Local Demands and Global Vision* (New York: Free Press/Macmillan, 1987); C. A. Bartlett and S. Ghoshal, *Managing Across Borders: The Transnational Solution* (Boston: Hutchinson Business Books, 1989); B. Kogut and U. Zander, "Knowledge of the Firm, Combinative Capabilities, and the Replication of Technology," *Organization Science*, 3 (1992), pp. 383–397; R. E. Caves, *Multinational Enterprise and Economic Analysis* (Cambridge: Cambridge University Press, 1996; Y. Doz, J. Santos, and P. Williamson, *From Global to Metanational: How Companies Win in the Knowledge Economy* (Boston: Harvard Business School Press, 2001).

7 B. Kogut and N. Kulatilaka, "Operating Flexibility, Global Manufacturing, and the Option Value of a Multinational Network," *Management Science*, 40 (1994), pp. 123–139; S. J. Chang, "International Expansion Strategy of Japanese Firms: Capability Building Through Sequential Entry," *Academy of Management Journal*, 38 (1995), pp. 383–407; S. J. Chang, "An Evolutionary Perspective on Diversification and Corporate Restructuring: Entry, Exit, and Economic Performance during 1981–89," *Strategic Management Journal*, 17 (1996), pp. 587–611; B. Kogut and S. J. Chang, "Platform Investments and Volatile Exchange Rates: Direct Investment in the US by Japanese Electronic Companies," *Review of Economics and Statistics*, 78 (1996), pp. 221–231.

8 Hymer, "International operations"; Caves, *Multinational Enterprise*; M. F. Guillén, "Experience, Imitation, and the Sequence of Foreign Entry: Wholly Owned and Joint-Venture Manufacturing by South Korean Firms

and Business Groups in China, 1987–1995," *Journal of International Business Studies*, 34 (2003), pp. 185–197.

9 R. Vernon, *Sovereignty at Bay: The Multinational Spread of US Enterprises* (New York: Basic Books, 1971).

10 W. J. Henisz and O. E. Williamson, "Comparative Economic Organization – Within and Between Countries," *Business and Politics*, 1 (1999), pp. 261–277.

11 B. Kogut, "Entering the United States by Joint Ventures: Competitive Rivalry and Industry Structure" (with H. Singh), in F. Contractor and P. Lorange (eds.), *Cooperative Strategies in International Business* (Lexington, MA: Lexington Press, 1988).

12 S. Balakrishnan and M. P. Koza, "Information Asymmetry, Adverse Selection and Joint-ventures: Theory and Evidence," *Journal of Economic Behavior and Organization,* 20 (1993), pp. 99–117; J. J. Reuer and M. P. Koza, "Asymmetric Information and Joint Venture Performance: Theory and Evidence for Domestic and International Joint Ventures," *Strategic Management Journal*, 21 (2000), pp. 81–88.

13 J.-F. Hennart and S. Reddy, "The Choice Between Mergers & Acquisitions and Joint Ventures: The Case of Japanese Investors in the United States," *Strategic Management Journal*, 18 (1997), pp. 1–12.

14 Reuer and Koza, "Asymmetric Information and Joint Venture Performance"; J. J. Reuer and M. P. Koza, "On Lemons and Indigestibility: Resource Assembly through Joint Ventures," *Strategic Management Journal*, 21 (2000), p. 195; J.-F. Hennart and S. Reddy, "Digestibility and Asymmetric Information in the Choice Between Acquisitions and Joint Ventures: Where's the Beef?," *Strategic Management Journal*, 21 (2000), pp. 191–193.

15 J. Reuer, "Collaborative Strategies: The Logic of Alliances," in *Mastering Strategy* (Harlow, UK: Financial Times/Prentice Hall, 2000).

16 This figure has been kindly provided by Mr. Peter Ruh, formerly head of the post-acquisition integration group at Cisco Systems.

17 P. C. Haspeslagh and D. B. Jemison, *Managing Acquisitions: Creating Value Through Corporate Renewal* (New York: Free Press, 1991); M. Zollo, "Process Routinization, Knowledge Codification and the Creation of Organizational Capabilities: Post-Acquisition Management in the Banking Industry," unpublished dissertation, Wharton School, University of Pennsylvania, 1998.

18 Y. Doz, "The Evolution of Cooperation in Strategic Alliance: Initial Conditions or Learning Processes?," *Strategic Management Journal*, 17 (1996), pp. 55–84.

19 J. March, "Exploration and Exploitation in Organizational Learning," *Organizational Science*, 2 (1991), pp. 71–87; J. March and D. Levinthal,

"The Myopia of Learning," *Strategic Management Journal*, 14 (1998), pp. 95–113.

20 Doz, "Evolution of Cooperation"; A. Arino and J. de la Torre, "Learning from Failure: Towards an Evolutionary Model of Collaborative Ventures," *Organization Science*, 9 (1998), pp. 306–326; Y. Doz and G. Hamel, *Alliance Advantage: The Art of Creating Value through Partnering* (Boston: Harvard Business School Press, 1998).

21 M. Koza and A. Lewin, "The co-evolution of strategic alliances," *Organization Science*, 9 (1998), pp. 255–264.

22 D. K. Datta and J. H. Grant, "Relationships between Type of Acquisition, the Autonomy Given to the Acquired Firm, and Acquisition Success: An Empirical Analysis," *Journal of Management*, 16 (1990), pp. 29–44; Haspeslagh and Jemison, *Managing Acquisitions*; Zollo, "Process Routinization"; P. Puranam, H. Singh, and M. Zollo, "A Bird in the Hand or Two in the Bush?: *Integration Trade-offs in Technology-Grafting Acquisitions*," *European Management Journal*, 21 (2003), pp. 179–185.

23 G. Hamel, "Competition for Competence and Inter-Partner Learning within International Strategic Alliances," *Strategic Management Journal*, 12 (1991), pp. 83–103; A. Parkhe, "'Messy' Research, Methodological Predispositions, and Theory Development in International Joint Ventures," *Academy of Management Review* 18 (1993), pp. 227–268.

24 Haspeslagh and Jemison, *Managing Acquisitions*.

25 M. Zollo and J. Reuer, "Experience Spillovers Across Corporate Development Activities," INSEAD Working Paper, WP 2003/98/SM.

26 Nelson and Winter, *Evolutionary Theory of Economic Change*.

27 M. Cohen and P. Bacdayan, "Organizational Routines are Stored as Procedural Memory: Evidence from a Laboratory Study," *Organization Science*, 5 (1994), pp. 554–568.

28 Zollo and Winter, "Deliberate Learning."

29 Ironically, Corning focused itself in the late 1990s into fiber optics, and lost many of these capabilities in a strategic about-face that resulted in poor returns.

30 P. Kale, "Alliance Capability and Success: A Knowledge-Based Approach," unpublished dissertation, University of Pennsylvania, 1999.

31 P. Kale, J. Dyer, and H. Singh, "Alliances and Acquisitions as Alternative Growth Vehicles: Why Alliances Outperform Acquisitions," paper presented at Fisher College conference on *Strategic Alliances*, June 2003.

32 J. J. Reuer, M. Zollo, and H. Singh, "Post-formation Dynamics in Strategic Alliances," *Strategic Management Journal*, 23 (2002), pp. 135–151; M. Zollo , J. J. Reuer and H. Singh, "Interorganizational Routines and

Performance in Strategic Alliances," *Organization Science*, 13 (2000), pp. 701–713.

33 K. Fowler and D. Schmidt, "Determinants of Tender Offer Post-acquisition Financial Performance," *Strategic Management Journal*, 10 (1989), pp. 339–350; J. Pennings and H. Barkema, "Organizational Learning and Diversification," *Academy of Management Journal*, 37 (1994), pp. 608–641.

34 Zollo, "Process Routinization"; J. Haleblian and S. Finkelstein, "The Influence of Organizational Acquisition Experience on Acquisition Performance: A Behavioural Learning Perspective," *Administrative Science Quarterly*, 44 (1999), pp. 29–57; M. Zollo and H. Singh, "Deliberate Learning in Corporate Acquisitions: Post-acquisition Strategies and Integration Capability in US Bank Mergers," forthcoming in *Strategic Management Journal*, December 2004; M. Hayward, "When Do Firms Learn from Their Acquisition Experience? Evidence from 1990–1995," *Strategic Management Journal*, 23 (2002), pp. 21–40.

35 Zollo, "Process Routinization"; Haleblian and Finkelstein, "Influence of Organizational Acquisition Experience"; Hayward, "When Do Firms Learn?".

36 Haleblian and Finkelstein, "Influence of Organizational Acquisition Experience"; Zollo and Reuer, "Experience Spillovers"; Hayward, "When Do Firms Learn?".

37 Zollo, "Process Routinization"; Zollo and Singh, "Deliberate Learning."

38 Zollo and Winter, "Deliberate Learning."

39 D. Jemison and S. Sitkin, "Corporate Acquisitions: A Process Perspective," *Academy of Management Review*, 11 (1986), pp. 145–164.

40 Haspeslagh and Jemison, *Managing Acquisitions*.

41 A. Pablo, S. Sitkin, and D. Jemison, "Acquisition Decision-making Processes: The Central Role of Risk," *Journal of Management*, 22 (1996), pp. 723–746; Jemison and Sitkin, "Corporate Acquisitions"; P. Haunschild and A. Davis-Blake, "Managerial Overcommitment in Corporate Acquisition Processes," *Organization Science*, 5 (1994), pp. 528–541.

42 B. Powell, P. Puranam, and H. Singh, "When Closing the Deal is Bad News: Why Due Diligence Might Fail," London Business School Working Paper, 2002.

43 D. Fubini, C. Price, and M. Zollo, *Leading Mergers* (forthcoming).

7 | Developing new products and services for the global market

REINHARD ANGELMAR
INSEAD

With the emergence of global markets and global market segments, it may seem that standardized products and services are a given. But as Reinhard Angelmar points out in this chapter, developing new offerings for global markets requires a deep understanding of segmentation and a careful design of the product development strategy. Companies need to balance the tradeoffs between the increased cost of differentiating products and the increased revenue that can be obtained from such differentiation. He discusses strategies for reducing the costs of differentiation through the use of platforms. He also considers strategies to boost the revenue from this differentiation through effective market segmentation, particularly focusing on the "must have" and "delight" benefits that are critical to a specific segment. This discussion moves global product development beyond simplistic recipes for globalization or standardization to a richer analysis of the strategies to develop profitable new products for specific global market segments.

IN the 1980s and 1990s, it was tempting to believe that with the emergence of global markets and media, globally standardized products would quickly follow. In his highly influential 1983 manifesto for globalization, Theodore Levitt argued that Western firms were over-differentiating their products.[1] He recommended that companies follow the example of Japanese firms, which had designed global products for global markets. The picture turned out to be much more complicated than Levitt, and many of the managers who followed his advice, anticipated.

The Japanese companies that Levitt upheld as a model to be emulated later moved away from global product standardization. Honda used to design and sell the same cars in Japan, the United States, and Europe. Because the customer needs in these three regions were and still are quite different, successful models sold well in only one of the markets. Unsuccessful models sold well in none because compromises across these markets ensured that everyone was unhappy. For example, the 1993 Accord was too cramped for US drivers, but not stylish enough

159

for the Japanese. When Honda restyled it for the United States, its US sales surged, but declined in Japan, where buyers complained that it had grown too large and dowdy.

Learning from these failures, Honda moved to a policy of regionally differentiated cars. The new Accord launched in 1997 and 1998 was different in each region. The American Accord was a "big, staid family car . . . The jazzy Japanese car (was) a smaller, sporty compact, aimed at young professionals. The European version (was) short and narrow and . . . expected to feature the sporty ride Old World drivers prefer."[2] Because the regionally differentiated cars were based on the same global platform, Honda was able to match the needs of different customer segments, thus increasing global revenues, without a stiff cost penalty. In fact, it was estimated that Honda's total development costs for this project were less than 25 percent of those of Ford in redesigning its Taurus.[3]

This example illustrates the importance of careful segmentation of global markets and the opportunities to tailor products to the needs of different segments. It also shows the importance of reducing the costs of such tailoring through strategies such as building on a common platform. There are three primary concerns in the development of new products and services for global markets:

(1) *Segmentation:* Identification of segments within and across countries and determination of which product differentiations have the biggest impact on the customers' responses in the different target segments.

(2) *Reduction in cost of tailoring:* Efforts to lower the costs of developing new products for different market segments through the use of platforms and other strategies.

(3) *Integration of market and design perspectives:* The integration of cost and market information for the design, development, and commercialization of new products for the global market.

We explore each of these issues that shape global product strategy in more detail below, with a particular focus on the balance of the costs and benefits of differentiation.

Global market segmentation

To be successful, a new product must meet customer needs. Analyzing and segmenting the global market with a view to identifying target customers for the new product can help identify common sets of needs and increase the chances that the new product will be successful in meeting these needs.

From local to global market segmentation

Many companies still practice local segmentation. Local segmentation consists of segmenting each country or region in which the firm operates. The variables for defining the segments (segmentation bases or criteria) often vary from country to country, or from region to region. This makes it difficult if not impossible to identify and assess segments across countries. The segments in each country or region are evaluated from a country or regional perspective, and new products are developed in response to perceived local opportunities. Some of these products may subsequently be successfully marketed in countries or regions other than the ones for which they were originally developed. But this happens mostly by chance, and not by design.

Local market segmentation to guide new product development is clearly suboptimal from a global perspective. Locally attractive segments and the new products developed for them may not be suitable for other markets. At the same time, locally unattractive but globally attractive segments are likely to be ignored. Segmenting the country markets in which the firm operates may blind the firm to trends emerging in other markets, and which may spread to other countries.

Global market segmentation is a vital input for new product development geared to the global market. Instead of segmenting separately each country or region, global market segmentation aims to segment customers in all countries. The shift from local to global segmentation accompanies the necessary shift from individual countries to the global market as the primary unit for strategic market planning.[4]

Global segmentation requires two decisions: first, choice of the units of segmentation (or level of aggregation) – should countries be segmented (macrosegmentation), or should individual customers around the world be segmented (microsegmentation)?;[5] and, second, regardless of which unit of segmentation is chosen, segmentation variables or bases for forming the segments must be defined.

Just like local segmentation schemes, global segmentation schemes should be evaluated against five criteria:

(1) *Measurability:* Can the size and other characteristics of the segments be measured?

(2) *Substantiality:* Are the segments large enough to be served profitably?

(3) *Accessibility:* Can the segments be effectively reached and served through promotion and distribution channels?

(4) *Actionability:* Can effective programs be formulated for attracting and serving the segments?

(5) *Differentiability or differential responsiveness:* Do the segments respond differently to marketing-mix elements and programs and, more specifically, to different product features?[6]

Global segmentation of countries

Country segmentation uses country characteristics as the basis for forming country groupings. Characteristics which have been used include demographics (e.g. population size, age structure, ethnic composition), socioeconomic variables (e.g. GNP per capita), political variables (e.g. type of political system), culture (e.g. Hofstede's characterization of countries by individualism versus collectivism, power distance, uncertainty avoidance, and masculinity),[7] and consumption-related variables (e.g. average per capita beer consumption).

The more the country segmentation variables are related to the new product development project in question, the greater the potential managerial relevance of the segmentation scheme. For example, country market segmentation for a new anti-depressant product might be based on the prevalence and incidence of depression in a country, the percentage of patients (overall, and by patient segments) who are diagnosed and treated medically, the distribution of anti-depressant prescriptions by specific indications, and the price and reimbursement conditions for anti-depressant drugs. Similarly, Waste Management International uses countries' environmental regulations and their enforcement as key segmentation variables, and the small Norwegian toothbrush maker Jordan uses per capita consumption of toothbrushes and competitive intensity.[8]

The main advantage of country segmentation is measurability: much information on country characteristics can be acquired quite easily from secondary data sources. Its major drawback is the questionable actionability for the purpose of guiding the new product development process toward promising target benefits, product concepts, and specifications.

Country segmentation is probably most useful in the very first phase of the new product development process, to assess the attractiveness of country markets for new product development, and to decide which countries to retain for a more detailed opportunity identification analysis.[9] Country segmentation can also be conceived as the first phase of a two-phase global segmentation process, with the second phase involving the global segmentation of individual customers.[10]

Global segmentation of individual customers

Global segmentation of individual customers can be based on general characteristics of the customers that are not explicitly related to the category and product of interest, and/or on characteristics which are explicitly related to it, so-called domain-specific characteristics.[11]

General characteristics for global market segmentation

General characteristics include variables such as demographics (individual demographics include age, gender, income, and occupation; organizational demographics include firm industry, size, and location), values, and lifestyles.

A number of global segmentation schemes based on the values or lifestyles of individual consumers have been proposed both by academic and industry research (e.g. VALS-2, Roper Starch Worldwide, and Eurostyles). For example, Roper asked about 1,000 people in 35 countries to rank 56 values by the importance they hold as guiding principles in their lives, and found six value segments:
(1) Strivers (12% of all individuals)
(2) Devouts (22%)
(3) Altruists (18%)
(4) Intimates (15%)
(5) Fun seekers (12%)
(6) Creatives (10%).[12]

Global segmentation schemes based on general characteristics have been shown to produce measurable and substantial global segments.[13] However, accessibility is often uncertain and, above all, actionability for new product development and differential responsiveness to new product options are generally doubtful.

Domain-specific characteristics for global market segmentation

Domain-specific characteristics refer to customer characteristics, attitudes, needs (benefits sought), and behaviors that are directly related to the product category of concern for new product development. Segments based on domain-specific variables generally have higher actionability and differential responsiveness than general segmentation schemes, while their measurability, substantiality, and accessibility vary from scheme to scheme. Among the various domain-specific segmentation variables, benefits sought by customers are the most relevant segmentation variable for new product development. The key benefits that the new product is to provide to customers, and their summary in a "core benefit proposition" form the basis for the development of the physical product, marketing strategy, and service policy, which should all be designed to fulfill the key benefits.[14]

Types of segments discovered through global customer segmentation

If the members of the resulting segments are diffused broadly across many different countries, this creates complex logistical or access challenges, particularly in categories where distribution costs constitute a large share of total costs, such as in retailing, and where perishability is high, as for fresh food and fashion products.[15] Because of such problems, this approach to segmentation can sometimes lead to segments that, although fine in theory, turn out to be very difficult to reach in practice. While the country is not a segmentation variable when one performs a global segmentation of individual customers, countries or regions must be used for profiling the resulting segments, since they play an important role for segment accessibility (communication and distribution), and the evaluation of segment attractiveness.

Global segmentation may result in four types of segments across countries (Table 7.1):

(1) *Global segments:* These segments are present in all countries. For example, lager beers accounted for between 67 percent and 100 percent of 2001 beer sales (value) in all major markets.[16] Procter & Gamble's consumer research identified the need for a long-lasting lipstick as a global need, and created a worldwide development project to target it.[17]

Table 7.1. *Types of global segments*

	Country A	Country B	Country C	...	Country X	Types of segments
Segment 1	x	x	x	x	x	Global segments
Segment 2	x	x	x	x	x	Global segments
Segment 3	x	x				Regional segment
Segment 4			x		x	Geographically dispersed segment
Segment 5		x				Country-specific segments
Segment 6					x	Country-specific segments

(2) *Regional/contiguous segments:* These segments tend to be present in certain contiguous regions, which favors segment accessibility. For example, a study which segmented European consumers on the basis of the importance of retail store attributes identified a segment concerned predominantly with service quality, and which covered part of northwest Europe, including the Netherlands, northeast France, southwest and northwest Germany, and parts of Belgium.[18]

(3) *Geographically dispersed segments:* These segments are present in multiple but non-contiguous regions. For example, the major markets in which dark beer has a larger than 10% share of the beer market comprise such geographically distant countries as the UK (27%), Canada (19%), South Africa (16%), Germany (14%), and Russia (12%).[19]

(4) *Country-specific segments:* These segments are present primarily in one or a few countries. For example, demand for Sony's AIBO, the world's first entertainment robot, was concentrated in Japan. Aside from a small number of American enthusiasts, most Americans did not "get it."[20]

Local tailoring for global segments

A good global market segmentation scheme for new product development results in a set of segments, each of which comprises customers who seek distinctive key benefits. It seems logical to match the possible types of market segments resulting from global market segmentation with new product types, namely:

(1) to develop globally standardized products for global segments;
(2) to develop regionally standardized products for (contiguous and non-contiguous) regional segments; and
(3) to develop country-specific products for country-specific segments.

As a consequence, large multinational companies targeting all three types of segments could be expected to manage a portfolio of new product development projects comprising, at the same time, global, regional, and country-specific projects. Although this often appears to be the case, a more nuanced analysis is required.

Even when segments can be defined based on common benefits sought by individuals across national boundaries, there may still need to be further refinement of these segments. While customers in the same benefit segment are seeking similar benefits, this does not imply that the product attributes that will best *fulfill* these benefits are necessarily the same for all segment members. This is because of differences in the context for use and in the customers themselves. For example, the driving characteristics of an automobile are moderated by the quality of the roads, as well as by the driver's skills. Similarly, the benefits which a consumer will derive from a mobile phone depend both on the quality of the network and on the consumer's understanding of the phone's various features. A consumer in a market with a poor cellular network may seek the same benefits as a consumer in a market with a good network, but the latter consumer will realize that benefit much more completely with the same phone.

Cultural differences can shape the meaning of certain benefits for consumers in different countries. For example, the women's magazine *Elle* aims to provide the same core benefits around the world, namely to inform women about fashion trends, and contribute to women's emancipation in their daily life. But to fulfill these core benefits in different countries, *Elle* publishes thirty-five different editions, which use about 20 percent common and 80 percent edition-specific content. Similarly, Banyan Tree Resorts & Hotels, an Asia-based international resort management group, defines service standards primarily in terms of service satisfaction rather than specific technical features such as times and quantities, allowing the process of service delivery to vary according to the local culture as long as a high level of overall service quality is achieved and the brand's promise is fulfilled.[21] This is an explicit recognition that while all its customers may value "service quality," this means different things in different countries. Differences in language and infrastructure may also require more extensive local tailoring of product or service attributes to meet local languages, voltage levels, plugs, or other specifications.

Consumers may also differ in the meaning which they attach to a particular product attribute and, as a consequence, the benefits which they perceive. For example, while Olivetti's slimline word processors were perceived as elegant and sophisticated in Europe, American customers saw them as fragile and effeminate.[22]

When there is significant variance in the relationships between product attributes and perceived or experienced benefits within the same segment, segmentation by benefits may be complemented by segmentation based on variables that capture the characteristics of the use context and of the customer. For example, individual differences in perceived relationships between product attributes and benefits, as well as between benefits and values can be measured and used to define segments that share similar attribute–benefit–value perceptions.[23] Alternatively, consumer preferences for concrete sensory product attributes may be measured directly, and provide the basis for defining homogeneous sensory preference segments, which are directly actionable.[24]

Segment evaluation and targeting

Having identified the market segment opportunities in the global market, the new product development team must evaluate the segments and decide which of them to target for new product development. New product development opportunities should be assessed from two perspectives:

(1) How profitable is the opportunity?

(2) How valuable are the competencies which the firm can acquire?

Profitability evaluation

Segment evaluation for profitability looks at segment attractiveness (size, growth potential, competitive intensity, profitability, risk), as well as the fit between the resources and competencies required for the successful development and profitable commercialization of a new product in each segment and the resources and competencies available to the firm.

The broader the country scope of a segment, the more challenging its evaluation, since competitive conditions are likely to vary significantly across countries. For example, the new drug Aromasin from Pharmacia (acquired by Pfizer in early 2003), which entered the global market for the treatment of advanced/metastatic breast cancer had to compete with a drug the daily treatment cost of which varied between €1.53 (Australia) and €13.08 (Germany), while the daily cost of non-drug care for the target condition varied between €7.15 (Spain) and €20.13 (UK). Mainly as a result of these differences, the cost-effectiveness of Aromasin compared to its main competitor varied between €1,353 (Germany) and €13,016 (The Netherlands) per life-year gained.[25]

Small firms may prefer to focus on one segment, whereas larger firms with a broader resource base may opt for a multisegment strategy, directing product development both at global segments and other segments with a narrower geographic scope. A focused strategy has the advantage of allowing the concentration of development resources, but carries a higher level of risk. One of the main sources of risk is competition, with the twin possibility of seeing the target segment invaded by competitors with a broader scope, or of losing out to competitors who concentrate on a subsegment.

Iridium illustrates the dangers of focusing on a relatively narrow subsegment. Iridium was a telephone service targeted at the prototypical internationally mobile segment, namely the international traveler, and designed to satisfy this segment's need for seamless, anytime-anywhere telephone service. To provide this benefit, Iridium invested over $5 billion in a satellite-based telecommunications infrastructure. By the time the system was launched, however, national and regional cellphone providers were offering a much cheaper roaming service. This satisfied the needs of these international executives, a significant subsegment of Iridium's target group, within the major urban areas around the world.

Iridium went bankrupt, it was acquired from the bankruptcy court for $25 million, and the reborn service was now targeted to organizations operating beyond the reach of land-based cellular systems. That included the military, fishing fleets, oil and gas companies and mining concerns. During the 2003 Iraq war, thousands of US soldiers and international media correspondents were making calls on Iridium phones from the Iraqi desert, where there were no landlines or cell towers.[26] The focus on these new segments made the company less vulnerable to competitive attacks from substitutes.

Competence acquisition evaluation

While profit is the first concern, a company may also choose to enter a segment to learn or build competencies it can leverage in other markets, even if the segment may be small and/or the firm may lack the resources to address it profitably. Such market segments have been called leading or lead markets,[27] or lead users.[28] Lead market segments tend to be ahead of other markets in the emergence of needs that subsequently diffuse to other segments. Developing products for such segments, therefore, allows firms to acquire competencies which increase their chances of competing successfully in these other, typically larger segments.

Which countries or customer groups are leading can change over time. For example, in mobile telephony, leadership has shifted over time from the United States to Europe, Japan, and now to Korea. With a mobile phone penetration of 70 percent, Korea is currently in the vanguard of new mobile phone technology and service. Examples of services with significant consumer uptake include music downloads, music videos, and mobile movies – serialized film clips that users download each day like a soap opera and watch on their handsets. A service that allows consumers to watch satellite TV on their phones is planned for 2004 rollout.[29]

Strategies for developing profitable new products

Providing benefits that a certain global or local segment of customers is willing to pay for is a necessary condition of successful new product development, but this is just part of the overall value creation equation. The other key concern is to deliver that benefit through a product or service *profitably*. New product development success is linked to the following four factors:
(1) delivery of key benefits to the target customers
(2) time to market
(3) development cost, and
(4) production cost.

Because it is generally impossible to maximize performance on all these factors at the same time, new product managers must make tradeoffs.[30]

Matching the key benefits desired by each segment of the global market, as suggested by the segment-matching logic, satisfies the first success factor, but may lower performance on the other factors. For example, Procter & Gamble's new product development was traditionally geared to getting the customer benefits absolutely right through extensive but slow market testing. "Ready, aim, aim, aim, aim, fire," was one description of this model, which P&G's top management attempted to change by putting greater emphasis on time to market.[31] This change of emphasis was motivated by a growing number of cases where P&G's new products had been beaten to the market by faster competitors, resulting in poor market performance of the P&G products. Launching an identical new product around the globe is one way to speed up time to market, as well as to lower development and production costs. However, there is the risk that a lack of fit with customer needs may result in low sales revenues and poor profitability.

A framework for analyzing new product development for the global market

The decision of whether to match new products to segments or, on the contrary, to standardize them, therefore, must be analyzed for its consequences for both the revenue and cost sides. These two dimensions are represented in the framework for considering these issues shown in Figure 7.1.

As a baseline, one may consider the situation where a single new product is developed for all the segments of the global market which the firm intends to cover. This baseline is the center point of the figure. For every proposed product adaptation or parallel project to improve the matching to segment needs, two questions must be answered:
(1) What is the likely impact on total product program revenues?
(2) What is the likely impact on total product program costs?

Changes relative to the baseline may leave total program costs constant, increase them, or reduce them. The additional program costs may include greater R&D costs and higher production costs due to a reduction in the number of shared parts. On the other hand, a departure from a single standard new product may lower total program costs when components for the product variants or parallel new products benefit from lower production costs, because of lower-cost materials or lower-cost production processes and locations, and when these cost savings more than compensate for the higher R&D costs generated by the additional product and process design.

Program revenues may also increase, decrease, or remain constant as a result of differentiation. Greater revenues may result from better matching of segment needs, or revenues may be reduced when flawed assumptions about the market or poor implementation lead to adaptations that actually worsen segment fit in comparison to a standard product.

In Figure 7.1, the northwest quadrant is a "trade-on" zone, where proposed changes relative to the baseline increase revenues and, at the same time, lower costs. Options with such an outcome are obviously ideal. The southeast quadrant represents a "disaster" zone, where options lead to lower revenues and higher costs. The northeast and southwest quadrants represent tradeoff zones. The northeast quadrant represents options which increase revenues but also costs, while the southwest quadrant has options which lower revenues and costs at the same time. The 45° line through the origin divides these two quadrants in such a way that the options above the line increase profits, options below the line reduce profits, and options on the line are profit-neutral, since changes in revenues are compensated by identical changes in costs.

Theodore Levitt's contention that Western international firms were "overdifferentiating" is represented by the double-arrowed line *A* in the lower half of the northeast quadrant. This reflects a view that the incremental costs of differentiation were higher than the incremental revenues. Levitt contrasted this policy with that of Japanese companies which designed standardized new products for the global market,[32] and he recommended that Western firms pursue a similar course, represented by the arrow connecting line A to the origin (the baseline).

Many large, international firms were indeed in the lower part of the northeast quadrant. One reason was the administrative heritage of their "multi-domestic" organizational structure, where many largely autonomous, fully integrated country organizations designed and developed new products for their domestic market without considering cross-country or regional standardization possibilities.[33] The second reason was the wave of cross-border mergers and acquisitions that accompanied the closer economic integration within the European Union, and the run for globalization during the 1990s. The combined result was that many international companies found themselves saddled with multiple new product development centers, each developing

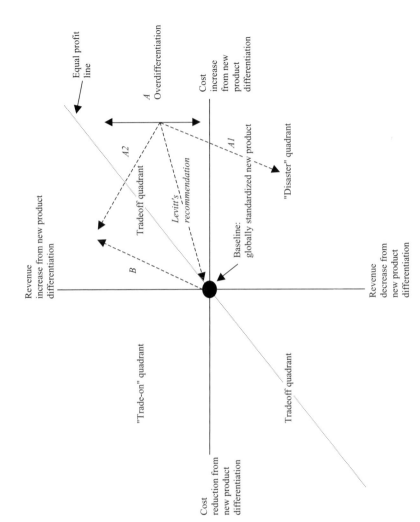

Figure 7.1. Profit impact of global new product strategy options.

new products for their respective target markets in an uncoordinated way.

Many of these companies did follow Levitt's advice and embarked on a process of increasing coordination and standardization of new products. Some succeeded, but others moved into the "disaster" quadrant instead, a move represented by line *A1*. Philips may be a case in point. Philips' administrative heritage of independent country organizations was largely dismantled by successive reorganizations and lay-offs, intended to improve coordination, concentration, and focus in new product development and production, and to reduce costs. These moves, however, also destroyed part of the precious technological and market knowledge that Philips had built up over many years and which had provided the basis for differentiated new products that matched local market needs. As a result, despite all the global rationalization and standardization moves, Philips' financial performance remained poor, and the company's global competitiveness was still in question.[34] Other companies such as Honda retreated from global standardization to a regionally adapted and differentiated new product policy, and were able to increase revenues more than costs, as represented by the arrow *B*.

A move into the upper half of the northeast quadrant, of course, is also attractive for companies that are currently in the lower half of this quadrant. This move is represented by arrow *A2*. It requires a selective interpretation of Levitt's message: focus the standardization effort on those new product aspects which have a high cost and low customer benefit impact, and make sure to match customer needs for aspects which are important to customers and where adaptation entails no significant penalties for cost and time to market.

Companies can influence where the product falls in this framework either by changing the cost of differentiating the product or by increasing the revenue generated by the differentiation. We now consider strategies for each of these activities.

Lowering the cost of development through systematic reuse

One basic strategy for lowering the cost of developing new products for different market segments consists in using products that have been developed for one segment, either in their entirety or in part, as a basis for entering new segments. The incremental costs of adapting already existing products for new segments are typically significantly lower than for an autonomous development, resulting in economies of scope.

International companies who, by chance, discover that locally developed products can be adapted to other markets benefit from such economies of scope. But why leave things to chance? The record company PolyGram created an international network of specialists whose main task was to analyze PolyGram's local products with a view to identifying the ones with the greatest internationalization potential.[35]

Using platforms

Platform-based new product development is another way of encouraging the systematic reuse of existing products or parts of them. A platform product is built around a preexisting technological subsystem.[36] Such platforms are used extensively in the automobile industry.[37] They support multiple manufacturing locations (e.g. the Fiat Palio is designed for emerging markets around the world and is built in several locations), variants of the same basic model (e.g. variants of Renault's Megane), products of several size segments (e.g. Ford's Ka is a sub-B segment car, derived from the Ford Fiesta's B segment platform), products for niche segments (e.g. the Audi TT is derived from the Volkswagen group A platform), products marketed under different brands by the same manufacturer (e.g. the Volkswagen group's VW, Seat, Skoda, and Audi brands), and products marketed under different brands by different manufacturers (e.g. the multipurpose vehicles Ford Galaxy, VW Sharan, and Seat Alhambra are all produced in a plant jointly owned by Ford and the Volkswagen group).

Beyond the automobile industry, platform-based new product development strategies are used in a growing range of industries, including non-assembled products and services.[38] Product life cycle strategies in the pharmaceutical industry, whereby a new chemical entity, over time, is used as the basis for targeting a growing range of diseases, for treating an increased variety of types of patient, through different types of formulations (e.g. oral, injection, ointment, transdermal), and possible combinations with other chemical entities, provide an example of platform-based new product development for non-assembled products.

The use of platforms in new product development reduces the incremental cost of targeting different market segments by lowering development costs (parts and assembly processes developed for one product need not be developed and tested again), manufacturing costs (machinery, equipment, and tooling can be shared across higher production volumes; economies of scale due to a larger volume of shared parts; easier switching between models; lower logistics and materials management costs due to the smaller number of parts).[39] In addition to lowering the incremental costs of developing new products for different market segments, platforms may also increase revenues by speeding up time to market, and by improving service levels on account of the simplified parts inventory management of shared components.[40]

However, platform strategies also involve a revenue risk. Shared parts may lead to the perception of a lack of differentiation, customers' knowledge of sharing may lead to the dilution of an upmarket brand's equity, and products with lower prices and margins may cannibalize the ones with higher margins. For example, traditional VW customers may buy Seat or Skoda cars instead, and Audi customers may buy Volkswagen cars.[41]

Lowering development costs through new technologies

Platform-based development lowers the cost of launching new products for different target segments by sharing resources across products. Another approach consists in lowering the development costs, independently of sharing, such that the targeting of small markets becomes profitable.

A targeted approach to drug development in the pharmaceutical industry can be used to illustrate this approach. Traditional methods of developing new chemical entities are estimated to result in R&D costs of about $800 million for the average new chemical entity that is brought to market.[42] Such high development costs impose a "blockbuster" model on the industry, whereby a drug is marketed to the largest number of patients, within the constraints of the indications approved for the drug. To ensure that a drug's potential is exploited to its maximum in the global market, pharmaceutical companies with insufficient market presence and promotional resources engage in co-promotion and co-marketing partnerships with other pharmaceutical companies.

Many drugs, however, are effective for only a fraction of the treated population, because of the difficulty of predicting individual differences in responses to drugs. New technologies (e.g. genomics) offer the prospect that drugs will be developed for narrowly defined patient populations, with a high probability of efficacy and low side-effects in these target populations. The narrow focus and improved disease understanding is expected to lead to significantly lower development costs, partly because the expensive clinical studies can be conducted on much smaller patient populations. The significantly lower costs of developing these new drugs, in turn, will make the targeting of many small segments economically feasible.[43]

Increasing revenue by identifying "must have" and "delight" features

The choice of which components should be shared across the different new products and which should be product-specific cannot be made on cost grounds alone but must take into account how the customers from the different target segments respond to these components.

A model developed by Noriaki Kano offers a typology of components and associated features based on how customers respond to them.[44] "Must have" features are taken for granted by customers in the product category of interest. Their presence provides no differentiation, but their absence severely compromises the product's prospects. For example, all cholesterol-lowering statin drugs used to be seen as having no severe side-effects. The problems encountered by Bayer as a result of deaths associated with its statin drug Baycol/Lipobay[45] shows the powerful negative impact of violating customers' expectations regarding such "must have" features. "The more (or less) the better" features increase customer preference, but generally with diminishing returns. For example, the more a statin drug reduces the bad cholesterol the better, but the medical community begins debating possible diminishing health benefits when the bad cholesterol is lowered beyond certain levels. Finally, when a new product fulfills needs which customers have difficulty articulating (latent needs) or do not expect to see satisfied, customers experience "delight." Customer response to the pill Viagra, when the only previous medical treatment consisted of an injection in the penis, illustrates such a "delight" response.

When developing new products for different segments of the global market, care must be taken to identify "must have," "the more (or less) the better," and "delight" attributes for each target segment. When product designers are unfamiliar with the target market, the "must have" attributes, which are taken for granted by segment members but unknown by the designers, can pose problems. Classic examples include the missing cup-holders in German luxury cars exported to the United States, or the Ford Taurus, which did not fit in Japanese parking spaces, a "must have" requirement for car registration in Japan.[46] The "must have" and "delight" attributes in one segment may not provoke the same responses in other market segments. For example, automobile navigation systems that identify upcoming traffic jams on the *Autobahn* and automatically suggest alternative routes may delight drivers on the congested arteries of Europe but hardly excite US drivers.[47]

How can developers understand the attributes that cause delight or are essential to consumers in a particular market? To discover the role of various product attributes in market segments with which the new product development team members are unfamiliar, observation of customers in their natural habitat is very useful.[48] The ultimate objective is for team members to immerse themselves in the customer environment so that they see the world with the customers' eyes. For example, to build a shared understanding about European customers, for whom Nissan was developing a new car, the company sent nearly 1,500 employees involved in its planning, design, testing, production, and marketing to Europe to acquire firsthand the taken-for-granted, difficult-to-articulate, tacit knowledge about the European automobile market, motoring culture, and road conditions.[49]

Building a shared knowledge of the customer's world among the key members of the development team is vital, as Whirlpool discovered. An "Asianized" refrigerator model developed at Whirlpool's US headquarters flopped in Asia despite the involvement of Singaporean engineers especially relocated to the United States for this project, because they were not able to share their knowledge effectively with their US colleagues who lacked direct Asian experience. But sharing was not an issue for another "Asianizing" project carried out in Singapore, and which was successful.[50]

Integrating cost and market information

These insights on opportunities to increase revenue or reduce costs need to be brought together into a coherent view of the potential value of the differentiation. Design and manufacturing engineers are often primarily focusing on the costs of responding to the differences between market segments and tend to prefer options that maximize standardization and sharing. Marketing, on the other hand, seeks to match the specific needs of each target segment with specific products and features, but these may sometimes be expensive to design or produce. As emphasized previously, good new product development decision-making requires that both logics – the external market as well as the internal cost-oriented logic – be integrated to arrive at profit-maximizing decisions.

Two methodologies exist that enhance the integration of the two logics:

Quality Function Deployment (QFD) methodology: QFD is a process for individual new product development projects that systematically links the needs of target customers to product features, and product features to production processes.[51] Information about the relative importance of different customer needs, the performance of competing products, and the cost of providing each feature are used to explore the tradeoffs involved in different new product design options. QFD is a valuable tool that provides a framework for organizing many different pieces of information, and for structuring the discussion between the product development team members from different functions.

Product Platform Planning process: This approach is similar to QFD, but focuses on a portfolio of products. While much academic and industry thought has been devoted to managing the development of individual products, the issues involved in coordinating the development of portfolios of new products have received much less attention. Platform planning processes structure the discussion between marketing units that seek to satisfy the specific needs of their target segments and the technological functions that want to make the best use of scarce technological resources. One of the proposed processes consists of the iterative refinement of three interlinked plans: the product plan, which specifies what products will be delivered when to each target segment; the differentiation plan, which specifies how each of the products will be differentiated from the others; and the commonality plan, which defines the common elements across the products.[52] Each iteration assesses the consistency and profit implications of the proposed set of plans, and uses the insights emerging from this to come up with better plans.

Top management involvement in new product portfolio coordination is essential. In many industries, the number and characteristics of the new products that a company offers in the global market are a main determinant of company success. Coordinating the new product development portfolio requires coordination across functional, product line/divisional, and country/regional boundaries. Only top management can provide the overall vision to guide coordination, and the power to resolve the inevitable conflicts that arise during this process.

Conclusions

It used to be thought that only large international or multinational companies were concerned with the global market and, therefore, with developing new products for this market. Companies were believed to go through a progressive internationalization process, whereby they gradually venture outside of their home country market, targeting countries with progressively increasing cultural and psychological distance from the home country market. Recent findings, however, have thrown doubt on this model by providing evidence that some firms aim for the global market from their very birth, so-called "born-global" firms.[53] The development of global products, therefore, is relevant for all firms regardless of their age, size, and prior international history.

Developing new products for the global market requires a fundamental shift from an orientation where new product opportunities are identified and assessed on a country-by-country basis to one where opportunities are perceived and evaluated on a global scale. Analyzing these diverse markets may be more complex, yet the fundamentals remain the same. Companies need to identify benefits that are of value to consumers and then develop products and services to provide those benefits in a profitable way.

Global market segmentation is the main tool for implementing this orientation. Although members of global segments may seek the same key benefits, the greater diversity of the members of globally defined segments may require the development of differentiated products. Consequently, targeting multiple segments of the global market can quickly escalate the complexity and cost of new product programs and hurt profitability. Thus, reconciling the need for responding to the diversity of the global market with the need for husbanding scarce development and production resources constitutes the main challenge of global new product development. Fortunately, methodologies are being developed that help to turn this complex challenge into a manageable task. The essential contribution of these tools consists in organizing information about the market, the technological possibilities, and costs in a way that provides a structure for a rational debate between the different organizational stakeholders to improve outcomes for all.

Notes

1 T. Levitt, "The Globalization of Markets," *Harvard Business Review*, May–June 1983, pp. 92–102.
2 K. Naughton and E. Thornton, "Can Honda Build a World Car?" *Business Week* 38, 44 (September 8, 1997), pp. 100–107.
3 Ibid.
4 S. P. Douglas, "Global Marketing Strategy in the 21st Century: The Challenge," *Japan and the World Economy*, 12 (2000), pp. 381–384.
5 Y. Wind and S. P. Douglas, "International Market Segmentation," *European Journal of Marketing*, 6 (1972), pp. 12–23.
6 P. Kotler, *Marketing Management*, 11th edn. (Upper Saddle River, NJ: Prentice Hall, 2003).
7 G. Hofstede, *Culture's Consequences: International Differences in Work-Related Values* (Beverly Hills, CA: Sage Publications, 1980).
8 M. Kotabe and K. Helsen, *Global Marketing Management Update 2000* (New York: John Wiley & Sons, 1998).
9 Ibid.
10 J.-B. E. M. Steenkamp and F. Ter Hofstede "International Market Segmentation: Issues and Perspectives," *International Journal of Research in Marketing*, 19 (2002), pp. 185–213.
11 M. Wedel and W. A. Kamakura, *Market Segmentation: Conceptual and Methodological Foundations* (Boston, MA: Kluwer, 1998).
12 T. Miller, "Global Segments from 'Strivers' to 'Creatives,'" *Marketing News*, July 20, 1998, p. 11.
13 Steenkamp and Ter Hofstede, "International Market Segmentation."
14 G. L. Urban and J. R. Hauser, *Design and Marketing of New Products*, 2nd edn. (Upper Saddle River, NJ: Prentice Hall, 1993).
15 Steenkamp and Ter Hofstede, "International Market Segmentation."
16 "Global Beer Overview," *Euromonitor* (2002).
17 C. A. Bartlett, *P&G Japan: The SK-II Globalization Project* (Boston: Harvard Business School Press, 2003).

18 F. Ter Hofstede, M. Wedel and J.-B. E. M. Steenkamp, "Identifying Spatial Segments in International Markets," *Marketing Science*, 21 (2002), pp. 160–177.

19 "Global Beer Overview."

20 Y. Moon, *Sony AIBO: The World's First Entertainment Robot* (Boston: Harvard Business School Press, 2002).

21 C. C. Hwee, P. Williamson, and A. De Meyer, *Banyan Tree Resorts & Hotels: Building an International Brand from an Asian Base* (Singapore: INSEAD, 2003).

22 J. K. Johansson, *Global Marketing*, 2nd edn (Boston: McGraw-Hill, 2000).

23 F. ter Hofstede, J.-B. E. M. Steenkamp, and M. Wedel, "International Market Segmentation Based on Consumer–Product Relation," *Journal of Marketing Research*, 36 (February 1999), pp. 1–17.

24 H. R. Moskowitz and S. Rabino, "Sensory Segmentation: An Organizing Principle for International Product Concept Generation," *Journal of Global Marketing*, 8 (1994), pp. 73–93.

25 P. Lindgren, B. Jönsson, A. Redaelli and D. Radice, "Cost-Effectiveness Analysis of Exemestane Compared with Megestrol in Advanced Breast Cancer," *Pharmaeconomics*, 20 (2002), pp. 101–108.

26 K. Maney, "Remember Those 'Iridium's Going to Fail' Jokes? Prepare to Eat Your Hat," *USA Today*, April 9, 2003, p. 3.

27 Johansson, *Global Marketing*.

28 E. Von Hippel, *The Sources of Innovation* (Oxford: Oxford University Press, 1988).

29 H. A. Bolande, "Korea Takes Cellphone to Next Level – With Music and Video Downloads, SK Telecom Rivals Media Companies," *Asian Wall Street Journal* (2003).

30 E. Dahan and J. R. Hauser, "Product Development – Managing a Dispersed Process," in B. Weitz and R. Wensley (eds.), *Handbook of Marketing* (London: Sage Publications, 2002), pp. 178–222.

31 Bartlett, *P&G Japan*.

32 A survey among seven large Japanese corporations covering forty-six diverse product categories suggested that new products were developed with the global market in mind from the start in 76 percent of the categories. H. Takeuchi and M. E. Porter, "Three Roles of International Marketing in Global Strategy," in M. E. Porter (ed.), *Competition in Global Industries* (Boston: Harvard Business School Press, 1986), pp. 111–146.

33 M. E. Porter (ed.), *Competition in Global Industries* (Boston: Harvard Business School Press, 1986); C. A. Bartlett and S. Ghoshal, *Managing Across Borders: The Transnational Solution* (Boston: Harvard Business School Press, 1989).

34 C. A. Bartlett, *Philips versus Matsushita: A New Century, a New Round* (Boston: Harvard Business School Press, 2001).
35 Y. L. Doz, J. Santos, and P. Williamson, *From Global to Metanational* (Boston: Harvard Business School Press, 2001).
36 K. T. Ulrich and S. D. Eppinger, *Product Design and Development*, 2nd edn. (Boston: McGraw-Hill, 2000).
37 The following passage on the use of platforms in the automobile industry is based on P. Wells, "Platforms: Engineering Panacea, Marketing Disaster?" *Journal of Materials Processing Technology*, 115 (2001), pp. 166–170.
38 M. H. Meyer and A. P. Lehnerd, *The Power of Product Platforms* (New York: Free Press, 1997); M. H. Meyer and A. DeTore, "Creating a Platform-Based Approach for Developing New Services," *Journal of Product Innovation Management*, 18 (2001), pp. 188–204; M. H. Meyer and D. Dalal, "Managing Platform Architectures and Manufacturing Processes for Nonassembled Products," *Journal of Product Innovation Management*, 19 (2002), pp. 277–293.
39 D. Robertson and K. T. Ulrich, "Planning for Product Platforms", *Sloan Management Review*, Summer 1998, pp. 19–31; Wells, "Platforms."
40 Robertson and Ulrich, "Planning for Product Platforms."
41 P. Wells, "Platforms."
42 J. A. DiMasi, R. W. Hansen, and H. G. Grabowski, "The Price of Innovation: New Estimates of Drug Development Cost," *Journal of Health Economics*, 22 (2003), pp. 151–185.
43 S. Arlington, S. Barnett, S. Hughes, and J. Palo, *Pharma 2010: The Threshold of Innovation* (Somers, NY: IBM Business Consulting Services, 2002).
44 The discussion of the Kano model follows Dahan and Hauser, "Product Development."
45 R. Angelmar, *Lipitor (B)* (Paris: INSEAD, 2002).
46 "Success Continues to Elude US Car Makers in Japan," *Asian Wall Street Journal*, 1, 7 (1997).
47 J. McDowell, "The Art of Global Marketing: Finding the Right Balance Between Global Strategy and Local Execution," *The Advertiser* (June 2002).
48 D. Leonard and J. F. Rayport, "Spark Innovation Through Empathic Design," *Harvard Business Review*, November–December 1997, pp. 102–113. Observational and other research methods for international marketing research are discussed in C. S. Craig and S. P. Douglas, *International Marketing Research*, 2nd edn. (New York: John Wiley & Sons, 2000).

49 I. Nonaka and H. Takeuchi, *The Knowledge-Creating Company* (Oxford: Oxford University Press, 1995).
50 Doz, Santos, and Williamson, *From Global to Metanational.*
51 See Dahan and Hauser, "Product Development" for a more complete discussion of QFD and references.
52 Robertson and Ulrich, "Planning for Product Platforms."
53 T. K. Madsen and P. Servais, "The Internationalization of Born Globals: An Evolutionary Process?" *International Business Review*, 6 (1997), pp. 561–583.

8 | Managing brands in global markets

GEORGE S. DAY DAVID J. REIBSTEIN
Wharton School

Should you create a uniform global brand or a set of independent local brands? While the world has moved closer to the idea of monolithic global brands envisioned by Ted Levitt more than two decades ago, not all brands have moved in that direction nor is it likely that they will. Some companies such as Coca-Cola or Starbucks have developed valuable global brands. Other companies such as Campbell Soup have many brands that are unique to local markets. Many companies such as Procter & Gamble, Unilever, or Toyota have a diverse mix of global and local brands. The authors point out that this diversity of approaches is the result of competing forces affecting branding strategy. The forces of increasing homogenization of customer requirements, globalizing competitors, and global marketing effectiveness are driving increased globalization; however, inherent market differences, entrenched local brands, growing channel power, and opposition to global brands are pushing companies toward local identity and adaptation. Decisions to use global and local brands are complex and depend upon a mix of factors, including products, industry, cultures, and competition. The authors discuss choices about developing brands along this spectrum and also examine the key strategies for managing brands globally using coordinating mechanisms that include global business teams, research-based brand planning processes, and metrics and incentives for encouraging collaboration.

A s mentioned in the previous chapter, in 1983 Ted Levitt took a strong and controversial position – that "the globalization of markets is at hand." He went on to forecast:

With (globalization), the multinational commercial world nears its end, and so does the multinational corporation. The multinational corporation and the global corporation are not the same thing. The multinational corporation operates in a number of countries, and adjusts its products and practices in each – at high relative cost. The global corporation operates with resolute constancy – at low relative cost – as if the entire world (or major regions of it) were a single entity: it sells things in the same way everywhere.

Implicit in Levitt's vision was the eventual dominance of global brands. These are brands with consistent names, identities, positioning, and target markets in every country. Twenty years later, what can we say about his vision? Has it come to pass – and if not, why not? How are global companies managing their portfolios of brands?

This chapter draws on twenty years of effort to apply Levitt's dictates. Our overall conclusion is that there are very few truly global brands, and that the forces promoting globalization and standardization are being blunted by countervailing forces that encourage adaptation and local identity. To make our case we will begin by reviewing the benefits of strong brands to the firm and to customers. This sets the stage for an analysis of global brands: what are their common features? What kinds of markets support them? And who are some of the leaders? We then switch perspectives and look at the strategies that global companies are following, and how they are coping with the countervailing forces. Finally, we will explore how global companies are managing their brands, and how organizational innovations are facilitating the coordination process.

A tale of two global brands

Developing brands for global markets is far more complex and nuanced a process than is reflected in Levitt's statement of the relentless progress toward globalization. The stories of the distinctive paths of two global brands, Unilever and MTV, illustrate some of the challenges and the richness of the solutions to this problem developed by global firms.

Unilever: rationalizing a brand portfolio[1]

Unilever barely grew during the 1990s, largely because its global marketing efforts and strategic resources were diffused over a bulky portfolio of 1,600 brands in more than fifty countries. This was a highly skewed portfolio, with 3 percent of the brands providing 63 percent of the revenues. This led Unilever to put brand rationalization at the center of a new growth initiative launched in February 2002. The objective was to boost the overall growth rate by drastically shrinking its portfolio to 400 brands, representing around 200 brand positionings, thereby allowing the company to concentrate resources on fewer brands. By the end of 2002, Unilever was halfway through the rationalization and was seeing the benefits of sales growth of 4.5 percent per year in the top brands which made up 90 percent of sales.

Unilever combined global, regional, and local branding strategies by placing the 400 core brands into three categories:

(1) *International brands* such as Dove, Lipton, and Magnum which have universal appeal to consumers in many countries, enabling common brand positioning and advertising campaigns.

(2) *Regional brands* that seek consistent global positioning but have different names in different countries, such as Flora spread in the UK, yet is sold under the Becel brand in Germany.

(3) *Local jewels* with strong and often unique positions in one country, such as Wishbone salad dressing in the United States and Persil detergent in the UK.

These brands were selected on the basis of:

(1) potential for growth – such as Bertolli, which began as an olive oil and has been extended to sauces and spreads;

(2) scale in terms of sales volume share and premium price potential to sustain competitive levels of investment; and

(3) brand power, reflecting the potential to be dominant in the market – a brand that retailers must have on their shelves to create traffic into the store.

The country brand teams were deeply involved in the process of selecting the core brands. The brands outside the core were either harvested for cash flow, de-listed, sold, or moved into a core brand. The freed-up resources could be used to drive growth of core global brands such as Dove (see box on "Leveraging an international brand").

MTV: adapting to local realities

MTV (Music Television Networks), a 24-hour music network that targets 16- to 34-year-old television viewers around the world, might look like the ideal candidate for the kind of uniform global branding Levitt foresaw. While MTV created a strong global brand identity, it took care to adapt its image and content to local markets. MTV is widely regarded as both the voice of American youth and an effective medium for reaching the lucrative youth market. By positioning itself as an aspirational brand, MTV attracts a loyal viewer base, and its ability to sense and respond to trends keeps the network close to its market.[2]

The network entered Europe in 1987 with pan-regional programming in English. Its content was freely available to local cable TV operators, with all revenues coming from advertising. By the early nineties, advertisers were pressing for localized content, either because they could not afford pan-European coverage, their products were only available locally, or they were not uniformly branded in all countries. This attracted strong local competitors in most markets, such as VIVA in Germany and MCM in France.

Leveraging an international brand

A classic example of the benefits of massing resources behind a few strong global brands is Dove, which began as a bar soap and is now extended to shampoo, body wash, and deodorants. This power brand began as a beauty bar, touting an extreme moisturizing quality. This claim was based on clinical evidence that Dove dried and irritated skin less than competitive soaps. This was especially appealing to the target segment of 35–50-year-old women who wanted to care for their skin. The brand message appealed broadly and eventually Unilever sold the brand in seventy-three countries with global sales of $800 million.

By 1999 the brand was aging. Competitors had caught up as the patents on Dove expired. The Olay beauty bar and body wash products were challenging Dove in the core moisturizing claim. In response, Dove was repositioned as a master brand that encompassed daily skin care, with three core elements: moisturizing, mildness, and gentleness, and a feminine positioning. Specific product extensions addressed consumer preferences for formulations that hydrate (body wash), provide value-added nutrients, cleanse, and promote youthfulness. By shifting benefits from "won't dry your skin like soap" to "helps you look and feel your best," and changing the attributes from "bar containing $\frac{1}{4}$ moisturizing cream" to a range of products "where everything works noticeably better for you," Unilever opened the way for new non-soap products such as deodorants, lip balms, moisturizing lotions, and sun care.

The Dove brand has benefited from having significant resources available to drive innovation that were gained through cost savings achieved through streamlining the brand portfolio. The payoff is the ability to grow at a sustained 5 to 6 percent, which is no mean feat in an intensely competitive and maturing product category.

By the mid-nineties growth had stalled, forcing a move to localized programming with a mix of common US content and artists, and local programming. Today MTV Europe (MTVE) has a presence in forty-one countries with multiple languages and formats and about half local music programming.

Local adaptation was enabled by (1) the recognition that the local advertising sales market was vastly bigger than the pan-European market, (2) the emergence of new technology and satellite capacity to enable separate satellite feeds to each country, and (3) a transfer of organizational power from a centralized headquarters in London out to the local markets. These moves paid big dividends: between 1997 and 2001, MTVE expanded its reach from 57.4 million to 100 million households. Ironically, given the concentrated investment in localization, advertisers cited MTV's pan-regional coverage as one of the key advantages that local advertisers could not match. Why did MTV not create a portfolio of independent local brands? Its strategy allowed it to address local content and advertising concerns, but still leverage a powerful global brand identity. The true key to success was to sustain the essence of the brand – as the voice of a generation, rebellious, anti-establishment, and creative, creating a global community of youth.

Both competitive opportunities and internal strengths – such as Unilever's local jewels – and external competitive threats – such as MTV's rivals – shape branding strategy. These and other forces, as discussed below, move the company toward more complex and localized branding at the same time that forces of globalization are pushing in the direction of Levitt's vision. By understanding the nature of these forces, managers can develop branding strategies that preserve their identities, yet address the realities of local markets.

The benefits of strong brands

What is the value of brands? A brand is an identifying name or symbol that distinguishes one maker from another and signals the source of the product. Branding with trademarks was originally used by trade guides in medieval Europe to assure the customers of the quality of their purchases and protect the producers from imitators. Brands build their meaning and value over time. Thus, livestock has long been branded to indicate ownership, in the same way as lobster pots are still "labeled" today. As the ranchers' customers started to learn that one rancher did a better job than others of raising his cattle, producing healthy, meatier beef, the brand started to have meaning in the marketplace.

For the consumer, a brand acts as a surrogate and a summary measure for all the attributes of a brand. Even in products as commoditized as those of the agricultural industry, we now see branding widely utilized as a way to designate the differences between one supplier and the next, indicating the distinctions that may not even be visible to the eye – witness, Perdue chickens, Perrier water, C&H Sugar, Dole bananas, Sunkist oranges, Star-Kist tuna, and now Starbucks coffee – none of which are even processed. The brand communicates a series of experiences, just like the consumer has experienced in the past. For future purchases, the evaluation process becomes simpler, as the brand name summarizes the set of product/service attributes for the buyer.

The companies using the brands also benefit in many ways, including:

(1) *Improving the efficiency of marketing:* A brand communicates many ideas and makes line extensions easier.

(2) *Intensifying customer loyalty:* Since the instant brand recognition reduces the choice evaluation and search process for the customer, the result is that well-known brand names increase customer loyalty levels.

(3) *Improving leverage with the trade:* Distributors are much more likely to accept a brand that is well known with already built-in demand than one that is totally new to the market.

(4) *Creating a true asset for the firm:* A brand name can be a strategic asset for the firm. Customers are willing to pay a premium for products with strong brands, as shown in Figure 8.1 (which illustrates the distribution for a brand where 68 percent of the customers are willing to pay a premium over the leading competitor). In the UK, accounting practice has allowed for showing the brand as an asset on the balance sheet. More recently, FASB, in the United States, has also said they will consider the brand being listed as an intangible asset, although finding the right measures is still a topic of intense discussion (see box on "Valuing brands").

As firms expand the markets they serve and the geography they cover, it is quite natural to use the brand name that has been established

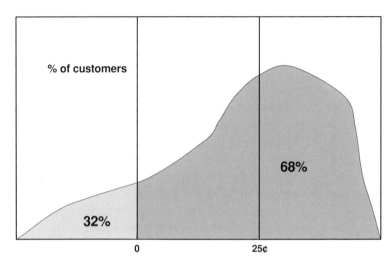

Figure 8.1. Distribution of price premium for a strong brand.

and accrued value. As the brand is stretched more thinly over broader markets and wider ranges of products, decisions about brands become more complex. What is the right branding strategy or portfolio of brands that will provide the most value to the company and allow it to achieve its strategic objectives?

Valuing brands

What's the value of a brand to a company? In general terms, the company benefits from a strong brand through improving the efficiency of marketing, intensifying customer loyalty, and improving leverage with the trade. A well-established brand name can be a strategic asset and a source of sustainable competitive advantage. Whereas competition can often match or respond to changes in pricing or features, or other marketing moves, it is difficult to respond to a strong brand. Measuring the precise value of a brand, however, is still a challenge. There are a variety of measurement approaches, including looking at contributions to stock price or the value that consumers place on the brand.

In some sense, the true value of a brand is not known until the company is sold, and even then separating the two is not always an easy task. An exception was the case of the sale of the Rolls Royce Company, in which Volkswagen purchased the physical assets of the firm, including plant and equipment, but BMW, in a magnificent coup, separately purchased the brand name for only a little over $60 million.[3] It is rare to have even this much clarity about the true value of a brand.

There are numerous approaches that have been used to value a brand without selling the firm. One is to look at the value consumers place on the brand through choice modeling or conjoint measurement. In this approach, consumers are given the task of choosing between varying sets of attributes, one being price and another brand. The procedure computes a part-worth/weight for each of the attributes. As such, it is possible to assess the value consumers place on the brand relative to competitors' products or services, and what additional price they may be willing to pay for a branded offering. Firms can use this information to determine whether to charge a premium or to lower price to capture more market share.

Another approach to valuing the brand is to look at the overall market value of the firm and subtract the value of tangible assets. The remaining value presumably comes from intangible assets, including the brand. How much is due to the brand? In a conjoint fashion, companies then assess the role of the brand to estimate the portion of the intangible earnings attributable to the brand. The riskiness of the brand (discount rate) is determined through a brand strength composite score based on an assessment of the brand and is applied across a projection of the forecast future brand revenue. Using this approach, Interbrand annually publishes the value of the leading brands across the globe, as shown in Table 8.1.

There is growing awareness of brand value and an increasing set of strategies for quantifying it. (The ones discussed above are just a few of the many approaches to valuing brands.) While these tools represent important steps forward, this is still clearly not an exact science. Assessing the value of the brand across different global markets and using quantitative measures to help assess whether to use a global brand or a local brand in entering a specific market are even more complex challenges. These initial approaches to assessing brand value offer insights into how these questions might begin to be addressed.

The emergence of global brands

As the brand moved from the hides of livestock to packages and advertising in fluid international markets supported by global media, some global corporations have created tremendous value by establishing strong global brands (see Table 8.1).

Table 8.1. *Value of global brands*

Brand	Value (billion $)
1. Coca-Cola	70.45
2. Microsoft	65.17
3. IBM	51.77
4. GE	42.34
5. Intel	31.11
6. Nokia	29.44
7. Disney	28.04
8. McDonald's	24.70
9. Marlboro	22.18
10. Mercedes	21.37

Source: Estimates by Interbrand, 2003.

When is a global brand most likely to work well? These outstanding global brands share many common features:
(1) they have a consistent name, that is easy to pronounce in all markets;
(2) company sales are globally balanced, and there is no truly dominant market;
(3) the essence and positioning of the brand is the same in all markets and cultures;
(4) they address the same customer needs, or the same target segment, in every market; and
(5) there is a high degree of similarity in execution (price, packaging, advertising, etc.) across countries.
In some ways, these large brands show the kind of "resolute constancy" that Levitt envisioned. Few brands, however, fully satisfy all these criteria. The result is a very wide spectrum of branding strategies from the development of global brands to the creation of very localized strategies.

In general, each of the global brands remains true to its target market regardless of which country they are in, serving the same set of basic needs. Disney represents family entertainment in all parts of the world, and Intel still represents the latest chip technology for computer OEMs throughout the world.

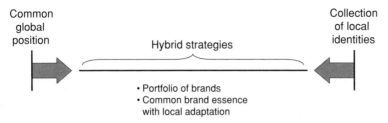

Figure 8.2. Brand strategy spectrum.

A branding continuum

Of course, not all global firms accomplish all of these steps completely. On the contrary, as discussed, they may find it necessary to modify what they do to the local conditions. We do recognize that there is a continuum covering the extent to which brands are global. As shown in Figure 8.2, we can position firms according to the degree to which they are currently global brands.

For example, in consumer goods, companies such as Coca-Cola, Procter & Gamble, and Nike, have all been well regarded as firms that have a global presence. Coca-Cola and Nike have done so with global brands, and a very firm standardization of their products and positioning in every country in which they operate. Procter & Gamble has elected to have different brands unique to individual countries, together with a handful of common brands. Other companies, such as Campbell Soup, have well-known brands, almost all unique to their specific markets. Their belief is that eating habits are very geographically specific and require local brands. The major exception to this rule is Godiva chocolate. Perhaps chocolate is a universal taste.

Market segmentation often leads to the creation of a portfolio of global and local brands. The high-end premium brands are quite the same throughout the world, yet each of the producers has developed unique models and brands for local markets, particularly at the low end. So, while automotive brands look very global in their nature, there are degrees of localization of products (such as right-hand steering wheels in Japan) and brands. There are numerous cases where the company name is used, but in other cases there are sub-brands that might be unique to a specific country. As an example, Toyota is a well-recognized brand name throughout the world, and some of the Toyota brands are also used globally, such as Lexus. On the other hand, they also have brands such as Crown, which has been one of the highest-selling models in Japan, and yet has never been offered under that name outside Asia. Similarly, Toyota's "semi bonnet" model is available exclusively in Europe and Taiwan, and the Spacio uniquely offered in Europe, Turkey, and Hong Kong, while the Avalon is not available in Europe, Africa, and most of Europe. Toyota and Lexus are the umbrella brands which are truly global and used consistently throughout the world.

Brands such as Starbucks, IBM, British Airways, Heineken, GE, Siemens, Marlborough, Intel, Prozac, Tagamet, and Viagra are probably the most global. They meet all five of the described criteria. Others, such as Nike, Nestlé, Wal-Mart, and Swatch, are all clearly global firms, but are not as global in their branding. Nike stresses different sports in different parts of the world. In 2002, in the context of the World Cup tournament, Nike, outside of the United States, ran local "Scorpion" logo tournaments all centered around football (the non-American variety). Whirlpool, similarly to Toyota, has both global brands, such as Whirlpool, and many local brands, such as Brastemp and Consul in Brazil, and Inglis and Lavatrici in Europe. Similarly, Nestlé offers Kit Kat in the United States and the Lion bar in Germany, while several products are sold globally under the Nestlé name. Swatch, while offering its products globally, is positioned differently – with the Swatch watch being perceived as a fashion accessory in many parts of Europe, while being viewed more as a teen item in much of the United States.

It should be noted that the branding strategy is not a static position, but a dynamic one, as firms strive to move along the continuum – not necessarily always to become more global. Some companies have had to reshape their brands as they have moved into broader markets. Wal-Mart's strong "made in America" positioning in the United States was dropped in both there and outside as it increasingly concentrated on non-US markets. While it still uses a common brand around the world, Wal-Mart allows for some local adjustment of the inventory stocked to the local market they are serving. So, while the positioning remains the same – a hypermarket with national brands and low prices – the inventory within each outlet may vary.

Brand strategies for globalizing companies

What are the factors driving companies into the arms of Levitt or away from his view of uniform global brands? The two extremes of the brand strategy spectrum in Figure 8.2 are increasingly seen as important outliers, but exceptions nevertheless to a general pattern of convergence toward a hybrid or global approach. We resist calling this a compromise position, for that implies vacillation and uncertainty. Think instead of an informed balancing of forces that favor global branding with countervailing forces that favor local identity and adaptation. The resulting hybrid strategy is exemplified by firms holding a portfolio of brands. Within the portfolio is a core set of regional or global brands, each with a common essence that is adapted to local market conditions, plus some strong country brands. The aim is to achieve *global brand leadership*,[4] based on coordinated management of each of the brands in the portfolio.

The remainder of this section brings together what has been learned about the forces that facilitate or inhibit the globalization of brands. As firms have become more adroit at balancing these forces, they have also learned how to manage complex brand portfolios. These lessons are the basis for the concluding section of this chapter.

Forces favoring global brands

These forces reflect the broader drivers of globalization reviewed in the introduction to this book. Those mattering most to brand strategies are the homogenization of customer requirements, the emergence of global competitors, and the cost advantages from global marketing efficiencies. But within these broad forces there are nuances that complicate the strategic choices.

Increasing homogenization of customer requirements
This is the driving force singled out most often as the reason markets are behaving globally. This is especially evident in preferences for up-market consumer goods such as Prada, Mont Blanc, and Burberry, that are becoming more similar as better education, higher discretionary incomes, wider communication, and global travel create international social groups whose members have comparable lifestyles. The

globalness of these markets is itself a signal of quality, expertise, and authority[5] that enables the buyer to show cosmopolitan taste. Products with a purely functional benefit, such as diapers, also seem to travel easily across borders. This homogenization is itself due to many forces, especially the ubiquity of media and entertainment.

The forces of homogenization *across* countries may also create more segments within each country, as lifestyles and incomes diverge. This opens up two segment possibilities with important implications for brand and marketing strategies. The first is the *universal* segment with essentially the same needs in each country. These customers are likely to be wealthy, mobile, and broadly informed. Thus, buyers of BMW autos in Japan, Germany, and Brazil all resonate the same way to the brand promise of "engineered for performance." Alternatively, the market could evolve toward *diverse* segments, where a common product can be sold only if it is positioned differently in each country. The latest Canon digital cameras target young replacement buyers in Japan, affluent first-time buyers in the United States, and older, more technologically sophisticated buyers in Germany.

Large corporate customers for business-to-business purchases tend to be global themselves, so companies selling to them often establish global brands. For technology and electronics equipment and other business-to-business markets, customers are global, making it easy for companies such as Microsoft, GE, Siemens, Philips, Intel, and Hitachi to create well-established global brands.

In some cases, uniformity of experience is at the core of the offering to customers. Starbucks believes very strongly that the products offered in each of their outlets, regardless of what part of the world they are in, must be identical. This includes the store layout, the product offered, and service training. Shell, with much less employee training – in fact, most of their service stations are not company-owned – is still offering products that are universal. Service firms, such as FedEx and British Airways, use their brands to convey consistent messages worldwide about service, while Disney's brand offers visitors in France or Japan a quintessential US experience (although even here there is some tailoring of the offering, if not the brand). Or, to take an example from another part of the world, Swedish company Absolut has used a uniform brand for its vodka in all parts of the world and has been very effective in distinguishing its colorless product from other offerings in what had once been essentially a commodity market.

Globalizing competitors

Many firms with diverse local brands and autonomous country operations have been forced toward greater standardization by the moves
of competitors. The trigger is the realization that a globally coordinated competitor is using the financial resources from one part of the
world to cross-subsidize a competitive battle in another. This financial advantage can usually be traced to an overall cost advantage
gained through standardization plus a higher price in a less competitive
market.

Even markets that prize domestic adaptation may evolve toward a
global approach if one competitor successfully forces the issue. The
major appliance market was long fragmented by differences in standards, preferences for energy source, size of kitchens, and cooking
and cleaning habits. At one point in the sixties, Electrolux even sold
the North American rights to its name. Ironically, it was Swedish-
based Electrolux that later led the global consolidation of the industry which forced the large US domestic firms such as Whirlpool and
GE to counter-attack by acquiring European and South American
brands. After becoming the world's largest appliance maker in 2000,
Electrolux bought its name back in the United States, in order
to double-brand the "Frigidaire-Electrolux," and also launch an
Electrolux-only branded line. The long-run intention is that Electrolux
will be the sole global brand heading a portfolio of strong regional or
country brands.

Improving global marketing effectiveness

When a brand can offer a promise that works in most markets, it can
achieve cost efficiencies and higher impact. A single campaign for IBM,
even when adapted to different languages, costs much less than it would
to create separate campaigns independently for each market. The aim
of the campaign is to promote a unifying IBM brand promise, "leading
the invention of technology and application to business problems,"
with one logo and one identity. By using a single advertising agency
worldwide, rather than spreading business across dozens of agencies,
they demand and get access to the very best creative talent, and obtain
more effective campaigns. Further cost efficiencies are gained through
cross-market exposure from media spillover and repeated exposure to
traveling business people.

Forces favoring local identity and adaptation

Countervailing pressures that challenge the basic premises of global advocates have slowed the march toward global brands and make the hybrid approach more appealing. Already some firms have found they overshot in their quest for a global identity and have retreated. As mentioned earlier in this chapter, Procter & Gamble (P&G) had historically used different brand names in different parts of the world for some categories. In an effort to globalize P&G's brands in 1999, CEO Durk Jager decided most products should be sold under the same name in all countries. This meant changing the name of P&G's dishwashing liquid in Germany from Fairy to Dawn, which was the name under which it was sold in the United States. This hurt their sales badly since German consumers did not know what the new name meant, and entrenched competitors took full advantage of the situation.[6]

We see four specific countervailing forces to be reckoned with, although their consequences vary by market.

Inherent market differences

One revisionist point of view is that "most often the need for global brands is in the mind of the producer, not the mind of the consumer."[7] The argument is that consumers are not actually converging toward common tastes, needs, and values, and existing differences are sustained by country-to-country variations in income, stage in the product life cycle, and competitive environment.

Evidence for sustained market differences comes from the experience of KFC which now has 5,000 US restaurants and another 6,000 abroad in eighty countries. They have learned they cannot open restaurants based on the US model and expect success in most of these countries. They have become adept at satisfying local tastes and negotiating changing cultural climates. In Japan, for instance, KFC sells tempura crispy strips, but in Holland they feature potato-and-onion croquettes. In France, pastries are sold alongside the chicken. In China, where KFC has more than 600 restaurants, the chicken gets spicier the farther inland you travel.[8]

What works for KFC will not necessarily apply to other products that are not so influenced by idiosyncratic food tastes and preferences. One study found that consumers would prefer a global brand because of its overt globalness if it is seen as providing higher quality – especially in markets where quality is hard to ascertain.[9] Globalness also helps when aspirational meanings and status are relevant, or the target segments are susceptible to reference groups.

Even if the brand's message is similar in different parts of the world, the brand's value to consumers may differ from one part of the world to the other because it is measured relative to other competitors. Wal-Mart, for example, is viewed as offering great "value" in many parts of the world, but in China, for example, many of the national brands that they carry and the food items stocked are not necessarily viewed as having the best price or being the freshest, since local providers can offer significantly lower costs for local produce.

Entrenched local brands

Global firms eventually hit a ceiling on the size of the segment in any country-market that is willing to buy global brands rather than local brands. This segment size varies considerably by country and product category, but it is usually well short of the total market. The ceiling depends on consumer resistance to paying a price premium for global brands, the stability of their purchasing requirements, and the strength of the local brands.

Conditions favoring local brands against an entry by a global brand are:

(1) unique needs within a market, such that a global solution misses the mark;
(2) low frequency of purchase, so brand equity passes from one generation to another through family tradition;
(3) low importance of advertising, which makes it harder for a global attacker to change loyalty patterns, or outspend local brands to gain distribution;
(4) high importance of salesforce relationships;
(5) a fragmented market where the buyers prefer to work with local operators or brands that cater to their particular needs; and
(6) there are few economies of scale in marketing, manufacturing, or sourcing, so the cost advantage of global firms is narrowed.[10]

When there are also strong local norms, local trade restrictions, and nationalistic sentiments, the global firm trying to penetrate a market where local brands are entrenched should suppress its global instincts and add the local brand to its portfolio. The new parent can then rejuvenate the local brand with R&D investments, transfer of best practices, and product innovation to protect their investment without disturbing the brand essence. The aim should be to achieve local leadership.

Growing channel power

One trend that is seemingly irreversible and ubiquitous in developed markets is the increasing concentration of retail buying power and the propensity to expand globally. Tesco, the leading UK grocer, has 42 percent of its floorspace outside the UK. In one way, this is beneficial to global brands which can serve multi-country accounts and have the sophistication to meet their complex information technology requirements. Thus, Henkel estimates that euro accounts represent 50 percent of its turnover. Yet, this same force eventually constrains global brands, owing to the adverse effects of heightened price sensitivity or buyer power by the mega retailer and greater private label activity.

Criticism of global brands

While the home country image might help a company like Starbucks, at other times it can become a liability as the brand develops or the political environment changes. Major brands have been the target of protests by groups opposed to globalization. The book *No Logo* became a focal point of the anti-globalization movement by implicating global brands and excessive corporate power as primary contributors to global poverty and economic exclusion.[11] When the book came out in 1999, it both reflected and accentuated the strength of the anti-sweatshop movement. High-profile logos such as Nike, Levi, McDonald's, Shell, and Disney became the simplifying symbols of exploitative labor practices, environmental abuses, corrupt investments, and a host of complaints about homogenization of culture and damage to local enterprises.

As the targeted companies responded with codes of conduct, improved labor practices, and other accommodations, the wrath of protesters has been deflected to other targets. But it was a wake-up call that heightened the sensitivity of global executives to the risks of high-profile brands (and especially of brands with strong US identities in the wake of the 9/11 tragedy). With this sensitivity, there has been a greater willingness to adopt a local coloration. Some have repositioned themselves, in the same way that BP-Amoco has tried to become known as an environmentally friendly energy provider.

Managing the brand strategy

If the objective is to achieve global brand leadership with a portfolio of strong brands, where should the company place itself on the spectrum of branding strategies? How can the tension between the competing desires for global standardization and for tailoring to local conditions be reconciled? This raises further questions about the coordinating and motivating mechanisms to get product managers, country managers, and other functions to work together: how will information be shared? What metrics and incentives are needed? And, how is the organization to be structured? As discussed at the opening of this chapter, Unilever and MTV converged on hybrid strategies from opposite ends of the spectrum. These strategies are not necessarily decided in advance and are often discovered through experimentation, research, and collaboration among different parts of the business worldwide.

How do companies coordinate these brand strategies? There is a myriad of organizational mechanisms that globalizing organizations can use to coordinate the strategies of individual brands and improve the allocation of resources across the brand portfolio. Success comes when there is:

(1) open sharing of best practices and insights;
(2) clear-cut managerial responsibility and accountability for brands to exploit scale benefits and combat local biases; and
(3) synchronized brand strategies that aggressively seek global leadership.

Coordinating mechanisms

Three of the principal mechanisms for achieving these aspirations are (1) global business teams, (2) research-based brand planning processes, and (3) metrics and incentives for encouraging collaboration.

Global business teams
Possibly the best coordinating tool is the cross-border team of individuals of different nationalities, working in different cultures, businesses, and functions, who come together to manage the brand portfolio.

However, it is hard to find the right balance of global efficiency and local sensitivity.

A popular solution in the nineties was to force the issue by creating global business units or divisions, thereby diminishing the country manager's role. Procter & Gamble, for example, handed all strategic questions about brands to new global divisions. Similarly, Dow Chemical created global businesses with responsibility for capital investments and market development. Visa did not go quite as far, centralizing only brand, risk, and interoperability issues, and leaving everything else to regional operations.

But any organization is a balancing of numerous contending forces, and it is easy to go too far in one direction. Thus, there is always a tension between staying flexible with small units while achieving economies of scale, facilitating coordination while cutting unproductive activities, and developing deep functional expertise rather than subordinating functions to process teams. Thus, as companies became more centralized, the country managers resisted the elimination and downgrading of their brands, and fought for a more significant role.[12] In response, firms have given more responsibility back to local managers within a complex matrix structure.

Procter & Gamble, for example, begins by differentiating high-income from low-income markets. In richer countries, the global business has responsibility for resource allocation and adapting the brand essence. But in poorer regions – where individual markets are less familiar and tougher to manage – the country manager has more clout. There are many variations on this theme, depending on the product. With shampoos, where consumers use the same product the same way in most of the world, the global business unit has greater influence. With other products such as laundry detergents, where local habits and competitive conditions vary more, the balance of the brand-building responsibility shifts from the global or regional division to country teams.

While global business teams are preferred for protecting and reinforcing the brand, they are not a panacea. All the problems of domestic teams are accentuated by geographic dispersion and language problems – misalignment of the goals of the members, a dearth of necessary market knowledge, and lack of clarity regarding objectives.[13] Many of these problems can be handled if there is a strong team leader, good communication, and a common brand-building process in place.

To ensure consistency of brand meaning and to extract potential economies of scale, some firms are supplementing the global business teams with global brand managers, or with stewards who work with teams of global brand managers.[14] This only works if those with brand responsibility have the requisite authority. One approach is to clearly distinguish those activities that must absolutely be globally standardized (such as the logo or the look and feel of the design) from those that are adaptable (the advertising strategy can be tailored to the local market as long as the common ad theme is used) or completely discretionary.

Research-based brand planning processes
A strong planning process balances top-down guidance that realistically challenges the brand or business team and ensures resources are available, with bottom-up inputs on specific market issues and strategy alternatives, and a flexible and adaptable calendar to guide the steps in the process.[15]

It is important to have a consistent plan framework for each market and product so all brand-building plans and presentations cover the same issues, use the same vocabulary, and have similar structures. The aim is not to have similar plans for each market – for this is where the art of adaptation is exercised – but to facilitate strategic thinking and nurture the essence of the brand. The appropriate structure depends on the culture and heritage of the firm as well as the realities of the market. What suits Guinness beer, that is distributed through intermediaries in 121 countries, would not work for an office products company with a portfolio of master and sub-brands sold through a mix of direct and retail accounts. None the less, the brand planning process for both companies will have a situation analysis, specify the brand essence and critical points of difference, and lay out the specifics of the brand-building programs.

An effective brand planning process also encourages – and even demands – the detection, capture, and sharing of market insights and best practices. A necessary condition is a deep grounding in research in every context in which the brand is perceived and relevant. Levi's does ongoing tracking with a common methodology to see whether local adaptations are required to serve the target segment of 15- to 19-year-old males. The brand has a distinct personality as original, masculine, youthful, rebellious, and American. It takes considerable care to stay true to that personality without conflicting with the local culture. Thus, in Japan, where rebellion is frowned on, that aspect of the personality is not emphasized.

Metrics and incentives for encouraging collaboration

Many companies today are moving to the use of "executive dashboards." This is a way to capture the overall standing of the business. It starts specifying the key performance measures, and then proceeds to identify the key drivers of the business. One of the important benefits of such a system is that it is very useful for articulating throughout the organization the key elements executives should be trying to affect. For large dispersed organizations, the dashboard is an excellent way to communicate the objects, and the status in each of the various businesses and the various parts of the world.

Most dashboards would have sales as one of the performance metrics, and would identify a set of drivers. One of the drivers of sales will be the brand's equity. This way the firm can continually monitor the health of the brand in the various parts of the world. The dashboard is an excellent way to gain collaboration on objectives, and to convey a sense of what is working in one part of the world that might be tried in others.

Conclusions

The saying, "All generalizations – including this one – are false," is especially apt when decoding patterns in the brand strategies followed by companies that are globalizing. One can find examples at every point along a spectrum from a "collection of local identities" at one end to a "common global position" at the other.

True global brands are relatively rare, yet there is no question we have been moving in the direction of Levitt's vision over the past twenty years, driven by the forces discussed above. On the other hand, with the counterbalancing forces leading to localization, it seems very unlikely that we will ever live entirely in the world of homogeneous brands envisioned by Levitt. Instead, companies will develop complex portfolios of brands that are carefully tailored to their markets, products, and competitive environment.

Being a global brand should not be an objective. As discussed, there are various levels of being truly global. It is not always achievable, nor desirable, to go the full extent, as some form of local adaptation may be necessary, either in the product/service that is offered or in the positioning relative to competition. This branding strategy also will change over time, influenced by shifts in the environment, moves by rivals, or the company's own strategies. By carefully examining the factors discussed in this chapter, managers can develop dynamic solutions to these changes and design the best set of branding strategies for their particular strategic challenges.

Notes

1 Sources include http:// www.unilever.com/; Unilever 1999 Annual Report, *Stewarding the Brand for Profitable Growth*, Washington, DC: Corporate Executive Board, 2001; C. McCarthy, C. Noguerra, G. Scola, and G. Sheen, "Dove: Building Brand Equity through a Brand Extension Strategy," unpublished paper, Wharton School, University of Pennsylvania, 2002; and C. Bittar, "Dove's Key Softening Agents," *Brandweek*, October 15, 2001, pp. M32–36.
2 Sources include K. Capell, *et al.*, "MTV's World," *Business Week*, February 18, 2002, pp. 81–85; R. Baird, "MTV Chief Faces Euro Challenge," *Marketing Week*, April 20, 1999, pp. 14–16; T. Duffy, "Since Its London Birth, MTV Europe's Empire Has Taken the Continent," *Billboard*, 109 (September 13, 1997), p. 55; Gordon Masson, "MTV Availability Reaches 100 Million Mark in Europe Enhanced Title," *Billboard*, 113 (July 21, 2001), pp. 10–12; and M.-L. Farmakides, S. J. Gunter, and L. Manus, "Going Global: MTV's Expansion into Europe," unpublished working paper, Wharton School, University of Pennsylvania, 2002.
3 T. Blackett, *Trademarks* (New York: Palgrave Macmillan, 1998).
4 D. A. Aaker and E. Joachimsthaler, *Brand Leadership* (New York: Free Press, 2000).
5 J.-N. Kapferer, *Strategic Brand Management*, 2nd edn. (Dover, NH: Kogan Page, 1997).
6 K. Brooker, "The Un-CEO," *Fortune*, September 16, 2002, pp. 88–96.
7 M. De Mooij, *Global Marketing and Advertising: Understanding Cultural Paradoxes* (Thousand Oaks, CA: Sage, 1998).
8 B. O'Keefe, "Global Brands," *Fortune*, November 26, 2001, pp. 102–110.
9 R. Batra, J.-B. Steenkamp, and D. Alden, "Global Brands: Consumer Motivations and Mechanisms," in Pedro Sousa (ed.), *Global Branding*, MSI Conference Summary, Report 00–114 (Cambridge, MA: Marketing Science Institute, 2000), p. 13.

10 J.-N. Kapferer, "Is There Really No Hope for Local Brands?" in Sousa (ed.), *Global Branding*, p. 6.

11 N. Klein, *No Logo: Taking Aim at the Brand Bullies* (New York: Picador USA, 1999). Another book in the same genre is F. Bové and F. Dutous, *Le monde n'est pas une marchandise*: Entretiens avec Gilles Luneau (Paris: Pocket, 2004).

12 M. Goold and A. Campbell, *Designing Effective Organizations: How to Create Structured Networks* (San Francisco: Jossey-Bass, 2001).

13 Govindarajan, V. and A. K. Gupta, "Building an Effective Global Business Team," *MIT Sloan Management Review*, Summer 2001, pp. 63–71.

14 Aaker and Joachmisthaler, *Brand Leadership*, p. 320.

15 G. S. Day, *Market-Driven Strategy: Processes for Creating Value* (New York: Free Press, 1990).

9 | Global marketing of new products

HUBERT GATIGNON
INSEAD

CHRISTOPHE VAN DEN BULTE
Wharton School

In rolling out new products across global markets, companies are increasingly using a big-bang approach of simultaneous launches in different parts of the world instead of a sequential approach of gradually progressing from the home country into the world. With a richer set of options for global market entry, the authors consider choices about where to enter and what strategies to use in rolling out new products. They discuss three ways to segment global markets – grouping countries based on country factors, grouping individual consumers into segments that may cut across borders, and grouping countries based on diffusion patterns of innovations. The third approach is particularly relevant for their subsequent discussion of strategies for product rollouts. The authors discuss two strategies for such rollouts: the sequencing "waterfall" and the simultaneous "sprinkler" strategies. In addition to the targeting and sequencing decisions, the authors examine four other strategic decisions taken at the time of launch that affect the diffusion of new products: preannouncements, market entry commitment, distribution and product standardization.

TRADITIONALLY, firms introduce new products in their home country first and only later start marketing them abroad. This is still the most typical pattern of launching new products. BMW, Matsushita, General Electric, Dell, Benetton, and the Body Shop are examples of well-established and newer firms using such a strategy.[1] Yet, with the globalizing of the marketplace, it is becoming more common to see a new product being introduced at the same time or within a very short period in a multitude of countries. This is most common among global firms, such as Microsoft, Sony, or Apple Computers. Microsoft, for example, launched Windows XP on Thursday, October 25, 2001 not only in New York and London but also in India, Malaysia, Singapore, and Australia, followed by a launch the following Tuesday in Taiwan, the Philippines, and Vietnam and a

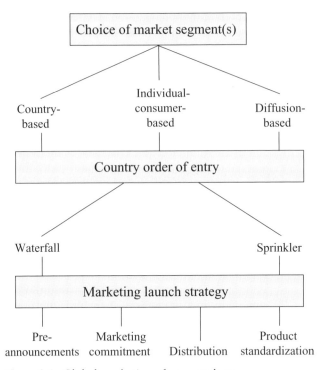

Figure 9.1. Global marketing of new products.

few days later in November in Hong Kong, Indonesia, China, and Japan. When releasing the movie *X2: X-Men United*, 20th Century Fox unveiled it in ninety-three countries within a period of forty-eight hours between April 30 and May 2, 2003. Simultaneous introduction seems increasingly popular not only among firms that already are global, but also among firms that are in the process of becoming so. AmericaOnline expanded simultaneously in Europe, Asia, and Latin America. Similarly, telecommunications companies tend to use simultaneous introduction strategies.[2]

The decision between sequential and simultaneous launch is just one of the issues that managers face in marketing new products globally. In a globalizing world, there are three questions that a firm with an innovation to bring to market must answer, as illustrated in Figure 9.1:

(1) Which segments should be targeted and how should these segments be defined (country-based, individual-consumer-based, diffusion-based)?

(2) Which country or countries should be selected for marketing the new product and in which order should they be entered?
(3) What marketing launch strategy or strategies should be used to enter these markets, including preannouncements, market entry commitment, distribution, and product standardization?

The answers to these questions depend on one's understanding of similarities and differences across the world's consumers. In this chapter, we first consider three approaches to segmenting the global marketplace, each providing a different perspective on strategies for rolling out new products. We then discuss how firms can take advantage of the globalizing phenomenon for launching new products and services. When relevant, we also touch briefly upon the issues raised by this global perspective and their consequences for consumers and society.

International market segmentation

The first challenge in designing a plan for introducing products and services internationally is to understand differences and similarities among markets. There are three basic approaches for international market segmentation:

(1) *Clustering countries based on country factors:* Identifying which countries are the most similar on a set of macro-level variables, including economic, political, demographic, and cultural dimensions.
(2) *Clustering individual customers, possibly across borders:* Looking for similarities and differences among individual consumers rather than among countries.
(3) *Clustering countries based on diffusion patterns:* Identifying which countries have similar typical patterns of diffusion of new products (how they gain market penetration); possibly extended by explaining these similarities.

The first two approaches have already been described by Reinhard Angelmar in Chapter 7, so we limit our discussion to their strengths and weaknesses in the context of global new product marketing. Then, we discuss the third approach, which is particularly relevant to the launch of new products.[3]

Clustering countries based on country factors has the advantages of being simple and of using easily available (and cheap) national statistics. This, in turn, allows one to repeat the exercise periodically and to update one's segmentation scheme. To the extent that economic, demographic, and political convergence occurs, it may result in a smaller set of segments over time. One of the limitations of this approach is its rather a-theoretical nature, which sometimes makes it difficult to interpret *post hoc* the rationale for the groupings. Furthermore, country segmentation ignores both heterogeneity among customers within the same country and, perhaps more critically, the commonalities among subsets of consumers in different countries. In addition, this approach does not lead to managerial insights as to how to introduce new products.[4] On balance, this method of segmentation leads to a coarse-grained view of the world markets, which may be appropriate for high-level descriptive purposes but does not provide input into either the globalizing debate or the management of globalizing firms.

The second segmentation approach, clustering individuals rather than countries, is much closer to traditional market segmentation practice. The major appeal of this approach is that it allows one to identify segments that cross national boundaries. This may prove especially useful when two conditions are met. First, the new product or service is targeted toward business users or toward particular types of consumer that one believes might exist in several countries – e.g. yuppies, video game enthusiasts, and two-income families with young children. Second, management does not believe that macro-level differences across countries (e.g. law and language) are major impediments to appealing to such customers living in different countries. Business users in different parts of the world, for instance, may be quite willing to use English-language software. Products subject to extensive regulation, on the other hand, may be less suitable for this type of segmentation approach, mass-market financial services being an example. The major disadvantage of this approach is that it might lead to a segmentation scheme that performs rather poorly on the accessibility and actionability criteria mentioned in Chapter 7. This will be the case when the segments run across several countries but media and distribution channels are very different across countries. Finding the right mix of media and distribution channels can quickly become very difficult in such circumstances.

The third approach, clustering countries based on diffusion patterns, consists in classifying countries according to the pattern with which new products are adopted by those countries' consumers. Its main appeal is that the segmentation scheme one obtains is based on the countries' prior history involving new product adoption and is therefore more specific to the task at hand. Like the first approach, it takes the country rather than the individual consumer as the unit of analysis, which has both advantages (cheap) and disadvantages (no within-country heterogeneity).

The approach works as follows. First, one takes data for several new products and countries, describing how each product gained market penetration in each country over time. Then, one summarizes each of these "diffusion paths" by means of a small number of parameter values. A popular approach is to fit a so-called Bass model that describes the shape of the diffusion path by two parameters: the coefficient of innovation capturing to what extent people are likely to adopt quickly regardless of social influence or word of mouth, and the coefficient of imitation capturing to what extent people's adoptions are affected by social influence and word of mouth that builds over time. Finally, one groups countries based on the similarity in their parameter values, i.e. their diffusion paths. This diffusion-based segmentation can result in substantially different segments than does clustering countries based on country factors.[5]

One important advantage of this approach is that the shape of the diffusion path has important implications for targeting and sequencing strategy. A second important advantage is that the coefficients of innovation and imitation vary across countries as a function of economic, demographic, and cultural differences, which means that some of the macro-level variables used in the more standard country-clustering approach may be reflected in the sales evolution path of new products. This provides one with a firmer basis for interpreting the resulting segments and provides one with a richer conceptual basis to formulate an effective introduction strategy, which we discuss later in the chapter.

The population's standard of living, as reflected in purchasing power (e.g. income per capita), health status, and literacy, is positively related to the coefficient of innovation.[6] In other words, countries with a higher standard of living adopt innovations faster without the need to rely on prior adopters. One study also found that the country's health status was negatively related to the extent of inter-personal influence, implying not only faster adoption early on but also a lesser role for word of mouth. This second result is not as reliable as the first, though, since it has been observed in a single study only and since poor health status (e.g. high death rates) is often highly correlated with low purchasing power and poor communication infrastructure. The exposure to mass media and other outside information, as reflected in the availability of newspapers, the degree of literacy, as well as in the cosmopolitan outlook of the country's citizens, is also associated with higher coefficients of innovation.[7]

One study found that the ease with which people can share information among themselves, as reflected in the availability of means of transportation and in the resulting mobility of the population, was associated with a higher propensity to imitate.[8] There are also some indications that the presence of multiple ethnic groups within a country is associated with a lower propensity to imitate.[9] The latter is consistent with the idea that people tend to communicate more with others like them ("birds of a feather flock together").

Some differences in diffusion patterns can be attributed to the nature of the products. This is especially so for labor-saving innovations as it concerns the role of working women.[10] Countries with a larger proportion of working women tend to adopt labor-saving innovations faster without being influenced by prior adopters.

Recent research has also documented systematic relationships between the shape of the diffusion path and national culture. First, in collectivistic rather than individualistic cultures, the propensity to imitate is higher[11] and that to innovate is lower.[12] The relative size of the propensity to imitate rather than innovate is also larger in collectivistic cultures where conformity to social norms is more important.[13] Second, in cultures that feel threatened by uncertain or unknown situations, the tendency to innovate is lower, both in absolute terms[14] and compared to the propensity to imitate.[15] Finally, the importance of innovation relative to imitation is also lower in more status-oriented cultures.[16]

In general, all these findings are consistent with both common sense and economic and sociological theory. Some of these studies, however, also indicate how one might use their results to forecast the parameters of innovation and imitation, and hence one's new product penetration path in different countries.[17]

Table 9.1. *Three international segmentation approaches*

Segmentation approach	Best use
Country factors	For product categories where national governments play a key role (such as telecommunications, medical products, and food items) or where national differences predominate in dictating acceptance and diffusion.
Individual consumers	For products targeted toward people with specific values and lifestyles (yuppies, video game enthusiasts, etc.) and for which law, language, and other national differences do not present major hurdles to acceptance.
Diffusion patterns	For new products that are rather slow in achieving full market acceptance and for which similarities in the speed of adoption across countries is of key interest.

Of the three types of segmentation, the standard one of clustering countries based on country factors may become decreasingly useful as markets continue to globalize and economic conditions in emerging nations improve. Although there are controversies regarding whether the rich countries get richer and the poor get poorer, there is general agreement that, except for some countries, the economic indicators are improving. Even if the disparity between the rich and the poor widens, it is likely that the role of economic factors is not linear and that the improvements in the poor countries will make the countries more similar, especially in terms of the adoption of innovations. This means fewer differences across countries and a decreasing role for traditional country segmentation. Furthermore, the increased mobility across borders and the accessibility of media on a global basis suggest that more segments will cross borders. So, one might expect more standardization of products and of launch strategy across countries, but some multiplicity or variety of products appealing to multiple segments existing within each country.

As summarized in Table 9.1, each of the three approaches to segmentation offers a different perspective on the market and each can be most valuable in certain situations. These approaches can be used separately or jointly to form a richer understanding of global markets and to develop marketing strategies for these markets.

Targeting and sequencing

It is still relatively rare for firms to enter many markets simultaneously. Typically, firms select specific markets on which to focus and enter them sequentially. Even though simultaneous market entry may be becoming more popular, as we mentioned at the start of this chapter, deciding which countries to target and in what sequence – if any – remains a fundamental issue.

The double question of which countries to select for entry and in which order to enter these target countries has received much attention in international business, as it is the "first and most important step in internationalizing the core business strategy."[18] We first discuss the issue of deciding which country or countries to target and then address the question of when a firm should introduce a product simultaneously and when there should be a clear sequence in the order of entry. We also discuss the implications of the globalizing forces on these marketing decisions.

Targeting

The first challenge is: Which markets to enter? Few companies live by the adage "the world is my oyster." In fact, companies tend to ignore major regions of the world completely.[19] For firms that seek to expand their scope, an assessment of the expected demand or market potential for the new product is often considered the fundamental criterion for targeting a country, although the competitive structure is an equally obvious consideration. Detailed checklists applicable to any product have been used to screen potential target countries but their validity remains mostly untested, especially in today's changing global markets. Such checklists also do not recognize that the determinants of country market potentials may often be idiosyncratic to particular innovations.

Broader competitive considerations may also influence entry decisions. Take the case of a firm considering entering a particular country that is the home base and main source of profitability of a global rival. Entering that country may trigger aggressive "cross-parry" moves by that competitor in other markets, and a firm might prefer not to enter that country even though it scores high on a standard checklist.

The challenge consists in assessing the market potential and competitiveness in sufficient detail to provide reliable sales estimates in a large number of countries where information specific to their new product is typically limited. In this situation, off-the-shelf checklists for market selection can be a valuable source of inspiration when designing one's own checklist tailored to the situation, but should be amended to reflect the situation the firm faces. The issue here is quite similar to the use of standard portfolio models in business planning (either within a single country or across several countries): the value of applying standard lists and tools lies as much, if not more, in the debate and reflection they engender among members of the management team as in the models' actual recommendations.

Sequence of entry

The decision on the sequence to enter selected target markets is not an easy one either. Given the high upfront investment in R&D, firms are often eager to generate cash as fast as possible. Moving quickly may also give the company more of a lead before competitors enter, which can be critical when other barriers to entry are absent. Under such conditions, textbook marketing principles suggest penetrating multiple markets quickly, the extreme form being entering them all at the same time.

A second consideration is the presence of spillover effects across countries. If the diffusion of a new product in Country B is in part driven by its success in Country A, then it makes sense to enter Country A first, use a penetration strategy (e.g. low introductory price) in that country, and only later enter Country B. The reason is that this strategy helps to get the word-of-mouth "snowball" rolling in Country A that will generate – at no extra cost to the firm – subsequent sales in Country B.

Waterfall vs. sprinkler strategies

How should a multinational firm introduce a new product into its global markets? Shlomo Kalish, Vijay Mahajan, and Eitan Muller contrast the sequencing or "waterfall" strategy with the simultaneous or "sprinkler" strategy.[20] The waterfall strategy consists of having new

Table 9.2. *Waterfall vs. sprinkler strategies*

Factors	Waterfall (Sequential)	Sprinkler (Simultaneous)
Product life cycle	Long	Short
Size of foreign market	Small	Large
Speed of market growth	Slow	Rapid
Innovativeness of target market	Low	High
Fixed costs of foreign market entry	High	Low
Competition in target markets	Weak	Strong
Coordination with competitors about entry timing	Coordination	Independent decision-making
Cross-country spillovers	Strong	Weak

Source: Based on Kalish, Mahajan, and Muller, "Waterfall and Sprinkler New-Product Strategies."

products trickle down in a cascade from the most to the least technologically advanced countries.[21] This is the pattern followed by many US-based multinational firms in the past: they initially focused on English-speaking countries, then on other industrialized countries, and finally on the less developed countries.[22] In contrast, the sprinkler strategy is the simultaneous entry into all markets. Even though large-scale simultaneous entries may still be rare, there is evidence that the lag between entries into foreign markets is decreasing.[23] The major argument in its favor is the increased worldwide competition.

The analytic model developed by Kalish, Mahajan, and Muller allowed them to perform an interesting study of the factors that favor one strategy versus the other, as summarized in Table 9.2.[24] In general, a waterfall (sequential) strategy is favored under the following conditions: (1) long product life cycle, (2) small foreign market, (3) slow growth in the foreign market, (4) low innovativeness in the foreign market, (5) high fixed costs of entry into the foreign market, (6) weak competitors in the foreign market, which could be the case if there are only local competitors, and (7) competitors coordinate their time of entry with each other. In addition, as discussed in the following section, the existence of cross-country spillover effects may have an influence on the choice of a strategy.

Trends in the evolution of global markets seem to provide increasing support for simultaneous (sprinkler) entry. Product life cycles and diffusion cycles tend to become shorter;[25] markets are becoming larger because of the increasing integration in various areas of the world; from the point of view of firms in industrialized countries, foreign markets tend to grow faster than that in the home country (e.g. China's growth over the last ten years); fixed costs of entry into foreign markets are decreasing with the availability of alternative distribution systems such as the Internet, better global logistics, and the greater familiarity with foreign markets; multimarket competition by international companies is more likely, with very few examples of firms that can attain absolute monopoly power in their global markets. Consequently, we should observe an increase in simultaneous entries. These trends do not mean that waterfall strategies are likely to be abandoned altogether, just that we can expect to see more use of simultaneous strategies and shorter time-lags between sequential entries in the future.

Cross-country diffusion and the lead (lag) effect

An additional factor affecting the choice of an entry strategy is the presence of spillover effects across countries, sometimes also referred to as "lead" or "lag" effects. Cross-border communication about the product – either through personal conversation or through exposure to foreign mass media – may improve consumers' awareness of the innovation before it is introduced in their own country and may reduce the risk they perceive in adopting early. The success of a product in the lead country may also continue to influence consumer opinion and adoption behavior in other (lag) countries after the product has been introduced in these countries. Such effects have been reported in a number of studies.[26]

Strong cross-country spillover effects favor the waterfall strategy because they reduce the costs of marketing communications in the lag markets. By using a sequential strategy, the company can rely on the free spillover effect from the lead market to generate awareness and a positive attitude toward the new product in the lag markets. However, there are important caveats in considering the impact of these spillovers. First, spillover effects may not be universally positive. For example, one study reported that lag time is positively related to the propensity to innovate and negatively related to the importance of social influence like word of mouth.[27] Second, there are some questions about whether these effects exist at all. Faster speed of adoption in a lag country need not result from cross-country communication. The lead–lag effect may simply reflect the passage of time and the concomitant changes in product design and quality, the availability of new, more advanced media vehicles and communication systems, and the general trend toward higher purchasing power.[28] If that is the case, there is no international snowball effect at work. Finally, lead–lag effects might not be genuine at all but simply a statistical artifact.[29] In short, while lead–lag effects provide a clever reason to enter markets sequentially rather than simultaneously, the existence of such effects is far from established. Managers would be advised to look critically at the odds that such effects exist for their own product, rather than simply take their existence for granted.

New product marketing mix strategies

In the previous sections, we discussed two key decisions:
(1) Choosing which market segment(s) to target
(2) Choosing the order to enter the chosen market segments.
The firm's decision about these two issues will affect how quickly its new products gain market acceptance. However, four additional strategic actions of the firm at the time of entry have been related to the speed of diffusion of an innovation:[30]
(1) Preannouncements
(2) Market-entry commitment
(3) Distribution
(4) Product standardization.

Preannouncements

Often, the marketing of a product precedes its availability in the market. Distributors, for instance, routinely receive requests from manufacturers that they pre-commit to carry products and services that are said to be under development and are promised at a future date. Preannouncements (vigorous promotion of non-existent products) have become common, and even a standard practice in some industries such as the software industry ("vaporware") and the movie industry (the endlessly forthcoming latest film from director X or star Y). These preannouncements can help companies gain an advantage with the consumer (who will wait for the product) and preemptively move against potential competitors (who will withdraw resources from their competing products or the market).[31] However, preannouncements may also have negative effects as consumers become frustrated with waiting or as they learn to see these initiatives as attempts to manipulate the market.

In addition to deliberate preannouncements, there are also opportunities for more "natural" preannouncements. These occur when the launch in a lead country serves as a preannouncement in lag countries. As we mentioned, companies might choose a more sequential strategy to benefit from this effect. Managers need to recognize, however, that if there is negative publicity as a result of the original launch, a sequential rollout might be dampened by this effect since they "preannounce" that the product does not perform as expected. In fact, studies of movie launches show that films that are likely to receive negative reviews benefit most from advance advertising, which may reflect a strategy of getting as many people as possible into the theater before they have time to hear the negative reviews and word of mouth.

Market-entry commitment

The commitment of a firm to a new product is a very important element of its overall entry strategy.[32] Strong commitment can send a credible signal to consumers, distributors, and competitors that the firm intends to build the market and to remain there for a long time. As a result, strong commitment may bring risk-averse customers and distributors faster into the market and may also act as a barrier to competitive entry. However, commitment usually comes at a steep cost. The greater the firm's commitment to entering a market or launching a new product or service, the more resources have to be devoted to it. This decreases flexibility and increases risks, and these concerns need to be weighed against the value of commitment in entering a new market.

There are several ways in which companies can demonstrate their commitment when entering a market:

Scale: Large-scale production and logistics facilities signal to competitors, distributors, and consumers that the firm expects that the market will be large enough and that the firm expects to remain there for a period long enough for it to recoup its investments. In an analysis of retail entries into foreign markets, Katrijn Gielens and Marnik Dekimpe provide empirical support for the positive long-term impact of the scale of entry on sales performance.[33]

Price: Setting low prices when introducing a new product is fairly common. It serves to achieve rapid market penetration, and shows to both consumers and competitors that the firm is committed to the market. The opposite strategy (initially high prices, or skimming) leads to slow diffusion and suggests that the firm may readily leave the market as prices drop. Such skimming is more common in the launch of new-to-the-world products.[34] For such highly innovative products, the firm itself may be uncertain about the ultimate size of the market and therefore may prefer to maximize short-term cash flow rather than offer low prices and bet that they will make money once the market has fully developed.

Product adaptation: Adapting the product to local market conditions increases the cost of entry. As a result, it can signal a commitment to particular markets.

Marketing communications: Often, a penetration strategy also involves large marketing communication expenditures. These increase awareness, improve the opinion about the product's value, and convert early prospects into actual adopters. Spending heavily on marketing communications may also be interpreted as a sign of the firm's commitment to the new product: customers, distributors, and potential competitors may reason that a firm would not knowingly invest heavily in a dubious innovation. In this respect, promotion reinforces a firm's reputation, which in turn reassures potential adopters about the (unknown) quality of the new product.[35]

Sales force: The firm's sales force is a critical factor in gaining acceptance among business buyers. High technology firms, notorious for outsourcing everything and keeping operations lean, none the less field extremely expensive sales forces.[36] The logic is that salespeople build relationships with prospects, and redeploy these relationships over successive innovations to reduce a prospect's uncertainty when introducing the latest generation of products. Given the high rate of technological change in these industries, the sales force's ability to speed up adoption justifies its high cost. An important decision is whether to build one's own sales force or to use third parties such as manufacturer representatives or independent resellers. Here again, using the high-commitment option (employees) has an advantage when dealing with new products. Salespeople frequently resist selling new products, particularly innovative ones, because it takes more effort to convince buyers, and independent contractors can be even more averse to this type of work than in-house sales reps. A company's own salespeople also serve a valuable role as market researchers and partners to marketers in new product development. For more established products and less technologically complex markets, firms often choose to use independent distributors in their go-to-market approach, as discussed in the next section.

These different ways to increase or decrease commitment make clear that commitment is not only part of one's competitive posturing but also intricately related to the design and execution of market-entry strategies. When there are significant barriers of consumer acceptance, regulation, or competition, high commitment may be necessary to break into the market at all. Where resources are constrained, the commitment may by necessity have to be less significant and managers should recognize that this will have an impact on entry success. The company can then carefully and deliberately weigh the potential of the market against the commitment required to enter.

Distribution

The firm's channels of distribution have substantial influence on how well the innovation connects with buyers in specific countries. Resellers and agents cultivate a reputation among their clientele. They put this reputation behind what they sell, even though they are not producers. Producers effectively rent this reputation, and find it particularly valuable in overcoming customer resistance to new products.

Producers may seek to build close, committed relationships with resellers and agents to secure not only quantity but also quality of effort: producers want their channels to present the innovation in a certain way to a targeted segment. Selective distribution is often an important means to this end. Resellers and producers employ selectivity in an elaborate "exchange of hostages": producers concede market exclusivity in return for category exclusivity (non-representation of competing brands), as well as other safeguards.[37] One reason why selective distribution is effective for selling innovations, particularly in final goods markets, is that representation by the "right" channels sends a quality signal to consumers.[38]

Producers trying to get resellers to carry their new products also face another problem: convincing the reseller that the product is a likely winner. In attempting to do so, they face a credibility problem: resellers know that producers have an incentive to tell them that all their new products are highly saleable, including those that producers know to be otherwise. How can channel members screen out false information? Slotting allowances, which have become an institution in grocery retailing, may be one way to achieve this.[39] Slotting allowances are fixed fees producers pay to "rent" shelf space to introduce new products (in addition to margins per unit sold). Resellers can use them to oblige producers to signal which new products truly are most likely to sell well. This is particularly important in fast-moving consumer goods categories where literally thousands of supposedly "new" products come out each year.

Variations in distribution channel structures and arrangements from country to country can have a significant impact on the diffusion of new products in different countries, making it difficult to completely standardize one's go-to-market strategy. A recent study found that even in a relatively homogeneous set of countries within the European Union, differences in the distribution infrastructure for consumer durable goods affected diffusion patterns.[40] In Germany, for example, sales in the all-under-one-roof value stores can benefit from sales in hypermarkets. The latter seem to give credibility and reduce consumer uncertainty about the innovation. In France, in contrast, the effect is negative. There, hypermarkets appear to spoil the market for the other channels. This may be due to the privileged position of hypermarkets in France where they have become ubiquitous. In markets with large specialized retailers, these firms act as scouts and bring innovations to market first while the other channels wait and see if the new product is successful. The findings from this study suggest that it would be ill advised to follow a standardized distribution policy, even within regions.

All these factors – channel selectivity, differences in slotting allowance practices, and differences in distribution infrastructures across countries – make distribution the strategy component that is most sensitive to differences across countries and regions. While global distribution companies might become more prevalent (e.g. Carrefour's or Wal-Mart's international development strategies), channel structures and practices generally remain strongly country-specific. The Internet is clearly the exception and, as it becomes more important as a way of distributing new products in certain categories, it may alter substantially the current practices.

Product standardization

Decisions about product standardization – offering the same item in all markets or adapting products to local environments – also have an impact on the diffusion of new products across national borders. For example, the initial reluctance of US automanufacturers to introduce right-hand-drive cars in Japan and adapt to the stringent aesthetic and quality demands of the market significantly slowed their progress there. Similarly, in the very early days of Honda's entry in the US motorcycle market, the company's sales were hampered by the fact that its large bikes were not adapted to suit the higher speeds at which bikes were driven in the United States.

While standardization creates economies of scale, adaptation exhibits sensitivity to local market needs. How the net impact on sales and profit balances out depends on the specifics of the situation. Apart from cost savings and sensitivity to local preferences, network effects also need to be taken into consideration. Examples include situations where the value of the product increases with the number of users and where compatibility is a critical factor in the innovation's development of the market. As transnational market segments become more prominent, there should be an increase in the proportion of standardized products across the world.[41]

The product standardization decision cannot be made independently from the entry sequencing decision. In general, the more standardized the product (such as Microsoft software or a movie release), the easier it will be to pursue a simultaneous entry (sprinkler) strategy. The more tailored the product, the more time it may take to develop all the product variants, and the firm may be eager to start selling in each market as soon as a good product variant is available for launch – in effect preferring a sequential (waterfall) strategy. On the other hand, the more tailored the product is to each country, the smaller the cross-country spillover effects are likely to be, which may make a simultaneous launch more appealing. (Other issues related to product standardization decisions are considered in more detail by Reinhard Angelmar in Chapter 7.)

Conclusions

We have discussed the key decisions involved in marketing a new product in globalizing markets. In making decisions about where and how to launch new products, managers should:

(1) *Use adequate segmentation:* International market segmentation is more than just grouping countries together. There are many ways to segment markets. In addition to considering similarities among consumers in different countries to create transnational consumer segments, similarities in diffusion patterns can also be a useful basis for grouping countries and segments within them. These different approaches to segmentation can offer a deeper understanding of similarities and differences across markets, and help present a richer set of options for targeting specific markets.

(2) *Consider interdependencies:* No market is an island. When making targeting and sequencing decisions, some thought must be given to potential interdependencies among countries. These consist not only of competitive and business portfolio considerations long emphasized in the strategy literature, but also of the influence that adoptions in one country may have on adoptions in other countries. As discussed above, among these interdependencies are competitive factors (entry in one country sparks a response in another) as well as potential lead–lag effects (awareness from the launch in one country helps in the launch in another). In considering entry into a given country, it is important to examine the broader context and develop strategies across countries.

(3) *Consider and assess the rationale of candidate strategies:* The forces leading to globalization are likely to lead to the increased use of simultaneous launches of new products worldwide. However, this should not be seen as a blanket prediction. We have discussed the mechanism

behind this prediction and managers should assess to what extent this mechanism applies to their own situation. Launching and marketing new products in globalizing markets will require more coordination, but this must not be confused with increased standardization. This is especially so for sales force and distribution strategies that tend to be heavily influenced by idiosyncrasies of specific markets. The specific entry strategy developed needs to reflect a consideration of a wide range of factors, including the company, the product or service, the competitive environment, and the characteristics of the country and segments targeted.

In multifaceted global markets, managers face more complex challenges in designing their market-entry strategies because of factors such as converging markets, cross-national market interactions, and the emergence of global segments across countries. At the same time, for managers who can recognize the opportunities, there are often a more diverse set of options for designing entry strategies within markets and across markets. Companies that might have had no choice but to pursue a sequential waterfall strategy may now have the option of considering a simultaneous sprinkler strategy for their product launches. A more thorough consideration of the factors shaping individual markets and the diverse options available, as discussed in this chapter, can offer a richer set of strategies for global market entry.

Notes

1 J. K. Johansson, *Global Marketing: Foreign Entry, Local Marketing, and Global Management*, 2nd edn. (Boston: Irwin McGraw-Hill, 2000).
2 Ibid.
3 H. Gatignon, J. Eliashberg, and T. S. Robertson, "Modeling Multinational Diffusion Patterns: An Efficient Methodology," *Marketing Science*, 8 (1989), p. 231.
4 K. Helsen, K. Jedidi, and W. S. DeSarbo, "A New Approach to Country Segmentation Utilizing Multinational Diffusion Patterns," *Journal of Marketing*, 57 (October 1993), pp. 60–71.
5 Ibid.
6 M. Dekimpe, P. M. Parker, and M. Sarvary, "Staged Estimation of International Diffusion Models: An Application to Global Cellular Telephone Adoption," *Technological Forecasting and Social Change*, 57 (1989), pp. 105–132; D. Talukdar, K. Sudhir, and A. Ainslie, "Investigating New

Product Diffusion Across Products and Countries," *Marketing Science*, 21, 1 (Winter 2002), pp. 97–114; C. Van den Bulte, "Want to Know How Diffusion Speed Varies across Countries and Products? Try Using a Bass Model," *Visions*, 26, 4 (2002), pp. 12–15; Helsen, Jedidi, and Desarbo, "New Approach."

7 Gatignon, Eliashberg, and Robertson, "Modeling Multinational Diffusion Patterns"; Helsen, Jedidi, and Desarbo, "New Approach"; Talukdar, Sudhir, and Ainslie, "Investigating New Product Diffusion."

8 Gatignon, Eliashberg, and Robertson, "Modeling Multinational Diffusion Patterns."

9 M. G. Dekimpe, P. M. Parker, and M. Sarvary, "Multimarket and Global Diffusion," in V. Mahajan, E. Muller and Y. Wind (eds.), *New-Product Diffusion Models* (Boston: Kluwer Academic Publishers, 2000); Talukdar, Sudhir, and Ainslie, "Investigating New Product Diffusion."

10 Gatignon, Eliashberg, and Robertson, "Modeling Multinational Diffusion Patterns."

11 D. C. Jain and S. Maesincee, "Cultural Influences on New Product Acceptance in Global Markets," Northwestern University Working Paper, 1998; and Van den Bulte, "Want to Know How?"

12 J.-B. E. M. Steenkamp, F. ter Hofstede, and M. Wedel, "A Cross-national Investigation into the Individual and National Cultural Antecedents of Consumer Innovativeness," *Journal of Marketing*, 63 (April 1999), pp. 55–69.

13 C. Van den Bulte and S. Stremersch, "Contagion and Heterogeneity in New Product Diffusion: An Empirical Test," University of Pennsylvania Working paper, 2003.

14 Jain and Maesincee, "Cultural Influences"; Steenkamp, ter Hofstede, and Wedel, "Cross-national Investigation."

15 Van den Bulte and Stremersch, "Contagion and Heterogeneity."

16 Ibid.

17 Talukdar, Sudhir, and Ainslie, "Investigating New Product Diffusion"; Van den Bulte, "Want to Know How?"

18 G. S. Yip, *Total Global Strategy II* (Upper Saddle River, NJ: Pearson Education Inc., 2003), p. 5.

19 V. Mahajan, M. V. Pratini de Moraes, and J. Wind, "The Invisible Global Market," *Marketing Management*, 9, 9 (2000), pp. 31–35.

20 S. Kalish, V. Mahajan, and E. Muller, "Waterfall and Sprinkler New-Product Strategies in Competitive Global Markets," *International Journal of Research in Marketing*, 12, 2 (1995), p. 105.

21 L. T. Wells, "A Product Life Cycle for International Trade?," *Journal of Marketing* , 32, 3 (July 1968), pp. 1–6.

22 W. H. Davidson and R. Harrigan, "Key Decisions in International Marketing: Introducing New Products Abroad," *Columbia Journal of World Business*, 12, 4 (1977), p. 15.

23 This observation was already made in Davidson and Harrigan, "Key Decisions in International Marketing," based on data from 1945 to 1976.

24 Kalish, Mahajan and Muller, "Waterfall and Sprinkler New-Product Strategies."

25 W. Qualls, R. W. Olshavsky, and R. E. Michaels, "Shortening of the PLC – An Empirical Test," *Journal of Marketing*, 45 (Fall 1981), pp. 76–80; C. Van den Bulte, "New Product Diffusion Acceleration: Measurement and Analysis," *Marketing Science*, 19, 4 (2000), pp. 366–380.

26 For instance, Kumar and Krishnan reported that the penetration in the lead country affected the number of adoptions in the lag country (V. Kumar and T. V. Krishnan, "Multinational Diffusion Models: An Alternative Framework," *Marketing Science*, 21 (2002), pp. 318–330; see also H. Takada and D. Jain, "Cross-national Analysis of Diffusion of Consumer Durable Goods in Pacific Rim Countries," *Journal of Marketing*, 55, 2 (1991), pp. 48–54) and Talukdar, Sudhir, and Ainslie, "Investigating New Product Diffusion," found that the coefficient of imitation tended to be higher in countries where a product was introduced later than in other countries. Puzzlingly, Talukdar and his associates also found a negative effect of lag on propensity to innovate, which might indicate that firms enter later in countries characterized by a lower propensity to innovate.

27 Helsen, Jedidi, and DeSarbo, "New Approach."

28 Van den Bulte, "New Product Diffusion Acceleration."

29 C. Van den Bulte and G. L. Lilien, "Bias and Systematic Change in the Parameter Estimates of Macro-level Diffusion Models," *Marketing Science*, 16, 4 (1997), pp. 338–353.

30 S. Kuester, H. Gatignon, and T. S. Robertson, "Firm Strategy and Speed of Diffusion," in Mahajan, Muller, and Wind (eds.), *New-Product Diffusion Models*.

31 J. Eliashberg and T. S. Robertson, "New Product Preannouncing Behavior: A Market Signaling Study," *Journal of Marketing Research*, 25, 3 (1988), p. 282. They also study the role of preannouncements *vis-à-vis* the distribution system.

32 P. Ghemawat, *Commitment: The Dynamic of Strategy* (New York: Free Press, 1991).

33 K. Gielens and M. G. Dekimpe, "Do International Entry Decisions of Retail Chains Matter in the Long Run?" *International Journal of Research in Marketing*, 18 (2001), pp. 235–259.

34 E. J. Hultink and A. Griffin, "In Search of Generic Launch Strategies for New Products," *International Journal of Research in Marketing*, 15 (1998), pp. 269–285.

35 A. Kirmani and A. R. Rao, "No Pain, No Gain: A Critical Review of the Literature on Signaling Unobservable Product Quality," *Journal of Marketing*, 64, 2 (2000), pp. 66–79.

36 R. G. McGrath, "A Real Options Logic for Initiating Technology Positioning Investments," *Academy of Management Review*, 22 (1997), pp. 974–996.

37 A. J. Fein and E. Anderson, "Patterns of Credible Commitments: Territory and Brand Selectivity in Industrial Distribution Channels," *Journal of Marketing*, 61, 2 (1997), pp. 19–34.

38 K. H. Wathne and J. B. Heide, "Opportunism in Interfirm Relationships: Forms, Outcomes, and Solutions," *Journal of Marketing*, 64, 4 (2000), pp. 36–51.

39 W. Chu, "Demand Signaling and Screening in Channels of Distribution," *Marketing Science*, 11 (1992), pp. 327–347.

40 H. Gatignon and E. Anderson. "Inter-channel Competition and New Product Diffusion: Market Making, Market Taking, and Competitive Effects in Several European Countries," INSEAD working paper no. 2002/88/MKT (2002).

41 N. Dawar and P. Parker, "Marketing Universals: Consumers' Use of Brand Name, Price, Physical Appearance, and Retailer Reputation as Signals of Product Quality," *Journal of Marketing*, 58, 2 (April 1994), pp. 81–95.

10 Global equity capital markets for emerging growth firms: patterns, drivers, and implications for the globalizing entrepreneur

RAPHAEL AMIT
Wharton School

CHRISTOPH ZOTT
INSEAD

The expansion and development of global financial markets has led to a rapid rise in foreign IPOs and listings. As the opportunities for financing ventures have increased significantly, so has the complexity of decisions facing entrepreneurs and others who need to tap into these markets. When equity can be sourced virtually anywhere in the world, how do managers make decisions about listing a German firm on the Neuer Markt, Nasdaq, or both? The authors draw upon academic literature and their own research on foreign IPOs on US and German exchanges, as well as interviews with senior executives at firms that chose to list on a foreign exchange. This chapter summarizes some of the key benefits that attract companies to list on foreign exchanges, including gaining access to capital, offering liquidity to existing investors, enhancing the company's reputation at home and abroad, providing currency for acquisitions in the foreign country, offering exit opportunities, dispersing ownership geographically, and achieving a higher valuation. Against these benefits, they present a set of costs, including underpricing and dilution, direct costs of the IPO, reporting requirements, and recurring costs. By weighing these costs and benefits entrepreneurs can develop informed strategies for taking advantage of globalizing equity markets.

The authors contributed equally to this chapter. Raffi Amit acknowledges the generous financial support of the Wharton e-business research center (a unit of WeBI), the Snider Entrepreneurship Research Center, and the Robert B. Goergen Chair in Entrepreneurship at the Wharton School. Christoph Zott gratefully acknowledges financial support from INSEAD. Both authors thank Iwona Bancerek and Amee Kamdar for their excellent research assistance, and Stacey Lange for her support. We thank the participants in the INSEAD workshop held during the development of this study for their insightful comments.

I n recent years, a new trend in the capitalization of relatively young, growth-oriented firms has emerged. These firms can now access foreign public equity capital markets. That is, these firms can raise funds in public capital markets in countries other than the ones where they were originally incorporated and headquartered. For example, Infosys Technologies Ltd., a global IT services company was the first Indian firm to be listed on the Nasdaq stock market. The Israeli company Check Point Software Technologies, which is the market leader in Internet security and firewall systems, had its initial public offering (IPO) on Nasdaq, and was added to the Nasdaq 100 index in 2000. Similarly, Lycos Europe NV, based in Holland, went public on the Neuer Markt in Germany.

While research on the globalization of public equity markets for financing entrepreneurial firms is only beginning to appear,[1] there has been an increase in non-domestic IPOs on both Nasdaq in the United States and the Neuer Markt in Germany. Since 1988, there have been 405 IPOs on the Nasdaq by non-domestic firms from 44 different countries, raising $50.35 billion of equity capital, or, on average, $125.5 million per issue. These non-domestic IPOs represented 8 percent of the total number of IPOs on Nasdaq between 1988 and 2001, and accounted for 19.5 percent of the equity capital raised by all IPOs on Nasdaq in that period. On the other hand, the younger Neuer Markt had a total of 313 IPOs, of which 44 (or 14 percent) were non-domestic. The non-domestic issuers raised $4.5 billion on the Neuer Markt, averaging $102 million per IPO.

As the total number of IPOs on Nasdaq grew, so did the number of foreign listings – from three non-domestic listings on Nasdaq in 1988 to thirty-four in 1998 and seventy-eight in 2000. These non-domestic listings amounted to 2 percent of the total number of companies listed in 1988, growing to 12 percent in 1998 and 19 percent in 2000, before dropping to about 9 percent in 2001. The growth of foreign listings even outpaced the overall growth of the IPO market. While the overall IPO market grew at a compound annual growth rate (CAGR) of 5.9 percent from 1988 to 1998, and 7.5 percent from 1988 to 2000, non-domestic listings grew at CAGRs of 24.7 percent and 28.5 percent respectively.[2]

This trend in the globalization of the public equity market for entrepreneurial finance, which has been mirrored in the simultaneous globalization of private equity markets, is particularly interesting as these markets are notoriously plagued by the presence of asymmetric

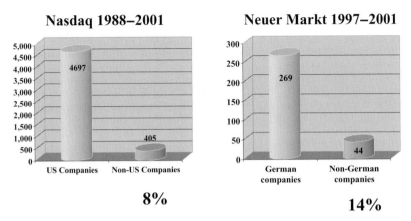

Figure 10.1. Domestic vs. non-domestic IPOs.

information (moral hazard, adverse selection). With foreign firms, the possibility of asymmetric information is heightened. As a result, the question of why markets for public entrepreneurial finance globalize so rapidly is interesting both theoretically and empirically. What can help explain this phenomenon? And what are the implications of these trends for the globalizing entrepreneur and for the leaders of corporate ventures? To illuminate one significant factor in the formation and rapid growth of entrepreneurial firms throughout the world, these are the questions that will be addressed in this chapter.

The next section examines patterns of globalization of equity capital markets as they affect entrepreneurial firms. We then consider the drivers and the tradeoffs inherent in globalization, examined through the perspective of entrepreneurial firms. We conclude with a section on implications for entrepreneurs of the globalization trend in capital markets.

Patterns of non-domestic IPOs

As noted above, our research shows that foreign IPOs – those by firms that have an original country of incorporation that differs from the country where their securities are listed – have increased on both the Nasdaq stock market in the United States and on the Neuer Markt (NM) in Germany (see Figure 10.1).[3] We focus on Nasdaq, which began trading in February 1971 (see Figure 10.2 for its evolution), because it is the largest and most developed market for high-growth firms. We also chose the Neuer Markt, which was established in March

1971   On February 8, Nasdaq begins trading.

1984   Small Order Execution System[SM] becomes ready for use to execute
        small orders automatically against the best quotations – making
        greater volume and efficiency in trading possible.

1994   Nasdaq surpasses the New York Stock Exchange in annual share
        volume.

1998   In conjunction with the Stock Exchange of Hong Kong, Nasdaq
        announces a partnership to provide investors worldwide with
        information about their respective markets on a new, joint Internet
        web service.

1999   Nasdaq becomes the largest stock market in the United States by
        dollar volume and repeatedly breaks share and dollar volume
        records. In June, Nasdaq signes an agreement in Tokyo with
        Softbank Corporation, jointly capitalizing a new company – Nasdaq
        Japan[SM]. This proves to be the first leg in Nasdaq's global strategy to
        link Asian markets with European and American markets.

2000   The restructuring spins off Nasdaq into a shareholder-owned,
        for-profit company. Nasdaq completes the first phase of its
        restructuring. Nasdaq formally opens the new Market Site in the
        heart of New York's Times Square. Nasdaq continues to be the
        engine for capital formation and job creation. Between 1997 and
        2000, it has brought 1,649 companies public, and in the process
        raised $316.5 billion. Nasdaq continues to build capacity for the
        trading volumes of tomorrow, with a capacity to trade 6 billion
        shares a day, a tenfold increase since 1997.

Figure 10.2. Evolution of Nasdaq. (*Source*: Nasdaq)

1997 (see Figure 10.3), because it was the largest and most liquid market in Europe for emerging growth companies during the time period
we consider. (In 2002, it was merged back into the Deutsche Börse,
following the collapse of the market for technology IPOs.)

Foreign companies accounted for 8 percent of IPOs on Nasdaq
between 1988 and 2001, and represented 14 percent of offerings on the
Neuer Markt between 1997 and 2001. While there has been variabil-
ity in the percentage of non-domestic listings on both exchanges, there
was a steady increase in the percentage of foreign listings until 2000
on Nasdaq and until 1999 on the Neuer Markt (see Figure 10.4). In

Origin	In March 1997, Deutsche Börse AG (the entity operating the FSE) established a new trading platform within the *Freiverkehr* segment, called the Neuer Markt.
Target	It serves small to medium-sized innovative growth companies, in particular in the telecom, Internet, multimedia, entertainment software, biotech, and other high-tech areas.
Performance	The Neuer Markt by far outperformed the other market segments and contributed significantly to the increase in IPO activity in Germany. It attracted more than 320 issuers, some 20 percent of which are foreign.
Platform	It has not only become Europe's largest market for IPOs of German innovative growth companies, but also a platform for high-tech companies from other European countries, Israel and the United States.

Figure 10.3. Neuer Markt.

2000, while there was a 27 percent decline in Nasdaq's domestic IPOs from the preceding year, non-domestic IPOs jumped 50 percent. The seventy-eight non-domestic IPOs – an all-time high for a single year – accounted for more than 19 percent of the total IPOs on Nasdaq in 2000.

While a few countries dominate each exchange, Figure 10.5 shows the increasing geographic diversity of countries listed on both Nasdaq and the NM (although it does level off in 2000). This trend points to the increased receptiveness of investors on both exchanges to embracing innovative companies from around the world, despite the greater asymmetry of information about these non-domestic companies. It provides evidence of the true globalizing nature of equity capital markets for promising entrepreneurial firms.

Drivers

These patterns of increasing use of non-domestic capital markets by entrepreneurial firms are driven by some of the broader trends toward globalization outlined in the introduction to this book. First, the *liberalization of capital markets* along with a general *harmonization of regulations*, such as capital market regulations, taxes, etc., clearly

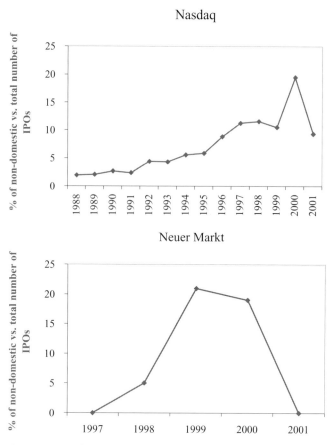

Figure 10.4. The increasing share of non-domestic IPOs on Nasdaq and the Neuer Markt.

foster cross-border flows of capital to support entrepreneurial companies. The creation of a common currency for the European Union, for example, reduced both currency risk and administrative barriers to investing, thereby facilitating cross-border investment in private local firms by non-local investors, both from within and outside the European Union. Second, *rapid advances in technology* and *accelerating information flows* make the investment process more efficient by enabling investors to meet their information needs and transact business at reduced cost. For example, firms can disseminate information to investors and analysts using teleconferencing technology, which

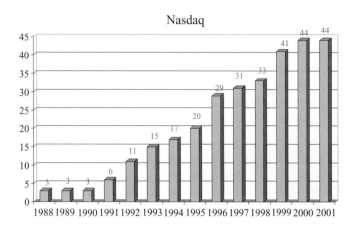

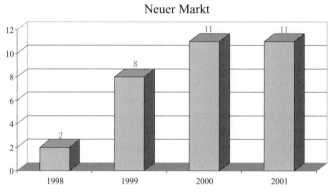

Figure 10.5. Number of foreign countries represented on Nasdaq and the Neuer Markt (cumulative IPOs). *Note:* Does not take into account delistings.

helps the latter avoid travel costs. Third, the trend toward an *increased mobility of products* implies that local firms are selling greater fractions of their output on global markets, which in some cases necessitates an enhanced presence in the foreign markets. One strategic rationale for raising funds in foreign markets, therefore, can be to improve a firm's visibility and brand recognition.

Some surprising findings

While the overall increase in foreign listings may be expected in the context of a globalizing world, there are some surprising findings from these data.

Many foreign listings come from countries with healthy domestic exchanges: These foreign IPOs spanned a wide range of countries of origin in both markets, as shown in Figures 10.6 and 10.7. By the end of 2001, there were forty-four non-US countries represented on the Nasdaq. Three countries, in particular, accounted for 53 percent of listings by foreign firms between 1988 and 2001: Israeli companies had 86 IPOs, Canadian companies had 73 IPOs, and UK companies had 54 IPOs. As shown in Figure 10.6, there was a total of 44 non-German companies from ten countries that listed their IPOs on the Neuer Markt; four countries accounted for 70 percent of these non-domestic IPOs: Austrian companies had twelve, US companies had five, and Israeli and Dutch companies had seven each.

This raises some interesting questions. Why would so many Canadian and UK firms find it advantageous, despite the high cost associated with such offerings, to list on Nasdaq even though there are well-developed capital markets in their home countries? Why would some US firms choose to list on the NM, despite having the most developed capital market for emerging growth firms at home?

The average age of foreign companies on the NM is less than that of their domestic peers, yet these younger firms have a higher average market cap: Another surprising finding is that the average age of foreign companies that list on the NM is less than the average of the German companies that list there, and these younger companies have a higher average market cap. The age of non-domestic firms on the Neuer Markt averages 9.7 years compared to 12 years for their German peers.[4] Investors faced with greater uncertainty about non-domestic companies might be expected to look for older firms with more historical data to compensate for the greater asymmetry of information. But this caution is absent, and there is no evidence of reluctance to make large investments in these younger companies, as might be expected. Quite the opposite. By comparing the average market capitalization to the age of the listing company, we observe an inverse relationship: the younger the company, the higher its market capitalization on the NM. Again, this is surprising, as investors have less historical information about younger companies. The fact that their capitalization is higher may reflect higher expectations about their future earning potential.

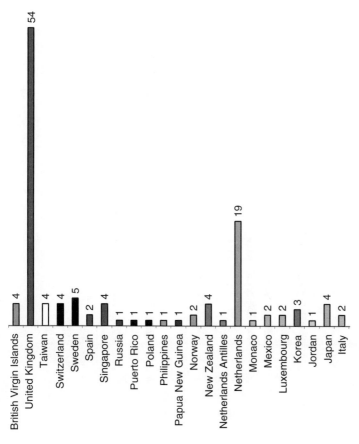

Figure 10.6. Number of non-domestic IPOs on Nasdaq by country of origin (cumulative number of listings for the period 1988–2001).

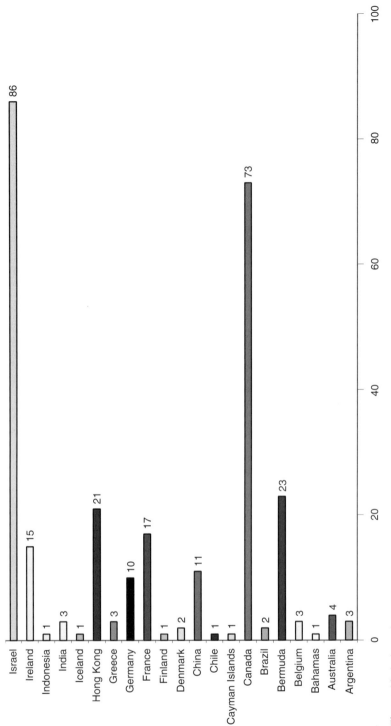

Figure 10.6. (*cont.*)

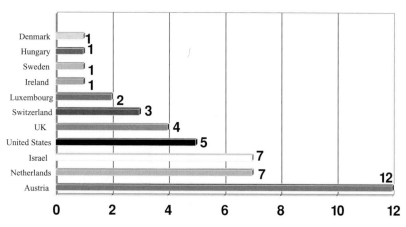

Figure 10.7. Number of non-domestic IPOs on the Neuer Markt by country of origin (Cumulative number of listings for the period 1997–2001).

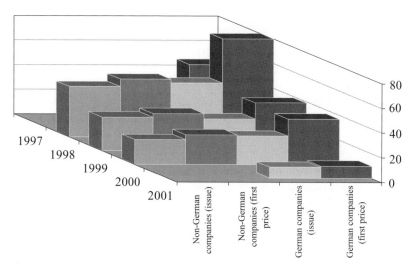

Figure 10.8. Issue price vs. first price (average), Neuer Markt, 1997–2001.

The "IPO discount" is not as steep for foreign firms: One of the costs associated with an IPO is the so-called "IPO discount," namely the issue price versus the closing price on the first day of trading.[5] We would expect non-domestic firms to suffer a steeper discount owing to the higher potential for asymmetry of information, but we found the opposite on the NM. From 1997 to 2000, the percentage difference

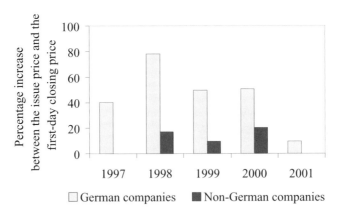

Figure 10.9. Percentage difference between the issue price and the first price, Neuer Markt, 1997–2001.

between the issue price and the closing price on the first trading day for non-domestic firms was smaller than for domestic firms (see Figures 10.8 and 10.9). This is particularly puzzling, as foreign firms on the NM, on average, are younger than domestic firms at the time of IPO.

Possible explanations could include the geographic dispersion of buyers. If the preference of German investors is to buy German stock rather than the stock of foreign companies, and if this preference is not anticipated by the bankers who price the new issue, greater under-pricing of domestic firms may result. Similarly, on the Nasdaq, we also found that non-domestic firms have a smaller percentage difference between the issue price and the closing price on the first trading day than domestic firms (see Figures 10.10 and 10.11).

Globalizing entrepreneurs: weighing the benefits and costs

What implications do these data and patterns have for entrepreneurs faced with the complex decision of where to conduct an initial public offering for their companies? The entrepreneur who wanted to raise public equity before the 1980s faced a relatively straightforward decision – an IPO at home (if there was a home market for young, entrepreneurial firms at all). Today, the opportunities are more diverse, making costs and benefits harder to assess. Should this entrepreneur stick to home markets or take the company's roadshow across borders

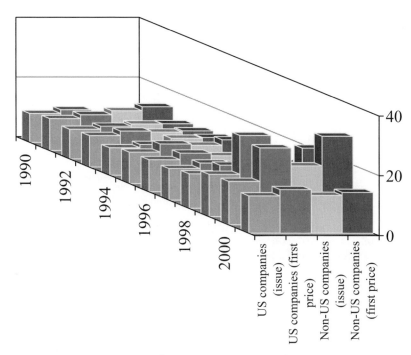

Figure 10.10. Issue price vs. first price (average), Nasdaq, 1990–2001. (*Note*: Analysis excludes seven companies for which first-price data are not available.)

to another market? How is this offering likely to be received at home and in the foreign market? There are no simple answers to this complex question, but by identifying the relative costs and benefits of sticking close to home or taking the offering abroad, managers can more fully analyze and weigh such decisions.

In the following subsections, we explore these costs and benefits in more detail. This discussion is informed by both the empirical research discussed above and academic literature, and is complemented by our own field research, including a questionnaire completed by senior executives of foreign firms that listed on the Neuer Markt.[6]

Benefits to entrepreneurs of listing their firms on a foreign exchange

Why have so many Canadian and British entrepreneurs taken their IPOs to Nasdaq? What are US and Israeli companies doing on the Neuer Markt? Many of these non-domestic companies are attracted to

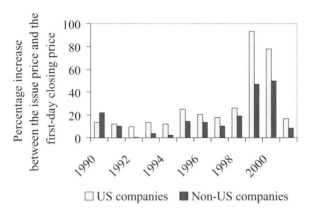

Figure 10.11. Percentage difference between the issue price and the first price, Nasdaq, 1990–2001. *Note:* Analysis excludes seven companies for which first-price data are not available.)

the various benefits of listing on a foreign exchange. Seven of these are discussed here.

Access to equity capital

First and foremost, entrepreneurs raise funds because they need capital to build and grow their firms, organically or by acquisition. Considering their need for significant cash infusions, entrepreneurs are more likely to consider a foreign listing when the amount of money they can expect to raise in the foreign market is higher than in their local capital market. In one particular case, for instance, a firm with founders who were citizens of a foreign country chose to list in that country because "the bankers felt that because of [their] roots and [their] expansion goals [they] could make a significant investment case," thus increasing the firm's odds of raising much needed capital.

However, it may be more difficult for entrepreneurial firms to gain access to foreign capital markets due to asymmetric information problems. Investors buying shares in these markets may find it more difficult to obtain, interpret, or evaluate relevant information on the company's management, products, services, and markets. As a result, the greater asymmetry of information about non-domestic firms tends to drive up the cost of capital for the entrepreneurial firm which attempts to list its securities on public non-domestic capital markets.

Liquidity for existing investors

Existing investors, including founders, senior managers, and employees who own stock (options), might wish to cash out some of their vested holdings in the company during its IPO and also in future rounds. (An IPO usually opens up the door for secondary offerings at some later point in time.) This "need for liquidity" argument is important in bull markets when the valuations of entrepreneurial firms are high. It also can be true in bear markets when investors may experience cash shortages or downright crises, and thus develop a preference for liquidity. To the extent that foreign capital markets offer a better chance to conduct a successful IPO (for example, because the local IPO market suffers from bad local economic conditions), entrepreneurs may prefer to list on a foreign exchange rather than on a local exchange.

Company shares and stock options are also an important incentive for employees and entrepreneurs to perform well. In general, the better the chances for a successful liquidity event such as an initial public offering, the more effective these incentives. Moreover, while existing strategic or financial investors may appreciate the possibility of liquidity, entrepreneurs may appreciate the opportunity to regain control of their firms[7] or to avoid control by private investors such as venture capitalists. Entrepreneurs might also benefit from a greater volume of transactions in a foreign market, as that tends to increase the market capitalization of the company and thereby reduce transaction dilution of the entrepreneurs at the IPO (see the discussion of valuation below).

Reputation, publicity, and visibility for entrepreneurial firms, abroad and at home

While Jay Ritter and Ivo Welch surmise that in general these factors play "only a minor role for most firms,"[8] in the particular case of non-domestic entrepreneurial firms trying to get a foothold in foreign product and/or factor markets, these considerations can be important. Our data indicate that strategic reasons motivate many entrepreneurial companies to list on non-domestic markets. They strongly desire to increase their reputation and build their presence in the foreign market in which they have chosen to list. This motivation for foreign listing has been confirmed in a number of interviews with executives. Executives of the Austrian company AT&S, which listed on the Neuer Markt in July 1999, suggested they chose the German market over the Austrian market because it enhanced the company's prestige and international

visibility, which helped it to recruit highly specialized foreign techni-
cians to positions in the company. A similar argument was made by
Highlight Communication, a Swiss company that listed on the NM.
Its leaders claim the listing allowed it to expand faster by increasing
its visibility and reputation. The Israeli company On Track Innovation
chose to list on the NM since it considered Germany to be its most
important market and consequently wanted to have increased visibility
there. Firms that listed outside their country of origin were able to make
useful contacts in the foreign markets, became better known, gained
prestige, increased their visibility and public relations, improved their
familiarity with the foreign product markets, and eventually increased
their sales and market share.

The challenge for most entrepreneurial firms is to overcome the lia-
bilities of smallness and newness,[9] which may be even more complicated in foreign markets, where a lack of track record and trading
history may weigh heavily against non-domestic entrepreneurial firms.
Foreign firms that want to establish credibility and legitimacy with
potential customers, suppliers, investors, employees, or creditors may
wish to do so by listing on the exchange of the target country, thus
signaling their trustworthiness, quality, and commitment to establish
a long-term presence in the market.

These moves not only enhance the company's reputation in foreign
markets, but also can add to its image at home. Some firms use a foreign
listing to create a corporate identity as an international company and
avoid being perceived as a local player. They reasoned that significant
market opportunities lay outside their local product markets, and these
could be captured only by expanding the firm internationally. These
firms wanted to create an image that was consistent with their expansion strategy. A related, but slightly different motive for foreign firms to
list on the Neuer Markt, for example, was to associate themselves with
the leading "new economy" exchange in Europe. They reasoned that
they would benefit from a reputation spillover and therefore would be
perceived as high-tech companies.

Interestingly, our qualitative interview data show that domestic firms
may benefit from being listed on a foreign exchange if their objective is
to acquire other domestic firms. Having an internationally recognized
brand can enhance the perception of the company by domestic players
as a reliable and valuable partner.

Companies also sometimes move to foreign markets to keep up with
rivals. For example, a Swiss firm decided to raise equity capital on the

Neuer Markt because "our competitors were on the Neuer Markt." It was presumably necessary to create a perception of competitive parity for customers, investors, and partners. These reasons for listing on a foreign exchange have not received much attention in either the finance or entrepreneurship literature to date.

Currency for acquisitions

Many firms that went public in the late 1990s pursued aggressive acquisition strategies, using their own company's shares, rather than cash, as a currency for acquisitions.[10] This tactic is particularly attractive for entrepreneurial, high-growth firms as it preserves cash reserves needed to fuel the company's growth. Of course, the prerequisite for success of such a financing approach is for the acquiring firm to be publicly listed, as the shares of private companies commonly trade at a significant discount relative to comparable public firms. This argument becomes particularly relevant for entrepreneurial firms that intend to acquire firms in a foreign market where the shares listed on their home exchange (e.g. Korea) might not be considered a valid currency. This would provide an incentive to firms focused on growth through acquisitions in foreign markets to list their shares in these markets.

Exit opportunities

Listing on a foreign exchange might increase the awareness of potential foreign acquirers of an entrepreneurial firm, while at the same time improving the target firm's bargaining position. This is because acquirers cannot exert pressure as easily on outside investors as on privately held firms.[11] In addition, the public market valuation puts a floor on the sales price, and the acquirer may actually have to pay a premium to convince public shareholders to take up the tender offer. An entrepreneurial firm might look at listing on a foreign capital market as possibly increasing the expected benefits from a trade sale in two ways: first, the decision to list on a foreign capital market may increase its chances of appearing on the radar screen of potential foreign acquirers; and, second, listing on the foreign market may result in a higher valuation than it would have had in its domestic capital market.

Dispersion of ownership

Increased dispersion of ownership may be attractive to entrepreneurs for several reasons. First, as Thomas Chemmanur and Paolo Fulghieri point out, diversified investors are generally willing to pay a higher price for a firm's shares than non-diversified investors, such as angel investors (i.e. individuals who invest their own money in privately held firms) or venture capitalists (i.e. institutional investors who invest other people's money in privately held companies).[12] Second, entrepreneurs may find it easier to deal with a more dispersed ownership base where no single shareholder wields too much power.

The two advantages mentioned above hold for all publicly listed firms when compared with privately held firms. Listing on a foreign market offers the added benefit of having a geographically dispersed shareholder base, which may reinforce the aforementioned advantages. It might also reduce volatility in the stock price because of differential patterns of behavior of cross-cultural investors in response to events in the company. Thus, an Israeli firm going public in the United States may benefit, for example, from having both American and Israeli shareholders – two different groups of investors who may respond differently to important events. The decision may also offer the American investors an opportunity for geographic diversification.

Valuation

Listing on a foreign exchange offers the possibility of achieving a higher valuation than might be possible in a domestic market. That is true if the foreign exchange has higher liquidity or if the entrepreneurial firm attracts international institutional investors to which it otherwise would not have access, thus increasing the demand for its shares. A higher valuation implies less dilution for the entrepreneurs when they raise new funds, and decreases the firm's costs of raising new funds.

Primary motives for foreign listings

Our survey results revealed that the most popular motive for these firms to list on a foreign exchange was to raise equity (100%), followed by strategic considerations to increase publicity and visibility (60%), and the desire to have access to international investors in order to increase the geographic dispersion of ownership (33%). About one-fourth of our sample firms (27%) were driven by liquidity concerns, and about the same number (20%) intended to use their shares as a currency for acquisitions. Surprisingly few firms mentioned as motives a higher valuation (7%) or the desire to increase exit opportunities by becoming an attractive target for acquisitions (0%).

When asked about realized (as opposed to expected) benefits, almost half the foreign firms (47%) discovered that they could use their shares as currency for acquisitions. This represented more than twice as many as had expected to derive this advantage from listing on a foreign exchange. By contrast, firms that hoped for increased liquidity seem to have been disappointed; only 7% noted it as a realized benefit.

These results shed interesting light on the frequently mentioned motives for public listing. Apparently, some of these motives matter more for non-domestic firms than for domestic companies. And the differences in importance that entrepreneurs attach to these motives can be substantial.

Costs and risks to entrepreneurs of listing their firms on a foreign exchange

The benefits of listing on foreign exchanges have to be weighed against the costs and risks of taking an IPO to these markets. We consider these costs under five headings, paying particular attention to whether these costs might be different for non-domestic as compared to domestic entrepreneurial firms:

Under-pricing and dilution
The reasons for under-pricing cited in the literature include the winner's curse,[13] the market feedback hypothesis,[14] and the bandwagon hypothesis.[15] These explanations are based on the existence of asymmetric information (or behavior) among various investors; they assume that there are informed and uninformed investors. In addition, they assume that the degree of asymmetric information between the issuing firm and the average investor does not vary.

Do the theories mentioned above predict differential under-pricing of domestic and non-domestic firms? And, if yes, what is the relative magnitude of the under-pricing? First, consider that the degree of asymmetric information between issuers and investors could be bigger for non-domestic than for domestic firms, because, for example, the evaluation of information given by non-domestic firms might be more difficult than the evaluation of the same information given by domestic firms. Following George Akerlof's adverse selection logic, this implies that the average quality of foreign issues will be lower than the average quality of domestic issues, as relatively more excellent foreign issues than domestic issues would tend to stay away from a market in which they do not receive a fair valuation.[16] Since the ratio of "bad" to "good" firms will be higher for foreign than for domestic firms, the winner's curse and the bandwagon hypothesis would predict greater under-pricing of foreign than domestic IPOs.

However, if there are reasons that would lead us to expect that the average quality of foreign firms seeking listing is *higher* than the average quality of domestic firms, then, based on the above theories, we would expect smaller under-pricing of foreign firms as compared to domestic firms. For example, very promising, rapidly growing foreign firms may not really have the choice to list on their domestic capital markets when the latter are too small to enable these firms to raise sufficient capital to fuel their rapid growth. In those cases, high-quality issues could find their way to global capital markets for entrepreneurial firms. Another argument that would lead to the same conclusion is that the cash costs (see below), as well as the opportunity costs, of going public (e.g. management time spent traveling) are higher for non-domestic firms, hence only those firms that are doing exceptionally well will incur these costs.

IPO costs

There are direct costs of undertaking an IPO that are non-trivial. The cash costs of going public include underwriting fees paid to the investment bankers (usually 7 percent of the total offering amount), filing fees (e.g. the Securities and Exchange Commission charges $92 for each $1m raised), listing fees (e.g. $100k–$155k for Nasdaq, depending on the number of shares offered), legal and accounting fees (typically $500k–$1m in the United States), printing expenses for the prospectus (typically $200k–$300k), costs incurred for the roadshow (typically $100k), directors' and officers' insurance (typically $500k–$1m), and other cash fees (e.g. for consultants, press conferences, etc.).[17] To these cash costs we must add the opportunity costs of management time spent on building and improving investor relations. Given the need for international travel and the barriers to intercultural communication,[18] these opportunity costs arguably are higher for foreign than for domestic firms. Our survey suggests that these costs are often underestimated.

Some of these costs are fixed, so that for small issues the proportional cost of going public (as well as that of secondary offerings) can be quite high. Entrepreneurs compare the costs of going public on various exchanges (including their domestic one), and, to the extent that the costs might be lower on a foreign than on a domestic exchange, they might prefer a foreign listing. One American firm in our sample, for instance, chose to list on the Neuer Markt rather than on Nasdaq chiefly because it had hoped to take advantage of lower listing costs.

Reporting requirements and other recurring costs

Further costs to be considered in going public include the potential costs of litigation, as well as recurring disclosure requirements (e.g. quarterly reports, audits, shareholder meetings), which some firms can only meet by hiring additional personnel (usually one or two new employees to take care of investor relations). The disclosure of company-specific information may also entail indirect costs by inviting imitators and attracting product market competition.[19] The increased scrutiny exercised by public shareholders can lead to a (perceived) loss of control and flexibility, and dealing with board issues can be perceived as time-consuming and costly. Other recurring costs include listing fees, fees for auditors, and fees for market makers.

Risk of negative spillover from failure of the exchange

Companies listing on a foreign exchange also face the risk that a new exchange might develop a negative reputation, and that this reputation will spill over to the listed companies. This was actually the case for Germany's Neuer Markt, which ceased to exist in 2002. Although the risk of negative reputation spillover is difficult to assess *ex ante*, it is clearly higher for newer exchanges than for more established ones with higher trading volumes and more stringent listing requirements. Conversely, to the extent that the domestic market for public entrepreneurial finance is new, and the respective foreign market is relatively more established, domestic firms might choose to move to a foreign market that is perceived to be more stable.

Employee tax penalties

There may be special tax penalties for employees of firms listing on a foreign exchange. For example, employees of Canadian firms listing in Canada get the first CA$500,000 of capital gains tax-free, but do not so if their company lists only abroad (e.g. in the United States). Listing abroad thus imposes a tax cost on the firm's employees who own company shares.

Globalizing entrepreneurship and venture capital

The data presented in this chapter clearly suggest that looking beyond domestic capital markets and tapping foreign equity capital markets is a viable alternative for some entrepreneurial companies. The data further suggest that entrepreneurs must carefully examine the tradeoffs in choosing whether to list on a domestic or on a non-domestic capital market. Tradeoffs are of three types: financial tradeoffs, specifically costs (cash costs, opportunity costs) versus benefits (amount of capital raised, trading volume, valuation); strategic tradeoffs, for which the costs of competition and imitation must be weighed against the benefits of legitimacy and credibility; and a third group, which can be considered entrepreneurial (i.e. company development). Here, the cost of the loss of focus on developing the company must be weighed against the benefits of increased opportunities for growth, both financial and in markets.

Our analysis suggests that the factors that seem to make globalizing entrepreneurs prefer a foreign listing to a domestic one are often strategic and organizational in nature. Many founders hope to raise the company's visibility in foreign product and factor markets both by raising equity in these markets and by establishing relationships, trust, and track records with foreign investors, investment banks, and institutions. In addition, a substantial number of entrepreneurial firms that (plan to) operate internationally have adopted, or strive to adopt, an international image. While being rooted (e.g. headquartered) in a specific country, these entrepreneurial firms consider themselves multi-national (e.g. pan-European rather than Dutch). By listing on a foreign exchange, they seek to enhance and make consistent their chosen corporate identity. These considerations confirm our belief that the emergence of global capital markets for entrepreneurs documented in this chapter goes hand in hand with broader trends toward globalizing product and factor markets.

Some companies have chosen a dual listings approach; that is, they have floated their securities, either simultaneously or sequentially, on both domestic and non-domestic capital markets. This approach, while more costly, enables companies to enjoy the potential benefits of a domestic listing, such as offering domestic investors easy access to the company's securities and providing employees with potential tax benefits, while at the same time enjoying the fruits associated with a foreign listing discussed above.

The emerging trend of globalizing public capital markets, which we documented in this chapter, has implications for private equity markets as well. Anticipating the possibility of exiting their investment in global capital markets, many private equity firms have opened branches or developed co-investment partnerships in non-domestic capital markets, thereby providing additional sources of capital to aspiring entrepreneurs. For example, over 340 leading US firms have an Israeli, European, or Asian focus.[20] These funds source investments globally and inject managerial and financial discipline early on in the development of the company. This discipline, coupled with the venture capitalists' knowledge of the US capital market, gives the investee firms easier access to the US public market. Hence there is an externality in the capital formation process for entrepreneurial firms: the opening of public markets to non-domestic firms makes it attractive for domestic private equity investors to make foreign investments. These investments, in turn, make it easier for the investees to access foreign public capital markets.

The emergence of global private and public capital markets for entrepreneurial firms is likely to accelerate the pace of commercializing innovations, and contribute to job creation and economic development. Furthermore, despite the overall slowdown of domestic venture capital and private equity investments since the peak year of 2000 when $94.4 billion were invested by US-based firms in 6,142 domestic and foreign transactions,[21] the globalization of US private equity firms continues. This trend, in turn, points to the expectation of investors that once the public market for young, emerging growth firms reopens, non-domestic firms will be able to gain access to the public market as well.

Notes

1 See, for example, A. Blass and Y. Yafeh, "Vagabond Shoes Longing to Stray: Why Foreign Firms List in the United States," *Journal of Banking and Finance*, 25(2001), pp. 555–572; and C. S. Eun and S. Sabherwal, "Cross-border Listings and Price Discovery: Evidence from US-Listed Canadian Stocks," *Journal of Finance*, 58 (2003), pp. 549–576.
2 The analysis examined the ten-year period 1988–1998, as well as the thirteen-year period 1988–2001, so as to control for the period considered by some to be a bubble in capital markets.

3 Data regarding IPOs on Nasdaq were collected from SDC Platinum, CRSP, Dealogic LLC, the Nasdaq website, and Compustat. Obtaining data on foreign IPOs on the Neuer Markt was more problematic as there is no central data depository. (Note that companies that transferred from another exchange are not included in the IPO count as they were already publicly listed. We excluded thirty-six companies from the NM analysis because of a former listing on another exchange or a lack of data.) Specifically, we obtained stock price and market-value data from Datastream, while other data were extracted from company filings that were available on the NM website and, in some cases, from the filing prospectus. For example, the issue price and the country of origin were obtained from the NM website and from the companies' filings. As the NM IPOs were in a foreign currency (either the DM or the euro), we converted the IPO listing price into US dollars using the inter-bank exchange rate on the day of the offering.

4 The age data on NM companies excludes eighteen companies because of a lack of information.

5 J. R. Ritter and I. Welch, "A Review of IPO Activity, Pricing, and Allocations," *Journal of Finance*, 57 (2002), pp. 1795–1828.

6 This is based on open-ended questionnaires sent to forty-four foreign firms who listed on the Neuer Markt; fifteen questionnaires were returned (giving a response rate of 34 percent). The questionnaires were completed in most cases by the firms' chief financial officers.

7 B. S. Black and R. J. Gilson, "Venture Capital and the Structure of Capital Markets: Banks versus Stock Markets," *Journal of Financial Economics*, 47 (1998), pp. 243–277.

8 Ritter and Welch, "Review of IPO Activity," p. 1796.

9 A. L. Stinchcombe, "Organizations and Social Structure," in J. G. March (ed.), *Handbook of Organizations* (Chicago: Rand-McNally, 1965), pp. 142–193.

10 P. Schultz and M. Zaman, "Do the Individuals Closest to Internet Firms Believe They Are Overvalued?" *Journal of Financial Economics*, 59 (2001), pp. 347–381.

11 L. Zingales, "Insider Ownership and the Decision to Go Public," *Review of Economic Studies*, 62 (1995), pp. 425–448.

12 T. Chemmanur and P. Fulghieri, "Investment Banker Reputation, Information Production, and Financial Intermediation," Columbia First Boston Series in Money, Economics and Finance working paper, no. FB-91-09.

13 In an IPO, a fixed number of shares are typically sold at a fixed price. If demand exceeds supply, rationing will occur. Assume there exists an asymmetry of information among investors. If the "less informed"

investors get all they ask for, that is because the more informed investors did not want the shares. Faced with this adverse selection issue, the less informed will only submit purchase orders if, on average, the issue is sufficiently discounted to compensate them for the bias in the allocation of new issues.

14 To induce the true revelation of an investor's valuation of the stock of a particular IPO, the investment bankers compensate the investor through under-pricing. Further, the investment banker must underprice issues for which favorable information is revealed by more than those for which unfavorable information is revealed.

15 Investors pay attention not only to information about the company in which they invest, but also to whether other investors are buying. If no one else buys, then an investor may not buy, even if she has favorable information.

16 G. A. Akerlof, "The Market for 'Lemons': Quality Uncertainty and the Market Mechanism," *Quarterly Journal of Economics*, 84 (1970), pp. 488–500.

17 J. A. Fraser, "The Road to Wall Street," *Inc.*, 24, 6 (2002), pp. 80–85.

18 One Dutch company that listed on Neuer Markt, for example, stated that "Germany has a completely different culture on investor relation-related activities than the Anglo-Saxon countries." As investors in small- and mid-cap stocks preserve a local (i.e. national) investment focus, a foreign company "has to attract the national financial press."

19 V. Maksimovic and P. Pichler, "Technological Innovation and Initial Public Offerings," *Review of Financial Studies*, 14 (2001), pp. 459–494.

20 Source: Venturescape (http://www.venturescape.com/).

21 Source: Venture One (http://www.ventureone.com/).

11 | *Cross-border valuation: the international cost of equity capital*

GORDON M. BODNAR
The Johns Hopkins University

BERNARD DUMAS
INSEAD

RICHARD MARSTON
Wharton School

How does a firm in one country evaluate an investment in a firm in another country, or how does it evaluate a foreign project that the firm itself is undertaking? Both questions are increasingly important as international mergers and acquisitions grow and as firms become more multinational in their operations. In domestic markets, managers would typically estimate future free cash flows to equity of the investment and discount these cash flows at some appropriate rate, using the classic Capital Asset Pricing Model (CAPM). The CAPM, however, has several problems when applied to global markets. First, it requires an equity premium, or the excess return of the broad equity market over the risk-free rate, which is quite complicated to determine in global markets. For example, should a US-based firm considering an acquisition in China use the equity premium from its home market or from China? Further, there are other forms of global risk that the CAPM ignores completely. How can managers take into account the broader risks of global markets such as currency risk and political risk? In this chapter, the authors examine ways to make the CAPM a more robust tool for assessing global investments. They propose ways for managers to address differences in equity premiums and integrate considerations of currency and political

We thank Stéphane Marchand, MBA student at INSEAD, for extremely valuable research assistance offered during the drafting of this chapter.

255

risks into the CAPM. Finally, they examine an approach that is especially useful in analyzing investments in developing countries.

I n July 1998, the Indonesian government decided to privatize a cement firm, PT Semen Gresik, opening the bidding to firms throughout the world. Cemex, a Mexico-based firm, competed with Holcim, a Switzerland-based firm, in the bidding process. In advising Cemex, the French investment bank Paribas proposed to base the bid on a discounted cash flow model using the Capital Assest Pricing Model (CAPM) as the basis for valuation. But which country's stock market premium should be used for this valuation, the Indonesian market's or the Mexican market's? The valuation might vary widely depending on whether the CAPM was applied to one market or the other. Would Holcim evaluate the Indonesian firm differently because it was based in Switzerland? How should Cemex take into account the political risk associated with the ending of the Suharto regime? The CAPM is not suited to measuring political risk, so how should the discount rate for the project be adjusted to account for this additional risk?

Domestic finance teaches us that the classic Capital Asset Pricing Model allows a systematic comparison of the costs of equity of various traded firms. The classic CAPM, however, recognizes but one source of risk and one risk premium to be charged on a share of stock, namely, the systematic risk or risk of covariation of the stock with the broader equity market, captured by the equity's β.[1] The discount rate for equity-financed projects is based on this β times the *equity market premium*, or the excess return of the broad equity market portfolio over the risk-free rate. In the international setting, it's not obvious which country's equity market premium should be used in the evaluation, that of the acquiring firm or that of the target firm.

If the world's stock markets were fully integrated, acquiring firms from different countries would evaluate an acquisition in the same way. Both Cemex and Holcim would base their discount rates for the acquisition on the same (worldwide) equity premium. Since both potential acquirers would measure the β of PT Semen Gresik *vis-à-vis* the same world index, they would use the same discount rate for the cash flows (in a given currency). If the cash flows expected by each bidding firm were identical, Cemex and Holcim would come up with the same valuation for the Indonesian firm. But what if markets are not fully integrated? What approach does one use then?

Diverse sources of risk

In the international setting, there are many dimensions of risk for which financial market participants require a premium. These are discussed in the following paragraphs.

The *world* stock market price risk. As discussed above, the classic CAPM says that this is the only systematic source of risk, but we intend to go beyond the classic CAPM. The index of traded securities that carries this risk is, of course, the worldwide stock market index. The fundamental source of this dimension of risk is the fluctuation in worldwide business activity.

The stock market price risk of each *country*. This risk is specific to the securities of that country, but systematic to all of them. The index that carries this risk is each country's stock market index.[2] The fundamental source of this risk is the fluctuation in the country's business activity. When world and country dimensions are taken into account jointly, the fundamental source of this dimension of risk is the fluctuation in the country's business activity relative to that of world business activity.

The stock market price risk of each *industry*. This risk is specific to the securities issued by firms of that industry, but systematic to all of them. The index that carries this risk is each industry's stock market index calculated across the world.[3] The fundamental source of this risk is the worldwide fluctuation in the industry's business activity.

Exchange rate risk affects many firms, depending on their foreign-exchange exposures. The index of return is provided by returns on foreign-currency deposits.

Political risk is the risk that the securities issued by entities of a country may be in default. It is the risk generally that legal financial contracts will not be enforced. A possible return index is provided by sovereign bond returns, and we discuss below the validity of using these returns as indices of political risk pricing.

Liquidity risk is a dimension of risk that is especially present in developing capital markets. It represents the risk that capital gains indicated by stock market quotes can never be realized, because an attempt to realize them would produce a negative price impact. An index can be provided by the difference in rates of return between less liquid and highly liquid company shares, or by differences in rates of return between country capital markets where liquidity is low and those where liquidity is high. We do not discuss this dimension of risk any further in this study.[4]

These systematic risks (risks to which many securities are exposed), are the only ones that can fetch a non-zero premium in the financial market. An investor who bears other dimensions of risk, that are specific to each security, receives no reward because he could have diversified that risk away. As discussed below, for each dimension of risk, it is not enough to surmise that it receives a non-zero price. We need also have in mind some index of security market prices that uniquely carries this risk and can, therefore, help us determine what the going price is. We can then incorporate these factors into an assessment of the cost of equity.

   In the following sections, we investigate these issues in more detail. We first examine how the cost of equity capital can be measured in an international context. Then we consider how to assess both exchange risk and political risk. While these discussions do not address all the sources of risk noted above, they illustrate the complexities of making cross-border valuations and demonstrate useful frameworks and tools for addressing these challenges.

Measuring the cost of equity capital

In November 1994, Westmoreland Coal Company, a US-based firm, intended to invest $540 million in an electric power project located in Zhangze, China. In the Chinese market, there is no comparable publicly traded project from which to calculate a local β. This is a common problem in many projects in developing economies. Should Westmoreland measure the β using the returns of electricity companies in the United States? How should it adjust those returns for the β of China's market *vis-à-vis* the US market? If so, should it use the China equity premium or the US equity premium? The choice of equity premium is a difficult one and it can have significant implications for investment decisions

   Equity premiums vary widely from country to country, as shown in Figure 11.1 which displays a record of equity premiums in sixteen

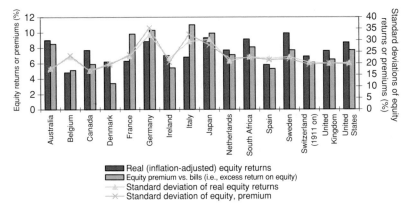

Figure 11.1. Equity returns around the world, 1900–2000, yearly observations, local currencies. (*Source:* Dimson, Marsh, and Staunton, *Triumph of the Optimists.*)

countries, measured in the respective local currency, based on one hundred yearly observations.[5] Because the currency units differ, these numbers are not directly comparable. Currency movements, however, are not so large as to alter dramatically the general picture. Their differences are economically meaningful: many more investment projects would be deemed acceptable when using the equity premium of Denmark (below 4 percent/year) than when using the equity premium of Italy (11 percent/year). Furthermore, differences would be even more stark if more countries were considered, or if subperiods of the twentieth century were examined.

None the less, many of these differences are not statistically significant,[6] and some researchers have hypothesized that the differences observed across countries were only differences arising from statistical sampling.[7] Investors in Italy during the twentieth century turned out to be lucky but they did not expect such a return. Therefore, one should not look at the numbers in Figure 11.1 as having differed *ex ante* or as representing expected returns that were required by investors. They are just differences in the realized averages. Under this hypothesis, the premium based on the largest number of observations, namely the world premium, is the best estimate we have.[8] It turns out to be equal to 6.2%.[9]

To the extent that equity premiums differ across the world in an economically meaningful way and to the extent that some are statistically significantly different from each other, one would like to know, when evaluating a project in a country, whether one should use the local premium (the premium observed in the country where the project is to be undertaken), the home premium (the premium observed in the country where capital comes from) or the world premium. One would also like to know whether the differences in premiums are the sign of some segmentation of the financial markets of the world along country lines. In other words, is capital cheaper in some places than others? If it is, a further recommendation can be provided concerning the market where capital should be raised.

Segmented or integrated?

The answer to whether the local, home, or world premium should be used depends whether we are ready to believe that the world financial market is fully integrated or, at the other extreme, fully segmented along country borders. If the world is fully segmented, investors of one country have access only to the securities issued by the companies that trade in that country. A "domestic CAPM" prevails in each country. According to that form of the CAPM, β is measured relative to the country's market index and the equity premium to be applied is the local market premium.[10] As we have seen, the choice of the equity premium can vary widely depending on whether the local premium (where the project is undertaken) or the home premium is used.

In the situation of complete market segmentation, it is necessarily the case that the shareholders of a company are home stockholders, unless the company is listed in several countries or has issued Depositary Receipts in foreign countries. If a firm contemplates an investment abroad, therefore, it should use the CAPM of its home country. It should measure the β of the foreign investment, or that of a comparable traded company, relative to its *home* equity market, but it should charge the market premium that prevails in its *home* market.

If the world is fully integrated, on the other hand, a company's stockholders come from many different countries because it is assumed that each one holds a globally diversified portfolio. For all investors, a "worldwide classic CAPM" prevails in which the return premium to any investment, when measured in a specific currency unit, is the same for all investors. This is because each security's β is measured *vis-à-vis* the world market index and the market premium to be used is the world equity premium.[11]

Table 11.1. *Segmented and integrated views of Thalès*

January 28, 1987 to January 28, 2002	*"Quantity of risk"* β *of Thalès* vis-à-vis *domestic/world market*	*"Price of risk"* *Equity premium on the domestic/ world market*	*Required premium (%/month)*
Segmented: view of US investor	0.789	× 0.654%	= 0.516
Segmented: view of French investor	1.065	× 0.529%	= 0.529
Integrated: required US dollar premium	0.870	× 0.267%	= 0.232

If a firm contemplates an investment abroad under a full integration assumption, it should use the "worldwide classic CAPM". It should measure the β of the foreign investment, or that of a comparable traded company, relative to the *world* equity market portfolio. It should charge the market premium for the *world* equity market portfolio.

Different views: an illustration

As an illustration, the first row of Table 11.1 shows the calculation of the required premium (or required excess expected rate of return) in dollar units on the French firm Thalès (ex Thomson-CSF) from the point of view of US stockholders in the hypothetical, full-segmentation situation in which they hold US assets only. This required premium is to be added to the current value of the riskless dollar rate of interest, to obtain a required rate of return. The next row, by contrast, shows the same calculation, with a different result, from the point of view of a French investor who holds only French assets, abstracting from the fact that a French investor would not want to calculate a required rate of return in dollar units.

Using an integrated perspective, the final row shows the required premium (or required excess expected rate of return) in dollar units from the point of view of worldwide stockholders for the hypothetical, full-integration situation in which they hold a worldwide, diversified portfolio of equity. This required premium is to be added to the current value of the riskless US dollar rate of interest, to obtain a required rate of return in US dollars. The risk premium obtained using this method is quite different from those using the segmented-market model. So the

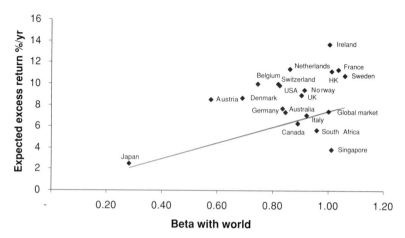

Figure 11.2. Testing the CAPM across countries: last twenty years' equity monthly data in US dollars.

valuation of a project would change markedly depending on which model applied. The reader might think that currency risk is absent from the analysis, but this is not true. If the β of Thalès were measured after being hedged for exchange risk, the result would be somewhat different.

A hybrid model: multi-β CAPM

Is the world integrated or segmented? On the basis of observations of the actual rates of return in the financial market, it is difficult to produce a definitive answer to this question. If the dataset includes only returns on the equity portfolios of various countries, a typical cross-sectional picture, shown in Figure 11.2, is not conclusive. However, if the dataset includes foreign-currency denominated deposits in addition to equity portfolios, the picture in Figure 11.3 emerges. A more distinct cross-sectional line can be drawn within the cloud of points.[12]

Given the inconclusive picture provided by Figure 11.2, we need to remain agnostic on the question of whether we should use a country risk premium (as is the case under full segmentation) or, instead, a world risk premium (under full integration). Driven by the desire to remain agnostic and by the belief that the world financial market

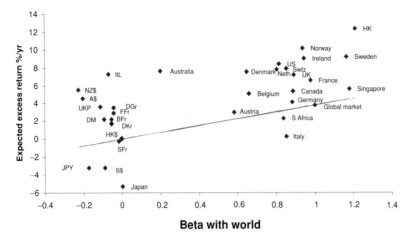

Figure 11.3. Testing the CAPM across countries and currencies: last fifteen years' monthly data in US dollars.

is probably neither fully integrated nor fully segmented, one might be tempted to use a CAPM including both kinds of premiums, determined on the basis of distinct βs and different prices of risk for each dimension of risk. This leads to the idea of a multi-β, or "hybrid," CAPM.

In a multifactor, or multi-β model, the measurement of risk is not one-dimensional. Instead, there exist several dimensions to which an investor is sensitive simultaneously. For instance, we mentioned above that a mean-variance investor should only care about a security's sensitivities (exposure) to its portfolio return. At the market level, this implies that the market requires a premium only for a security's exposure to the return on the market portfolio.

But when investors care only about the mean and variance of their return, it means that they do not care when they receive a high return and when they receive a low return. That may not be a realistic assumption. People may be interested in getting high returns from their world-wide, diversified portfolio when their own country is in recession but may be ready to accept lower returns from their portfolio when their own country is in expansion. This may be because they collect some other income (such as wages) intrinsically tied to the economic activity in their own country.[13] Under these circumstances, they may want to look carefully at their portfolio's exposure to their own country,

Table 11.2. *Required US dollar premium on Thalès according to the "hybrid model" incorporating world and country factors*

January 28, 1987 to January 28, 2002	"Quantity of risk" Joint $\hat{\beta}$s of Thalès vis-à-vis *two* markets	"Price of risk" Average excess return on the two markets	Required premium (%/month)
World market risk	−0.36	× 0.267%	= −0.097
French market risk	1.266	× 0.497%	= 0.629
Total			0.532

probably reducing the weight of their country's shares in order to diversify away from their other income. Alternatively, consider a different case in which investors may have a special liking for the shares of their own country's firms because they feel better informed about them.

Whatever may be the reason for it, it can happen that the financial market prices a portfolio or a security's exposure to countries differently from the way it prices exposure to the world financial market as a whole.

To implement a model of this sort, one must generalize the concept of β as a one-dimensional exposure to risk, to reach a concept of multidimensional exposure. This is easily done by using the tool of multiple regression.[14]

Let us illustrate with our example of Thalès how the "hybrid" model would incorporate the two factors. The βs for the two-factor model are reported in Table 11.2. The influence of the French market is evidently the dominant one, since the β for the world market is not even positive. Modifying the French-only model of Table 11.1 with the addition of a world market return as in Table 11.2 seems to make little difference. Thalès appears to be priced primarily with respect to the French market.

To gain some perspective on whether this phenomenon is a general one, we examined the values of the joint $\hat{\beta}$s for an arbitrary sample of firms of an arbitrary subset of countries: the United States, Belgium, France, and Poland. For each firm, we obtained the two joint $\hat{\beta}$s by regressing the firms' excess rates of return on the local and the world stock markets, as illustrated for US and French firms in Tables 11.3 and 11.4.[15] In these tables, the excess rates of return are measured in

Table 11.3. *Joint βs and hybrid pricing model for selected US firms*

| NAME | Average excess return (%) | Multifactor | | Risk premium for country risk (%) | Risk premium for world risk (%) | Total premium (%) |
		$\hat{\beta}$ stock-to-country	$\hat{\beta}$ stock-to-world			
Riskless US dollar return	0	0	0	0.00	0.00	0.00
US index	7.84	1	0	7.84	0.00	7.84
World	2.49	0	1	0.00	2.49	2.49
Abbott Labs.		0.56	−0.07	4.43	−0.18	4.25
American Home Products		0.68	−0.17	5.37	−0.44	4.93
Andersen Group		0.88	−0.10	6.90	−0.26	6.65
AT&T		0.86	−0.02	6.76	−0.04	6.72
Bank of America		1.42	−0.44	11.17	−1.09	10.08
Ford Motor		0.84	0.02	6.58	0.05	6.63
General Electric		1.16	−0.05	9.08	−0.12	8.95
Hewlett Packard		1.38	0.11	10.83	0.28	11.11
IBM		0.76	0.23	5.96	0.58	6.54
Johnson & Johnson		0.80	−0.13	6.28	−0.33	5.95
Motorola		1.40	0.19	10.98	0.47	11.45
Pfizer		0.84	−0.11	6.59	−0.28	6.31
Caterpillar		0.91	0.18	7.14	0.44	7.58
Nthn. Trust		0.92	0.14	7.20	0.35	7.54
Kimberly Clark		0.58	−0.02	4.51	−0.05	4.46
Wells Fargo & Co		0.94	0.00	7.39	−0.01	7.38
Coca Cola		0.76	−0.06	5.98	−0.14	5.85
Du Pont E I De Nemours		0.77	0.13	6.03	0.33	6.36
Intel		1.59	0.07	12.49	0.17	12.66
Walt Disney		1.23	−0.01	9.66	−0.02	9.65

Table 11.4. *Joint βs and hybrid pricing model for selected French firms*

NAME	Average excess return (%)	Multifactor β stock-to-country	β stock-to-world	Risk premium for country risk (%)	Risk premium for world risk (%)	Total risk premium (%)
Riskless French franc return	0.00	0.00	0.00	0.00	0.00	0.00
France Index	4.80	1.00	0.00	4.80	0.00	4.80
World	2.93	0.00	1.00	0.00	2.93	2.93
Accor		1.09	0.01	5.24	0.04	5.28
Air Liquide		0.83	−0.22	3.99	−0.65	3.34
AXA		1.42	−0.12	6.81	−0.37	6.45
Bouygues		1.41	−0.11	6.76	−0.32	6.45
Carrefour		0.84	0.06	4.01	0.18	4.19
Ciments Francais		1.14	−0.23	5.50	−0.68	4.82
Danone		0.83	−0.16	3.98	−0.46	3.52
Société générale		0.95	−0.07	4.57	−0.20	4.38
Total Fina Elf		0.61	0.06	2.94	0.19	3.13
Sanofi-Synthelabo		0.93	−0.23	4.46	−0.68	3.78
Suez		1.13	−0.21	5.44	−0.62	4.81
Pernod-Ricard		1.16	−0.49	5.58	−1.44	4.14
Peugeot		1.03	0.06	4.97	0.19	5.15
Michelin		1.08	0.09	5.18	0.27	5.45
Dassault Aviation		0.53	0.06	2.56	0.17	2.72
Pinault Printemps		1.26	0.03	6.05	0.08	6.12
Thalès (Thomson-CSF)		1.32	−0.34	6.34	−0.99	5.35
Valeo		1.07	0.12	5.13	0.34	5.46
Colas		1.10	−0.24	5.29	−0.72	4.57
Vivendi Universal		1.27	−0.22	6.08	−0.64	5.44

the local currency but the exposure $\hat{\beta}$ numbers would be similar if the rates of return had been measured in some other currency.[16]

For all countries, it was clear that the joint $\hat{\beta}$ *vis-à-vis* the local market is much larger than the joint $\hat{\beta}$ *vis-à-vis* the world market and that local-country risk premium dominates the pricing. This is a striking empirical fact, although it is a difficult one to understand in theoretical terms. Unless the world is segmented generally – and not just financially – why should local stock indexes have such a dominant influence on stocks in that country?

The CAPM by itself does not dictate what βs should be; it only indicates how expected returns should differ from one security to another given the structure of βs. However, βs come from somewhere; they are calculated from rates of return. In a broader dynamic-pricing theory, prices – not just expected returns – would be entirely calculated from the fundamental cash flows paid by the security under consideration.[17] In the context of such a theory, under the hypothesis of full integration, common stochastic discount factors are applied to all securities of the world. As these discount factors fluctuate, so do the prices of all securities. The theory is likely to tell us that securities are more exposed to the world market index than to country market indices, contrary to what we observed in our examination of the four countries.

Local pricing

The results in Tables 11.3 and 11.4 are consistent with other studies. A study by Bertrand Jacquillat and Bruno Solnik found that the price movements of a set of US multinationals are markedly related to those of the NYSE, while they are poorly related to the stock indices of the countries where the multinationals are active.[18]

There is also a well-known phenomenon of "local pricing" whereby, for unknown reasons, the securities traded on one stock exchange seem to follow the gyrations of that stock exchange index. For example, consider the pricing of the shares of Royal Dutch Shell.[19] Since 1909, the sister companies of the Royal Dutch Shell group have shared all dividends. Yet the stocks of the British company, Shell Trading and Transport, and the Dutch company, Royal Dutch Shell, have often fetched different prices (when expressed in the same currency). And, even more interestingly, the ratio of these prices follows the ratio of the stock price indices in London and Amsterdam. In other words, the local stock market influence seems to pertain even for sister companies sharing the same dividends.

Another example of local market pricing concerns closed-end country funds. These funds, which typically invest in the stocks of a single foreign country, are offered to investors in the US market as a convenient way to buy a diversified portfolio of the foreign country's stocks. When the prices of these closed-end funds are compared with the net asset value (NAV) of the underlying stocks, large differentials are often discovered. This by itself is not surprising, since these differentials cannot be "arbitraged away" unless the fund is forced to liquidate its holdings. But what is strange about the differentials is that they are correlated with the US market.[20] Why should the differential between closed-end fund prices and their NAV be correlated with the home market of the investors in the fund? The US market exerts an influence on closed-end fund prices even though the stocks in the fund are overseas.

We may have done well to have remained agnostic and, by applying the "hybrid" model, to have left open the possibility that the world financial market may, at least partially, be segmented. As is the case for many multifactor CAPMs, it is not easy to produce a rigorous theoretical foundation for the hybrid CAPM.[21]

The pricing of currency risk

The world CAPM that we have discussed is implicitly based on an important assumption – that every investor has the same currency. When we applied the CAPM in question to rates of return measured, for instance, in US dollars, we were implicitly assuming that all investors of the world were choosing their portfolios on the basis of anticipated US dollar returns, or that all investors were based in US dollars, presumably living and consuming the income from their portfolio in the United States. In reality, the world is populated with investors who live in different countries. This creates among them a degree of heterogeneity. When this heterogeneity is taken into account, we have the picture of the world financial investor population that is shown in Figure 11.4.

When the world investor population is heterogeneous in this manner, foreign-exchange risk cannot be priced in the same way as world-market risk. This difference arises for the following reason. As far as

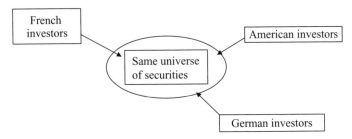

Figure 11.4. The world investor population.

world equity risk is concerned, every investor in the world essentially holds a long position. Firms issue stock securities to finance their investment and almost everyone buys those securities. The cases in which some investors short stocks only arise from a difference of opinion about the anticipated returns from stocks; in that case, other investors hold even more of the same stocks long.

To reap the benefits of diversification, investors of the world hold the stock securities of all countries. All these stock securities – but especially the foreign stocks – expose the investors not only to equity risk but also to currency risk. This latter risk may or may not be worth bearing depending on the equilibrium rates of return in the market for currency deposits. If it so happens that the currency risk imbedded in foreign stock securities is not worth bearing (which means that the cost of hedging is sufficiently low), investors who invest in foreign stocks will want to hedge this investment against currency risk.

In the market for currencies, the situation is vastly different because investors consider the deposit denominated in their home currency to be a riskless or quasi-riskless asset, since it guarantees a future purchasing power. Even if inflation in their country is very volatile, the home-currency deposit will often be the safest asset available.[22]

Provided their risk aversions are sufficiently high,[23] the investors of each country hold the home-currency deposit positively. They stand ready to hold it because they want to invest some of their wealth in what they view as a riskless asset. This is just an application of the familiar Tobin separation theorem, whereby investors choose the composition of a portfolio of risky securities and then, depending on their level of risk aversion, decide what fraction of their wealth to invest in the riskless and what fraction in the portfolio of risky securities. By

Table 11.5. *Required US dollar premium on Thalès according to the IAPM incorporating world and currency factors*

January 28, 1987 to January 28, 2002	"Quantity of risk" Joint $\hat{\beta}$s of Thalès vis-à-vis *two* factors	"Price of risk" Average excess return on the *two factors*	Required premium (%/month)
World market	0.856	× 0.267%	= 0.229
Euro deposit	0.303	× −0.038%	= −0.011
Total			0.217

holding the home-currency deposit, home investors maintain the home-currency rate of interest at a level lower than it would otherwise be. Foreign investors who are holding stocks of the country, in contrast, are candidates for hedging. They may wish to borrow the home currency, or, equivalently, sell it forward or generally hold it short. They will do so if the cost of hedging is sufficiently low. But a low cost of hedging is precisely what home-country resident investors tend to bring about since their situation induces them to hold the currency. The equilibrium that obtains is one in which foreign investors short the home currency, taking advantage of the vast pool of home residents who, by holding their home currency, stand ready to provide hedging services, at a cost which is lower than it would be in their absence.

International Asset Pricing Model

In this equilibrium, stock market risk is priced by investors who are all essentially holding that risk long, while each of the currency-risk dimensions is priced by investors some of whom structurally hold it long while others short it. Because of this structural difference, the equilibrium pricing of currency risk cannot be subsumed in the pricing of world stock market risk. It cannot be a redundant dimension of risk. To price it, we need a separate risk premium, with a price of risk that is determined separately from the price of world stock market risk. The result is the International Asset Pricing Model (IAPM).[24]

In Table 11.5, we illustrate the working of the IAPM on the Thalès example. Since the equity return on Thalès is measured in dollars, the table reports joint βs with respect to both the world stock market

Table 11.6. *Required euro premium on Thalès according to the IAPM incorporating world and currency factors*

January 28, 1987 to January 28, 2002	"Quantity of risk" Joint βs of Thalès vis-à-vis two factors	"Price of risk" Average excess return on the two factors	Required premium (%/month)
World market	0.856	× 0.271	= 0.232
Dollar deposit	−0.159	× 0.123	= −0.020
Total			0.213

and the euro deposit (representing the foreign-currency risk factor). Adding the resulting risk premium to the dollar rate of interest gives the dollar required rate of return on Thalès in a world market in which the investor population is heterogeneous.

In Table 11.6, we perform the same task using the euro as the measurement currency.[25]

All the CAPMs we have discussed prior to this section have one major weakness in common. If the CAPM in question applies to the rates of return measured in one currency, then the same CAPM will no longer hold after translation into another currency. If all securities line up when their returns are measured in one unit, they no longer will when measured in another unit. This deficiency is shared by any CAPM that does not include a separate term for a currency-risk premium. The International Asset Pricing Model enjoys a property of consistency under a change of measurement unit. One can show that the choice of the measurement currency, in terms of which the IAPM is stated, is immaterial.[26]

The IAPM is not without drawbacks, however. One drawback is that the list of non-measurement currency dimensions of risk to which a security may be exposed is potentially very long. Moreover, premiums for these currency risks are often much smaller than world market risk premiums[27] and the calculation of the currency risk is based on a price of risk that is estimated with a wide margin of error. This is because it is based on the average excess rate of return on just one asset, namely, the average excess rate of return on each of the foreign currencies considered one by one. This is in contrast to the price of world market risk, which is based on the average excess rate of return on the wide world market portfolio. By a statistical analog of the diversification effect, the average excess rate of return on a wide portfolio is a much better estimate of the corresponding expected excess return than would be the average return on a single asset.

The pricing of political risk

As far as financial market pricing is concerned, there is a strong similarity between currency risk and political risk. Both are borne differentially by the residents and the non-residents of a country. For similar reasons, therefore, it may be a good idea to recognize a separate risk premium for political risks. This again leads to a multi-β CAPM in which we would recognize a premium for world, or country, market risk and one or more premiums for political risk.[28]

But what index can properly represent the political risk factor? Niso Abuaf proposes to treat political risk by including foreign, sovereign bonds (or Brady bonds) in the multiple regression for the estimation of joint βs and, correspondingly, to estimate the market price of political risk.[29] There are both empirical and conceptual problems with this approach. The empirical problem is that, for the last fifteen years, the Brady bonds of some countries have had negative returns. The conceptual problem is that Brady bonds may not capture political risk properly. For one thing, they are partly backed by US Treasury bills. More crucially, the risk that a government will not repay may differ from the risk that a company of the country will see its stock return affected by political factors.

To illustrate the empirical problem with using Abuaf's approach, we apply his methodology to a sample of Latin American firms in Table 11.7. We calculate the required risk premium on a number of American Depositary Receipts (ADRs) which are written on Latin American stock securities and which are traded on the NYSE. This is done on the basis of the excess dollar rate of return on the corresponding Brady bonds of the respective Latin American country.[30]

The results in this table are problematic because, during the sample period under consideration, the average realized excess dollar rate of return on the Brady bonds turned out to be negative or, in several cases, implausibly small. It is unlikely that negative risk premiums or small positive risk premiums reflect the rates of return that investors expected and required on these securities. And the relative ranking of countries

Table 11.7. *A multi-beta model that prices political risk*

January 28, 1997 to January 28, 2002	Average excess return (%/year)	$\hat{\beta}s$		Required dollar excess return (%/year)	Country
		US stock index	US Brady bond index		
US – DS MARKET	0.320				
SALOMON BROS.BRADY BOND ARGENTINE – RETURN IND. (OFCL)	−12.68				
SALOMON BROS.BRADY BOND BRAZILIAN – RETURN IND. (OFCL)	3.15				
JPM ELMI + CHILE ($) – RETURN IND. (OFCL)	−4.29				
SALOMON BROS.BRADY BOND MEXICAN – RETURN IND. (OFCL)	4.33				
SALOMON BROS.BRADY BOND PHILIPPINE – RETURN IND. (OFCL)	1.82				
SALOMON BROS.BRADY BOND VENEZUELAN – RETURN IND. (OFCL)	1.20				

(cont.)

Table 11.7. *(continued)*

January 28, 1997 to January 28, 2002	Average excess return (%/year)	$\hat{\beta}s$ US stock index	US Brady bond index	Required dollar excess return (%/year)	Country
BBVA BANCO FRANCES SPN. ADR.		0.812	0.948	−11.76	Argentina
IRSA INVERSIONERS Y REP.S A GDR		0.710	0.839	−10.41	Argentina
METROGAS SPN.ADR.B 1 ADR = 10 B SHS.		0.066	0.432	−5.46	Argentina
TELF.DE ARGN.CL.B SPN. ADR 1 ADR =10 SHS.		0.824	0.834	−10.31	Argentina
TELECOM ARGN.B SPN.ADR 1 ADR = 5 SHARES		0.609	0.936	−11.68	Argentina
TSPA.GAS DEL SUR SPN.ADR1 ADR = 5 B SHS.		0.098	0.430	−5.42	Argentina
YPF D SPN.ADR 1 ADR = 1 SHARE		0.694	0.133	−1.46	Argentina
ARACRUZ PNB SPN.ADR 1 ADR = 10 B PF.SHS.		0.994	0.771	2.75	Brazil
CMPH.BRASL.DE DISTB.ADR.		0.333	1.704	5.48	Brazil
COPEL PNB SPN.ADR 1 ADR = 1000 SHARES		−0.203	2.472	7.73	Brazil
SID NACIONAL ON ADR 1 ADR = 1000 SHARES		0.726	1.488	4.93	Brazil

Table 11.7. *(continued)*

January 28, 1997 to January 28, 2002	Average excess return (%/year)	$\hat{\beta}s$ US stock index	US Brady bond index	Required dollar excess return (%/year)	Country
UNIBANCO GDR GDR=500 UNITS		0.683	2.420	7.85	Brazil
ANDINA 'A' SPN.ADR 1 ADR = 6 SHARES		0.657	1.255	−5.17	Chile
BBV BANCO BHIF SPN.ADR. 1 ADR = 10 SHARES		0.002	1.167	−5.01	Chile
BNC.CTL.HISPANO ADR DEAD – EXPD 16/04/99		0.524	0.153	−0.49	Chile
BANCO SANTANDER CHILE SPN.ADR.SVS.A		0.674	0.238	−0.80	Chile
CRISTALES SPN.ADR. 1 ADR = 3 NPV SHARES		0.092	1.783	−7.62	Chile
CTC 'A' SPN.ADR 1 ADR = 4 SHARES		1.113	1.959	−8.05	Chile
ENERSIS SPN.ADR. 1 ADR = 50 SHARES		0.737	0.946	−3.82	Chile
ENDESA CHILE SPN.ADR.		0.583	1.137	−4.69	Chile
SANTA ISABEL SPN.ADR. 1 ADR = 15 SHARES		0.719	1.083	−4.42	Chile
MADECO SPN.ADR. 1 ADR = 10 SHARES		1.072	3.498	−14.66	Chile

(cont.)

Table 11.7. *(continued)*

	$\hat{\beta}s$				
January 28, 1997 to January 28, 2002	*Average excess return (%/year)*	*US stock index*	*US Brady bond index*	*Required dollar excess return (%/year)*	*Country*
MASISA SPN.ADR 1 ADR = 30 SHARES	0.957	1.438	−5.86	Chile
BANCO SANTIAGO SPN.ADR.	0.389	0.639	−2.61	Chile
TELEX – CHILE SPN.ADR. 1 ADR = 10 SHS.	−0.610	0.134	−0.77	Chile
CONCHATORO SPN.ADR. 1 ADR = 50 SHARES	0.721	0.051	0.01	Chile
DESC 'C' 1 ADR = 4 SHARES	0.745	1.381	6.22	Mexico
ICA SPN.ADR 1 ADR = 1 SHARE	−0.218	2.762	11.89	Mexico
CERAMIC SPN.ADR. 1 ADR = 5 LTD.VTG.UNT.	0.078	1.781	7.74	Mexico
MASECA 'B' ADR 1 ADR = 15 SHARES	0.013	2.450	10.61	Mexico
RADIO CENTRO CPO SPN.ADR1 ADR = 9 CPO SHARES	0.459	2.301	10.11	Mexico
GRUPO CASA AUTREY 1 ADR = 10 SHARES	−0.431	2.913	12.48	Mexico
TMM L ADR.144A 1 ADR = 1 SHARE	0.925	0.152	0.96	Mexico
GRUPO TELEVISA SPN.ADR. 1 ADR = 20 SHS.	1.257	1.254	5.83	Mexico

Table 11.7. *(continued)*

January 28, 1997 to January 28, 2002	Average excess return (%/year)	$\hat{\beta}$s		Required dollar excess return (%/year)	Country
		US stock index	US Brady bond index		
SAVIA SA DE CV SPN.ADR 1 ADR = 4 SHARES		1.071	−0.517	−1.90	Mexico
VITRO SOCIED.SPN.ADR. 1 ADR = 3 SHARES		0.358	2.556	11.18	Mexico
PHILP.LONG DSN.TEL.SPN. ADR.1 ADR = 1 COM SHARE		1.114	0.168	0.66	Philippines
CORIMON CA SPN.ADR. 1 ADR = 500 SHARES		1.387	1.708	2.49	Venezuela
CANTV ADR 'D' 1 ADR = 7 SHARES		0.307	1.581	1.99	Venezuela

appears to be wrong. Surely the *ex ante* excess return on Argentina (which had defaulted twice since the early 1980s, even before its recent default) would be larger than the excess return on Mexico (which had avoided defaults since the early 1980s and has recently been upgraded to investment grade).

We might obtain more sensible estimates of the political risk factor if we replaced the realized returns on Brady bonds by an estimate of the *ex ante* excess returns that investors expected. In Table 11.7, the excess return on Mexican Brady bonds is 4.33%. This is similar to the 4% excess return on high-yield bonds in the United States from 1984 to 2001. If we use 4% as a lower bound on the *ex ante* excess return on Brady bonds, we can obtain estimates of the political risk premiums for each firm in Table 11.7 by applying the βs reported in that table. Although these numbers would be conditional on the 4% figure and therefore would have to be treated as illustrative only, they do indicate that political risk factors are potentially quite large.

How might these estimates be refined? We need to take into account differences across countries in the political risk premium rather than use a 4% figure for all countries. Several avenues might be explored:

Yield spread: First, we could consult yield spreads on Brady bonds. The spreads themselves provide upward-biased estimates of the excess return on Brady bonds because the spreads reflect the probability of default as well as the risk premium on the bonds. But the spreads might indicate the relative rankings of the country premiums.

Ratings: The same can be said of ratings of Brady bonds by services such as Moody's.

Objective indicators: Third, we could use models of country risk based on objective indicators. J. P. Morgan has a model for determining sovereign spreads based on a "scoring system" for both external and internal "country risk factors." External factors include exchange rate, current account/GDP ratio, external debt/GDP ratio, debt service as a percentage of foreign-exchange reserves, and interest services as a percentage of exports. Domestic factors include change in the growth rate of GDP, the inflation rate, growth or fiscal deficit as a percentage of GDP, real bank credit growth as a percentage of GDP. It is not clear how successful these factors would be in explaining political risk, but they could also help us to rank countries.

All of these approaches suggest the relative ranking of countries in terms of political risk, but none give us a quantitative measure of the *ex ante* risk premium. Clearly there is much work to be done in estimating political risk premiums.

Transposing required rates of return from one country to another

In many situations encountered in practice, the exposure measurements that are required for the application of the various CAPMs are not possible. For instance, if a US automobile manufacturer wants to build a plant in Brazil, it is not possible to obtain directly the βs of the project.

The usual escape is to find a firm operating in Brazil that would be comparable to the project. But such a firm may not exist. It is then necessary to measure stock-return relationships in one country (for instance, the United States), and then transpose them to another country (Brazil). This guesswork can be aided by a number of approximation methods, each one suggested by the form of a CAPM.

To illustrate the nature of the approximation, multiply Thalès' exposure to the French market risk (equal to 1.065; see Table 11.1) by the exposure of the French market to the world market (found to be equal to 0.975):

$$1.065 \times 0.975 = 1.0389$$

which differs from the full, direct exposure of Thalès to the world market, equal to 0.870. In the case of Thalès, there would be no point in settling for such an approximate number. If we need its β because we intend to utilize the world classic CAPM, we can measure it directly. The approximate procedure can become valuable, however, when attempting to price an asset that is not yet traded and for which no comparable firm exists. In the example of the US automobile plant in Brazil, we could go through the following steps:

- The β of the Brazilian plant *vis-à-vis* the world is approximately equal to the β of the Brazilian plant *vis-à-vis* the Brazilian stock market multiplied by the β of the Brazilian stock market *vis-à-vis* the world.
- The second term of that product can be calculated directly.
- The first term cannot be calculated since the Brazilian plan is not traded in the financial market. But we can assume further that the β of the Brazilian plant *vis-à-vis* the Brazilian stock market is similar in magnitude to the β of any automobile plant *vis-à-vis* the country stock market measured in another country. So, perhaps the β of GM *vis-à-vis* the US stock market can be used instead.[31]

How good an approximation is provided by this procedure?[32] Of the four countries considered here (France, the United States, Belgium, and Poland), the approximation works well except in Poland. Does that mean that there is a tendency for the approximation not to work well in countries whose capital market is not well integrated with the rest of the world? That would be bad news as developing capital markets may be the ones for which we need this approximation most often.

Another method that can be used to transpose returns from one country to another is based on the International Asset Pricing Model, in which, as we saw, currency risk plays center-stage. If we apply the two approaches (the hybrid model and IAPM) to evaluating Thalès' risk premium, we find intriguing results. In both cases, the risk premiums estimated for Thalès are remarkably similar to those of General Electric, another company engaged in the manufacturing of electrical equipment. But another feature of the results is important. The hybrid model leads to a much higher risk premium for Thalès (0.773%/month) than does the IAPM (0.235%). So we have not resolved the problem of choosing the "right model" for pricing a firm internationally. What the examples suggest is that the cost of capital for a French firm like Thalès may not be that different from that of an American firm like GE – as long as a similar model of pricing is used and the conditions under which the firm operates are taken into account. But the example leaves unresolved the issue of which model is right.

Conclusions

The main issue in determining the cost of equity capital in an international venture is the degree of integration of the world financial markets. If it is believed that some segmentation prevails along national borders, a home β and a home equity premium should be used. If it is believed that integration prevails, a world β and a world equity premium should be used. As discussed above, one way perhaps to remain agnostic on the issue is to use a hybrid CAPM containing several risk premiums for home and world risks.

The general approach that we have illustrated relies on an identification and separation of individual dimensions of risk: home vs. world stock market risk, industry risk (not discussed here), currency risk, and political risk. It is not enough to identify each dimension of risk. The price of each one must also be readable by watching the tickertape. Dimensions of risk must be recognized in such a way that there exist traded securities capable of indicating to us the price of each dimension. While there are no simple answers to the assessment of the cost of equity across borders, the tools described in this chapter offer a richer set of frameworks that can provide more insights than the classic CAPM so managers can engage in a more thorough analysis of the true risks and costs of international investments.

Notes

1 More recent forms of the CAPM recognize that there may exist more than one risk premium that the market charges on a share of stock. See E. Fama and K. French, "Multifactor Explanations of Asset Pricing Anomalies," *Journal of Finance*, 51 (1996), pp. 55–84.

2 As an alternative to calculating stock market index return for each country, which is an arithmetic average of the return on securities that trade on the stock market of the country, one can utilize a cross-sectional statistical technique that reveals the factor, i.e. the dimension of rates of return, that is common to all the securities of the country (here this can mean the securities that trade on the stock market of the country, or it can mean the securities of the firms that operate in the country). See the various models of the consulting firm BARRA, or S. Heston and G. Rouwenhorst, "Does Industrial Structure Explain the Benefits of International Diversification?", *Journal of Financial Economics*, 36 (1994), pp. 3–28. The drawback of this approach is that it posits that a firm listed in one country has an exposure equal to 1 to the country factor.

3 Here again, one can utilize a cross-sectional statistical technique that reveals the factor that is common to all the securities of the industry. This approach would posit that a firm belonging to an industry has an exposure equal to 1 to the industry factor.

4 On this point, see T. Chordia, R. Roll, and A. Subrahmanyam, "Commonality in Liquidity," *Journal of Financial Economics*, 56 (2001), pp. 3–28; and T. Chordia, M. Brennan, and A. Subrahmanyam, "Alternative Factor Specifications, Security Characteristics and the Cross-section of Expected Stock Returns," *Journal of Financial Economics*, 49 (1998), pp. 345–374.

5 E. Dimson, P. Marsh, and M. Staunton, *Triumph of the Optimists* (Princeton, NJ: Princeton University Press, 2002).

6 In Figure 11.1, the right-hand scale is for standard deviations. The lines, as opposed to the bars, indicate the standard deviations of the realized premiums of each year (the rate of return of that year in excess of the riskless rate in the local currency) or of the deflated return. The standard deviations of the estimates of expected values of equity premiums are equal to these numbers divided by $\sqrt{100} = 10$, since there are a hundred years of observations in this sample. This gives a visual impression of the degree of significance.

7 W. Goetzmann and P. Jorion, "A Century of Global Stock Markets," NBER working paper, no. 5901 (1997).

8 The world equity premium is weighted by the market capitalizations of the various countries, whereas the most reliable estimate (the most efficient,

in statistical language) should be weighted in inverse proportion to the variance of the average equity premium of each country.

9 Fama and French take that line of reasoning one step further. Even the most reliable estimate, say the world average, is only an estimate, or a realized number, not an expected rate of return. We may have legitimate reasons to argue that the realized average is too large or too small. Suppose, for instance, that it can be argued that required returns have slowly drifted down during the second half of the twentieth century. During that period, therefore, stock prices rose, producing higher than expected rates of returns. When we look at these realized returns *ex post* as estimates of *ex ante*, or expected, or required, returns, we make a mistake. E. Fama and K. French, "The Equity Premium," *Journal of Finance*, 57 (2002), pp. 637–659.

10

$$E[R_i - r] = \beta_{i/c} \times E[R_c - r] \tag{1}$$

In this expression, a beta measured relative to the local stock market, $\beta_{i/c}$, and the expected equity premium on the local stock market, $E[R_c - r]$, together determine the risk premium on the firm's equity, $E[R_i - r]$. As is well known, the coefficient β is equal to the slope coefficient of a simple regression, in this case, of the (excess) rate of return of a firm's equity in the stock market on the (excess) rate of return of the country market portfolio. It is the exposure of that firm's equity to the home market risk.

11

$$E[R_i - r] = \beta_{i/w} \times E[R_w - r] \tag{2}$$

where the beta is measured relative to the world stock market.

12 Modern tests of the CAPM would not be performed simply by taking a line through the cloud of points of Figure 11.2 or 11.3. Doing so assumes that the CAPM line one is trying to estimate never moves and that the position of each security on the line never changes. Modern tests would utilize variables (called "indicator variables," "instrumental variables," or "information variables") that track these movements. A CAPM with moving parts is called a "conditional CAPM." For an application to world data, see C. R. Harvey, "The World Price of Covariance Risk," *Journal of Finance*, 46 (1991), pp. 111–157.

When currencies are included in the dataset, the classic CAPM tends to be rejected by statistical tests, in favor of the more sophisticated models we are about to explore.

13 Non-financial wealth can also be broadly seen as the underpinning of the well-accepted multifactor CAPM of Fama and French, "Multifactor Explanations."

14 The following equation is an example of a multifactor model where the two "factors" are world rate of return risk, as in the integrated version of the classic CAPM, and country rate of return risk as in the segmented version of the classic CAPM. Accordingly, it relates the excess rate of return of the equity of firm i in country c, $R_i - r$, to the excess rate of return on the world market portfolio, $R_w - r$, and the excess rate of return on the country market portfolio, $R_c - r$:

$$R_i - r = \alpha_{i/c,w} + \hat{\beta}_{i/w} \times [R_w - r] + \hat{\beta}_{i/c} \times [R_c - r] + \varepsilon_{i/c,w} \tag{3}$$

In the above, we have placed a $^\wedge$ on the exposure coefficients to highlight the fact that they are not equal to the β coefficients that we have considered in the previous subsection. Those were coefficients in a simple regression. The coefficients in (3) are calculated jointly by the procedure of multiple regression applied to the time series (i.e. history) of past returns.

What we have just explained is a multifactor statistical model that simply captures the way in which random *ex post* returns relate to each other. A decomposition such as (3) can always be achieved. It is only a matter of getting the computer to calculate the β coefficients. This has no economic content. It does not tell us, for instance, what mean rates of return on securities should be such that investors would be willing to hold them.

The multifactor pricing model, however, gives us specifically that answer. It says that the expected rate of return of each security should be linearly related to the security's multiple exposures to the various dimensions of risk:

$$E[R_i - r] = \hat{\beta}_{i/w} \times E[R_w - r] + \hat{\beta}_{i/c} \times E[R_c - r] \tag{4}$$

$E[R_w - r]$ – expected value of the excess return on the world stock market – and $E[R_c - r]$ – expected value of the excess return on the country's stock market – are the risk premiums per unit of exposure risk, charged by the market to bear the systematic risks inherent in the local market portfolio, $R_c - r$, and the world market portfolio, $R_w - r$ respectively. The total risk premium required of any security i is the sum of two premiums: one for country risk equal to security i's exposure to country risk times the premium per unit of country risk, and one for world market risk equal to security i's exposure to world risk times the premium per unit of world risk. Again, the exposures to the two risks are partial, or joint, exposures (also called "loadings") calculated by a multiple regression.

15 Admittedly, some of the firms in our list are part of the local country stock index. That fact undermines a straight comparison of the sizes of the local and the world betas. Even when a firm is part of the local index, the betas we have calculated remain those that are relevant for CAPM application. Their relative sizes explain that the risk premium for country risk is almost always larger in the multifactor CAPM than the risk premium for world risk.

16 Compare, for instance, the $\hat{\beta}$s for Thalès in Table 11.5 (where they have been calculated in US$) and Table 11.6 (where they have been calculated in euros).

17 For one such theory applied to the international context, see B. Dumas, C. R. Harvey, and P. Ruiz, "Are Correlations in International Stock Returns Justified by Subsequent Changes in National Outputs?", INSEAD working paper (2000).

18 B. Jacquillat and B. Solnik, "Multinational Firms: A Poor Tool for International Diversification," *Journal of Portfolio Management*, 3 (Winter 1978), pp. 8–12.

    A recent paper by Diermeier and Solnik provides intriguing evidence about the relative influence of domestic and foreign markets. They develop a domestic stock index consisting of firms that are primarily exposed to the domestic economy only. They then find that the domestic index has a much smaller influence on firms in that market than does an index consisting of rest-of-world stocks. More research is needed to reconcile their results with the earlier work by Jacquillat and Solnik, and others, showing the predominance of home country influences on stock prices. J. Diermeier and B. Solnik, "Global Pricing of Equity: Analysts and Asset Managers Take Note: A Corporation's Stock Price Is Influenced by International Factors in Proportion to the Extent of the Company's Foreign Activities," *Financial Analysts Journal*, 57, 4 (2001), pp. 37–47.

19 K. Froot and E. Dabora, "How Are Stock Prices Affected by the Location of Trade?", *Journal of Financial Economics*, 53 (1999), pp. 182–216.

20 For evidence regarding such pricing, see C. Lee, A. Shleifer, and R. Thaler, "Investor Sentiment and the Closed-End Fund Puzzle," *Journal of Finance*, 46, 1 (March 1991), pp. 75–109.

21 This model is a strange mix of the full-integration and the full-segmentation CAPMs. An intermediate situation of partial segmentation may not lead to anything resembling the hybrid CAPM. In fact, it is not easy to define a situation of partial segmentation in the first place. Partial

segmentation is a configuration in which each individual investor has access to an incomplete but well-specified list of securities. Just specifying the situation in the first place requires information of dimensions $I \times N$, where I is the number of individuals and N is the total number of existing securities. For a full-fledged partial-segmentation equilibrium, see V. Errunza and E. Losq, "International Asset Pricing under Mild Segmentation," *Journal of Finance*, 40 (1985), pp. 105–124.

22 Case situations in which residents of one country regard a foreign-currency deposit as less risky than the home currency fall outside the theory that we are trying to develop.

23 See M. Adler and B. Dumas, "International Portfolio Choice and Corporation Finance: A Synthesis," *Journal of Finance*, 38 (1983), pp. 925–984.

24 $E[R_i - r] = \hat{\beta}_{i/w} \times E[R_w - r] + \hat{\beta}_{i/S} \times E[R_S - r]$ where $\hat{\beta}_{i/w}$ and $\hat{\beta}_{i/S}$ are the coefficients of a multiple regression of the rate of return of security i on the world market portfolio rate of return and on the rates of return of non-measurement currency deposits, all measured in some measurement currency, and where $E[R_S - r]$ is the expected excess rate of return on a non-measurement currency, also measured in the measurement currency. Currency risk is priced by the average excess returns on currencies. $\hat{\beta}_{i/S}$ can be interpreted as the "exposures" of security i to currency risks. See B. Solnik, "An International Asset Pricing Model," *Journal of Economic Theory*, 8 (1974), pp. 500–524.

The sources of the exposures to currency risks are analyzed in G. Bodnar, B. Dumas, and R. C. Marston, "Passthrough and Exposure," *Journal of Finance*, 57 (2002), pp. 199–232.

Key parameters are the firm's market share abroad, the product's elasticity of substitution with foreign products and the fraction of inputs imported from abroad, all captured in some cases simply by the fractions of revenues and costs originating from abroad and the rate of profit. See G. Bodnar and R. C. Marston, "A Simple Model of Foreign Exchange Exposure," in T. Negishi, R. Ramachandran, and K. Mino (eds.), *Economic Theory, Dynamics and Markets: Essays in Honor of Ryuzo Sato* (Kluwer: New York, 2001).

25 The exposure to the world remains unchanged at 0.856. The exposure to the currency, -0.159, is the result of the following formula: $-0.159 = 1 - 0.856 - 0.303$. This formula is exact, and can be demonstrated by calculus, for returns calculated on extremely short holding periods. When changing currency units, the currency exposure calculated from the point of view of the new currency is equal to 1 minus the sum of the exposures measured in the old currency.

The proof of this result is based on a simple approximation, which is exact in the limit as the length of the holding period becomes extremely small. Start with the statistical exposure relationship written in dollar units:

$$R_i^\$ - r^\$ = \hat{\beta}_{i/w} \times \left[R_w^\$ - r^\$ \right] + \hat{\beta}_{i/S} \times \left[R_S^\$ - r^\$ \right] + \varepsilon_{i/w,S}$$

We want to turn this relationship into one where returns are measured in euros. An excellent approximation to $R_i^\epsilon - r^\epsilon$ is $R_i^\$ - r^\$ - [R_S^\$ - r^\$]$. Let us calculate that quantity. First, we subtract $[R_S^\$ - r^\$]$ from both sides of the equation:

$$R_i^\$ - r^\$ - \left[R_S^\$ - r^\$ \right] = \hat{\beta}_{i/w} \times \left[R_w^\$ - r^\$ \right] + (\hat{\beta}_{i/s} - 1)$$
$$\times \left[R_S^\$ - r^\$ \right] + \varepsilon_{i/w,S}$$

But then we also want to express the world equity premium in euro units. An excellent approximation to $R_w^\epsilon - r^\epsilon$ is $R_w^\$ - r^\$ - [R_S^\$ - r^\$]$:

$$R_i^\$ - r^\$ - \left[R_S^\$ - r^\$ \right] = \hat{\beta}_{i/w} \times \left\{ \left[R_w^\$ - r^\$ \right] - \left[R_S^\$ - r^\$ \right] \right\}$$
$$+ (\hat{\beta}_{i/s} + \hat{\beta}_{i/w} - 1) \times \left[R_S^\$ - r^\$ \right] + \varepsilon_{i/w,S}$$

Finally, from the euro point of view, we wish to show on the right-hand side, not the excess dollar rate of return on a euro deposit but the excess euro rate of return on a dollar deposit. To the same degree of approximation, they are equal and opposite to each other. Hence we get, as claimed:

$$R_i^\epsilon - r^\epsilon = \hat{\beta}_{i/w} \times \left[R_w^\epsilon - r^\epsilon \right] + (1 - \hat{\beta}_{i/S} - \hat{\beta}_{i/w})$$
$$\times \left[R_S^\epsilon - r^\epsilon \right] + \varepsilon_{i/w,S}$$

26 See P. Sercu, "A Generalization of the International Asset Pricing Model," *Finance, Journal de l'Association Française de Finance*, 1 (1980), pp. 91–135.

27 None the less, Dumas and Solnik are able to show empirically, in a conditional version of the IAPM, that these premiums are statistically significant. Furthermore, while they may appear small when an average over many months is calculated, they fluctuate a great deal from month to month, and may not be small at all in any given month. This is the reason why their statistical significance can be demonstrated only in a conditional version of the IAPM, in which a number of indicator variables are used to track these movements. See B. Dumas and B. Solnik, "The World Price of Foreign Exchange Risk," *Journal of Finance*, 50 (1995), pp. 445–479.

28 For clarity of exposition, we consider each type of risk premium separately and discuss it in separate sections but they can obviously be

combined, provided that care is taken to estimate the βs in a joint multiple regression.

29 N. Abuaf, "The International Cost of Capital – The Empirical Evidence," Salomon Brothers, New York, 1997.

30 To clarify the calculation, the required excess rate of return on "BBVA BANCO FRANCES SPN. ADR.", -11.76%, is equal to: $0.812 \times 0.32\% + 0.948 \times (-12.68\%)$.

31 Needless to say, if leverage differs, a leverage adjustment must be performed.

32 The procedure was suggested by D. R. Lessard, "Incorporating Country Risk in the Valuation of Offshore Projects," *Journal of Applied Corporate Finance* 9, 2 (Summer 1996), pp. 52–63.

12 | Managing risk in global supply chains

PAUL R. KLEINDORFER
Wharton School

LUK N. VAN WASSENHOVE
INSEAD

With supply chains stretched around the globe, how can companies manage the inherent risks of moving raw materials, components, and finished products across diverse cultures, currencies, and regulations? This chapter discusses two basic types of risk management issue for global supply chains: matching supply to demand and addressing disruptions to supply chain activity. On the first issue, there is much to be learned from options-based thinking and flexibility/risk-sharing features of contracting theory. Innovations such as B2B marketplaces, in particular, offer opportunities to manage and mitigate risks. On the issue of disruption risks, a body of literature on so-called "operational risks" provides guidelines for best practice in the identification of potential vulnerabilities and an array of response mechanisms for spotting potential problems before they become disasters.

T HE Taiwan earthquake of September 1999 sent shock waves through the global semiconductor market.[1] The terrorist attack on the World Trade Center on September 11, 2001, also led to significant disruptions of global supply chains in many industries. As supply chains have become more complex and geographically dispersed, the risks of disruption have increased. In addition, increasingly lean designs and global supply chains, snaking through a network of suppliers to reach dispersed global markets, have created new risks in matching supply and demand.

These two types of risks – disruption and coordination (supply/demand matching) – have become increasingly important and complex in global markets. How can companies identify and better manage these risks? In this chapter, we examine the emergence of supply chain management, the nature of these risks, and strategies for addressing them.

Globalizing supply chains

Globalization has made supply chains more complex, with significant implications for design and risks. Up until the late eighties, the emphasis was on manufacturing and selling products to rather protected markets, but the creation of common markets and regional regulations in Europe and other parts of the world led companies to centralize and rationalize their products and production networks to increase standardization and achieve economies of scale. Manufacturing plants now had to produce a specific product line for multiple countries and markets.[2] Manufacturing turned from being focused on technology between four walls to being centered on the supply chain, legitimating its existence by playing an integrated role in the supply chain and new product introduction network of the company.

Parallel to the above evolution in the role of plants, in the late 1980s and early 1990s, we saw an evolution from logistics as an activity (i.e. bringing products from point A to point B) to supply chain management as a necessary function in integrating complex global networks of design, procurement, manufacturing, distribution, and sales. This occurred in parallel with increasing outsourcing of logistics activities to third parties for reasons of cost as well as scope ("logistics is not our core competence!"). Simultaneously, globalization trends pushed companies to look outside the box of their own company limits and pay attention to better coordination and integration of all activities along the total value chain. With globalization and increased outsourcing, the number of parties involved in bringing a simple product to a final consumer had significantly increased. Companies also started to recognize that all those parties contributed to the final customer experience in terms of costs, quality, speed, variety, and innovation. The pieces of this now more complex puzzle needed to be coordinated. End-to-end supply chain management was born.

The emergence of supply chain management

With the emergence of supply chain management came a broader view of the supply chain. A supply chain is essentially a network consisting of suppliers, manufacturers, distributors, retailers, and customers (Figure 12.1). The network supports three types of flows that require careful design and close coordination:

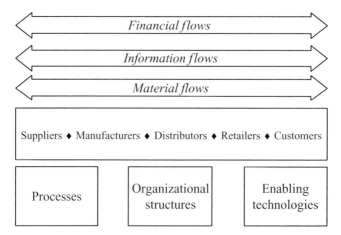

Figure 12.1. The supply chain.

(1) *Material flows*, which represent physical product flows from sup-
    pliers to customers as well as reverse flows for product returns,
    servicing, and recycling;
(2) *Information flows*, which represent order transmission and order
    tracking, and which coordinate the physical flows; and
(3) *Financial flows*, which represent credit terms, payment schedules,
    and consignment arrangements.
These flows are sometimes referred to as the "3Bs" of supply chain
management: boxes, bytes, and bucks. Although, traditionally, the
emphasis has been on "boxes," the physical flows in the supply chain,
all three flows are equally important. From a risk management perspective, disruptions can easily occur in any one of them. For example, a
regional financial crisis could have a significant impact on supply chains
that flow through the region even without a direct physical disruption
in the flow of materials.

As shown in Figure 12.1, the supply chain is supported by three
pillars:
(1) Processes, encompassing such value-adding activities as logistics,
    new product development, and knowledge management;
(2) Organizational structures, encompassing a range of relationships
    from total vertical integration to networked companies as well as
    performance management and reward schemes; and
(3) Enabling technologies, encompassing both process and informa-
    tion technologies.[3]

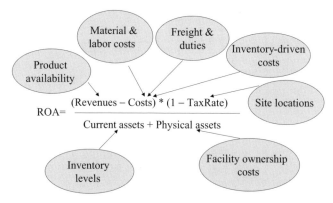

Figure 12.2. The supply chain's impact on ROA.

From the backroom to the boardroom

Logistics (the term comes from the French *maréchal de logis*, the military officer responsible for organizing all camp facilities for troops at war) traditionally focused on the physical management of material flows. New supply chain designs and a more strategic view of the supply chain in the organization placed a greater emphasis on information and financial flows, and the critical role of the supply chain in market mediation (matching supply and demand).

There has been increasing strategic attention to effective supply chain management. While this issue has not yet reached C-level attention in many companies, supply chain management in many industries has moved from the backroom to the boardroom. In the PC business, for example, razor-thin margins are forcing producers to give meticulous attention to costs. Stock market pressures have driven companies to improve their asset management. While supply chain management originally was considered a low-level, operational issue of making the goods available at minimum cost, it has evolved into a broader view of demand–supply matching, especially for dynamic, high-margin markets requiring responsive supply chains. Supply chain management has come a long way since the *maréchal de logis* in Napoleon's army.

There is increased recognition of the relationship between supply chain management and return on assets (ROA). Figure 12.2 illustrates how supply chain variables impact ROA. Traditional supply chain management would only consider costs as reflected by materials and manufacturing overheads, freights and duties, and conventional

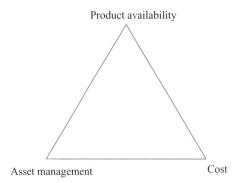

Figure 12.3. The supply chain's balancing act.

warehousing costs. With increasing internationalization, companies also started to look at site location for tax purposes and other benefits such as labor cost savings. Increasing risk of supply–demand mismatches led to more attention to inventory-driven costs. The latter are the costs of having the wrong inventories at the wrong time at the wrong place. Finally, Figure 12.2 shows the impact of supply chain management on assets. Decisions about what to keep in-house and what to outsource or send offshore influence facility ownership costs, and so do decisions on what technologies to use and where to locate facilities.

New risks

While supply chain management is receiving increased attention on the corporate agenda, the new risks resulting from supply chain innovations have not been adequately recognized. The modern supply chain challenge is to strike the right balance between product availability, cost, and asset management (see Figure 12.3), and there are risks that are inherent in striking this balance. Small inventories in lean supply chains are vulnerable to disruptions in revenue while large inventories in fat supply chains are vulnerable to high inventory-driven costs (such as obsolescence). The risks from the rise of outsourcing and pressure on asset base reduction in recent years have not been fully understood. These complex, lean, and global supply chains are often more vulnerable to major natural and man-made disasters and altered power balances. In the following sections, we examine two of these risks in more detail: supply–demand coordination and supply chain disruptions.

Strategies for addressing supply chain risks

Strategies for managing the risks of supply and demand coordination and disruption draw upon three general approaches that global companies have typically used to address supply chain risks.

(1) *Supply chain design:* Design issues include facility location and sizing, product allocation, inventory points, logistics, and using contracting innovations to manage volume and price risk along the supply chain better. Redesign activities to decrease cycle times and waste (usually in the form of excess inventory, equipment, or facilities) from supply chains have been the chief preoccupation of operations management researchers and practitioners throughout the 1990s. The key risk management question is: what is the appropriate balance between leanness and robustness to disruptions?

(2) *Contracting:* There has been a veritable revolution in the literature and practice of contracting in supply chains, through both innovations in standard, negotiated contracts between individual buyers and sellers, as well as via B2B and B2C exchanges.[4] Contracting and market instruments have been developed to convey better information on supply and demand, including price discovery and the reduction of transaction costs of buyer–seller interactions. From a practitioner's point of view, the integrated use of these Internet-based contracting mechanisms, as facilitated by the new exchanges, represents a real opportunity for improved risk management of the supply chain.[5]

(3) *Risk management systems:* The disciplines for analyzing, quantifying and managing disruption risks have also matured significantly in the past three decades. The field of risk analysis/management in industrial contexts consists of four integrated processes:
  (i) Identifying underlying sources of risk and determining the pathways by which such risks can materialize;
  (ii) Estimating the potential consequences of these risks under various scenarios;

(iii) mitigating these consequences and providing financing for residual risks; and (iv) Designing appropriate emergency response and crisis management systems.

This chapter will be concerned primarily with the first three of these processes.

These three general approaches to managing supply chain risks have been applied to the specific challenges of supply–demand coordination and disruption, as discussed below.

Managing supply–demand coordination risk

Arguably the central problem in supply chain management is efficient coordination of supply and demand, including price discovery and the reduction of transaction costs of buyer–seller interactions. In particular, a key concern of supply chain management has been to avoid the "bullwhip" phenomenon – in which delayed or distorted information leads to an amplification of demand volatility as one moves upstream along the supply chain from the market – which can lead to costly mismatches between demand and supply (shortages, obsolescence, poor capacity utilization).[6]

Technologies such as Web-based tools have helped improve coordination and remove information distortions. Effective supply chain contracts have also helped align incentives to mitigate mismatches between supply and demand.[7] These innovative designs have increased transparency and coordination. A classic example of the latter is the collaboration between Wal-Mart and Proctor & Gamble which has led to the now widespread practice of Vendor-Managed Inventory. Other innovations included Efficient Consumer Response and systems to support Everyday Low Pricing. Companies also developed modular products and processes to manage product variety and used late product differentiation or postponement to reduce supply–demand mismatches.

New technologies have also increased the "clockspeed" of supply chains in many industries,[8] but these faster speeds have also increased risks. These technologies have drawn many companies in many sectors into a higher-risk, higher-revenue situation. The stakes increase, and the tolerance for error decreases. Both clockspeed and bullwhip effects can jeopardize capabilities to react to sudden demand shifts and therefore entail high risks of costly supply–demand mismatches.

Leaner supply chains have also increased these risks. Implementation of powerful information systems linked across supply chain partners (Web-enabled ERP systems) and efforts to reduce supply chain costs have led to smaller inventories and, in general, to leaner supply chains. While these leaner supply chains reduce inventory costs, companies have started to experience some of the negative consequences of leanness when their efficiency-based supply chains were not able to react to changing market demands and led to severe service deterioration. With increasing industry clockspeed, globalization, decreasing product life-cycles, overcapacity, and maturing markets, the efficiency of supply chain management has often become less important than its effectiveness in supply–demand matching. Increasing complexity, more demanding customers, and low margins are increasingly making supply–demand mismatches extremely expensive (lost sales, obsoletes, idle capacity, high inventories), and many of the cost-squeezed lean supply chains are not exactly robust to even moderate environmental changes.

Strategies for managing supply–demand coordination risks

This has prompted some companies to revisit their lean supply chains, with a resulting set of innovations, including three-dimensional concurrent engineering for better supply chain design,[9] dynamic supply–demand balancing to reduce mismatches (particularly in fast-clockspeed industries), closed-loop supply chains for customer return and end-of-life management dictated by environmental regulations, and the revolution in B2B markets and exchanges. Let us briefly consider each of these major trends in supply chain innovations.

Three-dimensional concurrent engineering
Three-dimensional concurrent engineering (3D-CE) is a framework for dynamic supply chain design.[10] It acknowledges that with today's fast industry clockspeeds, every new product constitutes a high-risk, short-life project that should be designed as such. Hence, 3D-CE encourages concurrent design of the product, the (manufacturing) process, and the supply chain, and explicitly considers the interfaces among these three dimensions. Such concurrent engineering is, in turn, enabled by the architecture of the products, processes, and supply chains. Design choices can make products integral (e.g. an aircraft wing) or

modular (e.g. a PC). Manufacturing choices can make processes dedicated (e.g. catalytic crackers) or flexible (e.g. flexible manufacturing cells). Supply chain choices can make supply chains integral (e.g. oil refineries) or modular (e.g. PCs). These choices support or hinder the dynamic evolution of supply chain designs as a company faces new competition, technologies, or legislation.

Concurrent product/process design is by now a well-accepted concept with a vast literature on design-for-X, where X could stand for manufacturability, assembly, or disassembly. The product/supply chain interface has recently been highlighted through the market mediation role of supply chains.[11] A "functional product," with a stable demand pattern but thin margins (e.g. a tube of toothpaste), would necessitate a cost-efficient supply chain, while an "innovative product," with a highly unstable and short demand but attractive margins (e.g. a ski parka), would require a responsive supply chain. While cost reduction is the overriding concern in the former family of products, agility is vital for the latter, so the approach that works for one supply chain might be counterproductive for another. For example, implementing an *efficient* supply chain for a product requiring an *effective* supply chain may lead to low cost but it may also have very expensive consequences in terms of missed margins through lost sales.

Dynamic supply–demand balancing

Supply–demand mismatches are increasingly expensive. The name of the game is to have the right product at the right place at the right time with minimal inventories in the supply chain. Customers will happily switch to a competitor's product if the latter has the same functionality and price and if it is readily available. Customer loyalty is increasingly a thing of the past.

However, perfect supply–demand balancing is incredibly difficult in a world where, on the one hand, the supply base contains some single-source suppliers with long lead-time items and, on the other hand, technology and customer preferences change daily. Forecasting the right quantities of the right components is close to impossible. The game then becomes one of dynamically determining what product versions can be assembled with available components and matching that with what product versions can be sold at what prices. This is a game that companies like Dell have elevated to an art. Note that dynamic supply–demand balancing requires close collaboration between designers, buyers, production engineers, supply chain experts, finance and accounting staff, and sales and marketing people. Under dynamic supply–demand balancing, the supply chain becomes a central business process, or as an executive from Zara (another expert at this game) put it to us, "The supply chain is the business model."

It should also be clear that even when the supply–demand balancing process works well, mismatches still frequently occur. Since they are expensive, they represent substantial risks to the company's bottom line and require fast and adequate decision-making (e.g. in selling excess stocks of components through Internet auctions). Stated differently, dynamic supply–demand balancing is just as much about trying to get it right as it is about quickly repairing mistakes. It requires a nimble business process, keeping everyone's eye on the ball continuously.

Closed-loop supply chains

If one combines smaller product margins with short life-cycles and increasing environmental concerns, it becomes clear that perfect supply chain design and coordination may not be sufficient. The small margins in the forward supply chain may easily be offset by the increasing costs of product returns. The latter may take various forms from consumer convenience returns, to repair and maintenance returns, to end-of-use and end-of-life returns.

Although consumer return policies have traditionally been much more liberal in the United States, the emergence of Internet sales and the increasingly global footprint of retailers such as Wal-Mart are quickly spreading these practices globally. Wal-Mart encourages customers in the United States to return their products within ninety days of purchase if they are not fully satisfied, and there is every reason to believe that they will soon export this policy to Europe. For some Internet sales, convenience returns are as high as 35 percent, and for many consumer electronics products sold at retailer outlets, returns are between 5 and 10 percent. Most of these products suffer from large value erosion over time (e.g. a PC's sale price falls 1% per week) and they are returned in perfect working order. Therefore, in small-margin businesses like the PC industry, being able to resell these products quickly (e.g. via Internet auctions) or otherwise to recover maximum value from them becomes very important for global profitability.

In addition to returns, companies are increasingly expected to take responsibility for the full life-cycle of their products, including disposal, effectively extending the supply chain far beyond the purchase. Spurred by NGOs and consumer pressures, regulators have passed producer responsibility laws. The European Union, for example, recently adopted the WEEE (Waste Electrical and Electronic Equipment) Directive that makes producers responsible for organizing product takeback from consumers at no cost as well as for environment-friendly disposal. Companies such as Sony expect that this directive may cost them as much as 1–2 percent of revenues, which is enormous considering the small profit margins of some of their products.

Hence product takeback, value or material recovery, and effective disposal become important considerations in product and supply chain design and management. Note that this evolution again requires much closer cooperation between different functions and (external) partners. Indeed, until recently, neither design nor sales and marketing was interested in or concerned by product returns, even though both functions have a big impact on value recovery (e.g. through facilitating disassembly and pushing sales of recovered products and components).

All of the above reverse product flows need to be integrated in supply chain design and management considerations.[12] Companies will need increasingly to adopt a life-cycle approach to supply chain management and carefully to evaluate the corresponding risks. When added to our earlier statement about the need to design the product, the process, and the supply chain (3D-CE) simultaneously, this life-cycle argument, which adds all reverse flows to the normal forward supply chain flows, suggests calling this "four-dimensional concurrent engineering" (4D-CE). These return flows (for environmental or other reasons) make supply chains increasingly close to the core of the business (increased complexity, multi-functionality, impact on bottom line, and higher risk).

B2B exchanges and supply–demand coordination risk

The development of B2B markets and exchanges has advanced the potential of strategic management of coordination risks. These exchanges build upon the developments of Material Requirement Planning (MRP), Enterprise Resource Planning (ERP),[13] and supply-chain-wide Collaborative Planning, Forecasting, and Replenishment (CPFR) systems. These online markets and exchanges enhance normal procurement and negotiated supply relationships with market-based price discovery and fulfillment.

A central feature of B2B, especially for capital-intensive industries with non-scalable production facilities, is that contracting needs to take place well in advance of actual delivery. Failure to do so is a recipe for last-minute confusion and huge excess costs. This has given rise to a general recognition that most of a plant's or service facility's output should be contracted for well in advance. However, there is still a very important role for short-term fine-tuning of capacity and output to contract for, say, the last 10 percent of a plant's output or a customer's requirements. Doing so requires a conceptual framework, and supporting market instruments, that allows contracting to take place at various points of time, constrained by commitment and delivery options and flexibilities, and mediated by electronic markets where these are feasible.

B2B exchanges create possibilities for integrating contracting and market structure with operational decisions (capacity, technology choice, production) to help manage coordination risk.[14] While there are a variety of options for the design of these exchanges, a common feature of most electronic markets supporting coordination risk management in global supply chains is the following: any particular buyer has only a small set of sellers who compete for the buyer's business in the contract market, while still having access to a larger set (sometimes a much larger set) who compete in the shorter-term market (the spot market) and whose actions determine a competitive spot market price. The spot markets serve as a second source of supply as well as a means of evaluating the price levels of contract purchases.

These exchanges have been applied to electric power,[15] commodity chemicals, natural gas, semiconductors and plastics, and many other capital-intensive goods. B2B exchanges provide non-manipulable indices of value for various important operational choices (capacity, utilization, contracting, and technology) so that, for the first time, senior management and the market can see, in the light, how good company capacity, demand management, and fulfillment decisions are for sellers and how good procurement strategies are for buyers. Thus, if the historical probability distribution of the daily or weekly delivered spot price for a good is known, this provides both the means for better management of contracting decisions for this good and a clear benchmark for valuing short and long contract positions by either buyers or sellers. In the resulting integration of spot and contracting markets, contracting serves both the important role of reinforcing price discovery in the spot market as well as the obvious direct role of coordinating capacity commitments with anticipated demand.

Implications for the management of global coordination risks

What are the key implications of these innovations for global operations and strategy? The flexibility of three-dimensional, concurrent engineering and dynamic supply–demand balancing can help companies better anticipate and respond to changes in global supply and demand. The consideration of closed-loop supply chains can help companies address shifts in consumer patterns such as increasing returns or changes in regulations such as those requiring companies to be responsible for the entire life-cycle of a product. The integration of spot markets with global sourcing and contracting is revolutionizing both the valuation of supply chain contracts as well as giving rise to new risk-hedge instruments based on spot prices as underlying value indicators. Together these strategies are the bow wave of a revolution to integrate risk management with supply chain operations, procurement, capacity management, and technology choice.

Managing disruption risk

In addition to the risks of mismatch in supply and demand, disruption is an increasing risk in global supply chains. With longer paths and shorter clockspeeds, there are more opportunities for disruption and a smaller margin for error if a disruption takes place. We will discuss strategies for addressing two fundamental aspects of disruption risk: those arising from purposeful agents, including terrorism risks, and those related to accidental triggers, including natural hazards.

Strategies for addressing purposeful triggers

For purposeful triggers (e.g. those resulting from terrorist acts), a process that has been known in the military for some time is useful, that of role-playing, or "red–blue teaming" approaches. Under this approach, a company's own supply chain experts, equipped with whatever information is available, attempt to "attack" the supply chain to cause major disruptions. The Red Team in this exercise generates a set of scenarios that they believe can lead to serious disruptions. The Blue Team attempts to provide mitigation or countermeasures that are cost-effective against the Red Team's scenarios. A multi-level exercise at each link of the supply chain directed toward uncovering significant vulnerabilities can be very effective both in understanding the vulnerabilities of a supply chain to disruptions and in making members of the risk management team aware of what can be done either to mitigate these or at least to be prepared to respond to them. The exercise begins at the process level for critical processes and equipment, proceeds to manufacturing and warehousing sites, and finally moves to the division or company level. At each level, red-teaming generates vulnerabilities that are either resolved at that level or passed on to the next level for resolution.

In addition to risks such as terrorism, another source of purposeful disruption can come from shifts in regulations. For example, as noted above, the European Union's WEEE regulations on product takeback entail huge risks for companies. These shifts in regulation represent significant strategic shifts in the design and operation of supply chains. A similar scenario-based approach to red-teaming can help to assist in the discovery and mapping of regulatory shifts, political risks, and associated supply chain strategies. For many global products, global producers simply cannot afford to have separate designs for different countries or markets. As a consequence, for example, environmental legislation in Europe will change the designs of products sold in the United States and the rest of the world. Thus, directives like the WEEE are forcing companies to adopt strategic monitoring systems and responsive supply chains to ensure that their processes (and hence products and services crossing the world's borders) can economically anticipate and respond to these product and process constraints imposed by regulation and law.

Strategies for addressing accidental triggers

For accidental triggers, benchmarking (both internal and external) and industry or sectoral studies can provide an ongoing basis for understanding the sources of major disruption. The use of external, industrywide benchmarks for identifying sources of disruption risk is nicely illustrated in the work of Wharton Risk Center on the accident history data reported under 112(r) of the Clean Air Act Amendments. The tragedy at Bhopal in 1984, followed by a subsequent release of the same substance, methyl isocyanate, from a facility in Institute, West Virginia, resulted in great public concern in the United States about the potential dangers posed by major chemical accidents. This public concern was translated into law in section 112(r) of the 1990 Clean Air Act Amendments. This section sets forth the requirement that regulated facilities maintain a five-year history of accidental releases and submit this history to the EPA (beginning June 21, 1999). The data collected have been analyzed in a series of studies by researchers at the Wharton Risk Center, and this research has uncovered key financial and facility factors that appear to be precursors of supply chain disruptions.[16] Data analyses such as those based on 112(r) data and on the corresponding MARS (Major Accident Reporting System) data in the European Union represent a significant step in understanding the scope of accidents in the chemical and process industries and in promoting more effective accident prevention and mitigation.

When such sector-wide data are unavailable, companies must rely on internal company-centric approaches to identifying sources of operational risk and to managing accident precursors. Recent work on Near-Miss Management Systems provides a road-map for designing and implementing such company-centric approaches.[17] As in the quality arena (e.g. ISO 9000), the approach begins with identifying and blueprinting key processes in the supply chain, with appropriate vulnerabilities identified from red-teaming and historical data. Supply chain participants then define metrics for assessing the performance of each of the key processes in the supply chain on selected risk dimensions. Operating personnel use these metrics and their own judgment about observed abnormal conditions to report "near misses" that serve to identify potential vulnerabilities in its sites and overall supply chain. Just as in the quality arena, the key to effective near-miss management is for committed employees, using appropriate tools to monitor and track key processes, to see the results of their actions implemented in risk reduction activities over time. Coupling these risk identification and mitigation activities with ongoing environmental, health, and safety procedures integrates employees and managers into a fertile fabric that generates improved knowledge on their part of the risk precursors in the supply chain and of opportunities to mitigate these. Internal or external auditors play an important reinforcing role in assuring compliance with company policies.

Implications of disruption risk management

Companies with hazardous chemicals or with fire or health hazards used to be alone in their concern with operational disruptions. Not so any more. Terrorist attacks, the collapse of major banks through operational failures, accounting scandals, product liability lawsuits, and severe natural catastrophes have had the combined effect of focusing the attention of senior executives in many industries on worst-case scenarios that could disrupt normal operations, with potentially disastrous consequences for the company. The result has been a thorough reassessment of companies' ability to assess, mitigate, and, if need be, respond to hitherto neglected operational vulnerabilities. Senior risk officers, global supply chain managers, and CEOs have now recognized the critical importance of organizing and managing disruption risks. The classical discipline of risk management, augmented by newer approaches to deal with purposeful agents, has been the starting point for these new initiatives and, thus far, seems to be providing a solid foundation for further progress.

Implications and conclusions

Globalization and the application of new technologies and designs to supply chains have increased risks and made supply chain management a more central strategic concern. The two types of risks considered in this chapter, while important, are not the only risks to global supply chains. Among the other risks are currency and other financial risks, as touched upon by Gordon Bodnar, Bernard Dumas, and Richard Marston in Chapter 11. There also are risks from changing regulations and flows of information across borders, as considered by Ethan Kapstein and Stephen Kobrin in Chapter 15.

As discussed in this chapter, there is also a rich set of strategies for addressing these risks. These include innovations in supply chain design and in market institutions and contracting, as well as new technologies and business models designed to address supply chain risks. These risks can also be addressed through management system and planning innovations such as Near-Miss Management Systems and red-teaming for vulnerability assessment. Together, these innovations provide powerful tools for identifying and managing risks of supply–demand coordination and disruption.

While there is no simple approach to addressing these complex challenges, it is clear that risk management has begun to assume a much more important role in strategy. No longer is it the case that supply design decisions are made purely on the basis of cost and revenue determinants, or even on combined financial measures such as ROA. Rather, these simpler metrics are being augmented by detailed risk assessments measuring the impact of supply chain decisions on the entire distribution of profits and returns, including the potential consequences for earnings that might occur through disruptions to normal supply chain operations.

There is a host of interesting implications, arising from the above considerations, for practice and for research related to improving the practice of risk management of supply chains. These are yet to be explored as we attempt to determine what best practices have emerged in industry related to the risk management of supply chains. Such practices include: organizing to coordinate risk management at the SBU and corporate levels; new models of decision-making to accommodate/profit from risk; internal and external monitoring and management systems; integration of insurance with operational risk management; and the integration of such practices with existing process management practices and ERP systems. These represent significant challenges in striking the right balance between leanness and robustness of supply chains, and in managing the risks and increasing the returns of global supply chains.

Notes

1 I. Papadakis and W. Ziemba. "Derivative Effects of the 1999 Earthquake in Taiwan to US Personal Computer Manufacturers," in P. Kleindorfer and M. Sertel (eds.), *Mitigation and Financing of Seismic Risks: Turkish and International Perspectives* (Dordrecht: Kluwer Academic, 2001).
2 C. H. Loch, L. Van der Heyden, L. N. Van Wassenhove, A. Huchzermeier, and C. Escalle, *Industrial Excellence: Management Quality in Manufacturing.* (New York: Springer-Verlag, 2003).
3 L. N. Van Wassenhove and E. Yücesan, "The Impact of Web-Based Technologies on Supply Chain Management," *Achieving Supply Chain Excellence Through Technology (ASCET)*, 4 (2002), pp. 80–82.
4 G. Cachon, "Supply Chain Coordination with Contracts," in S. Graves, and T. de Kok (eds.), *Supply Chain Management*, Handbooks in Operations Research and Management Science, vol. XI (Amsterdam: North-Holland, 2003).
5 See A. Geoffrion and R. Krishnan, "Prospects for Operations Research in the E-business Era," *Interfaces*, 30.2 (March–April 2001), pp. 6–36; and P. R. Kleindorfer and D. J. Wu, "Integrating Long-Term

and Short-Term Contracting via Business-to-Business Exchanges for Capital-Intensive Industries," *Management Science*, 49, 11 (2003), pp. 1–19.

6 J. W. Forrester, *Industrial Dynamics* (Cambridge, MA: MIT Press, 1961); H. Lee, P. Padmanabhan, and S. Whang, "The Bullwhip Effect in Supply Chains," *Sloan Management Review*, Spring 1997, pp. 93–102.

7 See Cachon, "Supply Chain Coordination."

8 C. H. Fine, *Clockspeed: Winning Industry Control in the Age of Temporary Advantage* (Reading, MA: Perseus Books, 1998).

9 C. H. Fine, "Clockspeed-Based Strategies for Supply Chain Design," *Production and Operations Management*, 9 (2000), pp. 213–221.

10 Ibid.

11 M. Fisher, "What is the Right Supply Chain for your Product?", *Harvard Business Review*, March–April 1997, pp. 105–116.

12 V. D. R. Guide, Jr. and L. N. Van Wassenhove, *Business Aspects of Closed-Loop Supply Chains* (Pittsburgh: Carnegie Mellon University Press, 2003).

13 E. Silver, D. F. Pyke, and R. Peterson, *Inventory Management and Production Planning and Scheduling*, 3rd edn. (New York John Wiley & Sons:, 1998).

14 M. Cohen and N. Agrarwal, "An Analytical Comparison of Long and Short Term Contract," *IIE Transactions*, 31(1999), pp. 783–796; H. Mendelson, and T. I. Tunca, "Liquidity in Industrial Exchanges," Stanford University, Graduate School of Business Working paper (2003); Kleindorfer and Wu, "Integrating Long-Term and Short-Term Contracting."

15 L. Clewlow and C. Strickland, *Energy Derivatives: Pricing and Risk Management* (London: Lacima Publications, 2000).

16 See Paul R. Kleindorfer, James C. Belke, Michael R. Elliott, Kiwan Lee, Robert A. Lowe, and Harold I. Feldman, "Accident Epidemiology and the US Chemical Industry: Accident History and Worst-Case Data from RMP*Info," *Risk Analysis*, 23 (2003), pp. 865–881.

17 J. R. Phimister, U. Oktem, P. R. Kleindorfer and H. Kunreuther, "Near-Miss Management Systems in the Chemical Process Industry," *Risk Analysis*, 23 (2003), pp. 445–459.

13 | *Global recombination: cross-border technology and innovation management*

PHILIP ANDERSON
INSEAD

LORI ROSENKOPF
Wharton School

In a knowledge age, the flow of ideas and innovations around the world is essential to business growth and renewal, but also poses complex management and design challenges. How can companies manage the process of global innovation? This chapter examines the issue of "global recombination," moving ideas from one part of the world to another or combining sets of ideas into innovations. The challenge is that while knowledge must move globally, it is still often contained within tight, geographically anchored communities. The authors identify four essential elements for making recombination work: access to diverse knowledge elements; the capacity to absorb knowledge from communities of practice; the ability to adapt such knowledge to different local contexts before recombining it; and ensuring that localized pockets of knowledge are integrated so that recombination actually takes place. The authors provide frameworks for managers to explore how their enterprises are positioned to recombine knowledge that already exists to create value for customers and wealth for the enterprise.

THE original pioneers of the plastics industry were blindsided by a set of actors from outside their community. These pioneers in plastics were chemists who saw plastics as a high-end product that was a replacement for dwindling natural supplies of rubber, shellac, and ivory. To make the first plastic, a British scientist modified nitrocellulose (which in a particular form is guncotton) to create Celluloid. A community of chemists learned how to produce and improve Celluloid and focused on addressing challenges such as the price of certain raw materials and Celluloid's flammability; this led to tinkering with the solvent used in the reaction that produces Celluloid.[1]

Leo Baekeland, a Belgian chemist, was not part of this community. He had made his first fortune inventing a better photographic paper, and approached plastics from a completely different perspective. Using the technological frame of a photo chemist, he focused on finding entirely different ways to produce plastics, and aimed at producing an easily molded material suitable for mass industrial production. His Bakelite plastic first gained a foothold in the automobile and electrical industries, and gradually became a favorite of industrial designers who were looking for ways to make products look modern and streamlined. This constellation of actors produced a set of applications for Bakelite that helped it displace Celluloid as the world's most widely used plastic material.

How did this innovation from Belgium find its way to Detroit? How did the automobile engineers and other industrial designers have the capacity to absorb and apply this innovation? How can this type of innovation flow across national and industry borders be encouraged? Today these types of cross-border innovations are more critical to the success of enterprises, and the challenges of organizing innovation across diverse national borders and centers are more complex than when innovation was concentrated in a single Bell Labs or Xerox PARC. In globalizing markets, moreover, there are greater opportunities to draw together diverse sources of knowledge into new combinations. In this chapter, we consider strategies and organizational design needed to drive cross-border innovation and "recombination."

Globalizing innovation

Firms have been managing international R&D operations for decades, and much is known about how to do this well.[2] It is already accepted wisdom that R&D must globalize; for example, Walter Kuemmerle warns, "As more pockets of knowledge emerge worldwide and competition in foreign markets mounts, the imperative to create global R&D networks will grow all the more pressing."[3] How does globalization change the nature of industrial innovation? While the imperative for global innovation has been discussed, the process of building global networks that can combine and recombine ideas is less well understood. The answer to the question of how globalization changes innovation hinges on understanding how most innovation occurs. The economist Josef Schumpeter defined innovation as combining components in a new way.[4] Empirical studies have long suggested that most new technical advances spring from recombining elements that already exist.[5] Breakthrough advances often exploit little new knowledge – as Ron

Adner and Daniel Levinthal point out, technological discontinuities frequently arise from adapting known technology to a new market application.[6] For example, they note, wireless voice technology was largely based on existing wireless telegraphy know-how, but adapting the same underlying ideas to a new domain created important new industries, such as radio and mobile telephony.

Some radical advances indeed spring from wholly new ideas, but it is not clear how globalization will affect the underlying rate at which such inventions appear. Without doubt, globalizing will dramatically accelerate the pace of innovation that springs from recombining familiar elements or applying known technologies in new market settings. Our key message in this chapter is that those firms that learn how to recombine ideas from a broader variety of sources will be the most successful at using technological innovation to create value and generate wealth.

The recombinative dilemma: tapping local knowledge across global networks

The globalizing forces that lower barriers between geographies, cultures, and industries greatly broaden the scope for global recombination. One key factor is the increasing geographic and cultural diversity of firms' supply chains and customer bases. Both suppliers and customers influence and contribute to innovations within a value chain. The rapid increase in outsourcing software development to India, for example, is bringing a much broader range of experiences and ideas into the software industries. Similarly, when products and services are introduced to new regions, users often adapt them to local conditions.[7]

Another reason why globalization drives more innovation through recombination is that people are more mobile between regions than ever before. Graduate students and professionals in the sciences and engineering are particularly prolific at cross-pollinating ideas across countries and cultures.[8] The return of US-trained Taiwanese engineers to Taiwan, for example, contributed materially to the growth of Taiwan's high-technology sector. Such individuals did much more than simply transplant ideas "made in America" to their homelands. They recombined techniques, tools, and concepts that they absorbed abroad with different ideas and processes that have diffused among Taiwanese manufacturers.

Recombination also stems from the changing nature of work itself. More and more of the economic value created everywhere in the world stems from knowledge work and knowledge assets.[9] As James Brian Quinn points out, the most efficient worker in a factory might be four to five times as productive as the average worker, but in knowledge-intensive fields, the strongest intellects are often thousands of times as productive as average ones. Experts are supremely important in knowledge work, and they usually desire a good deal of control over their efforts. Consequently, they are often hard for single organizations to retain, preferring to be represented by agencies who redeploy their talents from one project to another.[10] As intellectual work becomes more and more important, innovation will be influenced to a greater degree by firms' ability to combine the contributions of experts, many of whom work independently and cannot be relocated at an organization's behest.

Recombinative innovation is vital for the globalizing firm, but it also poses a dilemma. On the one hand, to exploit the power of recombination, firms must be prepared to reach out globally, working with the best talent wherever they find it. Yet on the other hand, the ability to recombine ideas and transfer know-how retains an inherently local character. Thus, while "global knowledge networks" exist, they are aggregates or mosaics of local network clusters, and have been termed "small worlds."[11] In a small-world structure, well-integrated local clusters are connected via a sparse set of linkages across clusters. This characteristic structure arises because the geographic location of knowledge significantly influences how it is transmitted and who is able to absorb it.

For example, different regions develop distinctive zones of competence through long historical processes.[12] Many years ago, Akron, Ohio in the United States was the world center of tire and rubber manufacture. Production has long since moved elsewhere, but many major tire and rubber manufacturers maintain their headquarters in or near Akron, along with R&D facilities whose research capabilities originated in the US government's efforts to develop synthetic rubber during World War II. Hence, there exists today a "polymer valley" between Akron and Cleveland, Ohio, which is a world center for research in thermoplastics, driven by these large enterprises. Companies that want to benefit from this deep know-how must find a way to become part of this milieu to tap into this talent pool and the informal exchange of knowledge that takes place within it.

In contrast, Sweden never developed a significant chemical industry and is not a center for polymer innovations. However, Sweden did develop world-class pharmaceutical research capabilities based on pharmacological know-how, not chemical expertise. Four main clusters of firms emerged around centers of excellence in four major Swedish universities, and they produced a host of innovations such as the first beta blocker drug and the world's leading anti-ulcer medication. The Swedish pharmaceutical knowledge complex has different origins and revolves around different institutions than Ohio's polymer valley, but both regions consist of an integrated network of actors that have strong informal ties to one another. To absorb and recombine knowledge from such centers of excellence, a company must participate in them locally.

This is the recombinative dilemma: as globalizing progresses, recombinative possibilities expand geometrically, but to realize these possibilities, firms must become involved in knowledge networks that retain strong local orientations. One cannot simply declare, "We will seek out and utilize the world's top expertise wherever we find it." Where one finds it and how one accesses it matters a great deal.

Capabilities for global recombination

The type of recombination that prevailed during the 1970s and 1980s was termed "technology fusion."[13] Technologies such as mechatronics and fiber optics sprang from blending incremental improvements from several separate technical fields, leading to a product with features not found elsewhere in the market. Sometimes, technology fusion took place within a firm, as when Sony created the Walkman by integrating headphone technology with compact cassette player technology that had been created by different groups within the company.[14] More often, fusion grows out of long-term R&D ties among many companies in a variety of industries. One cannot simply mix different types of technology; fusion arises from relationships characterized by mutual respect, mutual responsibility, and mutual benefit.

Although technology fusion is still important, the skills and routines needed to recombine knowledge from different organizations are quite different from those needed to recombine knowledge from different technological areas.[15] Companies can develop both *combinative capabilities,* the ability to synthesize knowledge newly acquired with that which they already possess,[16] and *architectural competence,* the ability to access new knowledge from outside the firm and to integrate knowledge across organizational boundaries.[17]

Companies tend to emphasize first-order competence – learning how to become more expert in a familiar domain. In many cases deepening the company's existing knowledge base is productive and rational.[18] On average, firms are more successful when they build on familiar technologies to create new knowledge.[19] Specifically, patents that cite recently and frequently cited patent subclasses and that combine subclasses that have been combined often before tend themselves to be more heavily cited in the future. Patents that depart from familiar knowledge bases are less heavily cited. However, while firms that experiment with new subclasses or combinations of subclasses are less successful on average, they have a higher chance of producing a truly seminal patent. Consequently, firms that only build on their own familiar knowledge can be beaten to landmark discoveries by those that have more skill recombining innovations that cross accepted boundaries.

For this reason, it is important for companies to augment this first-order competence in deepening existing knowledge with a second-order competence in creating new knowledge by recombining knowledge across boundaries.[20] A study of the optical disk industry showed that exploration that spans organizational boundaries has more impact than exploration that occurs within organizational boundaries. Specifically, the more firms file patent applications that cite prior art from other organizations, the more likely their patents are to be heavily cited by subsequent inventors. This tendency is accentuated in systemic industries like telecommunications, where multiple parties must coordinate their technological developments.

Some firms are better than others at innovating through recombination, and when they can sustain a distinctive competence in this domain, they can gain a durable competitive advantage. We do not yet know exactly why some firms have more combinative capability, architectural competence, or second-order competence than others do. However, it appears that firms bent on winning the innovation game by maximizing recombinant innovation must do at least four things well, as illustrated in Figure 13.1:

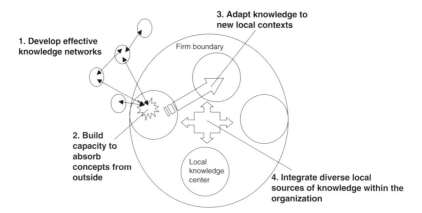

Figure 13.1. Four capabilities for successful global recombinative innovation.

(1) They must *connect* to external sources of ideas by building effective knowledge networks.
(2) They must *absorb* concepts they wish to recombine by participating in the communities that generate these ideas.
(3) They must *adapt* technologies by reinventing them as they are transferred from one local context to another.
(4) They must *integrate* the diverse sources of knowledge they have built in order to translate new combinations into commercial success.

We examine each of these capabilities in more detail in the following sections.

Building a network of connections

The first step toward creating a superior capacity to innovate by combining disparate ideas and knowledge sources is building the network of connections that exposes the firm to a rich variety of inputs.[21] To manage a network for advantage, a firm should analyze and diagram its social network. This can help identify who belongs to its network; assess its position in the network; look for unique combinations of knowledge instead of building ties to the same type of organization again and again; and look for ways to become more central in its network.

At first blush, the challenge of building a network would seem simple: build more ties and keep them as diverse as possible. However, more ties do not necessarily produce a stronger, more productive social network. Maintaining ties is costly, hence the adage that he who has too many friends has none. Other things equal, the more relationships a firm maintains, the less it can invest in any one of them.

High-performing firms do not tie themselves to every other relevant actor.[22] Instead, they strive to occupy "structural holes." Put another way, suppose A is connected to both B and C. If B and C are not directly connected to each other and no one else connects B and C, then A occupies an attractive position. It is the only one able to recombine inputs from both and to transfer ideas and information from one to the other. If B and C are already directly tied to one another, A would be better off investing its limited resources in some other tie where it can fill a structural hole, connecting actors that are not linked by anyone else.

A longitudinal study of the international chemicals industry showed that the more direct and indirect ties a firm had, the higher its patent count on average. However, the more that a firm occupied structural holes, the lower its output of patents.[23] Why? On the one hand, firms that occupy structural holes gather combinations of information that no other actor has. However, it can be difficult to build trust in a network when nobody you know is acquainted with anyone else. Densely interconnected networks foster the development of trust, because if one party takes advantage of another, everyone else in the network will hear the news. On the other hand, when everyone in a network is connected to everyone else, the flow of diverse, fresh insights from outsiders is attenuated. Network members are unable to learn novel things from "friends of friends," because they already know everyone that their friends know. Thus, the most effective networkers balance the benefits of dense interconnections and structural holes. In fact, recent research in the semiconductor industry demonstrates that firms embedded in the small worlds of global knowledge networks use knowledge gained via the less pervasive linkages *across* clusters as much as, or more than, the knowledge easily accessible *within* local clusters.[24]

Maintaining a diverse network matters, because interorganizational and interpersonal knowledge networks tend to become somewhat inbred. At any given time, people and companies familiar with a particular technology share a "technological frame," a consensus about how the technology is best deployed and what key problems or obstacles are interfering with its optimal employment.[25] Those who share a technological frame agree on a set of theories and strategies for solving these problems and on a set of criteria that define what an adequate solution would look like.

The leading experts in the technology are accepted members of the community that shares the frame. Usually, they have strong informal relationships with one another. They tend to ignore other actors who have a low level of inclusion in their technological frame. Such outsiders define goals, problems, and solutions quite differently, and it is they who are most likely to revolutionize an industry because they operate in a different technological frame, as we saw with the case of Leo Baekeland discussed at the opening of the chapter.

Innovators need to build connections with others who do not share the innovators' technological frame and involve customers in the innovation process. Many significant industrial innovations were originally pioneered by customers who were trying to solve their own problems.[26] Successful recombinative innovators build strong linkages to such "lead users," picking up and reinventing their home-grown solutions to adapt them to the needs of the broader market.

Globalizing suppliers have a particularly attractive opportunity to pick up ideas from customers that they can recombine, because customers themselves tend not to cross organizational boundaries when they innovate. A study of innovations developed by mountain bikers found that user-innovators almost always utilize information that was already in their possession or that they generated by themselves.[27] Users typically come up with an innovation to solve a problem they are facing, and they do not have much incentive to sell their home-grown solution to others with the same problem. As a result, they use information they already have "in stock" because it does not cost much and it is already adapted to their local context. Consequently, suppliers can create additional value by combining such ideas with those developed in other organizations or technological fields.

Technological communities and standard-setting
Additionally, innovators' networks should include the technological community and key actors who set standards, a group of stakeholders for a product class referred to as its "technological community."[28] This community can include suppliers, rivals, customers, research labs, patent agencies, regulatory bodies, professional societies, and trade associations, depending on the context. These communities are valuable not only for gaining access to knowledge and recombining it, but

also for establishing new standards based on a particular technology or innovation.

Technological communities are often linked together by cooperative technical organizations (CTOs), which both shape the direction of a technology and its key choices, and are in turn shaped by the challenges the technology poses. CTOs are especially likely to form during the period between a technological discontinuity and the emergence of a standard, or dominant design, because at such times the direction a technology will take is the subject of controversy. Firms and individuals are particularly likely to join CTOs at such times in order to influence the emerging technological frame.

Firms and individuals may join CTOs to promote the survival and growth of technological approaches they have adopted. For example, until the 1970s, most flight training for airline pilots took place in the air. Then two alternatives were introduced to allow pilots to train on the ground. Full flight simulators were very expensive devices that reproduced the motion of an airplane and simulated what the pilot would see out the windshield in order to create the most realistic experience possible. Flight training devices cost a fraction as much, but lacked the realism of full flight simulators because they used accurate instrumentation, but not motion and visual simulation. Despite their high cost, full flight simulators emerged as the dominant training technology and, by 1980, they were mandated by regulation. One reason why this technology became dominant is that the backers of full flight simulation formed CTOs to push their approach long before the sponsors of the rival technology created such cooperative organizations.[29]

Firms and individuals may also join CTOs because interactions among mid-level managers in industry technical committees help them identify opportunities for technical collaboration and potential alliance partners.[30] Membership in CTOs enhances a firm's combinative capability by giving it opportunities to meet and size up those with whom collaboration might create value. This is particularly important for firms that do not already have a large number of alliances. Technical committee participation lets them build the informal, interpersonal bonds needed to break into an industry's information-exchange network and eventually begin building a web of alliances.

Organizations that want to enhance their combinative capabilities also should build alliances to third parties who provide complementary goods and/or services, or who have the power to mediate disputes and enforce standard-setting. Third parties recombine their offerings with their partner's to take a product or service into niches that their partner alone could not reach. For example, Autodesk, the world's leading supplier of lower-priced computer-aided design (CAD) software, enrolled about 1,000 third parties in its partners program throughout the 1990s, with approximately a hundred firms leaving and a hundred joining in any given year.[31] Most of these third parties added specialized modules on top of Autodesk's package. For example, one partner built and marketed a program that could simulate how a building would fall down under various types of stress. This program was used after a terrorist bombing in Oklahoma City to locate likely places where people could survive the building's collapse, and rescue teams saved a number of lives as a result.

Innovators should also strive to connect to key third parties who can enforce standards and resolve disputes. For example, two separate coalitions of consumer electronics manufacturers sponsored rival standards for digital video discs (DVDs) in the mid 1990s.[32] Toshiba enlisted Matsushita (through its JVC subsidiary) and Pioneer to support its proposed standard, while Sony and Philips (the team that had pioneered the compact disk) pushed another standard. Each coalition tried desperately to enlist key third parties, such as movie studios and computer hardware manufacturers, in support of its standard. Ultimately, however, a large group of such third parties called for the two to agree on a compromise standard that would incorporate elements of each coalition's technology. On their behalf, IBM took a key role in brokering the emergence of a unified standard.

To summarize, the first step in developing the kind of combinative capability that can take advantage of globalizing is to build a robust social network. Both direct and indirect ties can enhance a firm's ability to innovate, but they are costly to maintain. A firm needs to balance the benefits of linking firms which are not otherwise connected with the benefits of belonging to a densely connected network where trust can flourish. Building connections outside one's technological frame is important to promote second-order learning, as is connecting to lead users, cooperative technical organizations, and key third parties.

Absorbing know-how from communities of practice

Being well connected is a necessary but not sufficient condition for effective innovation through recombination. A firm must also be able to absorb know-how from its social network. Just as some firms have greater combinative capability than others do, some have greater *absorptive capacity* than others.

Absorptive capacity is the ability to recognize new information, assimilate it, and apply it commercially.[33] This capacity is largely a function of possessing prior related knowledge and is especially important when knowledge cumulates. For example, it is difficult for students to learn calculus unless they have mastered algebra and analytic geometry. In a similar way, it is often difficult to absorb a complex body of knowledge unless one is actively involved in creating new knowledge in that domain.

It might therefore seem simple for a firm to optimize its absorptive capacity by ensuring that it always builds on what it already knows. However, building up absorptive capacity is more complex. A firm's absorptive capacity depends on its organizational form and certain types of combinative capabilities, not just on the content of its existing knowledge stock.[34] These include systems capabilities: policies, procedures, and documentation aimed at integrating knowledge via *ex ante* rules and procedures. They also include coordinative capabilities, which enhance knowledge absorption by building relationships among the members of a group. Finally, they encompass socializing capabilities, which forge a shared ideology that helps people make common sense of new knowledge.

For example, a longitudinal study of a prominent Dutch financial newspaper *Het Financieel Dagblad* (HFD) (similar to *The Financial Times* in the United Kingdom) found that it enhanced its absorptive capacity by changing its organization form and developing new capabilities in managing systems, coordinating units, and socializing individuals to work together informally. In 1996, HFD began creating a multimedia database and looking for ways to generate additional revenues from multimedia products. At first, the database simply contained electronic copies of the journal, but HFD's management found that selling digital content was very different from selling a newspaper. The firm was forced to change its functional structure, forming a new business development unit to build and market electronic products and search for other new revenue streams. It started a partnership with a software company to learn how to sell its database in a network environment. It instituted more formal policies for governing the assembly of the database than had been necessary to run the newspaper, and it learned how to manage cross-functional projects.

Firms can increase their absorptive capacity in general, but they must do more if they wish to become innovation leaders. The kind of knowledge innovators recombine often rests in a diffuse community of practice, consisting of firms and individuals engaged in sustained pursuit of a shared enterprise.[35] For example, technological-scientific communities have emerged in fields such as neural networks, medical lasers, and auto-immune disease.[36] Both industrial and academic researchers participate. In other communities, non-technical individuals can occupy key roles.

If absorptive capacity were only a function of possessing prior related knowledge, then firms could develop it by investing in more research and development. However, it is often important for the firm to be connected to the wider scientific community. In drug development, for example, while it is necessary to invest in basic R&D to build absorptive capacity, publicly funded research contributed to 75 percent of the twenty-one most important drugs introduced between 1965 and 1992.[37] Firms that hired the best people, encouraged them to be tightly connected to the public sector, and rewarded them for their rank within the public scientific community to which they belong were the most successful knowledge producers. Such practices not only improved their access to publicly funded research, but also improved the quality of their in-house research.

To absorb knowledge from a community, an individual and/or an organization must *actively* engage in the community's intellectual work. Reading journals and attending conferences is not enough. An innovative firm's researchers must be active collaborators with public and nonprofit sector researchers if they wish to be productive.[38] A study of biotechnology and semiconductor companies concluded that a firm's performance is higher when its scientists actively coauthor with the most prestigious scholars in their field.[39] Researchers found that individuals who coauthored articles with 327 star bioscientists with unusually high rates of publishing new gene sequences are much more likely to produce significant innovations. Team production, working together on a problem of mutual interest, is a prerequisite for capturing knowledge from the best people; reading publications and attending conferences does not suffice.

To absorb the knowledge made available via its social network, a firm needs to enhance its overall absorptive capacity by adopting an organization and set of combinative capabilities suited to the difficulty of what it has to learn. It must then identify and actively participate in communities of practice that hold knowledge it wishes to absorb in order to combine it in new ways. To get the most out of the communities of practice it works with, the firm must also engage in joint work with people from whom it wishes to learn, and support employees in engaging a community, imagining new practices and behaviors, and ensuring community members are properly aligned with one another.[40]

Adapting technologies to different local contexts

As noted above, "small-world" global networks emerge from linkages between local communities of practice, so firms and individuals need to absorb knowledge from a particular local context. To exploit the recombinative opportunities afforded by globalization, organizations must be able to port these concepts to different local contexts. Such an activity is often termed "technology transfer," but some prefer the term "knowledge exchange," because "transfer" may appear to be a one-way movement, while exchange implies two-way learning.[41]

Technology is almost never transferred from one location to another without modification. Rather, it is reinvented as it is implemented.[42] Each local context to which it is transferred has its own distinctive set of problems and actors and its own history. As a consequence, technologies must be adapted whenever they are shifted into new domains.

What guides successful adaptation and reinvention when knowledge is replicated in a new location? The two key drivers of successful adaptation appear to be the use of organizational templates and the movement of experienced personnel. An organizational template consists of the minimum set of information needed to drive value creation in a business model in any local context. For example, when firms replicate a successful business model, such as opening up new branches of a franchise, replication is often much more than the repeated application of a formula or recipe.[43] Replicators create value by discovering and refining a business model, adapting its components to different geographic locations, and routinizing knowledge transfer. In so doing, one can never step in the same river twice. Sidney Winter and Gabriel Szulanski argue that "Growth by replicating such a formula requires the capability to recreate complex, imperfectly understood and partly tacit productive processes in carefully selected sites with different human resources every time, facing in many cases resistance from proud, locally autonomous agents."[44]

When this set of information is replicated to a new location, the process is more effective when each replication is guided by a template, rather than being an exact copy. For example, between 1970 and 1993, BancOne bought over seventy banks and converted them to its management and reporting systems. A subsidiary, BancOne Systems Corporation (BOSC), chose a particular template for the new acquisition to copy, a sister bank, and by visiting their sister bank before the conversion, the employees of a new acquisition gained guidance as to BancOne's expectations. BOSC also established a "model bank" simulation showing how all of its front-office and back-office systems work. By experimenting with the simulation, the executives of a newly acquired bank could gain a clear picture of how these systems would run in its local environment.

In most cases, adapting know-how to a new context is best facilitated through the mobility of experienced people when the knowledge is tacit. For instance, in the late 1960s, a group of Canadian scientists invented the TEA laser. Several groups of physicists in the UK tried to build one, but found it impossible, even though the inventors had published their results widely. The ability to build a laser depended on the transfer of individuals with direct experience of operating it; making a working laser depended on a host of tacit knowledge that could be developed through experience, but not codified.[45] On the other hand, university-to-industry technology transfer may have been hindered in Germany because German universities are public institutions, and government regulations make it difficult for scientists to transfer temporarily to industrial locations.[46]

If firms emphasize the transfer of codified knowledge only, they may misunderstand and fail to absorb tacit knowledge. This focus on explicit knowledge was an apparent blindspot for some US firms in joint ventures between American and Japanese partners. As Andrew Inkpen and Adva Dinur observed, "Although in all cases the American firms formed JVs with an objective of learning from their Japanese partners, the learning expectation revolved around 'what' the Japanese firms knew, rather than 'how' and 'why' the Japanese firms knew what they knew . . . The American firms expected to find visible differences in the JV that could be analyzed and incorporated in the parent."[47] This focus on explicit knowledge led them to emphasize technology-sharing and to promote frequent interactions between the American parent and the joint venture, ignoring opportunities for tacit learning.

These authors concluded that the mechanism for sharing knowledge between partners in a joint venture needs to match the type of knowledge being shared. Tacit knowledge is best shared through personnel transfers, but unless the joint venture's strategy is closely integrated with and important to the parent's, individual knowledge may not be translated effectively into collectively held knowledge. When knowledge is explicit and codified, technology-sharing agreements and interaction between the alliance and its parents are effective knowledge-sharing vehicles.

In summary, once a firm has absorbed knowledge, it must adapt and reinvent it when it applies its learning to a new context. Applying knowledge to a niche with distinctive selection criteria and resources is an important source of innovation. Such applications are facilitated when firms use a template as a guide, instead of trying to copy knowledge precisely. Tacit knowledge is best transferred by introducing experienced people into the new context, while explicit knowledge can be transferred and adapted through more formal arrangements that do not involve personnel mobility.

Integrating internal knowledge pockets

We have discussed how recombinational innovation requires building a rich set of external connections, actively participating in communities of practice to absorb knowledge from them, and adapting and reinventing concepts when they are moved from one context to another. These local adaptations create many rich "knowledge pockets" that can be recombined to generate new innovations, but to realize such recombinations the firm must be able to integrate what it knows, porting concepts across internal organizational boundaries.[48] The ability of the organization to develop rich local sources of knowledge yet draw together these local worlds to drive innovation is at the heart of successful recombination. In other words, managers need to configure "small-world" structures within their global organizations.

For example, we have argued that to learn from Ohio's polymer valley or Sweden's pharmacology communities of practice, firms must participate in them locally. Units that are locally engaged (whether in a geographically based community or in a community that shares a technological frame) must be linked to one another within the firm, so that they can forge connections internally to capitalize on these diverse sources of knowledge. Furthermore, a global innovating network should connect all departments concerned, not just those tasked with R&D.[49]

One key to successful integration is building strong connections internally that make units with high absorptive capacity central to the intraorganizational social network. A study of twenty-four business units in a petrochemical company and thirty-six units in a food manufacturing company found that the most innovative units were those most central in the network but only if they had high absorptive capacity.[50] Units that were well networked but that had low absorptive capacity were not particularly innovative.

A second key is ensuring that project teams gain direct access to business units that possess related tacit knowledge. A study of 120 development projects in 41 units of a multinational corporation found that project teams obtain and reuse more non-codified knowledge and finish their projects faster when they have more direct paths to units with related knowledge.[51] The length of the path mattered more than the number of connections a project team had or the sheer amount of related knowledge resident somewhere in the firm. The presence of shorter path lengths between distant units implies that the shortcuts so important to small-world structures are in place. Because maintaining direct ties to many business units takes time and energy, such ties should focus on tacit knowledge, since codified knowledge could be transferred from business units even if the path from them to the project team was relatively lengthy.

A third key is implementing mechanisms to coordinate the integration of know-how across multiple innovation projects and to build common components that can be recombined across these projects. For example, Toyota transformed its product development to improve integration of knowledge across diverse projects. In 1991, Toyota's product development organization had sixteen design or functional engineering divisions and fifteen concurrent projects, managed via a matrix organization. Project managers found it very difficult to integrate the contributions of the functional divisions; to launch a new product a chief engineer had to coordinate forty-eight different departments. Coordination across projects was difficult because each project's chief engineer was given considerable autonomy.[52]

Toyota addressed these issues by creating four product centers, each responsible for managing several projects. One center took responsibility for rear-wheel drive vehicles, focusing on the development of luxury, high-quality cars. Another led development of front-wheel drive vehicles, emphasizing the development of innovative, low-cost cars. A third focused on utility vehicles and vans, looking to create new markets for Toyota in recreational vehicles. The fourth center developed components and subsystems designed to cut across vehicle projects and centers. Each of the three vehicle centers simplified to just six functional divisions (because the fourth center took on specialized components), and the center heads were explicitly responsible for coordinating multiple development projects within their own centers.

A fourth key is imbuing units that are to transfer know-how with an aggressive common mission and a shared sense of purpose. For example, Samsung grew from a producer of simple discrete semiconductor devices to the world's largest memory chip maker in a decade by exploiting the interactions between local US and Korean development teams.[53] After producing transistors and integrated circuits for consumer electronics for a decade, Samsung began moving into chip-making in the early 1980s. The company tried, without success, to license know-how from foreign producers and to obtain explicit knowledge by acquiring two troubled US companies. After these unsuccessful attempts, Samsung established parallel operations in Korea and in Silicon Valley, home of the most advanced chip manufacturing techniques. The two units shared a clear mission and an express charter to transfer knowledge from the US community of practice and from Samsung's technology suppliers.

First, Samsung imported chips from its US chip design licensor to Korea, and learned how to assemble them in its Korean facility, building on its prior knowledge of how to assemble LSI devices. Then, it set up an R&D outpost in Silicon Valley, staffed by five Korean-American PhDs who had worked for other semiconductor firms and by 300 American engineers. It closely linked this with an R&D task force in Korea via training, joint research, and consulting, to transfer know-how from Silicon Valley to headquarters. Both teams worked exceptionally hard in a crisis atmosphere to meet aggressive deadlines for developing a 64K DRAM, and this stressful process caused them to bond more closely and transfer know-how more effectively.

To move its chip design into production, Samsung contracted with a Japanese firm that had designed a semiconductor fabrication facility for Sharp. In a crisis atmosphere, Samsung constructed a working plant, largely copying Sharp, in one-third the time considered normal in Japan.

To produce the next generation of DRAMs (with 256 kilobytes of memory per chip), Samsung again set up two task forces, one in Korea and one in Silicon Valley. The Korean team obtained a license on a US chip design, but it used technology suppliers and its own 64K experience to develop its own manufacturing process. The US team developed its own chip design and its own process, in competition with the Korean team. The Korean team finished first and pioneered innovations in process design, but it ended up implementing the Silicon Valley design for mass production in Korea instead of the design for which it had obtained a license from the outside.

Samsung could have set up a learning outpost in Silicon Valley and relied on it to import knowledge. Instead, it used a shared mission to link its presence in a foreign community of practice to its process development operations at home. Samsung relied on both licensing and contracts to convey codified knowledge and on experienced people to communicate tacit knowledge, but these alone would not have sufficed to impart advanced chip-making capabilities to the firm. Tacit expertise developed by engagement with a local community of practice is best integrated into the rest of the organization when the units that must interact share a common vision and are impelled emotionally by a shared sense of purpose.

James Brian Quinn, Philip Anderson, and Sydney Finkelstein called this motivational force "care-why."[54] Firms invest the most money in codifying and transferring know-what and know-how, when know-why and care-why have much more influence on organizational performance. People and units inside the organization will recombine knowledge effectively if they share common objectives, so that the resulting innovation leads to mutual benefit.

Creating internal communities of practice
The creation of internal communities of practice can help weave together these external knowledge communities. Without this intentional weaving, active engagement with a local knowledge-generating community can lead to localized identities and a sense that non-local units in the same firm are "them" instead of "us." Consequently, innovative firms can foster recombination by creating internal communities

of practice that bind together internal participants who in turn reach out to different local communities. By belonging to internal as well as to externally oriented communities of practice, individuals develop a complex identity that transcends parochial motivational barriers to recombination.

IBM's Global Services unit illustrates the diverse ways these internal communities of practice can evolve. IBM Global Services established a knowledge management program in 1995, and by 2001 it had over 60 knowledge networks with 20,000 participants.[55] Each network connects practitioners worldwide who are concerned with a particular knowledge domain. Although each is sponsored by a business unit, none is a formal organization or a team. Each is linked via an IBM application developed on the Lotus Notes platform. Despite these commonalities, there is great variety in structure and style. For example, some use a highly formal approach to categorizing and storing knowledge in a knowledge base, while others use much looser structures. These communities also tend to evolve across five different states of existence, each with different behaviors and processes. A *potential* community forms when a nucleus of individuals concerned with the same knowledge domain locate one another, communicate, and begin to form relationships. It may transform into a *building* community when it defines itself and formalizes its operating principles. In this mode, members build a common understanding of what the community is and is not, why it is forming, and how it will function. The community then develops a memory of its shared history and purpose. Some communities then become *engaged* when they execute and improve a consistent set of processes that create more access both to its members and to what it knows. They transform into *active* communities when they understand, define, and assess what the community's collective work is contributing, to members and to the organization as a whole. Active communities also begin to build relationships with other communities. *Adaptive* communities use their knowledge to create competitive advantage, by generating and innovating new solutions, offerings, methods, processes, and groups.

These five kinds of communities do not necessarily follow one another in a life-cycle. IBM Global Services has developed many potential, building, and engaged communities, but only a handful of active communities and no genuinely adaptive ones (though a few communities exhibited some of the aspects of this state). Each type of community is capable of creating value for IBM Global Services, but after five years, the parent division remained uncertain how to encourage more communities to become active or adaptive.

IBM Global Services' experience with internal communities of practice suggests that it is possible for such informal groupings to take ownership of a knowledge domain and link participants who otherwise would not connect and recombine what they know. However, there is still much to learn about how to craft internal community structures that complement a firm's involvement in a set of external communities. Such internal communities should complement the other integrative mechanisms we have described: linking units with high absorptive capacity so they become central in the intraorganizational network; shortening paths from project teams to business units that possess related tacit knowledge; instituting mechanisms to combine knowledge across projects; and linking units designed to recombine knowledge by giving them a shared mission and sense of "care-why."

Conclusions

Globalizing presents those who would profit from technological innovation with an interesting set of opportunities and a considerable organizational challenge. There is vast potential for managers to create value by recombining knowledge found in niches that are not typically connected to one another. Yet realizing this potential requires managing the paradox that in a globalizing environment, knowledge production largely remains a localized affair and knowledge is located in communities of practice that are not themselves necessarily global.

Successful innovators must pay attention to all four elements that are vital to make recombination work: they must gain access to diverse knowledge elements they wish to combine; must absorb knowledge from communities of practice; must then adapt such knowledge to different local contexts before recombining it; and must ensure that localized pockets of knowledge are integrated so that recombination actually takes place. These are organizational challenges for general managers, not technical difficulties to be overcome by functional experts specializing in innovation. Senior executives reading this book and thinking about the consequences and implications of globalizing should ponder how well their enterprises are positioned to recombine knowledge that already exists but has not been brought together. Organizing to bring together ideas that have developed along separate lines in separate niches will provide them a fruitful wellspring of innovation that creates value for customers and wealth for the enterprise.

Notes

1 W. E. Bijker, *Of Bicycles, Bakelites and Bulbs: Toward a Theory of Sociotechnical Change* (Cambridge, MA: MIT Press, 1995).
2 See A. de Meyer, "Management of an International Network of Industrial R&D Laboratories," *R&D Management*, 23 (1993), pp. 109–120; or for a book-length treatment, R. Boutellier, O. Gassman, and M. von Zedtwitz, *Managing Global Innovation: Uncovering the Secrets of Future Competitiveness* (Berlin: Springer-Verlag, 2000).
3 W. Kuemmerle, "Building Effective R&D Capabilities Abroad," *Harvard Business Review*, 75, 2 (1997), p. 61.
4 J. Schumpeter, *Business Cycles* (New York: McGraw-Hill, 1939).
5 S. C. Gilfillan, *Inventing the Ship* (Chicago: Follett Publishing, 1935).
6 R. Adner and D. A. Levinthal, "The Emergence of Emerging Technologies," *California Management Review*, 45, 1 (2002), pp. 50–66.
7 S. Thomke and E. von Hippel, "Customers as Innovators: A New Way to Create Value," *Harvard Business Review*, 80, 4 (2002), pp. 70–85.
8 J. Song, P. Almeida, and G. Wu, "Learning-by-Hiring: Mobility and Knowledge Transfer?", *Management Science*, 49 (2003), pp. 351–365.
9 J. B. Quinn, *Intelligent Enterprise: A Knowledge and Service Based Paradigm for Industry* (New York: Free Press, 1992).
10 S. Albert and K. Bradley, *Managing Knowledge: Experts, Agencies and Organizations* (Cambridge: Cambridge University Press, 1997).
11 D. Watts, *Small Worlds* (Princeton: Princeton University Press, 1999).
12 P. Braunerhjelm, B. Carlsson, D. Cetindamar, and D. Johansson, "The Old and the New: The Evolution of Polymer and Biomedical Clusters in Ohio and Sweden," *Journal of Evolutionary Economics*, 10 (2000), pp. 471–488.
13 F. Kodama, *Emerging Patterns of Innovation* (Boston: Harvard Business School Press, 1991).
14 A. Morita, E. M. Reingold, and M. Shimomura, *Made in Japan: Akio Morita and Sony* (New York: E. P. Dutton, 1986).
15 L. Rosenkopf and A. Nerkar, "Beyond Local Search: Boundary-Spanning, Exploration, and Impact in the Optical Disc Industry," *Strategic Management Journal*, 22 (2001), pp. 287–306.

16 B. Kogut and U. Zander, "Knowledge of the Firm, Combinative Capabilities, and the Replication of Technology," *Organization Science*, 3 (1992), pp. 383–397.

17 I. M. Cockburn and R. M. Henderson, "Absorptive Capacity, Coauthoring Behavior, and the Organization of Research in Drug Discovery," *Journal of Industrial Economics*, 46 (1998) pp. 157–182.

18 T. Stuart and J. Podolny, "Local Search and the Evolution of Technological Capabilities," *Strategic Management Journal*, 17 (1996), pp. 21–38.

19 L. Fleming, "Recombinant Uncertainty in Technological Search," *Management Science*, 47 (2001), pp. 117–132.

20 Rosenkopf and Nerkar, "Beyond Local Search."

21 Rosenkopf describes in detail how to diagram and analyze a firm's social network. L. Rosenkopf, "Managing Dynamic Knowledge Networks," in G. S. Day and P. J. H. Schoemaker (eds.), *Wharton on Managing Emerging Technologies* (New York: Wiley, 2000), pp. 337–357.

22 R. Burt, *Structural Holes: The Social Structure of Competition* (Cambridge, MA: Harvard University Press, 1992).

23 G. Ahuja, "Collaboration Networks, Structural Holes, and Innovation," *Administrative Science Quarterly* 45 (2000), pp. 425–456.

24 L. Rosenkopf and P. Almeida, "Overcoming Local Search through Alliances and Mobility," *Management Science*, 49 (2003), pp. 751–766.

25 Bijker, *Of Bicycles, Bakelites and Bulbs*.

26 E. von Hippel, *The Sources of Innovation* (Oxford: Oxford University Press, 1988).

27 C. Luthje, C. Herstatt, and E. von Hippel, "The Dominant Role of Local Information in User Innovation: The Case of Mountain Biking," MIT Sloan School of Management, Working Paper 4377-02 (2003).

28 L. Rosenkopf and M. Tushman, "On the Organizational Determinants of Technological Change: Toward a Sociology of Technological Evolution," in B. Staw and L. Cummings (eds.), *Research in Organizational Behavior*, vol. XIV (Greenwich, CT: JAI Press, 1992).

29 L. Rosenkopf and M. L Tushman, "The Coevolution of Community Networks and Technology: Lessons from the Flight Simulation Industry," *Industrial and Corporate Change*, 7 (1998), pp. 311–346.

30 L. Rosenkopf, A. Metiu, and V. George, "From the Bottom Up? Technical Committee Activity and Alliance Formation," *Administrative Science Quarterly*, 46 (2001), pp. 748–772.

31 P. Anderson, "Autodesk," teaching case, Amos Tuck School, Dartmouth, NH, 1996.

32 P. B. De Laat, "Systemic Innovation and the Virtues of Going Virtual: The Case of the Digital Video Disc," *Technology Analysis and Strategic Management*, 11 (1999), pp. 159–180.

33 W. M. Cohen and D. A. Levinthal, "Absorptive Capacity: A New Perspective on Learning and Innovation," *Administrative Science Quarterly*, 35 (1990) pp. 128–152.

34 F. A. J. van den Bosch, H. W. Volberda, and M. de Boer, "Coevolution of Firm Absorptive Capacity and Knowledge Environment: Organizational Forms and Combinative Capabilities," *Organization Science*, 10 (1999), pp. 551–568.

35 E. Wenger *Communities of Practice: Learning, Meaning and Identity* (Cambridge: Cambridge University Press, 1998).

36 U. Schmoch, "Interactions of Universities and Industrial Enterprises in Germany and the United States – A Comparison," *Industry and Innovation*, 6 (1999), pp. 51–68.

37 Cockburn and Henderson, "Absorptive Capacity."

38 Ibid.

39 L. G. Zucker, M. R. Darby, and J. S. Armstrong, "Commercializing Knowledge: University Science, Knowledge Capture, and Firm Performance in Biotechnology," *Management Science*, 48 (2002), pp. 138–153.

40 Wenger, *Communities of Practice*.

41 Schmoch, "Interactions of Universities and Industrial Enterprises."

42 R. E. Rice and E. M. Rogers, "Re-invention in the Innovation Process," *Knowledge*, 1 (1980), pp. 499–514.

43 S. G. Winter and G. Szulanski, "Replication as Strategy," *Organization Science*, 12 (2001), pp. 730–743.

44 Ibid., p. 731.

45 H. Collins, "The TEA Set: Tacit Knowledge and Scientific Networks," in Mario Biagioli (ed.), *Science Studies Reader* (New York: Routledge, 1999).

46 Schmoch, "Interactions of Universities and Industrial Enterprises."

47 A. Inkpen and A. Dinur. "Knowledge Management Processes and International Joint Ventures," *Organization Science*, 9 (1998), p. 465.

48 Rosenkopf and Nerkar, "Beyond Local Search."

49 J. H. Tiessen, "Developing Intellectual Capital Globally: An Epistemic Community Perspective," *International Journal of Technology Management*, 18 (1999), pp. 720–730.

50 W. Tsai, "Knowledge Transfer in Intraorganizational Networks: Effects of Network Position and Absorptive Capacity on Business Unit Innovation and Performance," *Academy of Management Journal*, 44 (2001), pp. 996–1004.

51 M. T. Hansen, "Knowledge Networks: Explaining Effective Knowledge Sharing in Multi-unit Companies," *Organization Science*, 13 (2002), pp. 232–248.

52 M. Cusumano and K. Nobeoka, *Thinking Beyond Lean: How Multi-project Management Is Transforming Product Development at Toyota and Other Companies* (New York: Free Press, 1998).

53 L. Kim, "The Dynamics of Samsung's Technological Learning in Semi-conductors," *California Management Review*, 39 (1997), pp. 86–100.

54 J. B. Quinn, P. Anderson, and S. Finkelstein, "Managing Professional Intellect: Making the Most of the Best," *Harvard Business Review*, 74, 2 (1996), pp. 71–83.

55 P. Gongla, and C. R. Rizzuto, "Evolving Communities of Practice: IBM Global Services Experience," *IBM Systems Journal*, 40 (2001), pp. 842–862.

14 From corporate social responsibility to global citizenship

ERIC W. ORTS
Wharton School

Multinational companies must participate in the life of multiple countries, with different cultures and expectations for their citizens. At the same time, these companies are facing new demands to address global issues such as environmental concerns and poverty. In this context, what does it mean to be a "corporate citizen"? The author examines the emergence of the concept of corporate responsibility and citizenship, including the long-standing debate about whether a company owes its allegiance primarily to shareholders or to a broad community of stakeholders. He then considers what these concepts mean in a global context. While citizenship in a single nation has typically been defined by geography or ethnicity, global citizenship is a much more uncertain concept. The author discusses some of the challenges that face business in meeting conflicting national demands for citizenship, such as the troubles faced by Yahoo! when US users of its online auctions offered Nazi memorabilia on its website, accessible in France. The sale was protected under US First Amendment rights but banned under French law. The author also discusses the emerging concept of "cosmopolitan" or "global" citizenship. It is clear that companies must address global concerns, but each individual company must determine how to define global citizenship for itself and how to balance this identity with responsibilities that it may have to various local, national, and regional communities.

IN February 2002, thirty-six large multinational corporations (including Coca-Cola, McDonald's, and Siemens) issued a statement pledging a renewed commitment to "corporate citizenship." These companies promised to establish "responsible behavior [as] a core part of their business" and to forge "close links with all their stakeholders."[1] A number of recent books for managers also describe

I wrote an initial draft of this chapter while on a sabbatical as the Eugene P. Beard Faculty Fellow at Harvard University's Center for Ethics and the Professions. A previous version was presented at a conference on Corporate Governance and Sustainable Peace at the University of Michigan Business School.

the need to develop strategies for "corporate citizenship," and they tend to take a global perspective in making their recommendations.[2]

But what does the concept of "corporate citizenship" really mean? And how can one speak coherently of becoming a "global citizen" when the demands of national citizenship remain strong and when many companies operating in different countries often face conflicting demands under different claims of citizenship? This chapter attempts to shed some light on these questions by considering the evolution of ideas of business ethics, the emergence of a concept of corporate citizenship, and their implications for global management.

The emergence of the concept of corporate citizenship

The nature and scope of ethical responsibility within corporations change over time – or should change – as both the institution of the corporation and the society in which corporations are embedded evolve. In early times when business organizations were no more complicated than personal family structures or small partnership arrangements, one could usually describe the business ethics of a privately owned enterprise to be covalent with the ethical obligations of the individual business owners. Principles of fair business practice derived from ordinary ethical judgments based on religion or other personal ethical touchstones.

The historical development of complex business enterprises has significantly changed the ethical picture. Large public corporations can no longer be easily identified with the interests and moral views of a small group of owners. It is true that the importance of individual ownership, including family ownership, continues. Tycoons have been part and parcel of the dynamic of capitalist development from the age of "robber barons" to the present age of Bill Gates and Microsoft. But as business organizations use increasingly intricate corporate forms to manage relationships of contracts, capital funding, and networks of property, the expanding scope of the business enterprise in society demands a similarly expansive normative understanding.

Corporate social responsibility is a concept that attempts to bring a broader ethical understanding to the topic of business organization. Because corporate businesses are integral to the societies in which they exist, their managers owe a "responsibility" to society in general as well as to the interests of those running the business. As an idea, corporate social responsibility has early roots in Europe. In Germany in 1917, the industrialist Walther Rathenau argued that the business corporation could no longer be accurately described as "purely a system of private interests." Instead it had become "both individually and collectively, a national concern belonging to the community." Although the business corporation has continued to bear "the marks of an undertaking run purely for profit," it "for some time and to an increasing degree has been serving the public interest."[3]

The changing conception of the corporation as a social institution was reflected around the same time in the United States. In 1908, for example, John Dewey and his co-author James H. Tufts argued in their basic text *Ethics* that the rising size and influence of business corporations posed significant moral issues. In their words:

When . . . great corporations, each controlling scores or even hundreds of millions of capital, are linked together in common control, we have a tremendous force which may be wielded as a unit. It is easy to assume – indeed it is difficult for managers not to assume – that the interests of such colossal organizations are of supreme importance . . . The moral dangers attaching to such corporations formed solely for economic purposes are obvious, and have found frequent illustration in their actual workings. Knowing few or none of the restraints which control an individual, the corporation has treated competitors, employees, and the public in a purely economic fashion. This insures certain limited species of honesty, but does not include motives of private sympathy or public duty.[4]

Modern theories of business ethics and corporate responsibility arose to address these kinds of moral and social concerns that became especially salient with the growth of very large corporate business enterprises.

Conflicting views: in the service of shareholders or society?

Arguments for and against "corporate social responsibility" in management continued for the rest of the twentieth century and into the twenty-first. Another good example of the argument about whether corporations should include "social responsibility" as well as maximizing profits as a management objective appeared in a famous debate in the 1930s between two professors, Adolf A. Berle and E. Merrick Dodd, which was published in the *Harvard Law Review*. Berle maintained that the powers of business corporations should be "exercisable only for the ratable benefit of all the shareholders."[5] Dodd replied with a variation of the social responsibility theme. He claimed that the corporation is "an economic institution which has a social service as well as a profit-making function."[6] Although Berle later agreed that Dodd's view had prevailed, what become known as the "shareholder primacy norm" made a strong comeback in the latter part of the twentieth century.

Milton Friedman, in a classic contribution to American business literature, argued that "the social responsibility of a business is to increase its profits."[7] Contemporary principal–agent theories in corporate finance – in which shareholders of business corporations are seen primarily as the economic "agents" of corporations – have also strongly influenced US corporate law and management practice in recent times.[8] These economic and financial ideas helped to establish a very strong "shareholder primacy norm" in the United States.[9] This principle of managing for shareholder value has been reinforced through both formal law (in the articulation of corporate fiduciary duties as well as disclosures mandated by securities law) and softer normative methods of persuasion, such as business school education and business journalism.

At the time same, many practicing managers as well as business scholars continued to promote the view that a measure of corporate social responsibility is morally required – beyond what might reasonably be argued to contribute to long-term shareholder value. Law sometimes also changed in this direction, such as in the "corporate constituency statutes" adopted by many US states in the late 1980s and early 1990s that explicitly rejected a "shareholders only" view of corporate fiduciary duties.[10] An indication of the strength of a broader view can also be found in the work of many of those writing within the growing ranks of scholars in the emerging field of "business ethics."[11] The idea of managing corporations for "stakeholders" has gained recognition in theory as well as in the practical parlance of modern corporate managers.[12]

Elsewhere in the world as well, ideas of corporate social responsibility have found fertile ground. In Asia, the idea of a broad social purpose for business fits well with indigenous ethical views deriving from Confucian, Hindu, and other religious traditions. In Japan, corporate responsibility has particularly strong roots. It is expressed in a welfarist view of managing the firm first and foremost for employees, as well as with a deep concern for the overall social well-being.[13]

Many multinational corporations have also formally adopted a "stake-holder" concept as a guide for practice. A leading example is the Caux Round Table's Principles for Business, which were formulated and adopted by an international network of business leaders (primarily from Europe, Japan, and the United States). The Caux Principles state that business responsibilities extend "beyond shareholders" to include stakeholders, which are specified to include customers, employees, owners/investors, suppliers, the communities in which a business operates, and even competitors.[14] The Caux Principles refer to central moral principles such as the emphasis given in Western philosophy to "human dignity" and the Japanese idea of *kyosei* that recommends "a spirit of cooperation" in business so that individual and social interests will work together for the common good.[15]

While much has been written about the rise of corporate social responsibility and debates about corporate responsibilities, this chapter looks at the broader question of how these issues play out on a global stage.[16] If global companies such as McDonald's, Coca-Cola, and Siemens call themselves "corporate citizens," what does this mean? Does it mean the same thing in all parts of the world or different things in different places? What are the political, moral, and legal obligations of corporations in transnational operations and markets?

Citizenship

Citizenship begins, of course, as a political term. There are two political conceptions of citizenship that one can trace historically: a "blood and soil" kind of citizenship tied to territorial and kinship identification; and "civic citizenship" tied to the identification of membership within a particular form of political state.[17]

Conceptual matters get more complicated when we consider the idea of a "corporation" having citizenship. In law, it is now well established that business (as well as municipal and nonprofit) corporations possess legal "citizenship" in the sense that they have the legal power to own property, to make contracts, and to sue and be sued.[18] Corporations may even assert constitutional rights of different kinds. In the nineteenth century, the US Supreme Court agreed that corporations were "citizens" for purposes of asserting jurisdiction. Since then, the Court has progressively extended constitutional rights to corporations as "citizens." Corporations as well as natural persons may claim free speech rights under the First Amendment, freedom from unreasonable searches and seizures under the Sixth Amendment, and equal protection of the law under the Fourteenth Amendment.[19]

Conflicting demands of citizenship across borders

In a global society, the concept of citizenship is complex. The rights and duties of citizenship in one country differ significantly from those in another. Natural persons, of course, are usually citizens of one country or another – though cases of dual citizenship and even "people without a country" sometimes arise. The imputed "citizenship" of a corporation with operations in multiple countries poses more complicated and persistent issues. A firm's country of incorporation alone cannot resolve larger political, legal, and moral questions.

To begin with, a corporation may have to choose whether to comply with the legal obligations of one national or federal state rather than another – both of which may assert jurisdiction to govern behavior on a particular issue. "Conflicts of law" rules apply to resolve these disputes at the level of formal law.[20] But this phenomenon itself indicates how the idea of corporate citizenship becomes quickly complicated in the process of globalization.

For example, French law bans the sale of Nazi memorabilia to French citizens, while US law upholds the rights of citizens to trade in such items based on First Amendment protections of free speech. When several US sellers used the Yahoo! auction site to advertise Nazi memorabilia, the company found itself in the middle of these two views of citizenship, and on the wrong side of French law.[21] Is Yahoo! a citizen of the United States, in which case it should protect and uphold the values of free speech, or a citizen of France, in which case it should respect the prohibition on the commercial sale of Nazi relics? Can Yahoo! be a good citizen of both places, or does it have to choose? What does it mean in this context to be a global citizen?

In this case, Yahoo! litigated first in French courts and then in the United States. It lost in France and was ordered to make technical changes to its Internet auction site that would prevent French citizens from buying Nazi artifacts in violation of French law.[22] Yahoo! then turned to ask a United States court for relief from enforcement of the French order in the United States – and won on First Amendment grounds.[23]

In short, Yahoo! seems to have elected to resolve the matter through a legal strategy. But one wonders whether it would have been possible (as well as cheaper and morally superior) for managers at Yahoo! to have avoided extended international litigation by addressing the problem of international conflict with greater sensitivity in the design of its website. Google, for example, blocks selected sites in French and German in response to complaints on a case-by-case basis.[24] In any event, it seems clear that corporations with global reach through the Internet will need to develop internal policies – ideally with an ethical foundation – to address situations of conflicting national laws.

A purely legalistic approach to resolving corporate citizenship problems does not offer an easy or convincing solution. Such an approach to managing global issues regarding the Internet seems not only to have resulted in a questionable ethical position for Yahoo! in Europe, but also to be leading to another moral quagmire for the company in China. Recently, Yahoo! agreed to purge its website of material deemed "subversive" by the Chinese government.[25] From an ethical perspective, the idea that Yahoo! would flout a French ban on the sale of Nazi materials and then proceed to cooperate with Chinese censors is highly questionable. However one thinks the complex moral issues here should be resolved, the tribulations of Yahoo! demonstrate that simply "following law" is often insufficient to resolve the conflicting moral claims of international "citizenship."

The Internet is not the only source of competing claims of citizenship. As more and more companies establish global marketing, management, and financial structures, they should expect to confront a host of new issues related to "citizenship." For example, the recent Sarbanes–Oxley legal reform in the United States imposed new rules on corporations that listed securities in the United States. German companies were suddenly caught between the new US standards that required "independent" audit committees and a German corporate legal structure that made compliance with the US law impractical if not impossible. "Co-determination" law requires the supervisory boards of many large German corporations to have representatives of employees as well as managers and shareholders. German audit committees had not been established at least in part because of a fear that the labor unions would use them for bargaining leverage. The German companies petitioned the Securities and Exchange Commission for an exemption from the US requirement, and the SEC has granted a limited exemption, though it is not yet clear that the SEC had the statutory authority to do so.[26] However this situation is eventually resolved, it illustrates how competing legal obligations can force companies with global scope in operations to weigh competing claims of citizenship. Global companies need to decide whether and how to comply with different national laws that conflict. Simply "following the law" is often inadequate. One possible approach is for a company to support the development of an international legal framework to resolve conflicts. In securities regulation, for example, a company could lobby for an international agreement to specify which national (or supranational) regulator has responsibility for particular issues that cross borders.[27] In the absence of international agreements, however, companies are left to decide for themselves how to navigate the perilous waters of conflicting citizenships.

Is Daimler-Chrysler a German firm?

Larger conflicts of national citizenship arise for international corporations that develop extensive management and financial structures that cross national boundaries in a manner that makes it difficult to say where a company has what some European corporate law calls the "real seat" (*siège réel*) of corporate operations.[28] Daimler-Chrysler provides a leading example of this larger problem. Created through the merger of two major automobile companies – one German and one American – the question arises as to whether Daimler-Chrysler must choose between the two competing nationalities. Daimler-Chrysler is incorporated in Germany, but this fact alone is not dispositive. Major headquarters are maintained in Detroit as well as Stuttgart. Managers are drawn from diverse international backgrounds. Institutional investors around the world are major shareholders. The simple fact of incorporation in Germany – and of having a slight majority of German shareholders – does not yield a conclusive determination of Daimler-Chrysler as "German."[29] With global sourcing, sales, management, and investment, Daimler-Chrysler is "a firm with multiple national identities."[30] By the same measure, many other large automobile companies have similar characteristics. Toyota and Honda, for example, are arguably corporate citizens of the United States as much as Japan in terms of their customers, suppliers, employees, and investors. The implications of the global structure of automobile companies for corporate citizenship are profound. To describe Daimler-Chrysler as only "German" would ignore economic and social reality at almost every level. The large multinational structure of these kinds of companies requires forging a new identity as a "global citizen" – with all its attendant difficulties.

One central difficulty faced by multinational corporations developing global identities for themselves involves competing views of corporate governance. Older debates about corporate social responsibility return at the international level. In US companies, for example, high levels of executive compensation have been taken for granted as compared with more modest pay in continental European and Japanese corporations.[31] Should Daimler-Chrysler adopt an American or a German model of corporate governance in addressing this issue? Who should decide? Globalization puts pressure on different models of corporate governance within a single company, as well as more broadly in the global competitive environment. Again, the resolution of these issues cannot be avoided by an appeal to formal legal rules, because the legal systems themselves differ.

Even within Europe, it is hard for policymakers to come up with a common definition of the responsibilities of "corporate citizenship" in an environment of different national laws and cultures. Discussions about the nature of the relationship between society and business corporations have been intensified by European Commission proposals to "harmonize" national corporate laws to a common standard throughout the European Union. While a European Company Statute has been recently adopted that allows a firm to incorporate once at the European level and then have rights of operation throughout the Union, success in the endeavor of corporate governance harmonization has been mixed.[32]

The European debates have been marked by continuing disagreements about the nature of the corporation. Continental Europeans, including Germany and France, tend to view the large business corporation through the historical lens of political compromises made between labor unions and business interests. German co-determination in large public companies and its mandatory two-tier board structure is an example. It compares with the British approach, which sees the corporation much more as an entity managed solely in the interests of its owners, with a financial focus on shareholders. The European Company Statute suggests that a compromise may be worked out for the future, but it allows for flexibility for each company on issues of worker participation and competing models of corporate governance.[33]

The continuing importance of conceptual and empirical issues of corporate governance has also been recognized by the European Commission in funding major research efforts that will be designed to inquire into different conceptions of corporate social responsibility.[34] An implicit goal is to try to provide a common understanding of current theories and practice.

In a globalizing world, it is not surprising that conceptual discussions of corporate citizenship have moved beyond a legal framework. As corporations find themselves in many different countries and responding to different legal and political claims, those who manage corporations (and those who study them) will naturally begin to question the underlying moral arguments of citizenship. In brief, citizenship makes claims of loyalty on organizations as well as individuals. But in a business organization of global scope, the conflicting claims of national loyalty call for some kind of conceptual resolution beyond formal conflicts of law rules.

Global corporate citizenship

One potentially appealing approach to the globalization of business enterprises – and the natural persons composing them (including managers, employees, shareholders, and other investors) who are spread throughout the world – is for companies to conceive of themselves as having "global citizenship." The moral identification of a global corporation as a "citizen of the world" would have important implications for corporate social responsibility.

This idea of global corporate citizenship is similar to the concept of individual "cosmopolitan citizenship" that has been discussed by political theorists. A "cosmopolitan" rather than a "nationalist" person, according to the political theorist Brian Barry, is a "citizen of the world" and feels a moral obligation to other human beings regardless of nationality.[35] As an empirical matter, some movement toward "cosmopolitanism" has been identified among natural persons. The European Union, for example, is by definition multinational in its structure and affirmatively promotes the ideal of "the European citizen."[36] Even in Europe, however, most individuals do not yet regard themselves as strongly "cosmopolitan," though there has been some significant movement in this direction, especially among young people. One recent study found that although only a minority of Europeans felt a strong sense of cosmopolitan citizenship, the post-World War II generation was five times more likely to claim a cosmopolitan citizenship identity than their predecessors.[37]

Global corporate citizens would arguably have a broader perspective on social problems than the "citizens" of a single nation. The leading social problems for cosmopolitan corporate citizens would be global rather than local or national. For example, large global problems of environmental degradation (e.g. climate change and rampant species destruction) and radical divisions between rich and poor may figure more importantly from a global perspective than a concern about the well-being of a particular national economy and its national citizens. Even geopolitical issues of global war and peace that have been commonly thought to be within the exclusive competence of nation-states are arguably within the scope and moral responsibility of business management.[38]

This global view can be seen in the rise of the governance structures of the United Nations, the World Trade Organization, the World Bank, and the International Monetary Fund that have served to underpin the strong global economic growth of the late twentieth century. Not all regions of the globe have participated equally, and some parts (especially in Africa) have had little positive economic gain in recent decades. But in general, the legal and financial global framework of the so-called "Washington consensus" represented by the major international institutions has provided the basic stability needed for global economic investment and expansion to occur. How well these global institutions will perform in the future remains an open but very important question.[39]

A rising global self-conception can also be seen in the expansion of non-governmental organizations (NGOs). The number of NGOs with an international scope has increased from approximately 6,000 in 1990 to around 26,000 in 2000.[40] In the United States alone, there are about two million NGOs, and 70 percent of them have been created since 1970.[41] These numbers compare to about 63,000 multinational corporations having approximately 800,000 foreign subsidiaries.[42]

Ad hoc international movements have also organized around many of the same global concerns, with many of the "anti-globalization" protesters ironically taking a very cosmopolitan view of their own citizenship. Internet technology has greatly enhanced the means to organize such transnational groups, as the recent demonstrations in Seattle, Quebec, and Genoa attest. An international anti-globalization movement presents a key risk for global business managers in terms of possible consumer boycotts or even stronger direct protests, as well as a general threat to the stability of the underlying global infrastructure. These groups – and the writers who support them – are raising questions related to global citizenship with a force and visibility that make it difficult and unwise for companies and policymakers to ignore them.[43]

Given the institutional globalization of both business corporations and NGOs, one might hypothesize the gradual development of a new level of social integration. The legitimate players in a new global society may include not only the traditional nation-states of the Westphalian system of the international order, but also global corporations, global NGOs, and global quasi-governmental organizations such as the United Nations and the World Bank. One might go so far as to say that a new global civil society has arisen that has become partially independent of nation-states. Of course, the extent to which this global civil society exists is dependent on the true strength and breadth of present and future globalizing processes.

A winding road

Should corporations adopt a global "cosmopolitan" view of citizenship? Current tendencies toward globalization characterized as the emergence of a new global level of civil society – organized in terms of multinational business corporations and global NGOs (e.g. Greenpeace, Oxfam, World Wildlife Fund, Nature Conservancy, and Doctors Without Borders) – tempt one to recommend this perspective. Perhaps an ideal world along these lines is desirable. At present, however, it seems that a global political order is still rudimentary with an infrastructure not yet able to support a universal claim of cosmopolitan citizenship.

As noted above, the percentage of individuals who view themselves as "cosmopolitan" is still relatively small. The political conditions for global citizenship may also be more fragile than they appear. Although we have enjoyed a period of relative international peace, which has been an important underpinning of globalization, the "small war" exceptions to this rule indicate the sharp divisions that remain. Even before the outbreak of renewed hostilities in Israel and Iraq, lower-intensity "intrastate wars" were in progress in many places. By one estimate, at least fifty such wars were being fought in 1999–2000.[44] In the wake of September 11 – if no other event or statistic is persuasive – it is simply not viable to posit a pure version of "cosmopolitanism" as an alternative to national citizenship for most individuals and organizations.[45] At a minimum, it is important to recognize that the emergence of a global civil society cannot be a substitute for strong international governing structures forged through agreements among nation-states.[46]

However, the continuing relevance of national citizenship does not mean that other aspirations toward global identification should be forsaken. Instead, individuals as well as corporations should begin to transform themselves – and their self-conceptions – to include a broad sense of global problems and responsibilities. For corporations, an orientation of global citizenship has the benefit of a sense of entitlement – of rights as well as moral duties. NGOs have indeed begun to play a representative role for individuals concerned with various important issues – from the alleviation of poverty to environmental protection. But the political framework of the emerging global civil society remains vague. Democratic participation of citizens does not legitimate the exercise of power either by multinational corporations or NGOs. Yet the global problems that we face will not wait for global political governance. Instead, we must "muddle through."[47] Business corporations, NGOs, and nation-states must work to address major social problems together with multilateral governmental organizations such as the UN and the World Bank.

A middle course

In thinking about the "global citizenship" of corporations, as well as NGOs and broad-minded individuals, the political philosopher Dennis Thompson offers a useful perspective.[48] Recognizing the current tendency toward expansion of the liberal democratic model to include increasing portions of the globe, Thompson argues for a middle course in the conception of global citizenship. He rejects the utopian view of "cosmopolitanism" as problematic from a democratic as well as a practical point of view.[49] The legitimacy of multinational corporations and international NGOs does not derive directly from any democratic structure of government. And the international legal and political infrastructure that currently exists is so fragmented that it cannot be relied upon to be representative. Thompson proposes the alternative of "civil societarianism" – a view that transnational associations, including corporations and NGOs, might compose a new global order. He sees the growth of this new form of transnational civil society as "an important and promising development in international politics."[50] Again, however, "the politics in the traditional places – local and national government – is still of critical importance to democracy itself."[51] Thompson's recommendation is to strengthen institutions that enable the capacities of a "deliberative democracy" to develop regionally and locally as well as globally.[52]

This recommendation is consistent with arguments from other quarters, such as the United Nations, for business corporations to enter into partnerships or a "Global Compact" with other firms, nation-states, NGOs, and multilateral international organizations to address major global problems.[53] It is true that such *ad hoc* arrangements to tackle global problems may suffer a "democratic deficit" in terms of a political ideal of democratic representation and participation.[54] But again, there are a number of major global problems that cannot wait.[55] As noted above, these problems should be part of the broader agenda of any individual or corporation that sees itself as a citizen of global society.

In a recent book, Jean-François Rischard lists "twenty global problems" that require immediate attention in whatever manner we can devise to address them in the next twenty years.[56] He identifies three sets of large problems. First are global environmental "commons" problems such as global warming, biodiversity loss, fisheries depletion, deforestation, and water shortages. A second set of issues relates to "what we owe to each other" as ethical human beings.[57] These issues include global poverty, peacekeeping and security against terrorism, education, fighting infectious diseases, overcoming the digital divide, and the prevention and mitigation of natural disasters. Finally, there are issues of improving the global regulatory infrastructure, including taxation, biotechnology rules, global financial architecture, illegal drugs, intellectual property protection, e-commerce rules, and international labor and immigration law.

One does not need to agree with all of the items on this list, and we may disagree about how to prioritize these challenges to world society as we know it. But the conclusion from the point of view of forming a new conception of "global citizenship" is that business corporations, as well as individuals, NGOs, and governments, should all play a role in addressing these larger issues. Picking and choosing what one can do, and what one cannot, is part of a mature and healthy recognition of personal and organizational limitations. Business corporations cannot solve all of the world's problems. But given the gravity of many of the global problems facing us today, no group in society – especially powerful groups and individuals – can be excused for turning a blind eye to our current human situation. Creating a practical role as a "global citizen" for ourselves and the organizations in which we work is a compelling ethical calling.

Conclusions

Business leaders must act in a world in which there is no clear definition of global citizenship. Yet the expectations for companies to behave as citizens of the world are apparent and show no sign of diminishing. Whatever companies may feel about their obligations, they are increasingly seen as players on the global stage, and they will be forced to confront global issues – whether they are the environmental concerns faced by major petroleum companies or the demands for major pharmaceutical companies to provide low-priced drugs to AIDS patients in poor African countries. Companies are going to be seen and held accountable as global citizens, but business leaders have many choices to make about how they define that citizenship and how they articulate it to include responsibilities owing to various communities and shareholders.

This is not a new problem in a certain sense. Companies have long been recognized as "citizens" at multiple levels: local communities, states or provinces, and nation states. Managers have always had to juggle the competing demands of different expectations for citizenship. For example, when an automaker moves a plant from the United States to Mexico, the move might be seen as contributing to the viability of the auto industry, boosting returns for shareholders, and providing highly paid jobs in a developing nation. Or it might be seen as destroying a local community that had previously depended upon the plant for employment. A chemical company needs to ensure the safety of a plant in a small community even if it may suffer some expense to its global bottom line. These types of tradeoffs have always been made – at least implicitly. Global citizenship adds yet another level of complexity to the challenge of balancing multiple demands on business leaders made by a diverse group of shareholders and other stakeholders. In the case of global citizenship, the demands are broader, the "globe" less clearly defined, the regulations, and even regulatory bodies, shifting and uncertain. This makes the project of global citizenship somewhat more difficult than other levels of citizenship, but the difficulties are not intractable.

Developing an overall conception of "global corporate citizenship" can help companies to respond effectively to globalizing forces and participate in multiple societies. Global citizenship is not a universal set of principles that should somehow be recognized, adopted, and practiced by all companies operating on a global plane. Rather, each particular company should develop its own view of corporate citizenship and its own approach to being a "good citizen" according to its own best moral, political, and social view of its proper place in our shrinking and fragile world.

A company may take several practical steps in the direction of formulating its own solid identity as a "global citizen." First, it should identify the major social issues implicated in the company's daily operations or highlighted by the company's specialization. Priorities should be established, and concrete strategies should be developed. Second, a company should look for partners with similar priorities and interests – both other companies and entities in the nonprofit world and government. A third step is to adopt internal policies to involve a firm's employees, shareholders, and other important "constituents" in the process of building a unique personality as a "global citizen." Businesses that follow this path of engagement with the world and its social problems will develop a good reputation for being part of the larger solution rather than merely another thoughtless contributor to the world's problems.

Notes

1 A. Maitland, "Companies Pledge Better 'Corporate Citizenship,'" *Financial Times*, February 4, 2002; "Why Business Leaders Must Be Good Citizens, Too," *Financial Times*, February 9, 2002; "Outlook: Even Corporations Are Getting a Social Conscience," *The Independent*, February 9, 2002.

2 N. M. Tichy *et al.* (eds.), *Corporate Global Citizenship: Doing Business in the Public Eye* (Lanham, MD: Rowman & Littlefield, 1998); M. MacIntosh *et al.*, *Corporate Citizenship: Successful Strategies for Responsible Companies* (London: Financial Times and Pitman, 1998); D. T. McAlister and W. C. Downing, *Business and Society: A Strategic Approach to Corporate Citizenship* (Boston: Houghton Mifflin, 2003); S. A. Waddock, *Leading Corporate Citizens* (Boston: McGraw-Hill/ Irwin, 2001).

3 H. Kessler, *Walther Rathenau: His Life and Work* (New York: Harcourt, Brace and Co., 1930).

4 John Dewey and J. H. Tufts, *Ethics* (New York: H. Holt, 1908), pp. 498–499.

5 A. A. Berle, Jr., "Corporate Powers as Powers in Trust," *Harvard Law Review*, 44 (1931), p. 1049.

6 E. M. Dodd, Jr., "For Whom Are Corporate Managers Trustees?" *Harvard Law Review*, 45 (1932), pp. 1145 and 1148.

7 M. Friedman, "A Friedman Doctrine – The Social Responsibility of Business Is to Increase Its Profits," *New York Times Magazine*, September 13, 1970, p. 32.

8 For a good introduction to this literature, see L. Putterman and R. S. Kroszner (eds.), *The Economic Nature of the Firm: A Reader* (Cambridge: Cambridge University Press, 2nd edn. 1996).

9 See, for example, R. Romano, "What Is the Value of Other Constituencies Statutes To Shareholders?," *University of Toronto Law Journal* 43 (1993), p. 533. ("A fixed point of corporate law is that shareholders are, or should be, the ones whose interests count in corporate decision-making.") For a historical account of this development, see D. G. Smith, "The Shareholder Primacy Norm," *Iowa Journal of Corporate Law*, 23 (1998), p. 277.

10 I canvass this development in E. W. Orts, "Beyond Shareholders: Interpreting Corporate Constituency Statutes," *George Washington Law Review*, 61 (1992), p. 14.

11 For an argument contesting the view among some economists that "there is no need" for business ethics, see Amartya Sen, "Does Business Ethics Make Economic Sense?," reprinted in T. Donaldson *et al.* (eds.), *Ethical Issues in Business: A Philosophical Approach* (Upper Saddle River, NJ: Prentice-Hall, 7th edn. 2002).

12 Dozens of books and hundreds of articles have been devoted to the idea of "stakeholders" in business. T. Donaldson and L. E. Preston, "The Stakeholder Theory of the Corporation: Concepts, Evidence, and Implications," *Academy of Management Review*, 20 (1995), p. 65. Elsewhere, I explore with a colleague some limitations to the stakeholder concept.

E. W. Orts and A. Strudler, "The Ethical and Environmental Limits of Stakeholder Theory," *Business Ethics Quarterly*, 12 (2002), p. 215.

13 See, for example, Sen, "Does Business Ethics Make Economic Sense," p. 248 (citing sources attributing the success of the Japanese economic system to special characteristics of a "Japanese ethos" which draws on such sources as Confucian ethics and Samurai conceptions of honor).

14 Principle 1 carries the "beyond shareholders toward stakeholders" expression. Section 3 provides the list of stakeholders and a description of duties owed toward them. For the complete text of the principles, see http://www.cauxroundtable.org/principles.html (last visited September 13, 2003). To include one's business "competitors" in a stakeholder theory may seem odd on a first impression. Of course, this is not to say that one should manage a business for the direct economic benefit of one's competitors. Instead, the idea is to include one's competitors in the moral universe of those whom deserve moral consideration – such as fair, honest treatment.

15 Ibid., introduction.

16 For an overview of the topic, see P. Werhane and R. E. Freeman, "Corporate Responsibility," in Hugh LaFollette (ed.), *The Oxford Book of Practical Ethics* (Oxford: Oxford University Press, 2004), pp. 514–538. For a recent collection of essays on the topic of corporate social responsibility, see *Harvard Business Review on Corporate Responsibility* (Boston: Harvard Business School Publications, 2003). See also J. W. Anderson, Jr., *Corporate Social Responsibility: Guidelines for Top Management* (New York: Quorum Books, 1989) (including a historical account of the development of the idea).

17 For a critical discussion of this distinction between "blood and soil" and "civil" forms of nationalism (and their respective forms of citizenship identification), see B. Barry, "Statism and Nationalism: A Cosmopolitan Critique," in I. Shapiro and Lea Brilmayer (eds.), *Global Justice: NOMOS XLI* (New York: New York University Press, 1999), pp. 12–66.

18 See, for example, 8 Del. Code §122 (2003).

19 For overview treatments of the constitutional rights of corporations in US law, see D. Graver, "Personal Bodies: A Corporeal Theory of Corporate Personhood," *University of Chicago Law School Roundtable* 6 (1999), p. 235; C. J. Mayer, "Personalizing the Impersonal: Corporations and the Bill of Rights," *Hastings Law Journal*, 41 (1990), p. 577.

20 There are several basic texts treating the problem of conflicts of laws. See, for example, L. Brilmayer and J. Martin, *Conflict of Law: Cases and Materials* (Boston: Little, Brown, 3rd edn. 1990).

21 See E. Gulland, "All the World's a Forum," *National Law Journal*, February 11, 2002, at B13; E. A. Okoniewski, "Yahoo!, Inc. v. LICRA: The French Challenge to Free Expression on the Internet," *American University International Law Review*, 18 (2002), p. 295.

22 "L'Union Des Etudiants Juifs de France v. Yahoo!," *T.G.I. Paris*, May 22, 2000; "L'Union Des Etudiants Juifs de France v. Yahoo!," *T.G.I. Paris*, November 20, 2000.

23 "Yahoo!, Inc. v. La Ligue Contre Le Racisme et L'Antisemitisme," *F. Supp.* 2d 169 (N.D. Cal. 2001), p. 1181.

24 J. Schwartz, "Study Tallies Sites Blocked by Google," *New York Times*, October 25, 2002, p. C8.

25 "Yahoo's China Concession," *Washington Post*, August 19, 2002, p. A12.

26 J. C. Coffee, Jr., "Corporate Securities Leading Issues Under Sarbanes–Oxley, Part I," *New York Law Journal*, September 19, 2002, p. 5. The SEC's final rule discussed the special circumstances involving the partial exclusion for German companies. Final Rule, Standards Relating to Listed Company Audit Committees, 17 C.F.R pts. 228, 229, 240, 249 and 274, RIN 3235-AI75 (April 9, 2003).

27 With respect to disclosure in securities law, for example, one might choose among the following options for adopting a consistent regulatory approach: (1) focus on the nationality of the issuer of a security, (2) regulate a security in terms of the location of transactions, (3) focus on the nationality of the investors, (4) adopt global rules to be enforced universally, or (5) allow for choice of regulatory regimes by the issuers. M. B. Fox, "The Securities Globalization Disclosure Debate," *Washington University Law Quarterly*, 78 (2000), pp. 567, 568–569.

28 For an explanation of this approach, see W.-H. Roth, "Recognition of Foreign Companies in Siège Réel Countries: A German Perspective," in J. Wouters and H. Schneider (eds.), *Current Issues of Cross-Border Establishment of Companies in the European Union* (Antwerp: Maklu, 1995) pp. 29–46.

29 L. Mabry, "Multinational Corporations and US Technology Policy: Rethinking the Concept of Corporate Nationality," *Georgetown Law Journal*, 87 (1999), pp. 563, 629–632.

30 Ibid., p. 633.

31 Levels of executive compensation in US companies are at least twice as high as in their European and Japanese counterparts. S. J. Stabile, "One for A, Two for B, and Four Hundred for C: The Widening Gap in Pay Between Executives and Rank and File Employees," *University of Michigan Journal of Law Reform*, 36 (2002), pp. 115, 121 n. 22.

Ratios between executive compensation and rank-and-file salaries are even greater. In the US, corporate executives today make 400 to 500 times as much as ordinary workers, as compared with ratios on the order of 20:1 or less in Europe and Japan. See also G. S. Crystal, *In Search of Excess: The Overcompensation of American Executives* (New York: Norton, 1991), pp. 207–209; R. S. Thomas, "Should Directors Reduce Executive Pay?" *Hastings Law Journal*, 54 (2003), pp. 437, 441.

32 For an overview, see A. Kellerhals and D. Truten, "The Creation of the European Company," *Tulane European & Civil Law Forum*, 17 (2002), p. 71.

33 Ibid.

34 Researchers, including representatives of the INSEAD–Wharton Alliance, have recently been awarded a major grant from the European Commission to begin a major study in this area.

35 Barry, "Statism and Nationalism," p. 35. See also M. Cohen, "Rooted Cosmopolitanism," in M. Walzer (ed.), *Toward a Global Civil Society* (New York: Berghahn Books, 1995), pp. 223–233.

36 The topic of what it means to be a multinational "European citizen" is an issue of significant current academic as well as popular interest. See, for example, J. H. H. Weiler, *The Constitution of Europe* (New York: Cambridge University Press, 1999), p. 329 (discussing "a new concept of citizenship" as an important intellectual and practical challenge for the European Union). See also I. Ward, "The End of Sovereignty and the New Humanism," *Stanford Law Review*, 55 (2003), p. 2091.

37 P. Norris, "Global Governance and Corporate Citizens," in J. S. Nye and J. D. Donahue (eds.), *Governance in a Globalizing World* (Cambridge, MA: Brookings Institution Press, 2000), pp. 155–177.

38 I have made this argument with respect to the responsibility that corporations have in terms of their relatively direct involvement in warfare. E. W. Orts, "War and the Business Corporation," *Vanderbilt Journal of Transnational Law*, 35 (2002), p. 549.

39 For a strong criticism of the recent performance of the IMF and, to a lesser extent, the World Bank in promoting sustainable growth and prosperity in poor countries, see J. Stiglitz, *Globalization and Its Discontents* (New York: W. W. Norton, 2002). Even critics such as Stiglitz, however, recognize the importance of a global financial and legal architecture.

40 J.-F. Rischard, *High Noon: Twenty Global Problems, Twenty Years to Solve Them* (New York: Basic Books, 2002), p. 48.

41 Ibid.

42 Ibid., p. 138.

43 Some examples of the recent literature critical of globalization on polit-
ical grounds include the following: C. Derber, *People Before Profit: The
New Globalization in an Age of Terror, Big Money, and Economic Crisis*
(New York: St. Martin's Press, 2002); J. Gray, *False Dawn: The Delu-
sions of Global Capitalism* (London: Granta Books, 1998); N. Hertz, *The
Silent Takeover: Global Capitalism and the Death of Democracy* (New
York: Free Press, 2001); D. Korten, *When Corporations Rule the World*
(San Francisco: Berrett-Koehler Publishers; Bloomfield, CT: Kumarian
Press, 2nd edn., 2001); D. Model, *Corporate Rule: Understanding and
Challenging the New World Order* (Montreal: Black Rose Books, 2003).

44 Rischard, *High Noon*, p. 96.

45 It is instructive to consider the estimates of global indirect losses caused
by the September 11 attack. In addition to the thousands of people from
many different countries killed outright, an estimated 10 million people
in the world are expected to fall into poverty as a result of economic
slowdown caused by the terrorist attacks. Also, 20,000 to 40,000 children are expected to die because of delays in fighting malnutrition and
common diseases.

46 For a strong historical argument warning that some present claims for the
peacemaking capacities of global civil society risk repeating errors made
after World War I, see C. S. Meier, "International Associationalism: The
Social and Political Premises of Peacemaking After 1917 and 1945," in
P. Kennedy and W. I. Hitchcock (eds.), *From War to Peace: Altered Strategic Landscapes in the Twentieth Century* (New Haven: Yale University
Press, 2000), pp. 36–52.

47 Cf. C. E. Lindblom, "The Science of 'Muddling Through,'" *Public
Administration Review* 19 (1959), p. 79 (giving the classic version of
the argument in favor of the need to address public policy issues in the
absence of perfect institutions and with only imperfect information).

48 D. Thompson, "Democratic Theory and Global Society," *Journal of
Political Philosophy*, 7 (1999), p. 111.

49 Ibid., pp. 114–115.

50 Ibid., p. 116.

51 Ibid.

52 Ibid., pp. 119–120.

53 See http://www.unglobalcompact.org/Portal/ (last visited September 27,
2003).

54 The problem of a "democratic deficit" has been expressed in the context of supranational orders such as the European Union. See, for example, Peter L. Lindseth, "Democratic Legitimacy and the Administrative
Character of Supranationalism: The Example of the European Union,"

Columbia Law Review, 99 (1999), p. 628. Other international organizations are subject to similar criticism.

55 Worries about a "democratic deficit" may also downplay other important ethical values – such as survival or health – in comparison with the
political virtue of democracy.

56 Rischard, *High Noon*, p. 66.

57 See T. Scanlon, *What We Owe to Each Other* (Cambridge, MA: Belknap
Press of Harvard University Press, 1998).

15 | Colliding forces: domestic politics and the global economy

ETHAN B. KAPSTEIN
INSEAD

STEPHEN J. KOBRIN
Wharton School

While the economy is global, politics and political institutions are still, for the most part, local or national. This set of colliding regulatory and business forces creates tremendous complexity for global businesses that must work across a patchwork of fragmented national and regional regulations. In this chapter, the authors examine some of the complexities of this political and economic terrain through two cases. The first case considers the differences in views of the privacy of personal data between the United States and the European Union that have come to the fore in discussions of the Safe Harbor negotiations. The second case examines the challenges in developing a global information and communications technology (ICT) infrastructure, spearheaded by the US Global Information Infrastructure (GII) initiative. Both of these cases illustrate the challenges of managing global operations in a world of local politics and the importance of deeply held cultural beliefs in shaping the advance of global regulations. They also show that, paradoxically, in a globalizing world, domestic regulations are becoming increasingly important.

I N March 2003, Porsche, the German sports car manufacturer, abandoned plans for an offering on the New York Stock Exchange because of its opposition to the Sarbanes–Oxley Act. The Act, which was passed in reaction to the "Enron" corporate scandals, requires all firms *listed* on American markets to comply with new governance standards, including a requirement that chief executive officers attest to the accuracy of financial statements. Porsche argued that the *extra-territorial* application of Sarbanes–Oxley imposes unnecessary rules that are incompatible with German law.[1]

Sarbanes–Oxley applies to a very large number of European firms, including half of London's FTSE 500. The objective of Congress

Portions of this chapter are drawn from Stephen J. Kobrin, "Safe Harbors Are Hard to Find: The Trans-Atlantic Dispute, Territorial Jurisdiction and Global Governance," *Review of International Studies*, 2004.

353

was the protection of American investors, and there is no evidence that Congress intended to impose American rules and regulations on European firms. However, given the high level of integration of European and American markets, it is no longer possible to contain the impact of regulation within US borders. American capital markets have become "global" institutions. Any attempt to regulate the markets or the firms who participate in them will "spill over" into other jurisdictions; it will have a direct and significant impact on firms and individuals in other countries.

The problem is not limited to corporate governance issues or even the reach of American regulation. European law and regulation also has significant impacts in the United States. The Honeywell–GE merger, for example, was derailed by the European Commission, and European concerns about genetically modified foods have a direct effect on what American farmers plant and can sell overseas.

Porsche's problem is a reflection of an asymmetry between global economics and domestic politics that is most obvious in the transatlantic context, but is increasingly important in the world at large. In many respects, the economy is global; it is integrated transnationally. German firms that require substantial amounts of capital find that they have to list on American markets and virtually every multinational firm has to operate in both Europe and the United States.

Politics and political institutions, however, are still local and national; laws and regulations are made by national legislatures (or the European Union). While the nation-state's borders may no longer "contain" the economy, it is still the primary container of politics and society. Thus we find ourselves with an integrated economy, a single "economic space," governed by fragmented national and regional authorities.

And therein lies the rub. A transnational economy requires at least some degree of global governance. It requires international cooperation and harmonization, some minimal set of rules and principles that are compatible and non-conflicting. International cooperation is necessary in a wide range of issue areas including competition policy, corporate governance, and consumer protection.

In this chapter, we explore these challenges through two case studies. The first is the dispute between the United States and Europe over the privacy of electronically transmitted name-linked data, and the second is related to policies for the information and communications technology (ICT) sector. These cases make it very clear that global – or more specifically, transatlantic – economic governance is not simply a matter of government officials reconciling differences in law and regulation. One of the more dramatic effects of globalization is that the sharp line separating domestic and international affairs, a fundamental organizing principle of the modern international political system, is rapidly becoming a diffuse blur. International economic governance and domestic politics cannot be separated. Regulatory spillover is becoming the rule rather than the exception and in many issue areas important to corporations these policy externalities must be understood and managed by senior executives.

These cases reveal a paradox: the international liberalization of markets has increased rather than reduced the importance of domestic law and regulation. The domestic context and domestic politics must be taken into account if any effort involving international economic governance is to be successful. The nation-state is still the primary "container" of politics and society. Developing even a minimal set of international rules and principles may involve more than reconciling differing domestic regulations or even domestic interest groups. It may result in a confrontation between deep-seated values and belief systems which are fundamentally opposed to one another. Effective international cooperation may require that basic political and societal differences be reconciled. In that sense, the international and domestic contexts have merged into one.

Transatlantic economic integration

To set the stage for considering these cases, we first consider the extent of US–European economic integration. The United States and the European Union, the two largest economies in the world, are of roughly equivalent size, and account for 58 percent of the world's GNP.[2] The two economies are deeply integrated through foreign direct investment (FDI). Flows between the United States and the European Union, in both directions, accounted for about 30 percent of all flows of FDI between 1995 and 1999.[3] The sales of American firms' subsidiaries in the European Union total over $117 billion (1998) and those of European firms in the United States almost $107 billion (1999).

The vast majority of those firms transfer financial, credit, and marketing data and personnel records among their subsidiaries and between subsidiaries and headquarters electronically, so their viability depends on their electronic data networks. In 1999, 35 percent of the EU's exports of commercial services went to the United States and 33 percent of America's to the European Union.[4] While data on cross-border electronic transfers have proven hard to come by, it is relevant that between them the European Union and United States accounted for 84 percent of all Internet hosts and 54 percent of all users in 2001.

In summary, the EU and US economies are highly integrated, and electronic data flows are the medium which binds the network, or networks, together. That has two implications of interest here. First, given the magnitude and variety of "cross-border" transfers, it is unlikely that the impacts of "domestic" law and regulation are going to come to a full stop at the border; or conversely, if law or regulation is to be effective, its impact is going to have to reach beyond the domestic jurisdiction of any single country. Second, this high level of economic integration markedly constrains the freedom of action or independence of governments on both sides of the Atlantic. The cost of interrupting these "cross-border" flows, in terms of the impact on each economy, is not sustainable.

Yet while economic integration has advanced rapidly and fairly smoothly, political integration is far more troublesome. As discussed below, marked differences in the treatment of privacy on opposite sides of the Atlantic could have an impact on the economic flows.

The Safe Harbor dispute: a public debate over privacy

The United States and Europe are not only integrated by financial flows, but they are also woven together with information flows that pay scant attention to national borders. Electronic integration means that many transactions "spill over" jurisdictional boundaries. Multinational corporations (MNCs), for example, routinely transfer personnel, credit, and market research records across national borders. Airline profiles and reservation databases may "fly" with the passenger from one side of the Atlantic to the other. Use of a credit card or ATM bank card in Athens may require accessing a database in Atlanta. Last, and perhaps most troublesome, Internet transactions are – to a very real extent – space-independent. If a computer user in Mannheim accesses a website in Memphis, it is difficult to say whether the transaction is taking place in Germany or Tennessee. Given the high levels of electronic integration of the transatlantic economy, separate regulatory regimes to define and protect information privacy in the United States and Europe may not be feasible. Yet harmonizing these separate regimes can be problematic.

The issue of privacy is one of the places where these flows of capital and information collide with different cultural beliefs and regulatory approaches on opposite sides of the Atlantic. Information privacy entails an individual's control over the collection, processing, and use of name-linked data.[5] While concern about information privacy is not new, the information revolution and the ubiquity of cyberspace have significantly increased the risks to data privacy. Using the information infrastructure to communicate, order goods and services, or obtain information produces electronic data that can easily and inexpensively be stored, retrieved, analyzed, and reused.[6] Furthermore, rapidly emerging technology is providing new and very powerful means to sort, combine, and analyze data. Last and critically, data now exists in a networked environment: personal information collected, created, and processed on any computer on the Net is, at least in theory, accessible by every computer on the Net.

While this information provides benefits to consumers and businesses, it entails a tradeoff. Using E-Z Pass (an electronic payment device) allows motorists to speed through highway tolls at the cost of having their names and the date, time, and place recorded and saved in an electronically accessible database. Supermarket loyalty cards provide discounts and new product information targeted to a shopper's specific shopping patterns but result in a digital record of what they buy and where and when they buy it. The World Wide Web has opened up remarkable opportunities to anyone with a computer and a telephone line, but surfing websites provides copious data (through cookies and clickstream records) about which websites users have visited and even which books they have "browsed through." In each case, the very real benefits of the information age come at a cost in terms of a loss (real or potential) of personal privacy.

Conflicting views of privacy

How this tradeoff between the benefits and costs of the digital age is evaluated differs significantly in the United States and Europe. There are marked differences in what information privacy represents, its relative importance versus other issues such as economic growth or free speech, who is responsible for protecting it, and how it should be protected.

In the United States, data privacy is seen as alienable, a "commodity" subject to the marketplace; discussions of data privacy protection are often couched in terms of property rights. Data privacy is a "right" that inheres in the individual which can be traded for some other benefit such as discount coupons. The US approach to data privacy protection reflects a basic distrust of government; the primary emphasis is on using markets, self-regulation, and tort law to empower the individual to protect herself.[7]

US privacy protection is sporadic and unsystematic; what law and regulation that does exist is reactive and has been called a "patch-work" of rules that deal with specific sectors in a haphazard manner.[8] Aside from some specific efforts at legislated protection – the "Bork Bill" (1988), for example, protects data about an individual's video-tape rentals and the Cable Television Consumer Protection Act (1992) limits the disclosure of name-linked data for subscribers – regulatory protection of data privacy is very limited in the United States.[9]

The situation in Europe is quite different. Privacy is regarded as an inalienable human right that is protected by a comprehensive regime of explicit laws and regulation, enforced through oversight authorities. The European Data Directive (of which more later) is framed in terms of respect for the fundamental freedoms and rights of individuals; its concern is protecting the rights of citizens or data subjects rather than the property of consumers or computer users. Importantly, rather than empowering the individual to protect herself, Europeans are concerned with ensuring that society has the ability to protect the privacy rights of the individual.

The US–EU differences on how data privacy is defined and how it should be protected reflect deep-seated, fundamental differences in values and belief systems. These differences include whether privacy is seen as a commodity or as a right, and differences in views of individual and societal responsibilities, on the role and extent of markets, and in the degree of faith in technological solutions to societal problems.

Cross-national differences in values and beliefs are certainly not unusual and are always reflected in different systems of law and regulation. Very different limits on working hours in France, on the one hand, and the United States or Japan, on the other, result from markedly different ideas about the value and importance of work versus leisure and societal responsibility for unemployment, among others. The normal response to cross-border societal and cultural differences is "to each her own" in terms of regulation. But with the high levels of integration between the United States and Europe, a policy of separate and independent systems may no longer be tenable. Too much is at stake for businesses and the economies of the United States and Europe.

Thus both the European Union and the United States face a dilemma. While separate and different systems of protecting information privacy are increasingly problematic in an electronically integrated transatlantic economy, reconciling these differences requires dealing with basic conflicts in values and belief systems. International harmonization requires some marked changes in the domestic context and domestic politics. The problem has become very apparent in the context of attempts to resolve these differences through the Safe Harbor agreement between the United States and the European Union.

The Data Directive dilemma

In early 2003, the aggressive US anti-terrorism initiatives led to one very public dispute over data privacy that illustrates the complexity of the differences in regulation between the United States and Europe. As part of its anti-terrorist efforts, American authorities demanded access to passenger databases for all flights to the United States and threatened to subject the European airlines to fines if the data were not provided. The European Commission pointed out that this sort of access to personal data was not allowed under regulations based on the EU Data Directive, unless a passenger gave explicit permission for its release. A compromise was reached whereby the European Union agreed to allow the airlines to provide the data, provided the passenger consented, and the Americans agreed to insure it was only used for the intended purpose. (A failure to consent comes at a cost as passengers who do not agree to the data transfer are subject to extensive checks at US immigration.) This case illustrates the complex solutions that need to be developed in a world in which passengers can easily hop on a plane across the Atlantic, but personal data cannot so easily follow.

This issue of passenger information, however, was fairly easy to resolve compared to the more complex business issues that led to the imperfect compromise of the Safe Harbor agreement between the

Table 15.1. *Irreconcilable differences on privacy?*

European Union (Primary provisions of EU Data Directive)
- Data collected must be adequate, relevant, and not excessive in relation to the purposes for which they are collected and processed.
- Data may not be further processed in ways incompatible with the purposes for which they are collected.
- Recipients of information are entitled to know where the information comes from, how it was collected, whether responses were voluntary, and the like.
- Individuals have full access to all data linked to their name and the right to correct any inaccurate data. Individuals also have the right to "opt out" of further processing or transmission of personal data.
- Processing of sensitive data containing information about an individual's racial or ethnic origins, religious beliefs, union memberships, political opinions, sexual preferences, and the like cannot be processed without permission. In some cases, it cannot be processed even with the individual's permission.
- Each country must have one or more public authorities responsible for monitoring and enforcing the Directive.

United States and European Union. This agreement was an attempt to address challenges resulting from the EU Data Directive in the early 1990s, which demanded much stricter privacy protection than in the United States (see Table 15.1). The Data Directive, established to harmonize regulations within Europe, was enacted in 1995 and came into force in 1998.[10] It was established just before use of the Internet and the World Wide Web became widespread in both Europe and the United States, changing the use of data by consumers and by companies.

With technological shifts and the increasing integration between the United States and Europe, the Data Directive had much more far-reaching consequences than originally anticipated. For example, if a computer user in Germany logs into a website in Pennsylvania and agrees to exchange some personal information for a magazine article or a photograph, it is far from obvious where the transaction takes place and whose law applies (the European authorities argue that if the transaction "makes use of equipment" sited in Europe then the Directive applies).

Seeking a safe harbor

Given the degree of integration of the global economy and the ease of transmission of electronic data across borders, there was concern from the start about protection of the privacy rights of EU citizens if their personal information was transferred outside of the Union's borders. Thus, Articles 25 and 26 of the Directive deal with the transfer of personal data to third countries. The former prohibits the transfer of data unless the country in question takes steps to ensure an "adequate" level of protection for personal information. The latter deals with a number of "derogations" which allow for data transfer under certain stated conditions.[11]

While it was clear that the US data protection regime did not meet the Directive's criteria for "adequacy," it was also obvious to all concerned that any interruption in transatlantic data flows would be catastrophic economically. As a result, while negotiations began almost immediately after enactment (1995) to try to find a way to meet European notions of "adequacy" while maintaining the American reliance on the market and self-regulation, the Safe Harbor rules were not approved until mid-2000.[12]

The Safe Harbor agreement has a number of important characteristics. First, it is not an international treaty, but rather two unilateral actions: the United States issued the set of principles and the European Commission accepted them as a determination of adequacy under the terms of the Data Directive. Second, it is an attempt to bridge the EU–US differences through a scheme which provides "adequate" data protection while maintaining reliance on self-regulation and the market. Last, the agreement does not provide for a blanket determination of adequacy; rather, the US regime provides for a "safe harbor" which American organizations enter voluntarily to satisfy the adequacy requirement of the Directive.

American organizations can enter Safe Harbor either by joining a self-regulatory privacy program that adheres to Safe Harbor's requirements such as TRUSTe (http://www.truste.org/index.html) or the BBB Online Seal Program (http://www.bbbonline.org/), or by developing their own privacy policies that conform to the requirements and certifying this annually to the Department of Commerce. In either case, participating firms must develop and publish a privacy policy that notes that they adhere to Safe Harbor. The primary purpose of the self-regulatory organizations is to provide a mechanism for enforcement.[13]

The US federal government's enforcement of Safe Harbor's provisions does not rely on the direct application of privacy law or regulations. Rather, enforcement is indirect and depends on Federal Trade Commission prosecution for unfair or deceptive advertising or promises. Thus, at present, only companies which fall under the jurisdiction of the Federal Trade Commission or the Department of Transportation (air carriers and ticket agents) are eligible for Safe Harbor.

That leaves major sectors of the economy such as financial services and telecommunications out of the picture; they must rely on the Data Directive's Article 26 provisions for exemptions from the requirement of adequate protection, including situations where the data subject gives his or her informed consent to a specific transfer and where the transfer is necessary for the performance of a contract.[14]

Given its complexity and incompleteness, it is no surprise that Safe Harbor has not been seen as an overwhelming success on either side of the Atlantic. As of April 2003, only 320 American firms had enrolled in Safe Harbor and most were not major multinationals.[15] The relatively low number of firms that have signed up may reflect concerns about Safe Harbor, combined with a sense that, at least at this point, the penalties for non-compliance are not being enforced.

Neither side is happy. American firms believe that Safe Harbor goes much too far, that implementing it will be too costly, that it might stimulate pressure for similar legislation in the United States and that it might subject them to the reach of European law. There also appears to be considerable confusion about what the presumption of "adequacy" actually means; whether it extends, for example, to the national data authorities who still are responsible for implementing the Data Directive within their countries. In Europe, Safe Harbor was controversial from the start, with serious questions raised by both national data authorities and the European Parliament about the adequacy of data protection. A more recent European Commission staff working paper on the effectiveness of Safe Harbor expressed serious concerns about both implementation and the adequacy of data protection. They note that the number of organizations self-certifying under Safe Harbor is "lower than expected," and that many of those do not really satisfy the requirements of the agreement.[16]

Adversarial negotiations have not been successful to date in resolving the data privacy conflict. In fact, it is reasonable to argue that given the basic differences in values, it is unlikely that any negotiated solution is going to be perceived as legitimate by both sides. Resolving this dispute, and others where (1) the domestic context is critically important, and (2) there are fundamental social or cultural differences, requires a cooperative effort, an attempt to find an optimal solution for the larger "integrated" economic space, as we shall consider in our conclusions.

In the meantime, businesses will need to operate in a global environment of complex and shifting regulations. The low rate of participation in Safe Harbor indicates that many managers remain relatively unconcerned about this issue. Yet any business with significant information and financial flows between Europe and the United States, finds itself in the middle of this dispute, and could easily wake up one day on the wrong side of regulations from outside its domestic base. It is important to understand the dynamics of negotiations around these issues, monitor the progress carefully, and choose a strategy based on the careful assessment of political and economic risks. It is also important for business to become involved in the process of reconciling regulatory differences.

Domestic politics and international telecommunications

In March 1994, during a speech to the International Telecommunications Union in Buenos Aires, US Vice-President Al Gore proposed the concept of a Global Information Infrastructure (GII). He asserted that "we now have at hand the technological breakthroughs and economic means to bring all the communities of the world together . . . legislators, regulators and business people must do this: build and operate a Global Information Infrastructure."[17] While Gore did not provide any details as to how this GII would be built, he did suggest that it should be based on the principles that had guided the domestic National Information Infrastructure (NII) initiative, a centerpiece of US technology policy, which was seen as a key driver of economic productivity and growth.

The NII's underlying concept was to create "a seamless web of communications networks, computers, databases, and consumer electronics that will put vast amounts of information at users' fingertips."[18] That network would interconnect all modes of telecommunication and information transmitters and receivers: satellites, cables, fiber optic lines, telephones, cell phones, computers, and so forth. By developing this interconnectedness, competition among ICT providers would grow and new services would flourish, as had already happened with the Internet and with long-distance telephony, following the breakup of the AT&T monopoly in the early 1980s.

Although the NII was a domestic initiative, from its outset it was clear that the nature of telecommunications required a global view. President Clinton stated that "To remain competitive, America's high-tech industries need full access to overseas markets and effective protection of intellectual property rights." This reflected an implicit US ICT policy of globalizing the local, making the American ICT industry more competitive through investment and deregulation, and then unleashing that sector on the world in the context of a free trade environment. GII was a way to export the US revolution in telecommunications abroad.

US suppliers of telecommunications equipment and services played a leading role in pressuring the Administration to pursue greater market opening, which was needed to secure interconnection agreements with foreign Postal, Telegraph and Telephone providers (PTTs). The president of Bell Labs had written as early as 1985 that "Telecommunications technology is capital-intensive both for research and development and for manufacture. Global markets are increasingly required to justify these up-front expenses. Therefore, a clear and stable trade policy . . . is ever more important for industry . . ."[19] The American business sector lobbied actively to ensure that its telecommunications interests were advanced in global negotiations.[20] Trade policy analysts Barbara Fliess and Pierre Sauve assert that the multilateral telecommunications talks during the Uruguay Round of trade talks in the 1980s and 1990s "started out as a private sector initiative in the US . . ."[21]

GII was an incredibly ambitious undertaking at the technical, financial, and political levels. Technically, it would require nothing less than wiring the globe, making available high-speed interactive infrastructures which could be interconnected with various types of ICT hardware and software.[22] Financially, the investment – to be borne primarily by the private sector – would run into many billions of dollars, and private capital would only be forthcoming if the economic and regulatory environments of countries were reasonably stable. Politically, both domestic reform and multilateral agreements were likely to be difficult to achieve, in the face of entrenched postal, telegraph, and telephone monopolies (PTTs), unions, and other special interests that might fear for their rents in the presence of sectoral reform. As a consequence, many domestic political groups could be expected to fight the sort of opening measures that global interconnectedness implied.

Opposing forces

While US political and business leaders were at the vanguard of this globalization initiative, other parts of the world were understandably much less enthusiastic as a result of their domestic and political and economic structures. For example, consider the French Minitel system in comparison to the Internet. It may surprise some readers to learn that the French were the pioneers of electronic commerce, placing Minitel terminals in every French home, with which individuals could make travel and entertainment reservations, conduct banking transactions, and locate and purchase a wide variety of goods and services. The Minitel was amenable to electronic commerce because it was a "closed" system, controlled by the public telephone monopoly France Telecom, which extracted revenues from its use. The Internet, in contrast, employed an open architecture, which made it less secure but an ideal platform for new business development.

Minitel and Internet reflected the differing political and economic strategies developed in France and the United States to modernize their ICT sectors. Having invested heavily in Minitel technology, it was unlikely that France Telecom would readily wish to give up the rents it provided, by opening the market to foreign Internet service providers.

If one multiplies the French case many times over, we see how difficult it would be to achieve the GII agenda. At a minimum, it would require domestic *liberalization* and *privatization* of the ICT sector and *openness* of that sector to foreign trade and investment – in short, *market access* on the basis of *national treatment*. It would require international *standard-setting* on a wide range of technical matters (e.g. spectrum availability) and *multilateral agreements* on such issues as the removal of tariff and non-tariff barriers to trade and investment. These initiatives would stimulate the building of infrastructure and make its interoperability possible, but would require the presence of independent *regulatory authorities* and adequate private sector *investment* to network the globe. Were domestic political and economic actors in a heavily monopolistic industry really prepared to make such dramatic changes to their way of doing business?

Of course, there were political constraints on the American side as well. While freer access to the large US market has sometimes been used as a carrot to entice countries to open their domestic markets, there has been longstanding internal US opposition to foreign investment in the ICT industries. Indeed, recent efforts by the US Congress to block such investment remind us that domestic politics are alive and well in this sector on both sides of the Atlantic. Those attempts are contrary to the spirit of American commercial policy and, in many cases, the letter of international trade agreements. Ironically, just as the US Congress acted in 2000 to limit European investment in the American ICT industry, it called upon Mexico to open up its markets to US-based firms!

Strategies for advancing the US agenda

Against these opposing forces, the US government advanced its global policies both through international negotiations and by example. The break-up of AT&T in the 1980s and the subsequent Telecommunications Act of 1996, for example, sent a clear signal to the world that European-style PTTs, which monopolized telecommunications, should no longer be viewed as an appropriate economic model. They were businesses like any other, that had to be exposed to competitive disciplines if they were to innovate and contribute to national economic growth. To the extent that America's ICT sector blossomed owing to this policy, Washington's approach would become a model for the world. Countries that also wanted to have dynamic ICT industries would seek to adopt the American approach.

The main multilateral vehicle for advancing Washington's priority of sectoral openness in ICT was the newly created World Trade Organization (WTO). With the Uruguay Round trade agreement of 1994, global trade and investment in services (GATS) had been placed on the global economic agenda. The limited success of GATS within the Uruguay Round timetable, however, led several countries, chiefly the United States, to press member countries to continue their telecommunications negotiations on a voluntary basis. In May 1994, a Negotiating Group on Basic Telecommunications, open to all WTO members, was launched, charged with the objective of setting the rules for international trade and investment in this field.

Getting telecommunications – a public monopoly almost everywhere – on the Uruguay Round trade agenda was no simple matter during the mid 1980s, when the talks were launched in Punta del Este. A World Bank economist has written that "For telecommunications, resistance to trade negotiations . . . came from major players in the industry. After all, state-owned enterprises were the suppliers of telecommunications services in all but a handful of countries, and international telephony was conducted like a cartel . . . Against this background, the idea of using trade negotiations to promote the liberalization of telecommunications was an alien concept . . ."[23]

But openness was critical for the new American competitors to AT&T that were now offering long-distance service but needed secure interconnection agreements with foreign PTTs. As former US trade negotiator Geza Feketekuty has written, "International telecommunications firms in a country such as the United States that permits competition naturally find themselves in a poor bargaining position *vis-à-vis* foreign telecommunications monopolies." Sectoral rule-making was thus needed "to deal with market access problems faced by suppliers . . ."[24]

On December 13, 1996, the trade ministers meeting in Singapore reached an Information Technology Agreement (ITA), which served as the basis for the Framework Agreement on Basic Telecommunications of February 15, 1997. This latter agreement called for significant trade barrier reductions in telecommunications equipment and services, and it also called upon governments to ensure that domestic telecommunications companies do not engage in anti-competitive practices, and to permit interconnection at any technically feasible point on the telecommunications network on non-discriminatory terms and in a timely fashion.[25]

Beyond trade matters, the February 15 agreement included acceptance of a so-called "Reference Paper" on regulatory principles, heralding the introduction of multilateral trade disciplines into a whole new area of domestic economic management. The signatories to the Reference Paper agreed that independent national regulatory bodies would be established and charged with implementing pro-competitive policies, including interconnection rights, transparency, and non-discrimination. Turning these words into policy, however, has proved a difficult process, as recalcitrant PTTs, shielded from competition, have

balked at market opening. As a consequence, American firms that have
sought market access in Europe have often pursued the legal route by
filing with local regulatory authorities or seeking relief through the
European Union, but the grip of the local PTTs over the local loop has
remained quite strong.

Telecommunications pricing and other competitive dynamics are
also driving toward a more global view of the sector. Rates on
most long-distance telephone calls have fallen dramatically since the
Framework Agreement on Basic Telecommunications was signed, in
both the United States and other industrial nations.[26] This reflects
growing competition in that market segment from alternative long-
distance providers and call-back programs. Over time, these cost
pressures will force still-dominant national PTTs to become more
"consumer-friendly," offering lower prices and better service, and
spurring innovation.

Among globally active ICT companies, cellular phone and Internet
provision are currently the most hotly contested international markets,
followed by long-distance telephony, as mentioned above. American
companies, including the Baby Bells, are playing an active and growing
role in this globalization of the telecommunications industry, especially
as wireless providers. But some firms, with Bell Atlantic (now Verizon)
being a leading example, have also invested in foreign telecommunications enterprises; it (along with another regional Bell operating
company, Ameritech) has purchased a substantial block of Telecom
New Zealand. As Verizon writes in its international business "mission
statement":

> Markets around the world are opening up to competition as deregulation and
> economic development spurs the transformation of the (telecommunications)
> industry. The global need for expertise in building and managing complex
> networks dovetails with our demonstrated core competencies. The success-
> ful management of our domestic franchises, along with our size and scope,
> makes Bell Atlantic an attractive partner for international opportunities.[27]

Standard-setting

As with trade and investment, ICT standard-setting has also been
a focus of multilateral negotiations. The United States government's
approach to standard-setting in ICT has followed both intergovern-
mental and unofficial tracks. On the one hand, Washington has actively

participated in and sought to shape the outcomes of the deliberations of the International Telecommunications Union (ITU) – a body which, in addition to its work of reconciling international telephone charges, sets various technical standards for networks, equipment, and services. On the other, it has also created market structures and regulatory environments which have enabled private sector firms to establish their own standards through product domination.

Today, many of the private standards associated with ICT have brand names, like Microsoft's Windows, Intel's Pentium chip, and Sun Microsystems' Java software language. Others, like the Internet protocol TCP/IP, arose with that particular architecture and have proved to be remarkably durable in the face of challengers, even challengers – like the OSI protocol – supported by the ITU.[28] These provide perhaps the most obvious examples of the privatization of standard-setting in the new economy. Despite antitrust action against Microsoft, this privatization of standards by a handful of mostly American firms has raised concerns among some public officials and private sector participants in ICT overseas about the nature of the ideas and interests directing US government policy for this sector.[29] These concerns could call into question the legitimacy of Washington's policy approach in the future, if the perception widens that US leaders act solely on behalf of American private enterprise. Further, differing approaches to antitrust across the Atlantic could provide new sources of political conflict, as the United States and European Union find themselves at odds over whether certain firms and practices are anti-competitive.

Rapid growth

Whatever the role of global trade negotiations, ICT experienced tremendous growth in the United States during the Clinton Administration. It was a key driver of innovation and investment for the general economy (see Table 15.2). The market for telecommunications equipment and services more than doubled, growing from $250 billion in 1993 to $518 billion by the turn of the millennium. The United States alone represented over half the total of worldwide spending on information technology in 1999 of about $900 billion. According to the OECD, US investment in ICT software and hardware constituted over 50 percent of all business spending on new equipment by the century's end.[30] Venture capital investment in the information technology sector in 1999 was over $7 billion.[31] As a result of this activity, the

Table 15.2. *Information technology in the US economy*

ICT patents as percentage of total patents, 1999	31.0
US investment in ICT as percentage of total investment, 1999	52.0
Percentage of American workforce in ICT industries, 1999	5.0
Annual percentage growth of investment in ICT, 1990–96	23.8*
Percentage of economic growth attributable to ICT, 1995–99	30.0
Sales of ICT goods and services as a percentage of 1999 GDP	8.0

Note: By comparison, the annual growth of investment in ICT in France during this period was 11%, in Japan 14.5%, and in Germany 18.6%.
Sources: OECD, *Economic Survey of the United States, 2000* (Paris: OECD, 2000); Telecommunications Industry Association, *2000 Public Policy Report and Agenda* (see note 31); US Department of Commerce.

information sector created 200,000 new jobs between 1993 and 1999, and perhaps another 600,000 in related services.

Despite the limitations of the GII initiative in bringing about structural change in basic telecommunications or local telephony – there is, in fact, little competition to domestic PTTs along the local loop anywhere in the industrial world – cross-border trade and investment in IT has skyrocketed over the past five years, with equipment and service providers leading the way. Privatization and liberalization are also taking place, but market contestability within the telecommunications sector remains quite variable across both countries and sectors. The market for telecommunications equipment in particular has become globalized. In 1999, the United States exported some $23 billion of telecommunications equipment. Perhaps surprisingly, it imported even more, or $25 billion. When this sector is expanded to include information technology more broadly, the numbers jump fourfold, with trade in IT equal to over 12 percent of world trade, more than the comparable figure for agriculture.[32] Of interest, the top three suppliers of US telecommunications equipment were also the top three buyers – namely, Canada, Mexico, and Japan – suggesting the interdependent nature of this "intra-industry" trade.[33]

Conclusions

Both the data privacy issue and the ICT negotiations demonstrate the power of the "colliding forces" now at work – the frictions created when globalization hits up against domestic politics. Globalization means market access and competition; domestic politics often means rent-seeking and protection. Resolving the tensions between globalization and domestic politics will remain one of the great challenges facing business in the early twenty-first century.

Both the United States and Europe share a great material and moral interest in pursuing a free trade agenda, as do the companies within their borders. For both Washington and Brussels, bridging the "transatlantic digital divide" is crucial.[34] The United States needs a dynamic European economic partner, and the last thing its companies and its government need is for European courts and the EU to block the use of emerging technologies. Efforts to continue the "balkanisation" of ICT markets will only retard growth for the Atlantic and world economies. Similarly, conflicts over data privacy could risk creating a balkanised Internet.

In some cases, the differences may not be as extreme as presented by the two sides. Indeed, many Americans may share the sorts of concerns that are expressed by European data privacy legislation. Seeking permission from individuals before personal information about them travels across electronic wires – within and between countries – seems reasonable. With respect to information flows and also with respect to objectionable content, the Europeans have shown that they are perfectly willing to act decisively in the cause of consumer protection. On the other hand, the "safe harbor" negotiations are a recognition of the economic importance of flows of data across the Atlantic and the fact that despite its beliefs, the EU understands compromise is necessary.

The forging of mutually beneficial policies will require a process of give-and-take by the two sides, and that has been largely absent from transatlantic negotiations – in both the economic and security realms – in recent years. For example, ICT issues have proved so contentious that they were not even included on the agenda of the 2000 US–EU Summit. Clearly, these issues must be put back on the agenda, with each side offering something to the other.

The cases presented here are largely focused on the United States and Europe, both highly industrialized economies with many political and social similarities. Once one moves beyond these two regions, the problems faced in attempting to harmonize multilaterally will be much more severe. For billions of people across the developing world, modern ICT remains the stuff of science fiction, yet these sectors are often growing rapidly. While America and Europe must work hard to bridge the transatlantic digital divide, they will have to work even harder to ensure that the "new economy's" benefits are widely shared at the global level.

The "new" politics of trade and investment will be powerfully shaped by domestic political forces in the years ahead. Unlike the traditional politics of trade policy, in which domestic cleavages between export-oriented and protectionist interests could be exploited by governments on behalf of at least partial market opening, the domestic politics of globalization today involve extremely deep reforms of long-established national regulatory and market structures, or even cultural beliefs. The degree of intervention in domestic affairs is therefore becoming much greater, leading to new coalitions and to new political forces that are agitating for and against the existing trade and investment regimes.

Will these domestic forces ultimately lead to a regionalization of the world economy instead of toward further market integration? Probably not, but we believe that this dichotomy is too crude in any case to prove useful to decision-makers who must navigate these murky political waters. The real issues will involve the terms and conditions under which market access takes place, and there we see growing contestation.

Implications for managers

Ironically, multinational corporations will have to become increasingly cognizant of harsh domestic political realities if they are to thrive in the new economy. What are the implications for managers who need to act in this environment of hotly contested global negotiations and shifting regulation? Some of the insights for managers are discussed in the following paragraphs.

In a globalizing world, local regulations and policies are international in effect: Firms need to become much less "ethnocentric," and work hard to gain an understanding of the bases for regulation in other parts of the world, rather than dismissing them out of hand. As Porsche discovered with Sarbanes–Oxley and companies and regulators discovered in wrestling with data privacy issues, the regulations that were designed for local markets often have unintended consequences in other parts of the world. The financial reporting requirements developed in the United States affect businesses in Germany. The antitrust rulings by EU regulators have a significant impact on the strategies of companies in the United States. Managers need to look closely at the implications of regulations in countries outside their domestic base and carefully consider their potential implications. Managers also should play an active role in helping to shape these policies to the extent they can, or they could find themselves in a world in which it is very difficult to conduct business.

Government and business leaders can make significant headway in changing the global competitive playing field: While the GII has had limited success in overcoming local resistance to bring about structural changes in telecommunications, particularly along the local loop, US global trade and investment in telecommunications has grown rapidly since trade negotiations aimed at promoting market access were initiated. Privatization and liberalization also are proceeding apace. While it may be hard to assess the impact of the increased visibility and direct effects of these negotiations, especially given the strong technological and competitive drivers, the results are in line with the policies that were advanced. This could indicate the importance of agenda-setting in the discussion of global policy, even if strong formal agreements are hard to achieve. Managers and their firms should actively engage in multilateral negotiations of their own, working with private sector firms and organizations in other areas, to try to suggest resolutions to regulatory differences that are compatible with global business practices.

Determined local players can often hold back the tides of change: Managers should understand that even if multilateral agreements are achieved, they will only represent a partial solution to their problems. Domestic regulatory and legal structures will remain "sticky," and it may prove costly when attempts are made to reconcile them with multilateral guidelines. Local players often are part of the stickiness of domestic regulation. While all the legislation is in place in Europe and at the international level to promote global ITC changes, action is lacking as the PTTs seek to hold on to their privileged positions. France Telecom, for example, has balked at opening its local loop to competition, using the courts and regulatory authorities as a way of slowing down the liberalization process. And at a time when many European PTTs find themselves in grave financial difficulties, losing the rents off the local loop are the last thing they need. Yet, the competitive forces discussed above seem likely to erode these positions in the long run, opening markets to more competition.

Some deeply held aspects of cultural values or infrastructures represent intractable barriers, so managers will have to learn to live with them: The divide between the EU and the United States on privacy issues is based on deeply held values and beliefs about personal privacy, government involvement, and the importance of enterprises. While there may be some gradual meeting of the minds on such issues, differences may still remain for many years. This does not mean that business and political leaders will not keep working to find common ground, but managers need to accept that progress in this direction may be halting. This recognition of these differences is critical in developing realistic and pragmatic strategies for individual businesses.

While the headlines of globalization – announced in sweeping visions such as Gore's Global Information Infrastructure initiative – may seem to chart a steady progress toward convergence of regulations and markets, the fundamental reality of political and economic life is that transnational regulations are weak and transnational governing organizations remain instruments of nation-states. As a consequence, business leaders face a shifting patchwork of regional, national, and local regulations. The tensions between domestic politics and the global economy are left for businesses to work out, and corporate success will be defined by how well they do in resolving them.

Notes

1 L. Taylor, "US Law Stirs Wave of Pessimism," *Australian Financial Review*, January 9, 2003 (http://afr.com/).
2 World Bank, World Development Indicators Data Base (2002).
3 JETRO, *White Paper on Foreign Direct Investment* (Tokyo: Japan External Trade Organization, 2001).

4 World Trade Organization, *International Trade Statistics* (Geneva: World Trade Organization, 2002), Table III. 6.

5 J. Kang, "Information Privacy In Cyberspace Transactions," *Stanford Law Review*, 50 (1998), pp. 1193–1294.

6 Privacy Working Group, *Privacy and the National Information Infrastructure: Principles for Providing and Using Personal Information* (Washington, DC: US Information Infrastructure Task Force, 1995).

7 D. Banisar and S. Davies, "Global Trends in Privacy Protection: An International Survey of Privacy, Data Protection, and Surveillance Laws and Developments," *John Marshall Journal of Computer and Information Law*, 18 (1999), pp. 1–111; J. R. Reidenberg, "Resolving Conflicting International Data Privacy Rules in Cyberspace," *Stanford Law Review*, 52 (2000), pp. 1315–1371; M. P. Roch, "Filling the Void of Data Protection in the United Sates: Following the European Example," *Santa Clara Computer and High Technology Law Journal*, 12 (1996), pp. 71–96; P. P. Swire and R. E. Litan, *None of Your Business* (Washington, DC: Brookings Institution Press, 1998).

8 Kang, "Information Privacy."

9 The Online Personal Privacy Act is an attempt to regulate the collection, use or disclosure of personally identifiable information by Internet service providers, website operators, and certain third parties that use these entities to collect information. *Tech Law Journal* at http://www.techlawjournal.com/cong107/privacy/hollings/20020418summary.asp (accessed May 5, 2003).

10 Swire and Litan, *None of Your Business*.

11 The Council of the European Union. Common Position (EC) No /95 Adopted by the Council with a View to Adopting Directive 94/EC of the European Parliament and of the Council on the Protection of Individuals With Regard to the Processing of Personal Data and on the Free Movement of Such Data; Directive 95/EC of the European Parliament and of the Council on The Protection of Individuals with Regard to the Processing of Personal Data and on the Free Movment of Such Data.

12 H. Farrell, "Constructing the International Foundations of E-commerce – The EU–US Safe Harbor Arrangement," *International Organization*, 57 (2003), pp. 277–307; also H. Farrell, "Negotiating Privacy Across Arenas – The EU–US Safe Harbor Discussions," in A. Héritier (ed.), *Common Goods: Reinventing European and International Governance* (Oxford: Rowman and Littlefield, 2002) for a detailed discussion of the Safe Harbor negotiations.

13 Farrell, "Negotiating Privacy."

14 A more complete description of Safe Harbor can be found at http://www.export.gov/safeharbor/sh/overview.html.

15 The list of organizations enrolled in Safe Harbor can be accessed from http://www.export.gov/safeharbor/.

16 European Commission Staff, *The Application of Commission Decision 520/2000/EC of July 26 2000 Pursuant to Directive 95/46 of the European Parliament and the Council* (Brussels: European Commission, 2002).

17 A. Gore, "Remarks prepared for Delivery," International Telecommunications Union, Buenos Aires, March 21, 1994.

18 The White House, "The National Information Infrastructure: Agenda for Action," Office of the Press Secretary, September 15, 1993.

19 I. Ross, "Telecommunications," in A. Keatley (ed.), *Technological Frontiers and Foreign Relations* (Washington, DC: National Academy Press, 1985).

20 National Telecommunications and Information Administration, "NTIA/OIA International Activities," at http://www.ntia.doc.gov/oiahome/internat.html.

21 B. Fliess and P. Sauve, *Of Chips, Floppy Disks, and Great Timing: Assessing the WTO Information Technology Agreement*, Les Cahiers de l'IFRI, no. 26, Paris 1998, p. 29.

22 OECD, *Global Information Infrastructure – Global Information Society: Policy Recommendations for Action* (Paris: OECD, 1997), p. 19.

23 C. P. Braga, "Liberalizing Telecommunications and the Role of the World Trade Organization," *Public Policy for the Private Sector*, no. 120 (July 1997), p. 1.

24 G. Feketekuty, *International Trade in Services* (Washington, DC: American Enterprise Institute, 1988), p. 254.

25 For useful overviews of the WTO agreement, see P. Cowhey and M. Klimenko, "The WTO Agreement and Telecommunication Policy Reforms," report for the World Bank, Washington, DC, March 7, 1999; and W. Drake, "The Rise and Decline of the International Telecommunications Regime," Carnegie Endowment for International Peace working paper, 2000, at http://www.ceip.org/).

26 The details on these changes in international phone charges are available at http://www.fcc.gov/.

27 See http://www.bellatlantic.com/.

28 Drake, "Rise and Decline," p. 37.

29 For a useful overview of the shift to privatization of standard-setting in ICT, and of changes in the telecommunications regime more broadly, see Drake, "Rise and Decline."

30 *A New Economy? The Changing Role of Innovation and Information Technology in Growth* (Paris: OECD, 2000), p. 10.

31 Telecommunications Industry Association, *2000 Public Policy Report and Agenda*, p. 2, at http://www.tiaonline.org/.
32 Fliess and Sauve, *Of Chips, Floppy Disks, and Great Timing*, p. 14.
33 Telecommunications Industry Association, "US Exports of Telecom Equipment Top 22 Billion in 1999," March 29, 2000, at http://www.tiaonline.org/.
34 E. B. Kapstein and T. Marten, "Bridging the Transatlantic Digital Divide," US–France Analysis, Brookings Institution, Washington DC, January 2001.

16 Global implications of information and communication technologies (ICT)

ARNOUD DE MEYER
INSEAD

The emergence of new information and communication technologies (ICT) has created opportunities for changing business models and rapidly developing service innovations. In this chapter, the author examines the typical process of the emergence of new technologies – from improving the efficiency and quality of current operations to enabling a rethinking of products and services offered by the firm. He then explores some of the implications of information and communication technologies for the development of new models for global services. Among the opportunities are the facilitation of "overnight globalization," creating geographically independent knowledge-based services, making the customer the locus of innovation, and enabling peer-to-peer communities. Finally, he explores the implications of these technologies for the global management of the process of innovation itself.

WITH about a half-dozen employees in 1997, Celebrity Sightings, a website for fan clubs of teenage stars, could draw together teenagers in chat rooms from Australia, South Africa, Mexico, and the United States.[1] Internet technology allowed the company to violate one of the generally accepted principles of global service businesses: that services do not travel well and are difficult to export. The necessary interaction between the customer and the service provider required the provider to be located where the customer chose to be. International growth in the service industry and internationalization very often required duplication of assets, franchising, or other mechanisms to set up localized operations. This is very expensive and complex, but with the Internet, this internationalization has become technically easy and requires little investment. This has placed global markets within the reach of small or mid-sized firms and reduced the hurdles for larger companies to create experiments in diverse markets.

After the burst of the Internet bubble in 2000, many business leaders and managers may have thought that the period from August 1995 to

March 2000 would become a footnote in industrial history. Business practices and economic events seemed to be getting in line once again with the traditional views on management. But while some of the businesses and business models of the "new economy" ultimately failed, the emergence of new information and communication technologies (ICT) has had more far-reaching consequences for global business processes. It is not only opening up new opportunities, as discovered by companies such as Celebrity Sightings; these technologies are also opening up new avenues for innovation, changing the management of innovation, and enabling radically different approaches to the global management of technology itself. In this chapter, we examine some of these implications in global markets.[2]

The process of technological innovation

Earlier discontinuities such as the emergence of railway systems, electrical grids and telegraphy and telephony networks offer insights that can help us understand life-cycles for innovations that require an infrastructure and the implications of ICT for business. While the technology in itself could have been revolutionary, the broader impact comes from the emergence of a powerful new infrastructure and processes that support product and service innovations. Steam-powered machines existed before railways were developed, but it was the installation of an infrastructure that enabled these machines to run on a road with low friction and thus in an energy-efficient way. Once the system was installed, railway companies could start innovating with different types of services, and develop special travel arrangements such as vacation packages, overnight sleepers, mail services, etc. In the end, it led to the development of services offered by companies such as Thomas Cook or Compagnie des Wagons Lits which basically invented a whole new industry: travel for leisure and tourism.

Through the innovation of the railroad, the world was brought closer together (at least on continental land masses), creating new opportunities for innovation in business models and processes. The technology itself may involve a product (steam engines and railways) but the infrastructure enables service innovations (travel and tourism). Is something similar happening now with ICT-based innovations?

Typically when an infrastructure is put in place, albeit gradually, one can observe what Richard Barras has called a *reverse product life-cycle*, with three stages.³ First comes the application of the new technology and the technological infrastructure to increase the efficiency of the delivery of existing services. Second, the technological infrastructure is enhanced to improve the quality of services. Third, the technological infrastructure assists in generating wholly transformed or new services. As discussed below, ICT is beginning to create opportunities to engage in this third-stage transformation of services and this has implications for global business.

There is a fairly predictable pattern in which these transforming innovations primarily occur. One of the better models to begin to understand the technology life-cycle was proposed by William Abernathy and James Utterback.⁴ This well-known model identifies four stages in the development of a new technology:

(1) There is an initial fluid stage, in which there will be a high degree of activity in product innovations that are offered to the market. There are several reasons for this, but the main two are the low barriers to entry, and the difficulty of carrying out market research in emerging markets which means there is a need to experiment. This first phase usually leads to the emergence of a second stage, which has commonly become known as a dominant design.

(2) A dominant design has lots of scientific descriptions, but in brief it is a sort of milestone or quasi standard in an industry. In a sense, the product that becomes a dominant design embodies the requirements of many classes of users, even though it may not perfectly match the requirements of any one particular group of users. The emergence of the dominant design changes the nature of competition completely.

(3) In the third stage, one moves from competition based on the functionality of the product, to competition based on cost and quality. The challenge is no longer to define your product, but to offer a product similar to the competitor's at a lower price. That usually requires heavy investments in automation, business reengineering, and a much leaner organization. This is a period of intensive process innovation.

(4) In the fourth stage, innovation, both in process and product, becomes less relevant to survival in the competitive arena. At this point, the context for the product, and the amenities that come with it, are an essential element of the competition.

During the move from the fluid innovation phase to a dominant design, we sometimes see the definition of new boundaries for an industrial sector. As C. K. Prahalad suggested, the period after the discontinuity is a period during which the borders of sectors are very fuzzy.[5] Sectors are redefined, and the dominant players in the sector are thoroughly challenged. There are enormous opportunities for startups. Is Amazon in book sales, and thus a competitor for Barnes and Noble? Or are they honing a distribution system, which tomorrow can be used for many other products?

In the context of globalizing business, the borders that are being challenged are not only industry borders but also geographic borders. The new technology can create standards that are transnational, facilitating rapid transfer to other countries. Disjointed standards, such as competing cellphone standards in the United States and Europe, can limit the flow of innovations across borders. Harmonized standards can facilitate the flow of innovations and the integration of markets, as with cellphone standards within Europe.

The traditional geographical clustering of industries may change, and regions that used to be strong in delivering special products or services may lose their competitive advantages. Auctions used to be very local; for example, auctions for flowers in Europe were to a large extent concentrated in Holland. The eBay website has changed this geographic concentration of auctions totally. Speed is important, particularly in this fluid stage, when the world is moving toward a dominant design. We know from studying innovation processes that the earlier one enters an emerging business the greater the chances of success will be. Every emerging sector or application of new technologies goes through a phase where "anything goes": barriers to entry are low and entrepreneurs work through trial and error to find out what the customer wants. Moreover, the earlier the company experiments in the Internet world, the easier it will be to create externalities out of complementary assets, i.e. construct brand image, build up experience with electronic payments, etc., and thus create barriers to entry for others. The early entry of Amazon in the distribution of books has clearly given it advantage over Barnes and Noble or other latecomers.[6] This does not mean that these barriers cannot be overcome, but it will require resources and a lot of commitment.

Incumbents probably need to experiment with a *sequence* of efficiency improvement, followed by quality improvement in innovation, and then transformation of the business processes. But it makes a lot of sense to ride down this sequence in the shortest time possible in order to create hurdles for the other entrants.

The elusive customer

Speeding up the evolution from efficiency improvement to the development of new business models requires reducing the friction that slows the introduction of the innovation by producers or the adoption by customers. Traditionally we have two types of hurdle. The first type is adoption hurdles, which slow down the service provider in rolling out the innovation; these include the price/performance hurdle, the risk attached to the investment to be made by the service provider, and the ease of use (or lack thereof). The second type of hurdle is "realization" hurdles that limit the benefits users gain from the innovation even if they adopt it. These include:

- the market structure of the group of users: an oligopolistic market of users usually does not see an advantage in "rocking the boat" and will slow down the rollout of an innovation;
- the lack of potential opportunities created for the innovative adopter over the laggards; and
- the immobilization or resistance to change of the users.

Which of these hurdles have the greatest influence on the development of innovations based on ICT? It is not the market structure that creates problems. The market structure for ICT is in most cases to the advantage of innovation. The market for ICT applications is resolutely international and in many cases very fragmented. There are millions of potential users, and investment requirements for the early trendsetting customers are relatively low: a simple PC, a 3G-enabled mobile phone, and a subscription are sufficient.

The real hurdles have to do with the mentality of the users. How can they be persuaded to change their habits? Even if the convenience of trading on the Net, or buying products or services through the phone may be obvious, there remains a question whether such convenience outweighs the disadvantages. These disadvantages can be, for example, the delays in delivery, uncertainty about the quality, or perceived security issues related to paying by electronic means, etc. The software problems of Charles Schwab or E-trade in March

1999 had early on demonstrated the vulnerability of the convenience advantages.

The infrastructure in specific nations can speed or inhibit this adoption. For example, text messaging (SMS), which spread like wildfire in Europe and Asia, was slow to catch on in the United States, in part because of the fee structure and the lack of a large group of adopters using the service. Internet-based fraud with credit cards could also be another showstopper. Recently a number of websites that record sources of fraudulent credit cards listed Singapore as an important source of cheating. This immediately had a negative impact on the potential for Singapore consumers to purchase worldwide.

The potential benefits of Internet applications need to outweigh the costs of adopting. Buying two books from Amazon, investing in stock for € 5000 via the Internet and playing with it, or paying a parking fee over the mobile phone network may be fun experiments, but do they really change a consumer's behaviour? The breakthrough will only come when a consumer with a problem will think of the Internet first before searching for other possibilities. Such a fundamental change in behaviour will not come through a few excellent, but relatively isolated applications. Successful innovation may require bundles of related services, which act as a network via the Internet and which create a captive customer base.

The need for speed in implementing innovations and the differences in infrastructure and in the mentality of users and customers all over the world must have an impact on the way we think about testing and rolling out innovations based on ICT. Many of us may still have a view of the world based on the traditional international product life-cycle: a new product or service is first tested and introduced in a high-end market (e.g. the United States and some of the leading countries in Europe or Japan). Once it is successfully tested there, one then gradually rolls out the innovation in less and less "sophisticated" countries. The reach of ICT all over the world, and the differences in willingness to adopt a new way of behaving may change this perception. The most sophisticated market in the world for SMS is not in one of these leading industrialized countries, but in Manila (Philippines). Trying out new services based on SMS may well require companies to learn from how Filipinos react to the services, before launching them in Singapore or Tokyo.

Opportunities for innovation from ICT

What implications does the progress of ICT have for the management of global organizations? How can companies move from applying these technologies to raise the efficiency and quality of the existing business, to rethinking the business model itself?

The impact of ICT on business does not necessarily create *totally* new areas for innovation, but the application of these technologies will reinforce several important trends: facilitating rapid globalization in services, increasing the pervasiveness of rich knowledge-based services and making them more independent of geography, driving a shift to the user as the ultimate locus of innovation, and improving peer-to-peer business models.

Overnight globalization

First, as illustrated by Celebrity Sightings, global telecommunications technologies can facilitate overnight globalization. ICT can create a global infrastructure for service and delivery much more quickly and effectively, creating a world in which a small one-person company that offers a service on the Internet can cater to the world. E-Bay and Amazon offer similar examples in the consumer world, but B2B applications such as Covisint show that this new form of globalization is not limited to the consumer world.

The technology, of course, cannot address the preparation of the organization to offer an effective international service that is culturally and structurally adapted to the demands of customers from different continents. For a business such as Celebrity Sightings, serving global youth who share a common interest in international popstars, this local tailoring may be less significant, thereby increasing the value of the technology.

Infrastructure is also a concern. Although online businesses can reach global markets quickly, delivering products and services across geographic and cultural lines can be very challenging. Many of the failures in the Internet world, even of worthy business models, were due to the fact that the companies that launched the new services were not able to manage the international marketing, sales, and logistics. For example, Boo.com, an Internet-based fashion store, developed a presence in some eighteen countries almost overnight, but its operations and logistics system was unable to follow the demand and the company crashed quite quickly.[7] Effective implementation of new business models requires a new view on the rapid internationalization of small and medium-sized enterprises, and raises the question of how one can roll out services internationally with the resources of a small organization.[8] Because Celebrity Sightings' service began and ended with bytes, it did not face as many logistical challenges as a company such as Boo.com or a hotel or restaurant chain, which needs to deliver a product or service in a physical location.

But even in businesses that begin and end in bytes, the nature of the content often requires extensive tailoring. For example, services (e.g. Google or Yahoo!) have many websites tailored to the language and culture of specific countries. In this case, the content needs to be specific to the concerns, language, and the cultural and religious traditions of a given country. This is thus not simply a translation of the service from English into French, Arabic, or Japanese. Different cultures react very differently to the way information is accessed and structured. It is sufficient to compare the websites of, for example, the US-based television channel CNN and the French newspaper *Le Monde*. They offer similar information but they each do it in a style which is typical for US or French culture. The US intellectual tradition is inductive and starts from empirical observations. The French tradition is deductive, and will first conceptualize and then test the concept against the empirical facts. The way news stories are offered reflects these different cultural traditions. And it goes without saying that the reporting by British tabloids does not fit the behavioral norms of a strict Muslim society.

Geographically independent knowledge-based services

The emerging information and communication technologies (in particular, the performance offered by the Internet II protocols with natural language capabilities, the rapidly increasing potential of wireless technology and the opportunities created by mobile technology e.g. 2.5G and 3G – be it WCDMA or CDMA2000, but also meshed networks, etc.) will enable companies to offer rich knowledge-based services independent of time and location. National infrastructures obviously play a significant role in these developments. For example, the Republic of Korea is in 2003, by most standards and benchmarks, the leading user in the world of broadband services and one of the first markets where third-generation mobile services are available.[9] The early adopters of these services in Korea suggest that there are very real opportunities to create margins out of multiplayer games, snapping and sending pictures or video clips, the use of maps (i.e. mobile phones as GPS devices), or the downloading of movies and pornographic materials.

Most of these services are indeed already available in wired systems at home or at the office, but the introduction of mobile devices create two new dimensions for offering services: immediacy and geographical independence. Both these dimensions will increase dramatically the absolute capacity of the consumer or industrial user in accessing of knowledge-based services. The experience of the past years with the introduction of knowledge-based services for users in fixed locations indicates that with the right pricing strategies the users will quickly and massively adopt these new services.

The customer as locus of innovation

The Philippines have one of the most sophisticated markets for short messaging systems (SMS) in the world.[10] "Texting" has become part of the culture, and the number of text messages reached 100 million per day in 2002, a level higher than that of Europe and the United States combined. This very high use has led to a number of creative applications. The social security system uses SMS to provide access to contribution and loan transaction records. The Government Services Insurance System uses it to enable its members to check, within five minutes, loan balances, the status of a loan application, and the maximum amount that can be obtained as a loan. NGOs have used it to advocate their causes. A whole industry has been developed to offer new ring tones, images, and games, and SMS-TV has been a notable success. The more traditional location-based services are equally successful.

The operators stumbled on what appears to have become a goldmine. Between 35 and 40 percent of the revenues of the major cellular network providers in the Philippines are directly derived from SMS applications. And yet, virtually none of the innovative applications were introduced by them: all came from individual initiatives and thousands of small experiments.

ICT applications have a tendency to shift to some extent the locus of innovation towards the user and/or customer. The customer has become a very important source of ideas for creating new services.[11] This phenomenon is seen in other sectors,[12] but in ICT-based services the trend is becoming pervasive. Companies or nations such as the Philippines that can use technologies to harness the insights of users can drive innovation in domestic markets and abroad.

In addition to contributing ideas to the development of systems such as SMS in the Philippines, customers shape specific products to their needs through customization and product adaptation. Potential purchasers of consumer investment goods, for example, can simulate via the Internet the combination of options they prefer. Users of information sources can design both the interface and the content of the messages they want to receive, and mobile phone users design their ring tones and "faces" and offer them to other users. Many of these innovations may seem trivial, but they do form an enormous source of creativity.

How does this play out globally? What are the challenges and opportunities for engaging global customers in the design process? The biggest global challenge is probably that companies need to develop sensing devices in many more places than before, and often in quite unexpected places. Imagine that you had read an article in the early 1990s that argued that for the development of sophisticated SMS or MMS applications, a company like Nokia, Samsung, or NEC would have to set up an application laboratory in a place like Manila, that for flat panel displays you had better be connected to Korea, or for a better understanding of how call centers can be rendered more effective that India would be the place. You probably would have laughed; yet that is today's reality.

The biggest advantage is that you can get an involvement of the customer in the design and production process to an extent that was unthinkable before. A large European automotive manufacturer did the following experiment a few years ago. The company put the design of a future model on the Internet as well as a simple CAD tool to adapt the design of the car. This was made available to a few thousand potential customers for the car from all over Europe and Latin America. This group of international customers loved tinkering with the model features and made an unexpectedly high number of interesting suggestions for changing the design of the car. The car company hit two birds with one stone: the company received lots of great ideas, and it created a group of customers who saw the car as "their car" and were thus very interested in considering buying it.

The second opportunity is to involve the customer in the production process. Lately, we have been moving in the design of products and systems to a concept of delayed differentiation. The idea is that you try to keep a product as standardized as possible until late in the production process. The customization comes only in the last steps. For example, if you produce a computer printer you will design it such that the adaptation to the local market, e.g. the cable that connects it to the local electrical grid or the operating instructions in a specific language, will be added at the last step of the production process. Lots of this customization can actually be programmed and it is an obvious opportunity to offer the customer the possibility of adapting the product to his specific needs through Internet services. There is an opportunity to reduce costs, but also to offer a better service: it will be possible for a Japanese expatriate in France to adjust the machine bought locally in Paris to his or her Japanese wishes.

Enabling peer-to-peer communities

The information and communication technologies also allow companies to become facilitators of interactions between individuals, blurring the concept of a company and its customer even further. Auction services over the Internet have expanded tremendously the age-old habit of bartering personal services or selling secondhand products from one consumer to another. eBay has organized, institutionalized, and internationalized an activity that people used to practice in their local neighborhood. What used to be an *ad hoc* and highly inefficient and local activity (e.g. garage sales) has been transformed in a real system of services provided from international peer to international peer. As eBay has built its business around the world, it has brought buyers and sellers together across borders. As Eric Orts discussed in Chapter 14, these types of interactions can be problematic, as Yahoo! discovered when US sellers on its auction site offered Nazi memorabilia that were visible in France, in violation of French law. These systems also allow individuals to determine their own definition of community. Collectors of baseball cards or doll furniture can find one another regardless of where in the world they are located.

Blogger.com, another example of peer-to-peer services, hosts hundreds of thousands of weblogs, personal websites where people share insights and web links with all users. The potential creativity of what these distributed individual service providers offer is a true hotbed of innovative ideas. But perhaps more importantly, they lead to a sort of industrialization of an activity which used to be marginal and in the grey or black market. And it creates international communities of users that will stimulate each other and may lead to an increased creativity.

Even within a more traditional service such as Amazon.com's online marketplace, the advice of peers through product reviews and recommendations replaces the traditional role of the shopkeeper in providing advice. Services differ from normal production systems because of the overlap between service users and service providers. The most important design parameter of a service system is precisely the degree of "overlap" between customer and service delivery system. ICT, which provides many more degrees of freedom in the design of service delivery systems, can be used to either increase or decrease this overlap. E-trade is an example where the overlap is reduced to a large degree to what is essential. On the other hand, SMS-TV in the Philippines offers viewers a high degree of interaction with what is happening in the studio.

Managing global innovation

In addition to the strategic and market implications of ICT, these technologies also have an impact on the management of innovation itself. As noted by Philip Anderson and Lori Rosenkopf in Chapter 13, innovation and technology management, even when working globally, is in essence "parochial," centered around communities that are often geographically based.[13] This was a consequence of the tacit nature of technology and technological knowledge, in particular in its early stages of development. As a consequence, technology management put a lot of emphasis on co-location, face-to-face communication, dedicated teams, and interfaces based on informal interactions.

ICT can help companies facilitate the connections between communities and the integration of the resulting knowledge, particularly in a global context. These technologies can help companies "sense" worldwide, combine insights from diverse parts of the globe, link together diverse communities of knowledge and practice, and facilitate rapid worldwide deployment of these innovations.[14] Innovation in the mobile phone business could, for example, come out of the rapid combination of what the most sophisticated users of SMS in Manila (Philippines) do, the fashion in electronic products that is developed on California beaches, the miniaturization skills from Japan, and the patents from Qualcom in the United States.

The global scope of knowledge makes it very challenging to draw together these insights from developers and users, as well as third parties such as academic institutions. These globally diffused development teams need to meet five conditions:[15]

- Members need to have sufficient credibility with each other.
- Performing teams need to preserve diversity: too often one attempts to overcome the difficulty of distant locations by standardizing.
- The success of international teams is to a large extent based on their ability to keep the communications going, notwithstanding the difficulties due to cultural differences, geographical distance, and differences in time zones.
- Teams need moments to celebrate the fact that they are actually together, even though they are working in different locations.
- Around the internal networks within the international development teams and between the teams and the rest of the organization we often observe the emergence of international networks of outside partners (e.g. vendors, lead customers, or research institutions). A lead customer in one country may have had a subsidiary in another country that was in contact with another part of the development team.

Ten years ago, these conditions were difficult to meet, and only the best firms were able to implement effectively the concept of international product development. The effective deployment of new ICT can today help us to find ways to manage virtual teams across continents, to organise laboratories and other sources of technological innovation (e.g. partners, vendors, or research institutes) as a non-hierarchical network.

For example, many international organizations have invested heavily in support technologies (e.g. videoconferencing, computer conferencing, computer billboards, chat rooms, etc.). These do help to keep the credibility of the different partners high, on condition that one keeps in mind that (1) under the current circumstances and with the current scientists or managers, the initial credibility-building will still require face-to-face contact and (2) ICT tools increase the half-life of credibility, but do not extend it into eternity: most virtual teams realise that they regularly need to touch base face-to-face to remain productive.[16]

Sophisticated knowledge management systems also can help to preserve diversity in the team by capturing ideas anywhere in the network and making them available to others. These systems need to be embedded in the correct set of social dynamics. Imposing one system does not seem to work. Companies need to respect that a common system may be deployed differently in different cultural environments, while preserving the integrity of the database.

The effective deployment of these technologies creates the opportunity for a "virtual laboratory."[17] The idea behind this term is that the company's laboratory is only a subset of the group of people that work on the innovations for the organization: employees from vendors, lead customers, partner, and research institutes belong temporarily to the firm's development teams. Some of these are working in a contractual or hierarchical relationship with the organization. Others work in communities of interest together with employees. For example, a study of a Danish shipbuilder found that the company's own R&D capabilities were barely 20 percent of what they could mobilize for product and process development through outside networks. ICT is vital in connecting these networks and managing the knowledge that results.

Conclusions

The introduction of new information and communication technologies – including advanced mobile technology, the expansion of the capabilities of database management systems, and the increasing sophistication of Internet protocols – is a major discontinuity in the technologies used to design and implement services. As we move beyond the first stages of applying these technologies to improve the efficiency or quality of existing services to looking at creating process and service innovations, there are many opportunities to apply these technologies in globalizing business.

Because of their ability rapidly to build networks across geographic boundaries, these technologies can be particularly powerful in rethinking approaches to delivering global services. They can create opportunities for new businesses and transform the way existing businesses operate in global markets. These technologies also have implications for the global innovation process itself.

Most incumbent businesses will first have to go through a phase of efficiency improvement and quality enhancement of their existing business models before they can embark on new business models. But one can perhaps shorten drastically this "riding of the reverse life-cycle" if one analyzes the impact of hurdles to innovation, particularly the limitations of users in adopting. In an ICT-based economy, particularly with the shifting power toward the consumer and the increased importance of knowledge integration, managers should pay attention to the social dynamics of knowledge management systems, and ensure that IT is complemented by knowledge communities, switchboard operators, and a good knowledge architecture.

We live in a period in which the technology has not stabilized. In this "fluid phase" of the technological life-cycle we need flexible organizations, a willingness to question the boundaries of sectors, and a learning strategy rather than a traditional marketing- or customer-oriented strategy. As shown by the rapid growth of new ICT-based businesses in Korea or the fast rise of SMS and other services in the Philippines, there are tremendous opportunities for companies that can recognize the potential of these technologies and capitalize on them to draw ideas from diverse communities and connect with markets around the world.

Notes

1 L. Demeester and A. De Meyer, "Celebrity Sightings," INSEAD case study (1997).
2 In providing this answer we have relied on a series of case studies that we developed together with colleagues over recent years. Several of these were published in A. De Meyer, S. Dutta, and S. Srivastava, *The Bright Stuff* (London: Prentice Hall, 2001). Others are available through INSEAD or are in development. Among these are: "Charles Schwab, E*Trade and Merrill Lynch"; "Wal-Mart, Amazon.Com, and Barnes & Noble"; "GM and Auto-By-Tel" (all in De Meyer, Dutta and Srivastava, *The Bright Stuff*); "Celebrity Sightings" (see note 1 above); "MyWeb" (De Meyer and Chua, 2000); "Pinoy2Pinoy" (De Meyer and Bhardway, 2003); "Xerox: the Eureka Project" Dutta and Van Wassenhove, 1999); and "ARM Holdings plc" (Williamson and O'Keeffe, 2002).
3 R. Barras, "Towards a Theory of Innovation in Services," *Research Policy*, 15 (1986), pp. 161–173.

4 W. J. Abernathy and J. M. Utterback, *The Productivity Dilemma* (Baltimore: Johns Hopkins University Press, 1978).

5 C. K. Prahalad, "Managing Discontinuities: The Emerging Challenges," *Research Technology Management*, 41, 3 (May–June 1998), p. 14.

6 De Meyer, Dutta, and Srivastava, *The Bright Stuff*.

7 Ibid.

8 For discussion of meta-national organizations that might be helpful in this, see Y. Doz, J. Santos, and P. Williamson, *From Global to Metanational*, (Boston: HBS Press, 2002).

9 A. De Meyer, "ICT: Pockets of Leadership in East Asia," in S. Dutta, B. Lanvin, and F. Paua (eds.), *The Global Information Technology Report* (Oxford: Oxford University Press for the World Economic Forum, 2003), pp. 132–141.

10 "Pinoy2Pinoy."

11 De Meyer, Dutta, and Srivastava, *The Bright Stuff*.

12 E. Von Hippel, *Users as Innovators* (Oxford: Oxford University Press, 1988).

13 T. J. Allen, *Managing the Flow of Technology* (Cambridge, MA: MIT Press, 1977).

14 Doz, Santos, and Williamson, *From Global to Metanational*.

15 A. De Meyer, "Tech Talk: How Managers are Stimulating Global R&D Communication," *Sloan Management Review*, 32, 3 (Spring 1991), pp. 49–58.

16 Based on a small number of cases, we observed that the maximum time between two face-to-face events is around three months.

17 A. De Meyer, "Gérer la R&D en réseaux," *Le Journal de l'Ecole de Paris de Management*, 11 (Mai–Juin 1998), pp. 19–24.

17 Globalization and its many faces: the case of the health sector

LAWTON R. BURNS
Wharton School

THOMAS D'AUNNO
INSEAD

JOHN R. KIMBERLY
Wharton School

Previous chapters in this book have addressed particular challenges that firms face as they globalize, such as governance or branding or supply chain management. Or they have addressed themes in globalization such as the cross-border funding of entrepreneurial ventures or government responses to globalization issues. This chapter addresses the many faces of globalization as they play out in the management decisions within a particular sector of national economies – healthcare. The authors examine the complex forces driving and impeding globalization, and the opportunities they create for different players in different places in the world.

ROLF Schmidt, the CEO of a major global pharmaceutical company, looks out of his office at the twinkling lights of a major European city that has been its home for more than a century. The current conglomerate that occupies these offices bears little relationship to the sleepy little chemical company that was founded in the historic offices where the chief executive now paces late into the night. The company now operates across a global patchwork of complex regulations governing its pricing, advertising, and drug development and approval. Its research and development organization is stretched across diverse centers in the United States, Europe, and Asia. Its marketing initiatives are a combination of resource-intensive global brands and increasingly tightly tailored local brands. Its global supply chains and financing create new risks and make the company susceptible to unexpected shocks as it gears up for the rapid production of new drugs that have an ever-narrower window of opportunity.

The company is a social actor in diverse markets, the target of demands that it respond to AIDS in Africa and SARS in China and, in developed markets, to protests about the high costs of prescription medicines. At the same time, it faces intense global competition from an ever-consolidating set of major competitors. Because it operates across national borders, it must meet a set of diverse expectations of different regulatory bodies, even as the Internet and other technologies are drawing different parts of the world closer together.

Around the world, consumers expect higher quality healthcare, while nations and companies have only finite resources and capabilities to meet them. The company, and the governments of the nations in which it operates, are confronted by the "Iron Triangle of Health Care": the need continually to balance the requirements for higher quality, greater access, and lower (or certainly not greater) cost.[1] There are more technological opportunities to treat disease (such as genetic therapies), but these raise expenses and increase the risks of the high investments in improving traditional approaches to drug development, such as automated high throughput screening of potential compounds. At the same time, increasingly global markets are highlighting price differences from one country to the next. Consumers are becoming more aware and increasingly vocal in protesting these differences and legislators are listening, eroding patent protection, and opening the doors to imports.

These forces have been a driver of a wave of mergers, and tonight, Schmidt is reviewing a proposal from his staff for a potential merger with a US-based company. Despite the dismal results of the pharmaceutical mergers of the 1990s, there is still a compelling argument that drug-makers need a critical global mass to justify the investments required to sustain the high costs of development and commercialization. But can the company achieve its desired synergies from the merger? What structures and training will it need to cultivate for the leaders to realize these synergies? How would key investors in Europe and the United States respond to the deal? How will European workers react? Will the company be able to comply with Sarbanes–Oxley and still remain true to the values and laws of its European headquarters?

How should the deal be financed and what are the financial risks? How can company leaders ensure that knowledge is shared across this global network? How will the organization rationalize the resulting set of local and national brands in the portfolio of the combined firm? How can they manage the process of new product development to respond to local needs yet capitalize on the scale of the new company? How can they design their supply chains to maximize their efficiency while paying close attention to risks of shortages of new drugs or costly disruptions?

While Rolf Schmidt and his company are fictitious, the challenges he faces are real ones that major pharmaceutical firms and other companies need to address in globalizing businesses and markets. The complexities of the healthcare sector illustrate some of the challenges discussed throughout this book as well as the complex picture of globalization. In this chapter, we first consider the forces driving healthcare toward greater or lesser globalization, and then we examine some of the implications of insights from this book for the specific challenges faced by leaders in global markets such as Rolf Schmidt.

The globalization question: competing forces

One of the core issues that creates the context for Rolf Schmidt's deliberations is whether healthcare markets are becoming increasingly integrated or fragmented. The more integrated global markets are, the more potential there may be to achieve synergies from global operations. The more the markets are fragmenting, the higher the costs of tailoring the business, products, and marketing to individual markets. Companies are forced to adapt their business strategies and models to local conditions in ways that may inhibit their ability to leverage "recipes" or "templates," potentially lowering returns on investments in globalizing. Is the global healthcare industry drawing together or coming apart? There are compelling arguments on both sides of this issue.

Different answers for different organizations

Before addressing the specific forces that are driving the industry toward global integration or fragmentation, it is important to recognize that the situation varies for different kinds of organization that are

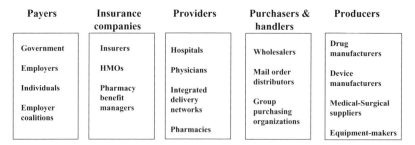

Figure 17.1. The healthcare value chain. (*Source:* Burns *et al., The Health Care Value Chain.*)

involved in the sector. Different organizations represent different stake-holders – providers, suppliers, payers, regulators, and consumers – and it appears that the extent to which they are likely to become truly global may vary by their position in the healthcare value chain and may, in fact, be limited to some degree by the nature of the transactions in which they are involved.

It is often argued, for example, that providing care is essentially a local activity and serious obstacles face any organization that tries to internationalize that service. Over the past three decades, hospital systems based in the United States such as HCA and NME (now called Tenet) have been unsuccessful in sustaining their expansion overseas. On the other hand, pharmaceuticals, medical devices, and information systems are products that may be less "local" in character and hence companies' investments in global development, manufacturing, distribution, and sales capabilities may be more likely to pay off. Indeed, an analysis of the healthcare value chain in the United States reveals that only the product manufacturers (right-hand side of Figure 17.1) operate in multiple national contexts; all other players operate domestically.[2]

We have, however, seen the recent emergence of global brands in healthcare delivery. Some organizations on the provider side, such as Harvard, Johns Hopkins, and Mayo in the United States, Capio in Sweden, Fresenius in Germany, and Générale de Santé in France, are launching ventures outside their home countries, trying to leverage their strong reputations for quality and technical excellence. Hopkins and Mayo, for example, look to various corners of the globe for patients who can afford their services, and have a variety of sourcing strategies in place. Harvard Medical International, a subsidiary of the Harvard Medical School, consults on the design and operation of hospitals in Greece, Turkey, India, China, and elsewhere, in some cases allowing the Harvard brand to appear on buildings in these distant locales. And Capio, Fresenius, and Générale de Santé all are attempting to leverage their hospital management know-how across national borders. These experiments are still being carried out, however, and variation in local habits, customs, and practices in health and medical care may limit the value of even such strong brands in global markets.

In examining globalization of healthcare, we also need to distinguish between the globalization of "players" and the globalization of "practices." The extent to which single firms operate in multiple nations is what we call the globalization of "players", and the extent to which actors operating in a single nation use practices that are common to other nations is what we call the globalization of "practices." In our view, the factors that can make globalization more or less feasible and attractive for health sector managers and enterprises vary depending on whether we are talking about players or practices. In either case, however, we see a variety of factors influencing globalization in the health sector, some of which inhibit the process while others promote it.

One thing is certain: healthcare is an important issue for every nation. The economic significance of the health sector is striking – expenditures on health account for between 6 percent and 14 percent of the GDP of most countries around the globe. Its social and political significance is extraordinary as well – commitments to maintaining and improving the health of populations are high on the list of national priorities for many, perhaps most, of these countries.

Factors promoting globalization

Multiple commonalities and convergent developments across countries are promoting greater globalization in the health sector. These include globalizing disease patterns; rapid spread of diseases; common global challenges; the rising percentage of elderly people; the rising costs of care and pressures for cost containment; demands for higher quality and safety; increasing consumer activism; calls for integrated healthcare; globalizing of managerial and policy knowledge;

globalizing inquiry in health science, policy, and management; and technological advances that transcend geography.

Converging global disease patterns

Recent analyses have begun to map worldwide expenditures on different diseases. Following the Pareto principle, these analyses have found that a small number of diseases (33 out of 269) account for nearly 50 percent of worldwide spending; and 70 diseases account for three-quarters of total spending.[3] Most of the high-cost diseases are prevalent throughout the modernized world. The most common disease-causing conditions in the future are likely to include obesity, hypertension, and atherosclerosis. Use of this information is enabling pharmaceutical firms to target their new product development efforts to those disease areas with large market and profit potential. To the extent that disease and illness are a product of environmental and behavioral factors such as obesity, sedentary lifestyles, smoking, and alcohol consumption, increasing cultural convergence may be expected to lead to greater similarity in disease patterns around the globe. Researchers at the World Health Organization recently reported that the number of new cancer cases worldwide is expected to increase by 50 percent over the next twenty years (from 10 to 15 million), in part because of the adoption of unhealthy Western habits by developing nations. In turn, such convergence may lead to increased globalization of treatment and prevention practices.

Rapid spread of diseases

Another driver of this convergence of diseases across nations is the increasing flow of people and products that spread disease rapidly around the globe. The most vivid illustration of this reality is, of course, the rapid and highly visible spread of SARS from China to many points around the globe in the spring of 2003. The breakdown of borders between countries and the increase of migration between them means that healthcare problems essentially become borderless, and disease patterns become more global. Increased air travel and shipping, population movements, and a shared food supply facilitate the rapid spread of infectious disease. Tourism now claims to be the largest global industry, accounting for 11.7 percent of global GDP in 1999.[4] The global movement of goods and services has also increased; US imports more than tripled in the last two decades, and food imports more than doubled in the last five years of the last millennium. Using new DNA fingerprinting technology, scientists have tracked drug-resistant tuberculosis strains originating in Eastern Europe, Asia, and Africa that are now appearing in patients in Western Europe and North America.[5] The worldwide prevalence of HIV is also striking: 28.5 million cases in Sub-Saharan Africa, 5.6 million cases in South and Southeast Asia, 1.5 million cases in Latin and South America, 1 million cases each in Eastern Europe/Central Asia and East Asia/Pacific Rim, and nearly 1 million cases in North America.[6]

Common global challenges

As shown by the global spread of diseases, globalization has introduced new challenges to advanced countries, as problems in one part of the world can spread to others through a variety of means such as terrorism, conflict, and environmental pollution. The World Health Organization's Commission on Macroeconomics and Health calls on both rich and poor nations to scale up their levels of monetary investment in access to essential health services in the Third World. The Commission also calls for knowledge investments in research on treatment protocols and interventions in low-income nations, technologies for fighting "killer diseases" (malaria, tuberculosis, AIDS), studies of epidemiological patterns in their countries, and human resource training. Others have similarly called for the United States and other Western nations to take a leadership role in fostering and investing in global public health.[7] A study by the US Central Intelligence Agency concluded that investments in improving healthcare can also enhance global security because poor health contributes to nation-state failures.[8] Global public health initiatives, such as detection of the emergence of new infection or a new form of antibiotic resistance introduced by terrorists, may become more central to Western countries' national security efforts.[9] Finally, investments in developing countries can provide market opportunities for Western firms while helping these nations.[10] These common global challenges create the need for global remedies, which could lead to greater integration.

The WHO Commission suggests that investments in health in Third World nations will serve to reduce poverty and mortality, and foster long-term economic growth.[11] Such growth would occur through several channels, including faster demographic transition (to lower fertility rates), greater investments in human capital, higher levels of household saving, greater foreign investment, and greater social stability. These suggestions are supported by econometric research that links health status indicators more closely to socioeconomic conditions (e.g. income per capita, literacy rates) than to investments in healthcare systems.[12] Other research has demonstrated the link between a nation's level of healthcare expenditure and both its income per capita and technological change (e.g. R&D spending in general and in healthcare).[13] The former finding suggests healthcare as a luxury good; the latter suggests the global role of technological progress in promoting higher levels of healthcare spending.

In addition to the advantages such progress affords these countries, other nations may also benefit. Indeed, the AIDS epidemic in the Third World may actually retard globalization by hindering access to cheap labor and fast-growing markets. On the one hand, AIDS strikes young and middle-aged adults, increases local firms' labor costs and healthcare outlays, and slows the growth rates of their countries. On the other hand, AIDS reduces the demand for goods and services by reducing household income and siphoning off any remaining disposable income for medical treatment.[14]

Rising percentage of elderly people

Diverse countries in the developed world face a graying of the population that will present them with a common set of healthcare challenges that might lead to a convergence of solutions. Between 2000 and 2030, the proportion of the population aged 65+ in the developed world is expected to rise from 1-in-7 to 1-in-4 (from 14.7% to 23.8%). This will increase outlays for pensions and healthcare services. For example, public spending on pensions and health benefits in the UK as a proportion of GDP is expected to increase, from 10.5% to 15.5% during the period 1995–2030. For the United States, this spending will rise from 10.5% to 17.0%; for Japan, from 11.5% to 23.1%; for France, from 17.6% to 25.5%, and for Italy, from 19.7% to 33.3%. Such spending levels had already outstripped public outlays on defense, education, and R&D in the G-7 nations as early as 1995. While public spending will be increasing, there will be fewer working-age adults available to support each elderly person, either in terms of their ability to pay taxes to finance these pensions and healthcare expenditures or simply to render care to the elderly at home. Between 2000 and 2030, the ratio of working-age adults (15–63 years old) to the elderly will drop from 4.5-to-1 to 2.5-to-1. The long-term decline in the percentage of the elderly living with their children, observed since the early 1950s, is likely to accelerate.[15]

What do these demographic developments portend? Rising public outlays will place further fiscal strain on national healthcare budgets in welfare states and increase calls for system reforms and new sources of capital. Countries will consider strategies that encourage workers to remain in the workforce longer, to increase the size of the working-age workforce, to increase fertility rates that ultimately feed the workforce, and to reconsider policies that currently discourage or retard immigration by working-age adults. Government leaders also will need to develop systems that provide long-term care and support chronic disease management.[16] These systems and supports will involve investments in home health and nursing home care, in community-based care models, and in programs that prospectively identify and target interventions to the chronically ill population. Firms that provide products or services that meet these needs should be in a stronger position to globalize, even taking into account the barriers to cross-national expansion that service providers face in the healthcare value chain. At the same time, these trends may also promote globalization of practices: nations may be eager to import models of care that other nations are using to meet the needs of their elderly.

Rising costs of care and pressures for cost containment

Healthcare costs are rising around the world, as a percentage of GDP, driven up by increasing elderly populations, rising income levels (which lead to greater levels of healthcare spending), increasing demand for healthcare services, and increasing investments in technology and research and development.[17] Such pressures will be exacerbated by shortages of trained healthcare professionals in many countries, which will lead to demand for higher wages. All of these forces will place greater strains on government budgets and lead to greater pressures for cost containment. Nations are likely to experiment with different mixes of strategic responses, including managed care, price caps on physician and hospital services, budgetary ceilings on system expenditures, higher consumer co-payments/contributions/cost sharing, increased investment in outpatient and home healthcare, greater focus on prevention and healthcare education, and reconsideration of the mix of public versus private sector involvement in healthcare (both financing and delivery). This set of common problems may lead to a drive for common solutions. For example, in the face of rising costs, Germany's public healthcare system recently introduced a fixed-fee payment plan for hospital procedures modeled on the system currently being used in Australia.[18] Cost containment may provide opportunities for globalization of firms as well. Greater opportunities will exist for firms that provide products or services that either directly or indirectly promote cost containment. For example, firms that can provide cost-effective, community-based disease management may be well positioned to implement such services in a number of countries. On the other hand, cost containment pressures may be so great that they make cross-national expansion financially unattractive.

Demands for higher quality and safety

There have been growing concerns in the United States regarding variations in medical practice and the lack of an evidence base for much of medical practice. Even where such evidence does exist, there are concerns about the failure of physicians to follow these findings and there is a growing recognition of systemically based errors in the practice of medicine.[19] Large US corporate purchasers (employers) have prompted the push for greater quality of care. Employers now demand greater value for their healthcare purchasing dollars and they have recently banded together in coalitions and are calling on providers to adopt various standards of practice (e.g. the Leapfrog Group). Similar concerns are now being voiced in the rest of the English-speaking world, fostered in part by new empirical documentation of regional variations in healthcare practices. A recent survey of sick adults in five countries (Australia, Canada, New Zealand, the United Kingdom, and the United States) found common patterns of dissatisfaction with various elements of the quality of care received: doctor–patient communication, medical errors, lack of coordination of care, and medication-related side effects.[20]

It is not clear how countries will reconcile the problem of rising costs with the demands for greater quality and access to more sophisticated treatments. To the extent that nations focus on different aspects of the challenge, their practices will diverge. For example, for years, the United States has focused on cost containment through its reliance on managed care and payment reforms (Prospective Payment System, the Balanced Budget Act). France, by contrast, has emphasized choice, flexibility, and coverage for all – with the result that its national health budget experienced a $2 billion shortfall in 2001, leading to measures that held down providers' wages and increased their hours of work. In contrast, there is also the possibility that, given the other factors we have discussed, nations will seek common solutions to the problems they face in balancing competing demands in the health sector, thereby providing a major impetus for globalization. The relatively recent adoption by several nations of a fixed-fee, prospective payment system, as noted above, supports this point of view. There is also some evidence that other countries are experimenting with single specialty hospitals for cardiac and orthopedic care, similar to those implemented earlier in the United States (MedCath Corporation) and even earlier in Canada (Shouldice Hospital). Such experiments are designed to improve quality outcomes, enhance patient choice, and promote efficiency.[21]

Increasing consumer activism

Concerns about quality, safety, and cost are leading consumers to play a much more active role in debating the conditions of healthcare in many nations. There is increasing evidence that patients are dissatisfied with their healthcare system's ability to meet their expectations. In a five-nation survey published in 2001, for example, 14–33 percent of the public felt that their system needed complete rebuilding, while only 9–25 percent felt their system worked well and needed only minor changes.[22] The majority expressed the opinion that while there were some good things in their system, fundamental change was needed. This common opinion across many countries could lead to calls for reforms that result in greater convergence.

Calls for integrated healthcare

One important result of several of the factors discussed above – including demands for higher quality and lower cost care and the need to deal with the needs of chronic care patients – has been calls for integrating healthcare services. In the United States, healthcare providers vigorously pursued integration during the 1990s, despite some skepticism about the wisdom of so doing.[23] Strategies for doing so have included horizontal consolidation of similar types of facilities (hospital systems), vertical combinations of different levels of providers (linkages between primary, secondary, and tertiary levels in a continuum of care), and vertical linkages of providers with insurers. The integration movement has now spread to much of the rest of the world, illustrating graphically the globalization of practices. The Singapore government has mandated that the majority of its hospitals coalesce into two competing, but equivalent, hospital systems. The delivery of integrated care has also become a national policy objective in many European countries. Scotland is seeking to reorganize its system using both horizontal and vertical integration models organized around Primary Care Trusts, Local Health Care Cooperatives, and Managed Clinical Networks.[24] England is likewise seeking to integrate primary and community health services around Primary Care Trusts.[25] Many of these countries (and others) are also pursuing integrated care through mechanisms familiar in the United States, such as disease management, care protocols, telemedicine, shared decision-making, and collaborative care models. The World Health Organization established a European Office for Integrated Health Care Services (in Barcelona) to promote the integration of health and social services and to improve the interplay among institutions, professions, and functions within a nation's healthcare system.[26] Both the WHO and the Health Services Research section of the European Public Health Association (EUPHA) have organized workshops on integrated healthcare.

The movement to integrated services provides an important opportunity for global companies because firms or practice models that prove effective in one nation may well cross national boundaries in much the same way as fixed-fee prospective payment plans. Much of the promise for integration rests on building bridges between systems of care and cure, between specialists and generalists, between ambulatory and acute care services, and in the development of "telematics," i.e. technologies that facilitate the exchange of information. Such technologies are now diffusing across Europe.[27] Firms or practice models that can address these challenges are the most likely candidates for globalization.

Spread of management and regulatory practices
Although healthcare tends to be highly regulated at the national level, and there are some 191 nations around the globe, each one of which regulates itself in this domain, the number of approaches to doing so is surprisingly small.[28] While there is less variation at the macro-level than one might expect, micro-level variations make a huge difference.

The extensiveness and the specifics of these commitments to improved health do vary from one country to the next, thus confronting firms with global aspirations doing business in the sector with complexities that firms in other sectors do not face to as great an extent.

Globalizing inquiry in health science, policy, and management

The development with perhaps the most far-reaching implications for promoting globalization of both players and practices along the health-care value chain is the increased globalization of inquiry in health science, policy, and management. As we have observed, nations around the world are facing similar challenges in health and the healthcare sector. Their responses to these challenges have varied considerably to date, but we anticipate increased convergence in these responses as a consequence of widespread information-sharing and the development of similar worldviews.

Globalizing of inquiry into healthcare has been spurred by the growing prominence of medical care policy in public sector agendas starting in the late 1980s and early 1990s. Ted Marmor suggests that three factors in particular account for this rise to prominence:

First, the financing of personal medical care became a major financial component of the budgets of mature welfare states. When fiscal strain arose, as during the prolonged recession of those years, policy scrutiny, not simply incremental budgeting, was the predictable result. Second, mature welfare states had, under almost all circumstances, less capacity for bold fiscal expansion in new areas. This meant that the management of existing programs (in new ways perhaps but in changing economic circumstances) necessarily came to occupy a larger share of the public agenda. Third, there was what might be termed the wearing out (perhaps wearing down) of the postwar consensus about the welfare state, namely the effects of more than two decades of fretfulness about the affordability, desirability, and governability of the welfare state since the early 1970s.[29]

There have been several manifestations of this convergence. First, we have seen the globalizing of health science, including biomedical research conducted by universities, research institutes, and pharmaceutical and biotechnology firms. Exchanges of human resources (e.g. scientists as visiting professors), exchanges of information and data (e.g. via the Internet, teleconferences, and traditional conferences), and the conduct of cross-national studies have all increased sharply, making health science a global enterprise. Though there clearly remains competition among research teams around the world, they are increasingly drawing on common research methods, tools, data, and information, contributing to what we consider globalization in practices. The remarkable speed with which the SARS bacterium was isolated and its gene sequenced is a particularly vivid example of this dimension.[30]

Second, there has been increasing globalizing of data collection on health and healthcare systems. Institutions such as the Organisation for Economic Co-operation and Development (OECD), the World Health Organization (WHO), and the World Bank have increasingly collected and made available comparative statistics on healthcare. For example, the OECD annually publishes a set of benchmark statistics on health status indicators in many countries (now numbering thirty),[31] and the OECD and the WHO have also developed frameworks for understanding how well national health systems perform.[32] At a more micro level, the Cochrane Collaborative has assembled a global electronic warehouse of information on randomized controlled trials across all areas of healthcare ("The Cochrane Library"). The Collaborative includes groups that review and update available evidence, methods groups that improve the validity and precision of the reviews, centers that maintain registries of researchers and promote collaboration among them, and local networks to involve consumers.

Third, concomitant with the increase in global data on health and health systems has been the proliferation of international forums and conferences on health management and policy issues for both academics and professionals. The Global Medical Forum, for example, assembles researchers and industry representatives from the entire value chain to promote a better understanding of the complex inter-relationship between the different healthcare systems of the world. INSEAD organizes a series of biannual conferences on "Innovation and the Future of Healthcare." And academic conferences have focused on such disciplinary areas as strategic management (held at St. Andrews University in Scotland) and organization theory (held at Oxford University).

Global survey research teams have recently formed to pursue cross-national studies in such diverse areas as access to healthcare,[33] quality of care,[34] hospital nurse staffing,[35] and the diffusion of technological innovation.[36] New journals have developed to address issues of common interest such as the *International Journal for Quality in Health Care* (launched in 1989) and the *International Journal of Integrated Care* (inaugurated in 2001). Professional associations such as the Health Industry Group Purchasing Association (HIGPA) have begun global conferences in both the United States and Europe, following the earlier lead of Arthur Andersen's (now Accenture's) Global Pharmaceutical Leaders Program. A number of major consulting firms now have "global" healthcare practices. Finally, major foundations such as the Milbank Memorial Fund have financed studies of the complex interactions between researchers and policy-makers in different countries. These studies show that public–private sector collaboration is heavily conditioned by a country's context: its history, culture, beliefs, and interests.[37]

Technological advances that transcend geography
Innovations in biomedical research, medical technology, and information technology are revolutionizing the healthcare sector. Many of these innovations, such as telemedicine or robotic surgery, make place or "site" less relevant than it has been historically for the delivery of care, creating opportunities that cut across national boundaries and leading to the formation of new ventures, be they for-profit, not-for-profit, public, or some amalgam thereof, to capitalize on them. Combined with increasing scalability, these new ventures invariably foster increased globalization of the healthcare sector.

Factors inhibiting globalization

As Rolf Schmidt considers the forces that might lead to greater integration of healthcare markets, perhaps increasing the value of his proposed merger and creating opportunities for global corporations to apply similar strategies in different parts of the world, he must also consider the other side of the issue. While there are many factors that are driving the global healthcare sector toward convergence, there are clearly countervailing forces. Several attributes of nations and their healthcare systems are certainly unique. These include a country's culture, values, and ideals – such as assuring every member of the population with universal access to necessary health services. They also include the developmental history of the country's health system – such as the decentralized and voluntaristic formation of the hospital industry in the United States. Some of the forces leading to greater fragmentation are discussed in the following sections.

Differences in culture, society and economics

Variation in national culture and in the social and economic organization of healthcare systems generally inhibits globalization of both players and practices. This variation undermines firms' ability to standardize the production and distribution of goods and services (hindering the globalization of players) and, similarly, such variation undermines an organization's ability to use practices that organizations in other nations have adopted (hindering the globalization of practices).

While, as noted above, pharmaceutical and medical equipment firms have been able to cross these boundaries more easily given their size and the nature of their business, variations in national culture and health system organization present especially acute problems for healthcare providers (hospitals and healthcare professionals such as physicians and nurses).[38] At a national level, culture affects how healthcare systems are organized. Many nations, for example, hold strong values about assuring universal access to necessary health services and this value is reflected in public ownership, governance, and funding of services. Moreover, national culture influences individuals' health-related behavior. For example, national culture influences decisions about lifestyle (smoking, drinking, diet, and exercise), the types of symptoms that prompt a visit to a physician, and how one interacts with a healthcare professional. Even manufacturers of commodity products such as tubes for specimen collection purposes need to customize to reflect sensitivity to different national cultures (e.g. need for spillproof containers in Europe versus unbreakable plastic tubes in Japan).[39]

Even industries such as pharmaceuticals, which may generally have more opportunities for globalization, still need to address varying and complex regulations and cultural norms around the globe. They need to tailor their advertising, or lack of advertising, to the specific market. They need to make their branding and packaging appeal to local consumers and vary their education according to the knowledge of, and comfort with, specific types of disease in different parts of the world. They may even need to focus their research and development on different types of conditions for different parts of the world and have to adjust their commercialization process to the specific regulatory constraints of different national systems.

Differences in approaches to treatment and technology adoption

These arguments may explain the observation that, at least to date, though nations often face similar types of illness and disease in their populations, they differ in the levels and types of treatment and service rendered.[40] For example, nations differ in the time and growth rate of new technology adoption, such as the take-up rate for new heart disease therapies (e.g. angioplasty), as well as the general population's interest in and support for new medical discoveries.[41] These differences should inform managers' decisions about introducing new products and services, or importing them from other nations, and, in some cases, might nullify plans to do so.

Different levels of spending

Nations differ not only in culture and in the organization of their healthcare systems, but also in the economics of healthcare, as indicated in their level of spending (e.g. as indexed by the proportion of GDP) on healthcare services, and in the means for financing this level of spending (user fees and insurance premiums, social insurance, or general taxation). In Europe alone, there are several relatively complex approaches to funding healthcare.[42] Both the level of funding and its complexity may present difficulties for firms seeking to become more global; at the very least, complex funding approaches tend to increase transaction costs for all players in the health sector, driving down efficiency. This may be more burdensome for small providers, organized as non-profit or even publicly owned entities and heavily regulated by their governments, than it is for larger, for-profit suppliers who may be better able to influence reimbursement policies.

Different concerns of developed and emerging economies

The Global Forum for Health Research and the Bill and Melinda Gates Foundation have noted that only 10 percent of medical research is devoted to the diseases that cause 90 percent of the world's health problems. This is primarily because there is less attention to the deadly diseases of emerging economies that lack the developed markets to support the development of treatments. To address this imbalance, the Gates Foundation has pledged $200 million to establish the Grand

Challenges in Global Health Initiative to convene top researchers to tackle global health problems. The National Institutes of Health in the United States will administer this initiative. Individual pharmaceutical companies also have addressed specific issues in emerging nations; an example is Merck's well-known development of a treatment of "river blindness." There is still a large gap between the concerns in developed nations, such as lowering cholesterol or addressing erectile dysfunction, which are the focal point of much commercial research, and the concerns of emerging economies about diseases such as tuberculosis and AIDS. To address this gap, major pharmaceutical companies have recently increased efforts to boost drug distribution to poor nations. For example, Eli Lilly has not only reduced the cost of its two traditional drugs for treating tuberculosis by 95 percent, but also developed a technology transfer program to allow other countries to make and sell their own supplies of the drugs. This is designed to increase the antibiotic supply, increase access, and improve affordability. And Pharmacia is negotiating with the non-profit International Dispensing Association of the Netherlands to sell inexpensive versions of its AIDS drug in poor countries.

The dark side of globalization

The factors that enable globalizing do not discriminate among the more and less desirable forms it may take. Whether it is "tourist healthcare" in Thailand, the global sourcing of nursing talent, global trafficking in organs, or the globalizing of the market for blood, there are a number of practices whose global reach is certainly worrisome. The shocking reports of human organs being harvested from prisoners in China for transplantation in patients elsewhere suggest that "market" forces are not an unmitigated good. The fact that the acute shortage of nurses in the United States is being addressed by importing nurses from the Philippines and elsewhere raises questions about whether the shortage in one country is simply being reproduced elsewhere. And stories about the spread of AIDS to farmers in rural China who are selling their blood to international blood collection and distribution ventures make one wonder about how supply and demand might be more effectively monitored and controlled. These faces in the shadows provide critics of globalization with plenty of ammunition. It is our view, however, that the factors enabling globalizing are neutral with respect to the ends to which they are applied, and it is up to the international community to define the limits of the permissible and desirable, and to determine how best to monitor and police activities that take place. That there are faces in the shadows is not an argument *per se* against globalization and these challenges may lead to greater global cooperation and integration if different nations and companies join together to address them.

The inertia of the current system

It is not just culture that limits healthcare reforms that might encourage globalizing but also the inertia of the status quo. The five-country survey cited above, which showed that consumers around the world are pushing for healthcare reform, also found that physicians in these countries are much less likely than the public to call for complete system overhauls. Such results suggest that professional groups that dominate the center of a healthcare system's value chain are not likely to drive systemic change, since such groups may be more satisfied with the status quo. For example, new evidence-based techniques in medicine often require fifteen to twenty years to diffuse fully to physicians in the United States. The inertia of physicians in the face of scientific evidence (often results from randomized controlled trials published in medical journals) becomes magnified in the face of major policy, regulatory, and reimbursement changes for which there is much less scientific basis. While there may be exceptions, physicians are likely to impede changes overall, including moves that would lead to greater global convergence. Existing systems in different parts of the world – supported by systems of education, regulation, and practice – may prove very difficult to change. In general, this will slow the process of convergence, a process that will be driven more by consumers and reformers demanding change.

Conclusions and management implications

What do these forces of global convergence and divergence mean for a manager such as Rolf Schmidt who is leading a global business in the healthcare sector? There are a variety of implications, including those which are discussed in the following sections.

Recognize the complexity

First of all, this mix of forces means that the context for global business is enormously complex. The opportunities for globalizing need to be examined for a specific company in a specific set of markets. As noted, the impact of globalization of a single sector such as healthcare affects different players differently. As we have seen, while service providers might face many obstacles in globalizing, pharmaceutical firms or device-makers might have a relatively easier time. By understanding the specific forces that are driving markets toward global integration and the contrary forces that are moving toward global fragmentation, managers can assess the potential impact for their firms. The opportunities depend on the nature of the industry, the players and processes involved, and the characteristics of individual national cultures and regulations. Also, these markets are in dynamic motion, so as the forces driving or inhibiting globalizing unfold, new opportunities will emerge from the interplay. Approaches that do not address these complex dynamics may lead to strategic errors in investments or cause managers to overlook strategic opportunities. What are the complex forces driving or impeding the move of your industry toward globalization and how do these forces create or limit specific opportunities for your firm?

Examine opportunities for rethinking the global business
A richer, more complex view of globalizing markets can help identify hidden strategic opportunities. For example, while conventional wisdom may be that healthcare service providers have few opportunities for globalizing, given the patchwork of different cultures and regulations, providers with global brands such as Mayo may be able to capitalize on forces such as converging consumer concerns for quality to establish global healthcare service operations. These provider initiatives are still very much experiments at this point, and their outcome is uncertain, but to see the possibility for such moves, the leaders of these organizations needed to break free of the view that it is nearly impossible to build a healthcare delivery business across national borders. Are there similar assumptions that limit your consideration of strategies in your industry? Are there ways to test these assumptions?

Examine opportunities for market entry
In addition to rethinking business models, opportunities can also be identified by looking at specific markets. For example, C. K. Prahalad and colleagues point out the potential for companies that "invest at the bottom of the pyramid"[43] by developing different business models and

products for emerging economies. They argue that two-thirds of the world's population (some 4 billion people) are too poor to participate in the global economy. Western firms can tap huge market potential and, at the same time, bring much needed development to these countries, through their investment decisions in local commerce and infrastructure development. To enter these markets, however, companies often need to rethink the design and delivery of their products and services to make them relevant and less expensive so they are within reach of consumers in these markets. Are there opportunities to enter these markets using a different approach and recognizing their distinctive cultures and concerns?

Carefully consider the costs of adaptation

Healthcare firms seeking to globalize must either invest significantly to learn about the culture and regulatory regimes of potential host nations (as well as develop the extensive social networks needed to do business there), or they must enter healthcare markets with local partners by means of strategic alliances or acquisitions. Consider, for example, that local licensing laws regulate who can provide care and that patients strongly prefer to receive care from professionals who are conversant in their native language. Healthcare providers seeking to globalize must hire local healthcare professionals to develop their local delivery networks or partner with firms that have this capability. There is a cost to this adaptation. Similarly, organizations that seek to adopt treatment or prevention practices and technologies, including medicines, from other nations must be aware of how local culture and regulations will affect their use.[44] In general, as is the case for other industries and sectors, the more that an organization doing business in the health sector must tailor its products and services to local markets and social conditions, the more expensive and difficult it is to globalize. What are the costs of adaptation in your industry and how do they limit your opportunities for globalizing?

Understand the contradictions

The central contradiction in consumers around the world demanding higher quality care, increased safety, *and* lower costs is a fundamental challenge for companies competing across or within global healthcare markets. Companies need to consider carefully how consumers are making tradeoffs among these competing goals, and how these tradeoffs may differ by country and in different economic periods. For example, a concern for lower costs may be expected to be greater in countries with a lower GDP or in economic downturns. Companies can also use these different concerns to segment the market. A business that can reduce costs will have an advantage in addressing segments that are most concerned about cutting expenses. On the other hand, organizations such as Mayo are betting that for at least a certain segment of the population, there will be the resources to pay for a "luxury" brand and that they can build a profitable business around this.

In addition to the clash of rising expectations and shrinking budgets, there are a variety of other balancing acts for nations and firms. There are increasingly more technological opportunities to treat disease (and now the genetic basis of disease), but such opportunities may be unrealized as nations confront the rising costs of care. There are increasing needs for chronic care and comprehensive care, while many nations have structured their healthcare systems around acute (inpatient) care. There are increasing calls for consumerism and patient-centered care, while healthcare delivery systems remain primarily provider-focused. There is an increasing recognition of the need for population-based healthcare planning and delivery, while most nations focus their healthcare resources on individuals. There is an increasing recognition of the importance of investment in information technology, and yet most information systems consist of disparate legacy systems that cannot easily speak to one another. Companies and nations are challenged to generate and utilize greater patient information, yet respecting patient privacy and maintaining confidentiality limit how this information can be used. Nations are confronted with the need to determine the appropriate balance among human resources, physical resources, technology, and pharmaceuticals in the overall mix of patient care.

Global markets have inherent contradictions, the most central of which is the simultaneous forces moving toward greater integration or toward fragmentation. Managers cannot resolve these contradictions, but must live with them. Understanding these contradictions can help managers better assess the risks and opportunities of their strategic initiatives. What are the global contradictions in your markets and how can you use them to segment the market or respond to changing economic conditions? What risks do these contradictions present for your firm?

The solutions that nations and companies craft to tackle these problems and tensions will be idiosyncratic and dynamic (i.e. shifting over time). Nevertheless, the issues that managers need to consider are quite similar, even if the strategies that they may pursue are very different. Managers need to examine the forces of globalization and countervailing forces. They need to understand the way these forces affect both players and processes. Finally, they need to understand the impact based on the position of their firm in the value chain of the industry.

There are very few players that can afford to ignore the forces of globalization and opportunities for globalizing. Even managers who are not facing a major decision, such as the merger presented to Rolf Schmidt, or currently have active global organizations need to make this a formal consideration in their strategy-making. There may be new opportunities outside of current markets or there may be new rivals who move in from abroad. This will be truer in the future. Notwithstanding the barriers to globalization discussed above, we conclude that these common perspectives are likely to fuel increased globalization of both players and practices in the years ahead.

The broad concern for healthcare around the globe is not only a reflection of its economic impact but also of its social impact. Even as they build or expand international businesses, globalizing companies need to be aware of this broader role. The challenge to the global community and to the business interests that are arrayed in and around the health sector will be to continue to promote practices and to encourage innovations that have the potential to maintain and improve the health of *all* people, not just those who can afford it.

Notes

1 W. L. Kissick, *Medicine's Dilemmas: Infinite Needs Versus Finite Resources* (New Haven: Yale University Press, 1994).
2 L. R. Burns *et al.*, *The Health Care Value Chain* (San Francisco: Jossey-Bass, 2002).
3 J. Northrup, "The Pharmaceutical Industry: A 2002 Perspective," presentation to the Wharton School, University of Pennsylvania.
4 World Travel and Tourism Council, *Key Statistics 2000*, available at http://www.wttc.org/economic_research/keystats.htm.
5 Ibid.

6 S. Rosen, J. Simon, J. Vincent, W. MacLeod, M. Fox, and D. Thea, "AIDS Is Your Business," *Harvard Business Review* (February 2003), pp. 81–87.

7 I. Kickbusch, "Influence and Opportunity: Reflections on the US Role in Global Public Health," *Health Affairs*, 21 (2002), pp. 131–141.

8 D. C. Esty *et al.*, "State Failure Task Force Report: Phase II Findings," *Environmental Change and Security Project Report*, no. 5 (Summer 1999), Woodrow Wilson Center, Washington, DC, pp. 49–72.

9 K. Shine and R. Anthony, "The Healthcare Doctrine," *Modern Healthcare*, July 14, 2003, p. 22.

10 C. K. Pralahad and S. L. Hart, "The Fortune at the Bottom of the Pyramid," *Strategy+Business* 26 (January 2002), pp. 54–67; C. K. Pralahad and A. Hammond, "Serving the World's Poor, Profitably," *Harvard Business Review*, September 2002, pp. 48–57; K. M. Lietzmann and G. D. Vest, "Environment and Security in an International Context: Executive Summary Report," *Environmental Change and Security Project Report*, no. 5 (Summer 1999), Woodrow Wilson Center, Washington, DC, pp. 34–48.

11 World Health Organization, *Macroeconomics and Health: Investing in Health for Economic Development* (Geneva, 2001), available at http//www3.who.int/whosis/cmh/cmh_report/.

12 C. Ramsey, *Beyond the Public–Private Debate: An Examination of Quality, Access, and Cost in the Health-Care Systems of Eight Countries* (Calgary: Marigold Foundation, 2001).

13 J. P. Newhouse, "Medical Care Expenditure: A Cross-National Survey," *Journal of Human Resources* 12 (1977), pp. 115–125; A. A. Okunade and V. N. R. Murthy, "Technology as a 'Major Driver' of Health Care Costs: A Cointegration Analysis of the Newhouse Conjecture," *Journal of Health Economics*, 21 (2002), pp. 147–159.

14 Rosen *et al.*, "AIDS Is Your Business."

15 P. G. Peterson, *Gray Dawn* (New York: Three Rivers Press, 2000).

16 "Note on the Impact of an Aging Population on the Ontario Health-Care System," University of Western Ontario, Richard Ivey School of Business, Case # 9B01B008, 2001; Robert Wood Johnson Foundation, *Chronic Care in America: A 21st Century Challenge* (Princeton, NJ: Robert Wood Johnson Foundation, 1996).

17 Okunade and Murthy, "Technology as a 'Major Driver' of Health Care Costs."

18 J. R. Kimberly, G. de Pouvourville, and associates, *The Migration of Managerial Innovation: DRGs and Health Care Administration in Western Europe* (San Francisco: Jossey-Bass, 1993).

19 L. T. Kohn, J. M. Corrigan, and M. S. Donaldson, *To Err is Human: Building a Safer Health System* (Washington, DC: National Academy Press, 1999). Committee on Quality of Health Care in America, *Crossing the Quality Chasm* (Washington, DC: National Academy Press, 2001); J. R. Kimberly and E. Minvielle, "Quality as an Organizational Problem," in S. S. Mick and M. Wyttenbach (eds.), *Advances in Health Care Organization Theory* (San Francisco: Jossey-Bass, 2003).

20 R. J. Blendon, C. Schoen, C. DesRoches, R. Osborn, and K. Zapert, "Common Concerns Amid Diverse Systems: Health Care Experiences in Five Countries," *Health Affairs*, 22 (2003), pp. 106–121; The Wanless Report on the National Health Service in the UK expressed concerns about long queues of patients seeking access to specialized services, arguing that the patient of the future will desire "safe, high quality treatment . . . [and] waiting within reason." Derek Wanless and HM Treasury, *Securing Our Future: Taking a Long-Term View* (London: HM Treasury, 2001), available at http://www.hm-treasury.gov.uk/Consultations_and_Legislation/Wanless/.

21 C. Becker, "Across the Pond," *Modern Healthcare*, September 15, 2003, p. 16.

22 R. J. Blendon, C. Schoen, K. Donelan, R. Osborn, C. DesRoches, K. Scoles, K. Davis, K. Binns, and K. Zapert, "Physicians' Views On Quality of Care: A Five Country Comparison," *Health Affairs*, 21 (2001), pp. 233–243.

23 S. Walston, J. R. Kimberly, and L. R. Burns, "Owned vertical integration and healthcare," *Health Care Management Review*, 21(1996), pp. 83–92.

24 K. Woods (2001), "The Development of Integrated Health Care Models in Scotland," *International Journal of Integrated Care*, 1(3), (http://www.ijic.org/).

25 N. Goodwin, "The Long-Term Importance of English Primary Care Groups for Integration in Primary Health Care and Deinstitutionalization of Hospital Care." *International Journal of Integrated Care* 1(1), (http://www.ijic.org/).

26 O. Grone and M. Garcia-Barbero, "Integrated Care: A Position Paper of the WHO European Office for Integrated Health Care Services," *International Journal of Integrated Care* 1(1), (http://www.ijic.org/).

27 Deloitte Touche Tohmatsu, *The Emerging European Health Telematics Industry: Market Analysis*. Report for Directorate General Information Society, European Commission, Brussels, 2000.

28 S. Globerman, H. Hodges, and A. Vining, "Canadian and the United States' Healthcare Systems Performance and Governance: Elements

of Convergence," *Applied Health Economics and Health Policy*, 1, 2 (2002), pp. 25–38; Organisation for Economic Co-operation and Development, *Measuring Up: Improving Health System Performance in OECD/Countries* (Paris: OECD, 2002).

29 T. R. Marmor, "Comparing Global Health Systems: Lessons and Caveats," in W. W. Wieners (ed.), *Global Health Care Markets* (San Francisco: Jossey-Bass, 2001).

30 M. Pottinger, E. Cherney, G. Naik, and M. Waldholz, "How Global Effort Found SARS Virus in Matter of Weeks." *Wall Street Journal*, April 16, 2003, p. A1.

31 Organisation for Economic Co-operation and Development, *Health Data 2001: Comparative Analysis of 30 Countries* (Paris: OECD/CREDES, 2001).

32 Organisation for Economic Co-operation and Development, *Measuring Up*. World Health Organization, *The World Health Report 2000. Health Systems: Improving Performance* (Geneva, 2000).

33 R. J. Blendon, C. Schoen, C. M. DesRoches, R. Osborn, K. L. Scoles, and K. Zapert, "Inequities in Health Care: A Five-Country Survey," *Health Affairs*, 21 (2002), pp. 182–191.

34 Blendon *et. al.*, "Physicians' Views on Quality of Care."

35 L. H. Aiken, S. P. Clarke, and D. M. Sloane (2002), "Hospital Staffing, Organization, and Quality of Care: Cross-National Findings," *International Journal for Quality in Health Care*, 14 (2002), pp. 5–13.

36 The Technological Change in Health Care (TECH) Research Network, "Technological Change Around the World: Evidence From Heart Attack Care," *Health Affairs*, 20 (2001), pp. 25–42; M. Kim, R. J. Blendon, and J. M. Benson, "How Interested are Americans in New Medical Technologies? A Multicountry Comparison," *Health Affairs*, 20 (2001), pp. 194–209.

37 Milbank Memorial Fund, *Informing Judgment: Case Studies of Health Policy and Research in Six Countries* (New York: Milbank Memorial Fund, 2001).

38 V. Roberts, J. Calhoun, R. Jones, F. Sun, and M. Fottler, "Globalization of U.S. Health Care Services: Assessment and Implementation," *Health Care Management Review*, 25, 3 (2000), pp. 24–25.

39 C. Christensen, "Becton Dickinson: Worldwide Blood Collection Team" (abridged), Harvard Business School, case No. 9-698-058.

40 Ibid.

41 The Technological Change in Health Care (TECH) Research Network, "Technological Change Around the World."

42 E. Mossialos, A. Dixon, J. Figueras, and J. Kutzin (eds.), *Funding Health Care: Options for Europe*, European Observatory on Health Care Systems, series (Buckingham, England: Open University Press, 2002).

43 Pralahad and Hart, "Fortune at the Bottom of the Pyramid"; Pralahad and Hammond, "Serving the World's Poor, Profitably."

44 J. Eisenberg, "Globalize the Evidence, Localize the Decision: Evidence-Based Medicine and International Diversity," *Health Affairs*, 21 (2002), pp. 166–168.

18 | *Conclusion: The continuing process of globalizing*

HUBERT GATIGNON
INSEAD

JOHN R. KIMBERLY
Wharton School

W HILE our focus in this volume, as stated at the outset, has been to aid managers in understanding and improving the process of globalizing their companies, we must recognize that there is a much broader context in which these decisions are made. World political structures are changing rapidly and often unpredictably in the post-Cold War era. The rules for humanitarian intervention or the pursuit of terrorists are being written both by individual political leaders and supranational organizations such as the United Nations, the World Trade Organization and the European Union, and the outcomes in shaping the environment of business remain uncertain.

Business used to be a player on a world stage. Increasingly, however, business has become a shaper of that world stage. For better or for worse, the globalizing of business is inextricably linked to the globalization of society. Corporations have become such central players in the process of globalization that they have been portrayed both as essential engines of progress and as wanton destroyers of value, depending on who is making the judgment.

Beyond globalization to "McDonaldization"

Global corporations are thus seen as having tremendous powers for good or for evil. On the positive side, Thomas Friedman observed in 1999 that "No two countries that both had McDonald's had fought a war against each other since each got its McDonald's."[1] His so-called "Golden Arches Theory of Conflict Prevention" was an exaggeration, perhaps, but he makes the point that the spread of global businesses can lead to greater political stability.

On the other hand, the same company's ubiquitous fast-food logo has become a target of attack for global protesters angry at Westernization.

George Ritzer's 1993 book, *The McDonaldization of Society,* uses a corporate brand to represent a certain process of globalization. Casting the discussion of "globalization" as "McDonaldization" shows how inextricably intermingled globalization is with the expansion of individual corporations. In this work, the globalizing of a company has become a focal point for the discussion of the globalization of the planet (of course with an emphasis on many of the things that are wrong, in the author's view, with both the company and the planet).[2]

Ritzer's more recent work, *The Globalization of Nothing,* takes this argument even farther, arguing that the ubiquitous corporate logos are a sign of increasingly dehumanized services and society.[3] He argues that we are moving from the "something" of local, indigenous culture to the "nothing" of dehumanized and centrally controlled homogenization. While we may not agree with this assessment, the questions raised in these and other critiques of modern business highlight the intense challenges and responsibilities that are now placed at the feet of global corporations. Can we expect businesses to be responsible for providing *meaning* to citizens of cultures around the world? In the postwar United States, no one expected McDonald's or Coca-Cola to deliver more than a Big Mac or a Coke. Has something changed? Whether global companies like it or not, they are in the middle of the street protests about globalization. It does not matter whether they *should* be expected to deliver more of "something," but they *are* expected to serve a much deeper role as citizens of the diverse countries in which they operate. The corporation often has to step into the vacuum of global political and economic infrastructures, and corporate executives were among the first to deplane when markets such as Russia and China began to crack open.

A business to run

Even as commentators and protesters bandy its name about in the media or on the streets, McDonald's – the company, not the corporate icon – still has a business to run. In January 2003, the company announced the first quarterly loss since it went public in 1965. While the company had spent considerable time and expense focusing on issues such as corporate responsibility, including issuing a "corporate social responsibility" report, it was not global protesters that brought about these financial challenges. The problems were not a direct result of citizens being upset with the "McDonaldization" of society; rather, they arose from a strategy of rapid growth in a mature industry. The company that had rapidly built more than 30,000 restaurants in more than 100 countries now faced some basic business challenges. It needed to throttle back on its expansion.

At a meeting with investors in April 2003, chairman and CEO Jim Cantalupo said that "The world has changed. Our customers have changed. We have to change, too."[4] He subsequently announced that the company made a strategic shift "concentrate on building sales at existing restaurants rather than adding new ones."[5]

The debates over globalization and its consequences are fascinating in the abstract. For managers, however, the abstractions have very concrete implications. The challenges in a globalizing world are far more complex; the decisions are more fraught with risks. While the attacks of street protesters and critics may be important, ultimately the business succeeds or fails according to its ability to create value for customers at a reasonable profit. Early on, McDonald's was a master in recognizing and seizing the opportunities for carrying its brand, products, and service into far-flung markets. It was able to create local infrastructures of suppliers to support its standardized offering in different parts of the world. Globalizing was a key part of its continued success as its domestic market began to mature. But the world continued to change. The company's success going forward depends on its decisions about growth, market entry, and global branding. While these strategic decisions may not be driven by the discussions of globalization that appear daily in the international headlines, they are made in a global context.

Insights for managers

The preceding chapters offer a variety of insights for managers on globalizing. While we will not attempt to summarize them on a chapter-by-chapter basis here (this is done briefly in Chapter 1 and at the beginning of each chapter), there are certain overriding themes and insights that cut across the various chapters that we would like to highlight by way of conclusion.

Take a globalizing view of world markets and operations
A global perspective helps identify opportunities to access more markets, expand sales, and realize economies of scale and scope. These

opportunities often come from taking advantage of the interdependencies between countries offered by worldwide operations. Although complex to understand, the benefits of a global as opposed to a multi-country approach, as described in the various chapters of this book, are overwhelming. And although it is not always possible or desirable to develop global approaches, consideration of these opportunities should be a constant part of developing business strategies.

Avoid going to extremes

As we have seen in several of the chapters in this volume, at various points in time, there have been some who have argued that companies should move to a completely uniform global strategy and others who have been equally vehement about the importance of a localized strategy. From branding to product design to leadership to supply chains, the answer is often somewhere in between. As Mauro F. Guillén points out in his book *The Limits of Convergence*, globalization does not lead to common organizational patterns or best practices across firms in different nations. The distinctive economic, political, and social features of national economies shape the trajectories of individual companies in specific countries.[6] On the other hand, national differences do not necessarily lead to the fragmented world portrayed by Samuel P. Huntington in *The Clash of Civilizations*.[7] The real impact of globalization is much more complex, and the solutions are far more nuanced. There are times when it makes sense to create global brands, but other times when these brands are not effective. These decisions have to be made on a case-by-case basis, and in the context of careful analysis of risks and opportunities, not on the dogmatic adoption of a simplistic position on globalization.

Carefully assess the risks

Global business presents new and sometimes unexpected risks. The insights of Paul Kleindorfer and Luk Van Wassenhove on supply chain risks in Chapter 12 and the analysis of financial risks by Gordon Bodnar, Bernard Dumas, and Richard Marston in Chapter 11 highlight two areas of particular importance to managers. These new risks mean that we need to take a fresh look at models such as CAPM to see how they need to be modified in this environment. By better understanding the nature of these risks, we can find more appropriate ways to address them, thus avoiding the trap of being either too cautious or not cautious enough.

Appreciate the broader context

The process of globalizing is a process of changing and expanding context. A player that had defined itself in terms of a domestic market now has to redefine itself for diverse national markets. National regulations are an important part of that context, and the patchwork of national regulations that governs global business is a significant source of risk and, sometimes, opportunities. The idiosyncrasies of these regulations, as highlighted by Ethan Kapstein and Stephen Kobrin in Chapter 15 create significant challenges for business leaders. Changing technologies, as discussed by Arnoud de Meyer in Chapter 16, further complicate the situation, as technological advances can overleap or erase borders, creating international moral and legal dilemmas for companies that do not even leave their domestic turf. Finally, the rising expectations for companies for "global citizenship," as seen in the discussion by Eric Orts, demands an even broader context for corporate actions.

Leadership has never been more important

The complexity of global decisions, the rapidity of change, and the patchwork of national cultures that need to be brought together into a corporate culture make leadership more important than ever. As Mike Useem points out in Chapter 3, in times of rapid change, leadership can make the most difference. Yet the qualities of leadership need to be adapted to the demands of specific cultures, as Mansour Javidan, Günter Stahl, and Robert House note in Chapter 4. While corporate governance may not converge to a Western model, the forces of institutional investors could be expected to lead to more homogenization and these investors will play a role in the development of businesses around the world. At the end of the day, the process of globalizing for any company is the result of a set of very difficult decisions made in the CEO's office and corporate board rooms, and by countless leaders throughout the organization. The global strategy is implemented across complicated, far-flung organizations and leaders need to be able to chart a clear and thoughtful path through this turbulent world.

Finally, business leaders need to recognize that they have a role in shaping the global context for their businesses. A global environment that is in flux means that there are opportunities to be active in affecting the way global economics and regulations develop.

Research challenges

While the chapters in this volume offer many useful insights on globalizing business, there is much more that needs to be known. Some of the key challenges for researchers in this area are set out in the following sections.

Develop better global data sets

Broad and long-term studies such as the global leadership research project reported on in Chapter 4 are few and far between. Even when global data exist, it is often hard to wrench meaningful conclusions from them. The sheer complexity and quantity make analyzing global business very difficult, and teasing out management implications is even more challenging, given the many different countries and companies involved. To what extent, for example, do insights on business in France apply in China? Or do those from Singapore apply in Germany? Furthermore, we need to insure that research efforts are aligned with the pace of change in business. Data collection and analysis must be linked realistically to the temporal context of the problems being examined. Otherwise, we risk elegant irrelevance.

Create global research publications and centers

As noted in Chapter 1, incentives need to be created for faculty involvement in research on global issues in business. Faculty tend to be rewarded for progress in their disciplines, and the multidisciplinary character of global issues thus can become a distraction from career advancement. Furthermore, there are relatively few outlets for scholarly research on global issues. We need to develop new publications, supported by both academics and managers, to provide a forum and incentive for researchers to explore these areas. Further, schools that are intensely focused on disciplinary research need to create centers, departments, and other mechanisms (such as this book) to encourage global research. While there has been a positive trend toward *integration* of global topics into the business school curriculum – it should be a part of all business decisions – this approach, which works well for education, may not be the most practical approach for global research. The drivers of disciplinary research are such a strong part of the academic culture that without some countervailing force, there will be little momentum for the kind of research that is so vital in this age.

Document the benefits of globalizing businesses to the citizens of the world, especially those from less-favored nations

Although there is a plethora of macroeconomic research attempting to demonstrate the benefits of global business to poor countries, the controversy remains as to the effects of globalization in general, as demonstrated by a recent study for the IMF.[8] For the most part, these studies fail to identify causality because of the cross-sectional nature (comparison across countries) of the analysis. An analysis of the effect of management policies and practices over time is needed to evaluate changes in population welfare. This requires in-depth, time-series analysis of data from individual firms in the process of globalizing.

Conclusions

We hope that this book has provided new insights on how managers can put into practice management principles that will allow us better to serve the people of the world while optimizing the firms' long-term interests at the same time. The two are certainly not mutually exclusive. Even many anti-globalization protesters recognize the positive effects of a globalizing world, arguing for an altered approach to globalization rather than an abandonment of it. These views are not in conflict with the view of management taken in this book where, for the long-term benefits of their enterprises, globalizing firms must adopt a management vision that is global in the scope of activities (i.e. recognizing and taking advantage of all the interdependencies that exist across countries) but also global in responsibility toward the citizens of the world.

A dialogue is necessary between the proponents and opponents of globalization. Failures such as the meeting at Cancún in the summer of 2003 are devastating for the development of many nations and those citizens that suffer from poverty. It should be clear from this book that globalizing does not mean simple standardization of products or services, prices, or brands.[9] It is not synonymous either with broad macroeconomic policies elaborated and implemented by international institutions (largely dominating what has been written recently on globalization).

Economic development is indispensable for improving the conditions of poor populations, and such development requires strong and effective international businesses. For economic development to occur, we need corporate leaders who can effectively manage the globalizing process by coordinating management across countries, including assessing interactions across markets, developing brands and products, managing global financial risks, and designing supply chains. To manage a globalizing process efficiently for the long term, firms must take into account the multiple publics with which they are concerned, including shareholders, customers, employees, society at large, and the environment (this includes reactionary forces against globalization). One objective we hope to have achieved in this book is to improve the dialogue between the various actors in the international arena (whether private firms, governments, international institutions, or non-governmental organizations) by providing a better understanding of how firms that increasingly operate at a global level are managed.

The very practical guidelines summarized in this concluding chapter should be a springboard towards greater collaboration between academic, business, and political leaders, encouraging improved decision-making for the good of all.

We invite you to join in this ongoing discussion. This is a central focus of the Alliance between Wharton and INSEAD, and we intend to continue to explore this issue through research and further publications in the years ahead. We welcome your suggestions for research topics, cases to study, and approaches so that we all can continue to learn from this great experiment.

Notes

1 T. L. Friedman, *The Lexus and the Olive Tree* (New York: Anchor Books, 2000), p. 248.
2 G. Ritzer, *The McDonaldization of Society* (Thousand Oaks, CA: Pine Forge Press, 1993).
3 G. Ritzer, *The Globalization of Nothing: So Many Making So Much of So Little* (Thousand Oaks, CA: Pine Forge Press, 2003).
4 "Did Somebody Say A Loss?" *Economist*, April 10, 2003; also at http://www.economist.com/displaystory.cfm?story_id=1705522.

5 McDonald's Corporation press release, April 28, 2003; also at http://www.mcdonalds.com/corporate/press/financial/2003/04282003/index.html.
6 M. F. Guillén, *The Limits of Convergence* (Princeton, NJ: Princeton University Press, 2001).
7 S. P. Huntington, *The Clash of Civilizations and the Remaking of World Order* (New York: Simon & Schuster, 1997).
8 E. Prasad, K. Rogoff, S.-J. Wei, and M. A. Kose, "Effects of Financial Globalization on Developing Countries. Some Empirical Evidence," International Monetary Fund working paper, March 17, 2003.
9 Ritzer, *The McDonaldization of Society*.

Author index

Aaker, D. A. 205, 206
Abernathy, W. 380
Abuaf, N. 272
Aditya, R. N. 101, 102
Adler, M. 285
Adler, N. J. 103
Adner, R. 308
Agrarwal, N. 305
Ahuja, G. 313
Aiken, L. H. 420
Ainslie, A. 225, 226, 227
Akerlof, G. A. 247
Albert, S. 327
Alden, D. 205
Allen, T. J. 393
Almeida, P. 313, 327, 328
Amit, R. 17, 35, 52
Anderson, E. 21, 228
Anderson, J. W. Jr. 348
Anderson, P. 18, 324, 328, 389
Angelmar, R. 15, 182, 209, 224
Anthony, R. 418
Aoki, M. 47
Appeldoorn, B. van 47
Arino, A. 157
Arlington, S. 182
Armstrong, J. S. 329
Ascarelli, S. 76
Avolio, B. J. 101

Bacdayan, P. 157
Baird, R. 205
Balakrishnan, S. 156
Balligand, J.-P. 48
Banisar, D. 375
Barham, K. 102
Barkema, H. 158
Barnett, S. 182
Barney, J. 21
Barras, R. 379

Barry, B. 340, 348
Barsoux, J.-L. 103
Bartholomew, S. 103
Bartlett, C. 107, 155, 180, 181, 182
Bass, B. M. 101
Batra, R. 205
Beck, T. 33
Becker, C. 419
Belke, J. C. 305
Benson, J. M. 420
Berger, S. 46
Bergh, D. 69
Berle, A. A. Jr. 347
Bernstein, A. 21
Bhandway, S. 392, 393
Bijker, W. E. 327, 328
Bilter, C. 205
Binns, K. 420
Black, B. S. 252
Black, J. S. 102, 103
Blackett 205
Blass, A. 251
Blendon, R. J. 419, 420
Bodnar, G. 17, 285, 303, 425
Boer, M. de 329
Bolande, H. A. 181
Bonchikhi, H. 127
Boutelier, R. 327
Boyer, R. 46
Bradley, K. 327
Brady, D. 21
Brake, T. 102
Branson, D. 47
Braunerhjelm, P. 327
Breeden, D. 114
Brefort, L. 75
Brennan, M. 281
Brilmayer, L. 348
Brooker, K. 205
Buckley, P. J. 155

Burkhart, R. 155
Burns, L. R. 20, 398, 417, 419
Burt, R. 328
Byrne, J. A. 75

Cachon, G. 304, 305
Calhoun, J. 420
Campbell, A. 206
Capel, K. 205
Carlsson, B. 327
Casper, S. 47
Casson, M. C. 155
Caves, R. E. 155
Cerny, P. G. 26–46
Cetindamar, D. 327
Chang, S.-J. 48, 155
Chatterjee, S. 69
Checa, N. 21
Chemmanur, T. 245
Cherney, E. 420
Chesnais, F. 46
Chordia, T. 281
Christensen, C. 420
Chu, W. 228
Chua 392
Clarke, S. P. 420
Clewlow, L. 305
Cockburn, I. A. 329
Cockburn, I. M. 328
Coffee, J. C. 46, 349
Cohen, M. 157, 305, 350
Cohen, S. 47
Cohen, W. M. 155, 328
Collins, H. 329
Collins, J. C. 82, 101, 102
Conger, J. A. 83, 101
Conyon, M. J. 64
Corrigan, J. M. 418
Courtney, M. 7
Cowhey, P. 376
Craig, C. S. 182
Croffi, J. 47
Crystal, G. S. 349
Cusumano, M. 329

D'Aunno, T. 20
Dabora, E. 284
Dabuko, G. D. 418
Dahan, E. 181, 182, 183
Dalal, D. 182

Darby, M. R. 329
Datta, D. K. 157
Davidson, W. H. 226, 227
Davies, S. 375
Davis, J. H. 59
Davis, K. 420
Davis-Blake, A. 158
Dawar, N. 228
Day, G. S. 16, 206
De Laat, P. B. 328
De Mooij, M. 205
Dekimpe, M. 220, 225, 226
Demeester, L. 392
Demirgüç-Kunt, A. 33
Derber, C. 351
DeSarbo, W. S. 225, 226, 227
DesRoches, C. 419, 420
DeTore, A. 182
Dewey, J. 333
Dickson, M. 102
Diermeier, J. 284
DiMasi, J. A. 182
Dimson, E. 259
Dinur, A. 320
Dixon, A. 421
Dodd, E. M. Jr. 347
Donaldson, M. S. 418
Donaldson, T. 347
Donelan, K. 419, 420
Dore, R. 46, 47
Dorfman, P. W. 102
Dosi, G. 155
Douglas, S. P. 180, 182
Downing, W. C. 347
Doz, Y. 106, 155, 156, 157, 182, 183, 393
Drache, D. 46
Drake, W. 376
Du Pont, E. I. de Nemours 265
Duffy, T. 205
Dumas, B. 17, 284, 285, 286, 303, 425
Dutta, S. 392, 393
Dvorak, P. 74
Dyer, J. 157

Eden, D. 101
Egidi, M. 155
Eisenberg, J. 421
Eliashberg, J. 22, 225, 226, 227
Elliott, M. R. 305

Engardio, P. 21
Eppinger, S. D. 182
Errunza, V. 284
Escalle, C. 304
Esty, D. C. 418
Eun, C. S. 251
Evans, P. 103

Fama, E. 281, 282, 283
Farmakides, M.-L. 205
Farrell, H. 375
Fein, A. J. 228
Feketekuty, G. 367
Feldma, H. I. 305
Felton, R. F. 75
Fields, K. J. 48
Figueras, J. 421
Fine, C. H. 305
Finkelstein, S. 158, 324
Fisher, M. 305
Fleming, L. 328
Fliess, B. 364, 377
Fligstein, N. 47
Forrester, J. W. 305
Fottler, M. 420
Foucauld, J.-B. de 48
Fowler, K. 158
Fox, M. B. 349, 418
Fraser, A. J. 253
Fredrickson, J. 65
Freeman, R. E. 348
French, K. 281, 282, 283
Friedman, M. 334
Friedman, T. 4–5, 21, 422
Froot, K. 284
Fubini, D. 158
Fulghieri, P. 245

Garcia-Barbero, M. 419
Gassman, O. 327
Gatignon, H. 16, 21, 22, 225, 226, 227, 228
Geoffrion, A. 304
George, V. 328
Gervais, P. 183
Ghemawat, P. 227
Ghoshal, S. 107, 155
Gielens, K. 220
Gilfillan, S. C. 327
Gilson, R. J. 252

Gimeno, J. 56, 75
Globerman, S. 419
Goetzmann, W. 281
Goffee, R. 101
Goldstone, J. A. 418
Gompers, P. 68
Gongla, P. 330
Goodwin, N. 419
Goold, M. 206
Gorindarajan, V. 206
Gourevitch, P. 72, 75
Gowan, P. 46
Grabowski, H. G. 182
Granovetter, M. S. 22
Grant, J. H. 157
Graver, D. 348
Gray, J. 351
Gregersen, H. B. 102, 103
Griffin, A. 227
Grone, O. 419
Guide, V. D. R. Jr 305
Guillén, M. F. 11, 13, 21, 22, 47, 48, 72, 77, 155, 425
Gulland, E. 349
Gunter, S. J. 205
Gupta, A. K. 206
Gupta, V. 102
Gurr, T. R. 418
Guth, R. A. 74

Haleblian, J. 158
Hall, B. J. 61, 75
Hall, P. 46
Hamel, G. 157
Hammond, A. 418, 421
Hanges, P. J. 102
Hansen, M. T. 329
Hansen, R. W. 182
Harff, B. 418
Harrigan, R. 226, 227
Harrison, J. 69
Hart, S. L. 418, 421
Harvey, C. R. 282, 284
Haspeslagh, P. 156, 157, 158
Haunschild, P. 158
Hauser, J. R. 180, 181, 182, 183
Hausmann, H. 46, 47
Hayward, M. 158
Heckeren, J. van 75

Heide, J. B. 228
Helsen, K. 180, 225, 226, 227
Henderson, R. M. 328, 329
Henisz, W. J. 156
Hennart, J.-F. 156
Herstatt, C. 328
Hertz, N. 351
Heston, S. 281
Higg, D. 70
Hill, M. A. 56, 75
Hippel, E. von 327
Hodges, H. 419
Hofstede, F. ter 180, 181, 226
Hofstede, G. 180
House, R. J. 14, 58, 100, 101, 102,
    426
Huchzermeier, A. 304
Hudnut, A. 75
Hughes, S. 182
Hultink, E. J. 227
Huntington, S. P. 425
Hwee, C. C. 181
Hymer, S. H. 155

Inkpen, A. 320
Ishii, J. 68

Jacquillat, B. 267, 284
Jain, D. C. 226, 227
Javidan, M. 14, 100, 101, 102, 426
Jedidi, K. 225, 226, 227
Jemison, D. 156, 157, 158
Joachimsthaler, E. 205, 206
Johansson, D. 327
Johansson, J. K. 181, 225
Jones, G. 101
Jones, R. 420
Jönsson, B. 181
Jorion, P. 281
Jürgens, U. 48

Kale, P. 148, 157
Kalish, S. 215–216
Kamakura, W. A. 180
Kang, J. 375
Kano, N. 176
Kanungo, R. 101
Kapferer, J.-N. 205
Kapstein, E. 19, 303, 377, 426
Kassinis, G. 65
Kedia, B. L. 102

Kellerhals, A. 350
Kessler, H. 347
Khermonch, G. 21
Kickbusch, I. 418
Kiedel, R. W. 102
Kim, L. 330
Kim, M. 420
Kimberly, J. R. 20, 127, 418, 419
Kirmani, A. 228
Kissick, W. L. 417
Klein, N. 206
Kleindorfer, P. R. 18, 304, 305, 425
Klimenko, M. 376
Kobrin, S. 19, 303, 426
Kodama, F. 327
Kogut, B. 155, 156, 327
Kohn, L. T. 418
Korten, D. 351
Kose, M. A. 430
Kotabe, M. 180
Kotler, P. 180
Kouzes, J. M. 101
Koza, M. P. 156, 157
Kraakman, R. 46, 47
Kripalani, M. 21
Krishnan, R. 304
Krishnan, T. V. 227
Kuemmerle, W. 307
Kuester, S. 227
Kühlmann, T. M. 102
Kulatilaka, N. 155
Kumar, V. 227
Kunreutherm, H. 305
Kutzin, J. 421

Lazonick, W. 47
Lee, C. 284
Lee, K. 305
Lehnerd, A. P. 182
Leonard, D. 182
Lessard, D. R. 287
Levine, R. 33
Levinthal, D. 156, 308, 328
Levitt, T. 15–16, 159, 171, 172, 173,
    184–185, 186, 188, 192, 195, 204
Levy, M. 418
Lewin, A. 157
Liebman, J. B. 61, 75
Lietzmann, K. M. 418
Lilien, G. L. 227
Lindblom, C. E. 351

Lindgren, P. 181
Lindseth, P. L. 351
Litan, R. E. 375
Loch, C. H. 304
Losq, V. 284
Lowe, R. A. 305
Luthje, C. 328

Mabry, L. 349
MacIntosh, M. 347
MacLeod, W. 418
Madsen, T. K. 183
Maesincee, S. 226
Maguire, J. 21
Mahajan, V. 215–216, 226
Maitland, A. 346
Maksimovic, V. 253
Maney, K. 181
Manus, L. 205
March, J. 156, 259
Marengo, L. 155
Marmor, T. R. 407
Marston, R. 17, 285, 303, 425
Marten, T. 377
Martin, J. 348
Masson, G. 205
Mayer, C. L. 348
Mayer, R. C. 59
McAlister, D. T. 347
McCarthy, C. 205
McCarthy, J. 21
McDowell, J. 182
McGrath, R. G. 228
Meier, C. S. 351
Mendenhall, M. E. 102, 103
Merck, G. 82
Metiu, A. 328
Metrick, A. 68
Meyer, A. De 19, 127, 181, 327, 392, 393, 426
Meyer, M. H. 182
Mian, S. 59
Michaels, R. E. 227
Miller, T. 180
Minvielle, E. 418
Mitton, T. 68
Model, D. 351
Moon, Y. 181
Morin, F. 43, 48
Morita, A. 327
Morrison, A. J. 102, 103

Moskowitz, H. R. 181
Mossialos, E. 421
Muchin, K. 76
Mukherji, A. 102
Muller, E. 215–216, 226
Murthy, V. N. R. 418

Naik, G. 420
Naughton, K. 160, 180
Nelson, R. 130, 157
Nerkar, A. 327, 328, 329
Newhouse, J. P. 418
Nobeoka, K. 329
Noguerra, C. 205
Nonaka, I. 183
Norris, P. 350
Northrup, J. 417

O'Keefe, B. 205, 392
O'Sullivan, M. 13, 46, 47, 48, 72
Okoniewski, E. A. 349
Okunade, A. A. 418
Olshavsky, R. W. 227
Orts, E. W. 18, 347, 350, 388, 426
Osborn, R. 419, 420
Osland, J. 102

Palo, J. 182
Papadakis, I. 304
Parker, P. M. 225, 226, 228
Parkha, A. 157
Parthiban, D. 56, 75
Peck, S. I. 64
Pennings, J. 158
Peterson, R. 305
Phimister, J. R. 305
Pichler, P. 253
Podolny, J. 328
Porras, J. I. 101, 102
Porter, M. E. 181
Posner, B. Z. 101
Pottinger, M. 420
Powell, B. 150
Powers, W. C. Jr 74
Prahalad, C. K. 155, 381, 414, 418, 421
Prasad, E. 430
Pratini de Moraes, M. V. 226
Preston, L. E. 347
Price, C. 158
Pucik, V. 102, 103

Puranam, P. 58, 101, 150, 157
Pyke, D. F. 305

Qualls, W. 227
Quinn, J. B. 309, 324

Rabino, S. 181
Radice, D. 181
Raghuram, G. R. 58–59
Ramírez, G. G. 58, 101
Ramsey, C. 418
Rao, A. R. 228
Rayport, J. F. 182
Redaelloi, A. 181
Reddy, S. 156
Reibstein, D. 16
Reingold, E. M. 327
Reuer, J. J. 156, 157, 158
Rhodes, M. 47
Rice, R. E. 329
Rigamonti, E. 43, 48
Rischard, J. F. 344, 350, 351
Ritter, J. R. 243, 252
Ritzer, G. 423, 430
Rizzuto, C. R. 330
Roberts, V. 420
Robertson, D. 182, 183, 226
Robertson, T. S. 22, 225, 226,
   227
Roch, M. P. 375
Rogers, E. M. 329
Rogoff, K. 430
Roll, R. 281
Romano, R. 347
Rosen, S. 418
Rosenberg, T. 12, 21, 22
Rosenkopf, L. 18, 313, 327, 328, 329,
   389
Rosenman, Z. 76
Ross, I. 376
Roth, W.-H. 349
Rouwenhorst, G. 281
Ruiz, P. 284
Rupp, J. 48

Saba, T. 102, 103
Sabherwal, S. 251
Santos, J. 106, 155, 182, 183, 393
Sarvary, M. 225, 226
Sauve, P. 364, 377

Scanlon, T. 352
Schmidt, D. 158
Schmidt, V. 48
Schmoch, U. 329
Schoen, C. 419, 420
Schoorman, D. 59
Schultz, P. 252
Schumpeter, J. 307
Schwartz, J. 349
Scola, G. 205
Scoles, K. L. 420
Sen, A. 347, 348
Sercu, P. 286
Shamir, B. 101
Sheen, G. 205
Shimomura, M. 327
Shine, K. 418
Shinn, J. 72, 75
Shleifer, A. 284
Silver, E. 305
Simon, J. 418
Singer, J. 74
Singh, H. 15, 45, 150, 157, 158
Sitkin, S. 158
Skilling, J. 50
Sloane, D. M. 420
Smith, D. G. 347
Snow, J. 65
Sohnenfeld, J. A. 74
Solnik, B. 267, 284, 285, 286
Song, J. 327
Soros, G. 5, 21
Soskice, D. 46, 47
Srivastava, S. 392, 393
Stabile, S. J. 349
Stahl, G. 14, 102, 103, 426
Staunton, M. 259
Steenkamp, J.-B.E.M. 180, 181, 205,
   226
Stiglitz, J. E. 21, 350
Stinchcombe, A. L. 252
Story, J. 22
Strange, S. 29, 46, 47
Stremersch, S. 226
Strickland, C. 305
Stroh, L. K. 103
Strudler, A. 347
Stuart, S. 76
Stuart, T. 328
Subrahmanyam, A. 281

Sudhir, K. 225, 226, 227
Sun, F. 420
Surko, P. T. 418
Swartz, M. 74
Swire, P. P. 375
Szulanski, G. 319, 329

Takada, H. 227
Takeuchi, H. 181, 183
Talukdar, D. 225, 226, 227
Tan, H. H. 59
Taylor, N. 374
Tener, S. 75
Thaler, A. 284
Thea, D. 418
Thomas, R. S. 349
Thomke, S. 327
Thompson, D. 343–344
Thornton, E. 160, 180
Tichy, N. M. 347
Tiessen, J. H. 329
Troubh, R. S. 74
Truten, D. 350
Tsai, W. 329
Tufts, J. H. 333
Tushman, M. 328

Ulrich, K. T. 182
Unger, A. N. 418
Urban, G. L. 180
Useem, M. 14, 26, 46, 74, 426
Utterback, J. 380

Vafeas, N. 65
Van den Bosch, F. A. J. 329
Van den Bulte, C. 16, 225, 226, 227
Van der Heyden, L. 304
Van Wassenhove, L. 18, 304, 305, 392, 425
Vernon, R. 156
Vest, G. D. 418
Vincent, J. 418
Vining, A. 419
Vitols, S. 47
Volberda, H. W. 329
Von Hippel, E. 181, 328, 393

Waddock, S. A. 347
Waldholz, M. 420
Waldman, D. A. 58, 101

Walston, S. 419
Wanless, D. 419
Ward, I. 350
Warglien, M. 155
Wathne, K. H. 228
Watts, D. 327
Wedel, M. 180, 181, 226
Wei, S.-J. 430
Weiler, J. H. H. 350
Welch, J. 14, 62, 75, 243, 252
Wells, L. T. 226
Wells, P. 182
Wenger, E. 329
Werhane, P. 348
Westphael, J. 65
Williamson, O. E. 156
Williamson, P. 106, 155, 181, 182, 183, 392, 393
Wills, S. 102
Wind, Y. 180, 226
Winokur, H. S. Jr. 74
Winter, S. 130, 155, 157, 158, 319, 329
Wójcik, D. 48
Woods, K. 419
Woolcock, S. 47
Wright, N. S. 101, 102
Wu, D. J. 304
Wu, G. 327
Wulf, J. 58–59

Yafeh, Y. 251
Yermack, D. 63
Yeung, A. K. 103
Yip, G. S. 226
Yücesan, E. 304
Yukl, G. A. 84, 101

Zaman, M. 252
Zander, U. 155, 327
Zapert, K. 419, 420
Zaun, T. 74
Zedtwitz, M. von 327
Zhang, C. 75
Ziemba, W. 304
Zingales, L. 252
Zollo, M. 15, 45, 155, 156, 157, 158
Zott, C. 17, 35, 52
Zucker, L. G. 329

Subject index

20th Century Fox, global launch 208

Abbott Laboratories 60, 265
Absolut 196
absorptive capacity 317–319, 322
Accenture 409
Accor 266
accounting rules 10
acquisition currency, and foreign
    exchange listings 245, 246
adaptation, and market entry 223
AIDS, and globalization 402,
    412
Air Liquide 265
Alcatel 43
alliance management function 148,
    153
alliances and acquisitions 132–137,
    152, 154
  feasibility 132
  learning issues 146–149; barriers to
    150, 153–154
  long-term consequences 137–138
  post-entry dynamics 140–145, 152
  see also automotive industry
Amazon.com 381, 383, 384, 389
American Home Products 265
AmericaOnline 208
Ameritech 368
Amtlicher Handel 37
Andersen Group 265
angel investors 246
anti-globalization protests 12, 341,
    422–423, 428
  and consumer power 6
Apple Computers, product launch 207
architectural competence 311
Argentina
  convergence in corporate
    governance 43

cultural practices 90–91, 93–94
currency peg with USA 42
Aromasin 168
Arthur Andersen Global
    Pharmaceutical Leaders Program
    409
Asahi 147
Asia, role of stock market 32
assertiveness 87; see also cultural
    practices
asymmetric information, in foreign
    capital markets 242, 247
AT&T 243, 265, 364, 366–367
Audi 174, 175
Autodesk partners program 316
automotive industry, use of alliances
    and acquisitions 138–140
Axa 266

B2B
  coordination risk management
    298–299
  and B2C 293
Baby Bells 368
Baekeland, Leo, and bakelite 306–307,
    314
Balanced Budget Act 404
bandwagon hypothesis 247, 248
Bank of America 265
BankOne Systems Corporation 320
banks' decline in shareholdings 30, 39
Banyan Tree Resorts and Hotels 166
Barnes and Noble 381
Bass model 211
Baycol/Lipobay 176
Bayer 176
BBB Online Seal Program 361
Belgium, corporate governance 29
Bell Atlantic (later Verizon) 368
Bell Laboratories 307, 364

benefits, perception of 167
Benetton 207
Berle, A. A., debate with Dodd, E. M. 333
Bhopal tragedy 301
Bill and Melinda Gates Foundation, the 411
Blogger.com 388
BMW 190, 196, 207
BNP 36
board of governors
  composition of 63, 66
  environmental violations 65
  experience of outside directors 65
  ownership levels 69
  size 63–64, 66
  see also directors *and* governance policies
Body Shop, the 207
Bogle, John (Vanguard Group) 65
Boo.com 384
Bork Bill 358
born-global firms 179
BP 71, 201
Brady bonds 272–278
brands
  planning process 203–204
  rationalization 185
  strategy, hybrid approach 198
  value of 188–189; measurement 190–191
British Airways 194, 196
Buffett, Warren (Salomon) 51, 74
bullwhip phenomenon 294
Burberry 195
business elite, global 26
business ethics, need for 334, 423
business expertise, global 98
business process outsourcing (BPO) 6
Business Roundtable 64
  guidelines for directors 65
business schools 105
  brand image 119–120
  combination strategies 114–115
  competition 123–124
  export models 109–111, 113
  funding 122–123
  global faculty 116–118
  governance boards 122
  import models 108–109, 113
  international students 104–106, 118–119
  leadership challenges 115
  location 26
  need for global perspective 106–107, 126
  network models 112–113, 114; management of 120–122
  partnership models 111–112, 113
Business Week 106

C&H Sugar 189
Cable Television Consumer Protection Act (1992) 358
Cadbury, Sir Adrian 70, 76
California Public Employees' Retirement System 55
Campbell Soup 184, 193
Canon 147, 196
Cantalupo, J. (McDonald's) 424
Cap Gemini 43
Capio 398, 417
capital, movement of 25
Capital Asset Pricing Model (CAPM) 17
  currency measure 271
  domestic 260
  exposure measurement 278–280
  hybrid 263–265, 266, 267, 268, 283–284
  political risk 272, 273
  risk measurement 256–257
  tests of 282
  worldwide 260, 262, 263
capital markets 7–8, 17
  liberalization 233
capitalism, varieties of 27
care-why 324, 326
Carrefour 223, 266
Caterpillar 265
Caux Principles 335
Celebrity Sightings 378, 379, 384–385
Celluloid, invention of 306
Cements Français 266
Chad–Cameroon oil pipeline 5
chaebol, see South Korea
Check Point Software Technologies 230

Chicago GSB 107
  brand image 119
  overseas program 109–111
Chile, tax on short-term capital 8
China
  economic development 11
  foreign direct investment 53
  World Bank report on governance
    63
choice modeling 191
Cisco Systems 15, 134, 135
Citigroup 100
citizenship, global 19
civil societarianism 344
Clean Air Act Amendments 301
clockspeed, of supply chains 294
closed-loop supply chains 297–298,
  300
clustering, *see* segmentation
CNN 385
Coca-Cola 130, 184, 192, 193, 265,
  423
  and corporate citizenship 331,
    335
Cochrane Collaborative 408
Colas 266
Collaborative Planning Forecasting
  and Replenishment Systems 298
collectivism 88–89; *see also* cultural
  practices
Columbia University, *see* London
  Business School
combinative capabilities 311
communication and information
  technologies, effect on
  globalization 8
Communications Workers of America
  7
Communist bloc, dismantlement 9, 11
Compagnie des Wagons Lits 379
Compaq 70
competitors, and market entry 214
Compustat 252
Conference Board 65
conflicts-of-law rules 336
conjoint measurement 191
consolidation, increase in 11
cooperative technical organizations
  (CTOs) 315
core ideology 82

core vs. periphery governance choice
  134
Corning 15, 107
  alliance management 146–147
corporate citizenship 331, 335
  and corporate social responsibility
    332–335
  cross-border 336–340
  global 340–346
corporate constituency statutes 334
corporate governance
  convergence between countries 23,
    24–26, 28–29, 40, 72–73;
    implications for managers
    44–46
  empirical evidence on change
    28–29
  global role 13
  national differences 26–28, 72
  reforms 43, 62–63
  see also board of governors, global
    competition, institutional
    investors, *and* stock markets
Corporate Governance Quotient 71
corporate scandals 29, 45
corporations, global
  influence on economy 24
  influence on society 422
cosmopolitan citizenship 340–341,
  343
  and corporations 342–343
cost of capital, *see* equity market
  premium
country managers, role of 202
country-specific segments 165
Covisint 384
Crédit Lyonnais, and government
  control 8
cross-border innovation 307
cross-cultural relationship skills 98
CRSP 252
cultural practices 2, 12, 85, 87, 89,
  90–91, 96–97
  Argentina 93–94
  convergence 10
  cross-national differences 96
  Denmark 91–93
  diffusion path 212
  employee information 96
  Singapore 95–96

currency risk 268–270
customer loyalty 189
customer requirements
    branding 195–196
    production process involvement 388
    source of ICT innovation 386–387

Dae-Jung, President Kim 40
Daewoo 40
Daimler-Chrysler 14, 138–139
    conflicts of citizenship 338–339
Danone 266
Dassault Aviation 266
data collection, healthcare 408
Datastream 252
Dealogic LLC 252
Degussa AG 60
Dell 207, 296
democracy portfolio 68
democratic deficit 351, 352
demographics, use in market
    segmentation 163–164
Denmark, cultural practices 90–93
Deutsche Aktieninstitut 38
Deutsche Bank 53
developing countries, shift to
    manufactures 8
development costs, new technologies
    175
dictatorship portfolio 68
diffusion path, *see* segmentation
directors
    choice of 65
    leadership role 51
disease
    global patterns 400
    rapid spread 400–401
Disney 5, 119, 192, 196, 200, 265
disposal, company responsibility 297
disruption, of supply chain
    accidental triggers 301–302
    implications for companies 302–303
    shifts in regulations 301
    terrorism 300–301
distance learning 124
distribution channels, and market
    entry 223
Doctors Without Borders 342
Dodd, E. M. debate with Berle, A. A.
    333

Dole bananas 189
domain-specific characteristics 164
domestic politics, and transnational
    economy 354–355
Dove Soap 187
Dow Chemical 202
drug development costs 175–176
Duke University, Fuqua School of
    Business 114
dynamic demand–supply balancing
    296–297, 300

eBay 384, 388
economic development, and emerging
    markets 10–11
economic integration
    lack of global infrastructure 5
    USA–Europe 355–356
Economist, The 114
Economist Intelligence Unit 40
elderly, and public spending 402–403
Electrolux 197
electronic data networks
    and domestic law 355
    information privacy 356–357;
        cross-national differences
        358–359, 371–372, 374;
        European approach 358; US
        approach 358
    see also European Data Directive,
        privacy legislation, *and* Safe
        Harbor agreement
Eli Lilly, drug costs 412
Elle magazine 166
employee shareholding 35, 36, 38
Enron 353
    bankruptcy 49–51, 63, 66
    board membership 67
Enterprise Resource Planning 298
entrepreneurial firms, use of
    non-domestic capital
    benefits 241–246
    costs and risks 247–249
    markets 230, 231–233, 250–251
environmental issues
    global citizenship 341
    global regulation 10
environmental legislation, *see* Waste
    Electrical and Electronic
    Equipment Directive

envisioned future 82
equity capital 17
  dual listings approach 250
  finance 29
  foreign exchange 242, 246
equity market premium 256, 261, 282
  choice of risk 258–260
equity markets, impact of globalization
  14, 51, 52–53
  trends in 32, 54, 233, 251
  see also entrepreneurial firms *and*
    foreign public equity capital
    markets
equity ownership 55–57, 307
ERP systems, Web-enabled 295
ESCP-EAP 112
ethnic groups, and imitation 212
E-trade 382, 389
European Commission, harmonization
  of corporation laws 339, 340
European Company Statute 339
European Data Directive 358,
  359–361, 362
European Public Health Association
  406
European Union 422
  citizenship 340
Eurostyles 163
evolutionary models 131
exchange rate risk 257
executive compensation levels 339
executive dashboards 204
exit opportunities, and foreign
  exchange listings 245, 246
experience spillovers 143–144
E-Z Pass 357

Fastow, Andrew S. (Enron) 50
FedEx 196
Fiat 174
Fidelity 55
financial crises 7
  Asia 68
financial flows 290
financial markets, global integration
  and corporate governance 25
  efficiency 26
  entrepreneurial ventures 17
Financial Times, The 104, 105
flexibility, of alliance or acquisition 132

Ford Motor 160, 174, 177, 265
  takeover of Halla Machinery 40
foreign direct investment (FDI), rise of
  53, 54, 355
foreign ownership, of corporations
  36–37
foreign public equity capital markets
  access to 230
  domestic exchanges 236
  see also entrepreneurial firms
Forrester Research Inc. 21
Framework Agreement on Basic
    Telecommunications 367–368
France
  corporate governance 29, 43
  foreign listings 35, 36
  role of stock market 31, 32, 34–37,
    42
  stock options 36
  see also mergers and acquisitions
    activity *and* privatization
France Telecom 365, 373
Fresenins 398, 417
future orientation 87; see also cultural
  practices

Gartner Research 7
Gates, Bill (Microsoft) 332
Gates Foundation, see Bill and
  Melinda Gates Foundation
gender egalitarianism 87
General Agreement on Tariffs and
    Trade (GATT) 9
General Electric 14, 60, 62, 64, 100,
    192, 194, 196, 197, 207, 265, 280
Générale de Santé 398, 417
genetic modification 354
geographic clustering, and Internet 381
geographic expansion, of firms 131
geographically dispersed segments 165
Germany
  foreign listings 37
  IPO market 37
  management stock options 36
  role of stock market 31, 32, 42
  share ownership structure 38–39
  unification 9
  see also mergers and acquisitions
    activity *and* employee
    shareholding

Ghosn, Carlos (Nissan) 83
global brands 16, 186, 192, 193,
    204–205
  common features 192
  degree of globalization 194
  marketing 15–17
global business teams 201–203
global competition 30
global economics
  and domestic politics 354–355,
    370–374
  implications for firms 372–374
global environment, changes in 3
Global Forum for Health Research 411
Global Information Infrastructure
    initiative 353, 363–365, 370, 373,
    374
  opposition to 365–366
global infrastructure, lack of 5
global investors, concerns of 2–4
global knowledge networks, *see*
    recombination *and* small
    worlds
Global Leadership and Organizational
    Behavior Effectiveness (GLOBE)
    project 14, 86–89
Global Medical Forum 408
global mindset 99–100
global models 108
global security, and healthcare 401
global segments 164, 165
  local tailoring 165–167
global sourcing 18
global systems 4
globalizing
  definition of 4
  importance 20
  and society 422–423
GM, takeover of Daewoo Motor 40;
    see also NUMMI venture
Golden Arches Theory of Conflict
    Prevention 422
Google 385
  and international law 337
Gore, Al 363, 374
  protest targets 200–201
governance choice, post-agreement
    135–136
  cognitive traits 136
  cultural traits 137

Governance Metrics International 70,
    71
governance policies 66–69
  arbiters of 69–72
  and composition 69
government regulation, and corporate
    governance 49
Greenpeace 342
Grove, Andrew (Intel) 65
Guinness 203
Gutfreund, John (Salomon) 51, 73

Harvard 107
  international participation 109
  medical school 398, 417
HCA 398
Health Industry Group Purchasing
    Association 409
health management 408–409
  adaptation costs 415
  complexity 413–414
  contradictions 415–417
  global opportunities 414
  market entry opportunity 414
health product manufacturers 398
healthcare provision
  economic significance 399, 400,
    402–403, 407, 411
  fragmentation causes:
  cultural variations 410–411;
    spending levels 411; system inertia
    413; treatment approaches 411;
    undesirable trends 412–413; value
    chain 398; varying national
    concerns 412
  globalization 20, 397–399, 417;
    consumer activism 405; costs of
    403–405; innovation 211; inquiry
    into 407–408; integration 405;
    investment in third world 401;
    management and regulation 406;
    quality demands 404–405;
    technological advance 409;
    undesirable trends 412–413
health science, globalization 407
HEC, New York University and
    London School of Economics 111
hedging costs 269–270
Heineken 194
Henkel 200

Het Financieel Dagblad, absorptive
capacity 317
Hewitt Associates 59
Hewlett Packard 15, 70, 134, 265
alliance strategy 147
Highlight Communication 244
Hitachi 196
HIV, worldwide 401; *see also* AIDS
Holcim 256
homogenization 196
Honda 15–16, 159–160, 173, 223
and corporate citizenship 338
Honeywell–GE merger 354
horizontal alliances, integration levels
141
hostile takeovers, increase in 29
humane orientation 89
Hyundai 39
takeover of KIA 40

IBM 192, 197, 265
brand 194
knowledge management 325
outsourcing 7
unified standard 316
ICT
adoption hurdles 382
impact of infrastructure 379–380
interaction between individuals
388–389
management of innovation 389–391
rapid growth of 369–370
realization hurdles 382–383
US global policy 366–368
IMD 109
Indian School of Business 110
information flows 8–9, 212, 234, 290
informational asymmetry 133
Infosys Technologies 230
innovation
network-building 312–316
process of 379–382
speed of diffusion 116, 383
INSEAD
alliance with Wharton School
111–112, 114, 118, 122, 429
brand image 119
conferences on healthcare 408
graduate jobs 106, 119
international board 122

overseas campus 112, 114, 118
research centers 116
INSEAD Quarterly 120
institutional diversity, importance 27
institutional investors
and competition 26
convergence of corporate
governance 72–73
increase in 29, 30, 51–52, 56
interest in governance 57–58
Institutional Shareholder Services 70
institutionalised learning 147, 149
instructor-led learning 124
integration, *see* segmentation
integration levels
development of capabilities 149,
153
optimal mix 144–145
of organizations 141–142
and relationship quality 143–144,
152
Intel 192, 194, 196, 265
standards 369
intellectual property 18
interaction, and alliances between
firms 133
Interbrand 191
interdependence, increase in 11
internal communities of practice
324–326
International Asset Pricing Model
(IAPM) 270–272, 285
returns between countries 280
International Dispensing Association
of the Netherlands 412
*International Journal for Quality in
Health Care* 409
*International Journal of Integrated
Care* 409
International Monetary Fund 7, 12
and corporate governance 26, 341
and integration 7
International Telecommunications
Union 363, 369
incentives for CEOs 29
Internet 8, 19
auction services 388
contracting 293
effect on market entry 223
exports of services 378–379

fraud 383
infrastructure 384
international law 337
and Minitel 365
protest organization 342
see also electronic data networks
investment
capital market liberalization 7–8
worldwide 269
investor activism 56
investor population, foreign exchange
risk 268
IPO discount 239–240
IPS costs 248–249
Iridium 168
Italy, role of stock market 31
ITT 107

Jager, Durk (Procter & Gamble) 198
Japan
cross-holdings 53
role of stock market 32
Japan Airlines 64, 69
Jobs, Steve (Apple Computers) 83
Johns Hopkins 398, 417
Johnson & Johnson 265
joint ventures, levels of integration 141
Jordan 162
*Journal of International Business
Studies* 116
JP Morgan 278

Kennedy, John F. 62
KFC 198
KIA, bankruptcy 40
knowledge codification 149, 151, 153,
154
knowledge entrepreneurs 126
knowledge exchange 319
knowledge intensity, and
recombination 309
knowledge management 148, 391
Knowledge@Wharton 7, 21, 120
knowledge-based services,
geographical independence
385–386
Kosdaq 40

L'Expansion 36
labor mobility 9

labor-saving innovations, diffusion
pattern 212
Latin America, role of stock
market 32
Lay, Kenneth (Enron) 50, 62, 73
Le Monde 385
lead-lag effect 217–218
lead markets 169
leadership
accountability 59–60
development programs 60–61
global competencies 97–99
of global firms 14, 85–86, 99–100
governance principles 62–63, 73–74
institutional investors 55, 58–59
need for flexibility 96
Leapfrog Group 404
learning-by-doing 146–147, 149, 153
Levi's 200, 203
LG 39
lifelong learning 125–126
liquidity
foreign capital markets 243, 246
risk 257
local brands 199–200
Local Healthcare Co-operatives 406
local pricing 267–268
logistics, supply chain management
289, 291–292
London Business School, and
Columbia University 111
London School of Economics, *see*
HEC
Lycos Europe 230

Maersk Air 66
Major Accident Reporting System
(MARS) 302
Managed Clinical Networks 406
management
compensation 59, 60, 61
lessons for 424–427
need for research 427–428
managers, with finance background 30
Mannesmann, takeover by Vodafone
37
manufacturing, shift from agriculture 8
market access, ICT industries 366
market differences 198
market efficiency 189, 197

market entry 16
  commitment 209, 219
  decision-making 214–215, 224–225
  entry sequence 215; waterfall vs.
    sprinkler strategy 208, 215–217,
    223
  scale of production 220
  see also distribution channels
    preannouncements, product
    standardization, *and*
    segmentation
market feedback hypothesis 247
market information, and design
  perspectives 160
market segmentation, *see*
  segmentation
marketing communications 220
Marlborough 192, 194
mass media, and innovation 212
material flows 289
Material Requirement Planning
  298
Matsushita 207
  DVD standards 316
Mayo 398, 414, 416, 417
McDonald's 5, 119, 192, 200,
  422–424
  corporate citizenship 331, 335
McKinsey studies 57–58
MCM 187
MedCath Corporation 405
Mercedes 192
Merck, and river blindness 412
mergers and acquisitions (M&A)
  activity 42, 171
  France 35
  Germany 37–38
  South Korea 40
Michelin 266
Microsoft
  brand 192
  outsourcing 7
  product launch 207, 223
  standards 369
migration paths, differences in 16
Milbank Memorial Fund 409
Minitel, and Internet 365
MIT, and video conferencing
  110
Mitsubishi 53

Mizuho Securities 74
mobility of personnel, and
  recombination 308, 320–321
Mont Blanc 195
Moody's 278
Motorola 265
MTV 186–188, 201

Nasdaq 17, 231, 232
  foreign IPOs 230, 231–233, 234,
    235, 237
  listing costs 241, 242, 248
National Information Infrastructure
  (NII) 363
Nationsbank 15
Nature Conservancy 342
Near-Miss Management Systems
  302
NEC 387
negative spillovers, foreign exchange
  listing 249
Nestlé 194
Netherlands
  corporate governance 29
  role of stock market 32
Neuer Markt 17, 37, 42, 231, 233
  average age of foreign companies
    236
  foreign IPOs 230, 231, 235, 239,
    243, 244
  listing costs 239, 240, 249
  negative reputation 249
  see also IPO discount
New York University, *see* HEC
Nike 193, 194, 200
Nissan 177
NME (now Tenet) 398
Nokia 100, 106, 192, 387
non-governmental organizations
  (NGOs), expansion of 341
Northern Trust 265
NUMMI venture 138, 139–140

Olivetti 167
On Track Innovation 244
Online Personal Privacy Act 375
Organization for Economic
  Co-operation and Development
  (OECD), and healthcare 408
organizational templates 319

organizing expertise, global 98
Orix Corporation 71
OSI protocol 369
outsourcing 3
  and recombination 308
  see also business process outsourcing
    and logistics
overnight globalization 384–385
overseas programs, business education
  110
Owens Illinois 147
ownership dispersion, foreign
  exchange listings 245–246

Paribas 256
partner-specific experience, of alliances
  148
passenger information 359
pensions, spending on 402–403
Perdue chickens 189
performance orientation 89; *see also*
  cultural practices
Pernod-Ricard 266
Perrier water 189
personality traits, of leaders 99
Peugeot 266
Pfizer 168, 265
pharmaceuticals
  challenges of globalization 395–397,
    410
  drug distribution to poor nations
    412
  global market opportunities 401
  and governments 19
Pharmacia 168
  and AIDS drug 412
Philips 130, 173, 196
  DVD standards 316
Pinault Printemps 266
Pioneer, DVD standards 316
platforms, in product development
  174–175
political globalization, and corporate
  governance 26
political risk
  measurement 256, 257
  pricing 272–278
political stability, and global business
  422
PolyGram 174

Porsche 353, 354, 372, 374
postal, telegraph and telephone
  monopolies (PTTs) 365, 366–367,
  368, 370, 373
power distance 88; *see also* cultural
  practices
Prada 195
preannouncements 209, 218–219
pricing, and market entry 220
Primary Care Trusts 406
principal–agent theories 334
privacy legislation; *see also* electronic
  data networks
privatization
  Argentina 41
  France 34
  standard-setting 369
Procter & Gamble 164, 170, 184, 193,
  198, 202
producer responsibility laws 297
product development
  adaptation 220
  cost and market information
    177–179
  cost reduction 173–176
  customer response 176–177
  delivery of benefits 169–170
  national markets 16
  profitability evaluation 167–168, 172
  segment matching 170–173
  see also global segments *and*
    segmentation
product distribution, and branding 189
product launch, sequential or
  simultaneous 207–209, 214
product mobility 9, 235
product platform planning process 178
product returns 297
product standardization 172, 209
  and diffusion 223–224
Prospective Payment System 404
protests, *see* anti-globalization protests
Prozac 194
public health initiatives, global 401
public share offerings, France 34
publicity, and foreign exchange listings
  243–245, 246

Qualcom 390
quality function deployment 178

R&D 18
  global networks 307
  investor pressure 56
Rathenau, Walther 333
recombination 307–308
  from different organizations
      310–312
  and globalization 308–310, 312
  integration of knowledge pockets
      321–324
  network-building 312–316
  see also small worlds *and* technology
      fusion
red–blue teaming 300
regional differentiation, of products
      160, 165, 180
regulation
  harmonization of 10, 233
  spillovers 354, 355
relationships
  between organizations 142–143
  development of 148–149
  see also integration
religious differences 12
Renault 174
reporting requirements 249
Repsol-YPF 41
reputation, of firms, and foreign
      exchange listings 243–245
resource-based learning 124
retail buying power 200
reverse product life-cycle 379, 392
risk
  and competition 168
  management of 17–19, 293,
      303–304
  sources of 257–258
  see also equity market premium *and*
      supply chains
Rolls-Royce 190
Roper Starch Worldwide 163
Ruh, Peter (Cisco Systems) 156
Ruiz-Quintanilla 102
Russia, impact of opening markets 11

Safe Harbor agreement 359, 361–363,
      371
sales force, and market entry
      220–221
Salomon 51

Samsung 39, 147, 387
  knowledge exchange 323–324
Sanofi-Synthelabo 266
Sarbanes–Oxley Act (2002) 4, 63, 337,
      353, 372, 396
SARS virus 400, 408
Scandinavia, corporate governance 29
Scandinavian Airlines 66
SCH 41
Schwab, Charles 382
SDC Platinum 252
Seat 174, 175
security 3, 12
segmentation, of market 160
  and equity premium 260–262,
      280
  global 161–162, 179; of countries
      162–163, 209, 212–213; diffusion
      patterns 209, 210–212, 213, 224;
      see also lead-lag effect
  of individuals 163, 209–210, 213
  types of 164–165; local 161; partial
      284
selective distribution 222
self-fulfilling prophecy 137
Seoul National University 115
September 11, 2001 3, 4, 200, 288, 343
  global loss 351
share ownership
  data on 29
  employee remuneration 35
  increase in 29
shareholder primacy norm 334
shareholder value 25, 28, 30
shareholders, and corporate
      governance 49
Sharp 324
Shaw, George Bernard 82
Shell 100, 196, 200, 267
Shell Trading and Transport 267
shipping, and global economy 5
Shouldice Hospital 405
Siemens 100, 147, 194, 196
  corporate citizenship 331, 335
Singapore, cultural practices 90–91,
      95–96
Skoda 174, 175
slotting allowances 222
small worlds 309–310, 313, 319, 321
  importance of shortcuts 322

Smith, Darwin (Kimberly-Clark) 82
Smith, Sir Robert 70
SMS-TV 389
social responsibility, of corporations
  11–12
Société Générale 266
  employee ownership 36
Sony Corporation 64, 69, 165
  DVD standards 316
  product launch 207
  technology fusion 310
  waste disposal 298
South Korea
  1997 financial crisis 40
  chaebols 39
  control of banks 8
  convergence in corporate
    governance 40, 44
  economic development 11
  foreign ownership of shares 40
  role of state 39
  role of stock market 39
spillover effects, *see* lead-lag effect
stakeholders, and corporate
    responsibility 334
Standard & Poor's Governance
    Services 70, 71
standard of living, innovation 211
standardization, of global products
    159, 170–173
  and competition 197
  see also global segments
standards
  harmonization of 381
  in ICT industries 368–369
Starbucks 184, 189, 194, 196, 200
Star-Kist tuna 189
state ownership, withdrawal 30;
    see also privatization
stock-market price risk 257
stock markets
  collapse of indices 29
  economic importance of 31–34
  foreign listings 35, 52
  source of finance 30, 43
  see also individual countries
structural holes 313
student exchange programs 111
Suez 266
Sumitomo 53

Sun Microsystems, standards 369
Sunkist oranges 189
Sunkyong 39
supply chains 18, 291, 292
  asset returns 291–292
  design 293
  flow types 289–290
  globalization trends 289
  risks 292–293; management of
    293–294, 303
  see also clockspeed, closed-loop
    supply chains, disruption, *and*
    logistics
supply–demand coordination 294–295
  management of risk 295–300
Swatch 194
Sweden
  role of stock market 31, 32
  vote against euro 6

Tagamet 194
tailoring costs 160
Taiwan earthquake 288
tax penalties, for employees 249
TCP/IP 369
technological communities, and
    innovation networks 314–316
technological frames 313, 328
technology fusion 310
technology life-cycle model 380
technology
  facilitates globalization 5, 8–9, 234
  familiarity and innovation 311
  innovation rate 30
  see also knowledge exchange,
    outsourcing, recombination, *and*
    small worlds
Telecom New Zealand 368
telecommunications, China 20; *see also*
    Global Information Infrastructure
Telecommunications Act (1966)
    366–367
Telefónica 41
telematics 406
terrorism, *see* disruption
Tesco 200
text messaging (SMS) 383, 386, 390
Thalès 261–262, 264, 266, 270, 271,
    279, 280, 284
Thomas Cook 379

three-dimensional concurrent
    engineering (3D-CD) 295–296,
    300
  and lifecycle approach (4D-CD) 298
TIAA-CREF 55, 70
time horizon, of alliance or acquisition
    134
Tobin separation theorem 269
Tobin tax 8
Toshiba, DVD standards 316
Total Fina Elf 266
tourism, spread of disease 400
Toyota 14, 53, 61, 184, 193
  corporate citizenship 338
  and knowledge exchange 322–323
  see also NUMMI venture
trading system, international, and
    political economy 5
transactional leadership 81
transformational leadership 81–82, 84
transportation costs, decline in 9
TRUSTe 361
tuberculosis, spread of 401, 412
Tyco 63, 66
  board membership 67, 69

uncertainty 132
  avoidance 88
  see also cultural practices
underpricing 247–248
Unilever 130, 184, 185–186, 201;
    see also Dove Soap
unionization, decline in 30
United Kingdom
  cultural practices 90–91
  employee shareholding 36
  public share offerings 34
  role of stock market 31, 32, 42
United Nations
  global compacts 344, 422
  governance structure 341
United States
  employee shareholding 36
  global ICT policies 366–368
  role of stock market 31, 32, 42

Valeo 266
VALS-2 163
valuation, foreign exchange listing 246
value-based leadership 81, 84–85

characteristics 82–84
cultural barriers 80
  see also cultural practices
Vanguard Group 55, 65
venture capitalists 246
Venture One 253, 256
Venturescape 253, 256
Verizon 368
vertical alliances 141
Viagra 176, 194
virtual laboratories 391
Visa 202
visibility of firms, foreign exchange
    listing 243–245, 246, 250
vision, of leaders
  articulation of 82
  communication of 83
  confidence of leader 83
  empowerment of executives 84
  role-model behavior 84
  self-fulfilling prophesy 83–84
VIVA 187
Vivendi 43
Vivendi Universal 14, 266
Vodafone 37
Volkswagen 9, 174, 175, 190

Wal-Mart 85, 194, 199, 223, 297
  and vendor-managed inventory 294
war, and globalization 342
Washington Alliance of Technology
    Workers 7
Washington consensus 3, 341
Waste Electrical and Electronic
    Equipment Directive (WEEE) 298,
    301
Waste Management International 162
Watkins, Sherron (Enron) 50
Wells Fargo & Co 265
Wharton School 107, 116
  brand image 119
  graduate jobs 106
  and INSEAD 111–112, 114, 118,
    122, 429
  leadership programs 61
  regional boards 122
  risk center 301–302
  technology transfer 110
Weiss Center for International
    Financial Research 116

Whirlpool 177, 194, 197
winner's curse 247, 248
World Bank
  and corporate governance 26, 341
  and healthcare data 408
World Health Organization 400,
    408
  Commission on Macroeconomics
    and Health 401
  European Office for Integrated
    Health Care Services 406
World Trade Organization 12, 422
  Cancún negotiations 6, 428
  GATS 366–368
  governance structure 341

influence of lobbies on negotiations 6
market liberalization 7
problems 5
product mobility 9
telecommunications 366
World Wildlife Fund 342
WorldCom 63, 66
  board membership 67

Xerox 307

Yahoo! 385
  and French law 336–337, 388

Zara 297